College of General Studies at Boston University

UNDERSTANDING
MOVIES AND MUSIC

Custom Edition for Freshman Humanities

Compiled by Cheryl C. Boots, Ph.D.
Boston University

Taken from

Understanding Music, Third Edition
by Jeremy Yudkin

Understanding Movies, Ninth Edition
by Louis Giannetti

Cover Art: *Untitled 30*, by Mark Kelly
Laundry Day, by Thomas Barron

Taken from:

Understanding Music, Third Edition
by Jeremy Yudkin
Copyright © 2002, 1999, 1996 by Jeremy Yudkin
Published by Prentice-Hall, Inc.
A Pearson Education Company
Upper Saddle River, New Jersey 07458

Understanding Movies, Ninth Edition
by Louis Giannetti
Copyright © 2002, 1999, 1996, 1993, 1990, 1987, 1982, 1976, 1972 by Pearson Education, Inc.
Published by Prentice-Hall, Inc.

This special edition published in cooperation with Pearson Custom Publishing.

Printed in the United States of America

10 9 8 7 6 5 4 3 2

ISBN 0-536-73875-0

BA 997513

BL

Please visit our web site at *www.pearsoncustom.com*

PEARSON CUSTOM PUBLISHING
75 Arlington Street, Suite 300, Boston, MA 02116
A Pearson Education Company

❖ Contents ❖

This text has been taken from:
Understanding Movies, Ninth Edition, by Louis Giannetti

This text has been taken from:
Understanding Music, Third Edition, by Jeremy Yudkin

Photography

Paramount Pictures and Touchstone Pictures

*People inscribe their histories, beliefs, attitudes, desires
and dreams in the images they make.*
—ROBERT HUGHES, ART CRITIC

Overview

The three styles of film: realism, classicism, and formalism. Three broad types of cinema: documentaries, fiction films, and avant-garde movies. The signified and the signifier: how form shapes content in movies. Subject matter plus treatment equal content. The shots: apparent distance of the camera from the subject. The angles: looking up, down, or at eye level. Lighting styles: high key, low key, high contrast. The symbolism of light and darkness. Color symbolism. How lenses distort the subject matter: telephotos, wide-angle, and standard lenses. Filtered reality: more distortions. Special effects and the optical printer. The cinematographer: the film director's main visual collaborator.

Realism and Formalism

Even before the turn of the last century, movies began to develop in two major directions: the **realistic** and the **formalistic**. In the mid-1890s in France, the Lumière brothers delighted audiences with their short movies dealing with everyday occurrences. Such films as *The Arrival of a Train* (4–3) fascinated viewers precisely because they seemed to capture the flux and spontaneity of events as they were viewed in real life. At about the same time, Georges Méliès was creating a number of fantasy films that emphasized purely imagined events. Such movies as *A Trip to the Moon* (4–4) were typical mixtures of whimsical narrative and trick photography. In many respects, the Lumières can be regarded as the founders of the realist tradition of cinema, and Méliès of the formalist tradition.

Realism and formalism are general rather than absolute terms. When used to suggest a tendency toward either polarity, such labels can be helpful, but in the end they're just labels. Few films are exclusively formalist in style, and fewer yet are completely realist. There is also an important difference between realism and reality, although this distinction is often forgotten. Realism is a particular *style,* whereas physical reality is the source of all the raw materials of film, both realistic and formalistic. Virtually all movie directors go to the photographable world for their subject matter, but what they do with this material—how they shape and manipulate it—is what determines their stylistic emphasis.

Generally speaking, realistic films attempt to reproduce the surface of reality with a minimum of distortion. In photographing objects and events, the filmmaker tries to suggest the copiousness of life itself. Both realist and formalist film directors must select (and hence, emphasize) certain details from the chaotic sprawl of reality. But the element of selectivity in realistic films is less obvious. Realists, in short, try to preserve the illusion that their film world is unmanipulated, an objective mirror of the actual world. Formalists, on the other hand, make no such pretense. They deliberately stylize and distort their raw materials so that only the very naive would mistake a manipulated image of an object or event for the real thing. Style is part of the show.

1–1a. The Perfect Storm (U.S.A., 2000), *with George Clooney, directed by Wolf-gang Petersen.* (Warner Bros.)

Realism and Formalism. Critics and theorists have championed film as the most realistic of all the arts in capturing how an experience actually looks and sounds, like this thrilling recreation of a ferocious storm at sea. A stage director would have to suggest the storm symbolically, with stylized lighting and off-stage sound effects. A novelist would have to recreate the event with words, a painter with pigments brushstroked onto a flat canvas. But a film director can create the event with much greater credibility by plunging the camera (a proxy for us) in the middle of the most terrifying ordeals without actually putting us in harm's way. In short, film realism is more like "being there" than any other artistic medium or any other style of presentation. Audiences can experience the thrills without facing any of the dangers.

Dames presents us with another type of experience entirely. The choreographies of Busby Berkeley are triumphs of artifice, far removed from the real world. Depression-weary audiences flocked to movies like this precisely to get away from everyday reality. They wanted magic and enchantment, not reminders of their real-life problems. Berkeley's style was the most formalized of all choreographers. He liberated the camera from the narrow confines of the proscenium arch, soaring overhead, even swirling amongst the dancers, and juxtaposing shots from a variety of vantage points throughout the musical numbers. He often photographed his dancers from unusual angles, like this **bird's-eye shot.** Sometimes he didn't even bother using dancers at all, preferring a uniform contingent of good-looking young women who are used primarily as semi-abstract visual units, like bits of glass in a shifting kaleidoscope of formal patterns. Audiences were enchanted.

1–1b. Dames (U.S.A., 1934), *choreographed by Busby Berkeley, directed by Ray Enright.* (Warner Bros.)

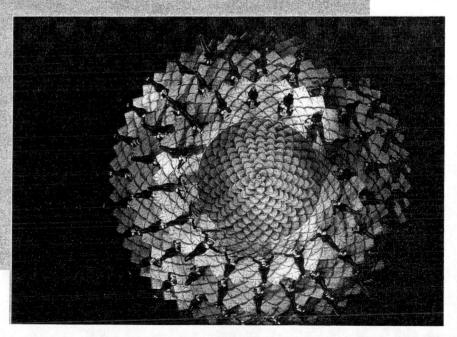

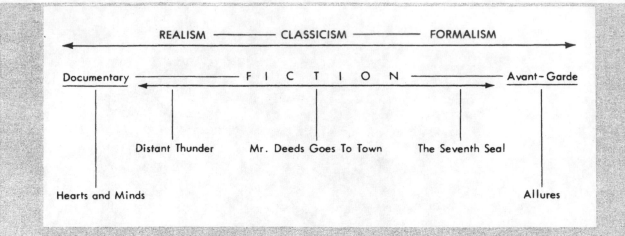

1–2. Classification chart of styles and types of film.
Critics and scholars categorize movies according to a variety of criteria. Two of the most common methods of classification are by style and by type. The three principal styles—realism, classicism, and formalism—might be regarded as a continuous spectrum of possibilities, rather than airtight categories. Similarly, the three types of movies—documentaries, fiction, and **avant-garde** films—are also terms of convenience, for they often overlap. Realistic films like *Distant Thunder* **(1–4)** can shade into the documentary. Formalist movies like *The Seventh Seal* **(1–6)** have a personal quality suggesting the traditional domain of the avant-garde. Most fiction films, especially those produced in America, tend to conform to the **classical paradigm.** Classical cinema can be viewed as an intermediate style that avoids the extremes of realism and formalism—though most movies in the classical form lean toward one or the other style.

We rarely notice the style in a realistic movie; the artist tends to be self-effacing, invisible. Such filmmakers are more concerned with *what's* being shown rather than how it's manipulated. The camera is used conservatively. It's essentially a recording mechanism that reproduces the surface of tangible objects with as little commentary as possible. Some realists aim for a rough look in their images, one that doesn't prettify the materials with a self-conscious beauty of form. "If it's too pretty, it's false," is an implicit assumption. A high premium is placed on simplicity, spontaneity, and directness. This is not to suggest that these movies lack artistry, however, for at its best, the realistic cinema specializes in art that conceals art.

Formalist movies are stylistically flamboyant. Their directors are concerned with expressing their unabashedly subjective experience of reality, not how other people might see it. Formalists are often referred to as **expressionists,** because their self-expression is at least as important as the subject matter itself. Expressionists are often concerned with spiritual and psychological truths, which they feel can be conveyed best by distorting the surface of the material world. The camera is used as a method of commenting on the subject matter, a way of emphasizing its essential rather than its objective nature. Formalist movies have a high degree of manipulation, a stylization of reality.

4

Most realists would claim that their major concern is with *content* rather than *form* or technique. The subject matter is always supreme, and anything that distracts from the content is viewed with suspicion. In its most extreme form, the realistic cinema tends toward documentary, with its emphasis on photographing actual events and people **(1–3)**. The formalist cinema, on the other hand, tends to emphasize technique and expressiveness. The most extreme example of this style of filmmaking is found in the avant-garde cinema **(1–7)**.

1–3. *Hearts and Minds* **(U.S.A., 1975),** *directed by Peter Davis.*
The emotional impact of a documentary image usually derives from its truth rather than its beauty. Davis's indictment of America's devastation of Vietnam consists primarily of TV newsreel footage. This photo shows some Vietnamese children running from an accidental bombing raid on their community, their clothes literally burned off their bodies by napalm. "First they bomb as much as they please," a Vietnamese observes, "then they film it." It was images such as these that eventually turned the majority of Americans against the war. Fernando Solanas and Octavio Gettino, Third World filmmakers, have pointed out, "Every image that documents, bears witness to, refutes or deepens the truth of a situation is something more than a film image or purely artistic fact; it becomes something which the System finds indigestible." Paradoxically, in no country except the United States would such self-damning footage be allowed on the public airwaves—which are controlled, or at least regulated, by governments. No other country has a First Amendment, guaranteeing freedom of expression. *(Warner Bros.)*

Some of these movies are totally abstract; pure forms (that is, nonrepresentational colors, lines, and shapes) constitute the only content. Most fiction films fall somewhere between these two extremes, in a mode critics refer to as **classical cinema (1–5).**

Even the terms *form* and *content* aren't as clear-cut as they may sometimes seem. As the filmmaker and author Vladimir Nilsen pointed out: "A photograph is by no means a complete and whole reflection of reality: the photographic picture represents only one or another selection from the sum of physical attributes of the object photographed." The form of a shot—the way in which a subject is photographed—is its true content, not necessarily what the subject is perceived to be in reality. The communications theorist Marshall

1–4.   *Distant Thunder* (India, 1973), *directed by Satyajit Ray.*

In most realistic films, there is a close correspondence of the images to everyday reality. This criterion of value necessarily involves a comparison between the internal world of the movie with the external milieu that the filmmaker has chosen to explore. The realistic cinema tends to deal with people from the lower social echelons and often explores moral issues. The artist rarely intrudes on the materials, however, preferring to let them speak for themselves. Rather than focusing on extraordinary events, realism tends to emphasize the basic experiences of life. It is a style that excels in making us feel the humanity of others. Beauty of form is often sacrificed to capture the texture of reality as it's ordinarily perceived. Realistic images often seem unmanipulated, haphazard in their design. They frequently convey an intimate snapshot quality—people caught unawares. Generally, the story materials are loosely organized and include many details that don't necessarily forward the plot but are offered for their own sake, to heighten the sense of authenticity.   *(Cinema 5)*

McLuhan pointed out that the content of one medium is actually another medium. For example, a photograph (visual image) depicting a man eating an apple (taste) involves two different mediums: Each communicates information—content—in a different way. A verbal description of the photograph of the man eating the apple would involve yet another medium (language), which communicates information in yet another manner. In each case, the precise information is determined by the medium, although superficially all three have the same content.

In literature, the naive separation of form and content is called "the heresy of paraphrase." For example, the content of *Hamlet* can be found in a college outline, yet no one would seriously suggest that the play and outline are the same "except in form." To paraphrase artistic information is inevitably to change its content as well as its form. Artistry can never be gauged by subject

1–5.   *Mr. Deeds Goes to Town* (U.S.A., 1936), *with Gary Cooper (with tuba), directed by Frank Capra.*

Classical cinema avoids the extremes of realism and formalism in favor of a slightly stylized presentation that has at least a surface plausibility. Movies in this form are often handsomely mounted, but the style rarely calls attention to itself. The images are determined by their relevance to the story and characters, rather than a desire for authenticity or formal beauty alone. The implicit ideal is a functional, invisible style: The pictorial elements are subordinated to the presentation of characters in action. Classical cinema is story oriented. The narrative line is seldom allowed to wander, nor is it broken up by authorial intrusions. A high premium is placed on the entertainment value of the story, which is often shaped to conform to the conventions of a popular genre. Often the characters are played by stars rather than unknown players, and their roles are sometimes tailored to showcase their personal charms. The human materials are paramount in the classical cinema. The characters are generally appealing and slightly romanticized. The audience is encouraged to identify with their values and goals.   *(Columbia Pictures)*

matter alone. The manner of its presentation—its forms—is the true content of paintings, literature, and plays. The same applies to movies.

The great French critic André Bazin noted, "One way of understanding better what a film is trying to say is to know how it is saying it." The American critic Herman G. Weinberg expressed the matter succinctly: "The way a story is told is part of that story. You can tell the same story badly or well; you can also tell it well enough or magnificently. It depends on who is telling the story."

Realism and *realistic* are much overtaxed terms, both in life and in movies. We use these terms to express so many different ideas. For example, people often praise the "realism" of the boxing matches in *Raging Bull*. What they really mean is that these scenes are powerful, intense, and vivid. These traits owe very little to realism as a style. In fact, the boxing matches are extremely stylized. The images are often photographed in dreamy slow motion,

1–6. *The Seventh Seal* **(Sweden, 1957),** *with Bengt Ekerot and Max von Sydow, cinematography by Gunnar Fischer, directed by Ingmar Bergman.*

The formalist cinema is largely a director's cinema: We're often aware of the personality of the filmmaker. There is a high degree of manipulation in the narrative materials, and the visual presentation is stylized. The story is exploited as a vehicle for the filmmaker's personal obsessions. Formalists are not much concerned with how realistic their images are, but with their beauty or power. The most artificial genres—musicals, sci-fi, fantasy films—are generally classified as formalist. Most movies of this sort deal with extraordinary characters and events—such as this mortal game of chess between a medieval knight and the figure of Death. This style of cinema excels in dealing with ideas—political, religious, philosophical— and is often the chosen medium of propagandistic artists. Its texture is densely symbolic: Feelings are expressed through forms, like the dramatic high-contrast lighting of this shot. Most of the great stylists of the cinema are formalists. *(Janus Films)*

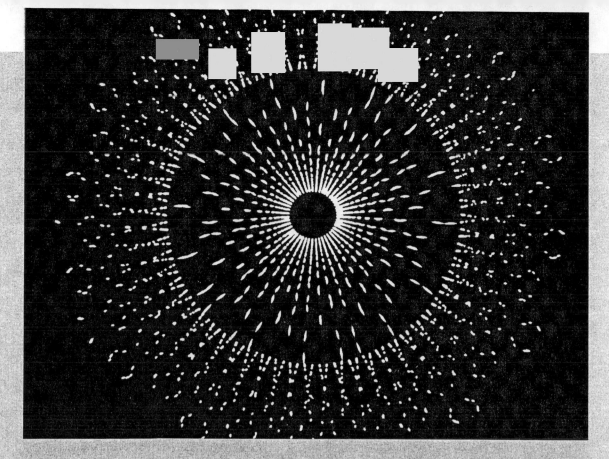

1–7. *Allures* (U.S.A., 1961), *directed by Jordan Belson.*
In the avant-garde cinema, subject matter is often suppressed in favor of abstraction and an emphasis on formal beauty for its own sake. Like many artists in this idiom, Belson began as a painter and was attracted to film because of its temporal and kinetic dimensions. He was strongly influenced by such European avant-garde artists as Hans Richter, who championed the "absolute film"—a graphic cinema of pure forms divorced from a recognizable subject matter. Belson's works are inspired by philosophical concepts derived primarily from Oriental religions, but these are essentially private sources and are rarely presented explicitly in films themselves. Form is the true content of Belson's movies. His animated images are mostly geometrical shapes, dissolving and contracting circles of light, and kinetic swirls. His patterns expand, congeal, flicker, and split off into other shapes, only to re-form and explode again. It is a cinema of uncompromising self-expression—personal, often inaccessible, and iconoclastic. *(Pyramid Films)*

with lyrical crane shots, weird accompanying sound effects (like hissing sounds and jungle screams), staccato editing in both the images and the sound. True, the subject matter is based on actual life—the brief boxing career of the American middleweight champion of the 1940s, Jake La Motta. But the stylistic treatment of these biographical materials is extravagantly subjective **(1–8a).**

At the opposite extreme, the special effects in *Total Recall* are so uncannily realistic that we would swear they were real if we didn't know better. In the scene pictured **(1–8b),** for example, we see a plump bald character magically transformed into Arnold Schwarzenegger after he removes his lifelike headpiece. Such fantasy materials can be presented with astonishing "realism" thanks to the brilliance of Dream Quest, one of the most prestigious special effects organizations in America.

9

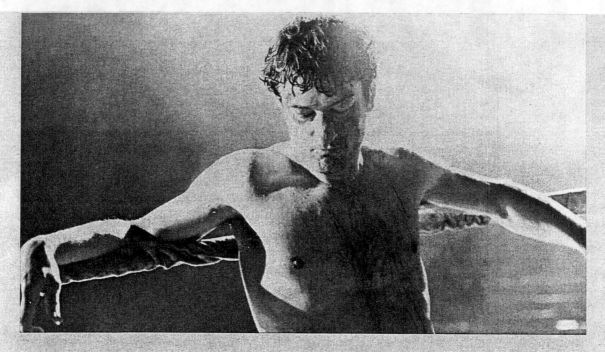

1–8a. *Raging Bull (U.S.A., 1980), with Robert De Niro, directed by Martin Scorsese.*
(United Artists)

1–8b. **Total Recall** (U.S.A., 1990), *with Arnold Schwarzenegger, directed by Paul Verhoeven.* *(Tri-Star Pictures)*

Realism and formalism are best used as *stylistic* terms rather than terms to describe the nature of the subject matter. For example, although the story of *Raging Bull* is based on actual events, the boxing matches in the film are stylized. In this photo, the badly bruised Jake La Motta resembles an agonized warrior, crucified against the ropes of the ring. The camera floats toward him in lyrical slow motion while the soft focus obliterates his consciousness of the arena.

In *Total Recall,* on the other hand, the special effects are so realistic they almost convince us that the impossible is possible. If special effects look fake, our pleasure is diminished. In short, it's quite possible to present fantasy materials in a realistic style. It's equally possible to present reality-based materials in an expressionistic style.

10

Form and content are best used as relative terms. They are useful concepts for temporarily isolating specific aspects of a movie for the purposes of closer examination. Such a separation is artificial, of course, yet this technique can yield more detailed insights into the work of art as a whole. By beginning with an understanding of the basic components of the film medium—its various language systems, as it were—we will see how form and content in the cinema, as in the other arts, are ultimately the same.

The Shots

The **shots** are defined by the amount of subject matter that's included within the **frame** of the screen. In actual practice, however, shot designations vary considerably. A **medium shot** for one director might be considered a **close-up** by another. Furthermore, the longer the shot, the less precise are the designations. In general, shots are determined on the basis of how much of the human figure is in view. The shot is not necessarily defined by the distance between the camera and the object photographed, for in some instances certain lenses distort distances. For example, a **telephoto lens** can produce a close-up on the screen, yet the camera in such shots is generally quite distant from the subject matter.

Although there are many different kinds of shots in the cinema, most of them are subsumed under the six basic categories: (1) the **extreme long shot,** (2) the **long shot,** (3) the **full shot,** (4) the medium shot, (5) the close-up, and (6) the **extreme close-up.** The **deep-focus shot** is usually a variation of the long or extreme long shot **(1–9).**

The *extreme long shot* is taken from a great distance, sometimes as far as a quarter of a mile away. It's almost always an exterior shot and shows much of the locale. Extreme long shots also serve as spatial frames of reference for the closer shots and for this reason are sometimes called **establish-**

1–9. *Okaeri* (Japan, 1995), *directed by Makoto Shinozaki.*
The setting dominates most extreme long shots. Humans are dwarfed into visual insignificance, making them appear unimportant and vulnerable. Shinozaki's desperate lovers seem oppressed even by Nature—vast, stark, merciless. *(Dimension Films)*

1–10. *Mary Shelley's Frankenstein* (U.S.A., 1994), *with Robert De Niro (under wraps) and Kenneth Branagh, directed by Branagh.*

At its most distant range, the long shot encompasses roughly the same amount of space as the staging area of a large theater. Setting can dominate characters unless they're located near the foreground. Lighting a long shot is usually costly, time consuming, and labor intensive, especially if it's in deep focus, like this shot. The laboratory had to be moody and scary, yet still sufficiently clear to enable us to see back into the "depth" of the set. Note how the lighting is layered, punctuated with patches of gloom and accusatory shafts of light from above. To complicate matters, whenever a director cuts to closer shots, the lighting has to be adjusted accordingly so that the transitions between cuts appear smooth and unobtrusive. Anyone who has ever visited a movie set knows that people are waiting most of the time—usually for the director of photography (D.P.) to announce that the lighting is finally ready and the scene can now be photographed. *(TriStar Pictures)*

ing shots. If people are included in extreme long shots, they usually appear as mere specks on the screen **(1–9)**. The most effective use of these shots is often found in **epic** films, where locale plays an important role: westerns, war films, samurai films, and historical movies.

The *long shot* **(1–10)** is perhaps the most complex in the cinema, and the term itself one of the most imprecise. Usually, long-shot ranges correspond approximately to the distance between the audience and the stage in the live theater. The closest range within this category is the *full shot,* which just barely includes the human body in full, with the head near the top of the frame and the feet near the bottom.

The *medium shot* contains a figure from the knees or waist up. A functional shot, it's useful for shooting exposition scenes, for carrying movement, and for dialogue. There are several variations of the medium shot. The *two-shot* contains two figures from the waist up **(1–11).** The *three-shot* contains three figures; beyond three, the shot tends to become a full shot, unless the other figures are in the background. The **over-the-shoulder shot** usually contains two figures, one with part of his or her back to the camera, the other facing the camera.

12

1–11.   *As Good As It Gets* (U.S.A., 1997), *with Jack Nicholson and Helen Hunt, directed by James L. Brooks.*
Above all, the medium shot is the shot of the couple, romantic or otherwise. Generally, two-shots have a split focus rather than a single dominant: The bifurcated composition usually emphasizes equality, two people sharing the same intimate space. The medium two-shot reigns supreme in such genres as romantic comedies, love stories, and buddy films.   *(TriStar Pictures)*

The *close-up* shows very little if any locale and concentrates on a relatively small object—the human face, for example. Because the close-up magnifies the size of an object, it tends to elevate the importance of things, often suggesting a symbolic significance. The *extreme close-up* is a variation of this shot. Thus, instead of a face, the extreme close-up might show only a person's eyes or mouth.

The *deep-focus shot* is usually a long shot consisting of a number of focal distances and photographed in depth **(1–10).** Sometimes called a *wide-angle shot* because it requires a **wide-angle lens** to photograph, this type of shot captures objects at close, medium, and long ranges simultaneously, all of them in sharp focus. The objects in a deep-focus shot are carefully arranged in a succession of planes. By using this layering technique, the director can guide the viewer's eye from one distance to another. Generally, the eye travels from a close range to a medium to a long.

The Angles

The **angle** from which an object is photographed can often serve as an authorial commentary on the subject matter. If the angle is slight, it can serve as a subtle form of emotional coloration. If the angle is extreme, it can represent the major meaning of an image. The angle is determined by where the *camera* is placed, not the subject photographed. A picture of a person pho-

13

tographed from a high angle actually suggests an opposite interpretation from an image of the same person photographed from a low angle. The subject matter can be identical in the two images, yet the information we derive from both clearly shows that the form is the content, the content the form.

Filmmakers in the realistic tradition tend to avoid extreme angles. Most of their scenes are photographed from eye level, roughly five to six feet off the ground—approximately the way an actual observer might view a scene. Usually these directors attempt to capture the clearest view of an object. **Eye-level shots** are seldom intrinsically dramatic, because they tend to be the norm. Virtually all directors use some eye-level shots, especially in routine exposition scenes.

Formalist directors are not always concerned with the clearest image of an object, but with the image that best captures an object's expressive essence. Extreme angles involve distortions. Yet many filmmakers feel that by distorting the surface realism of an object, a greater truth is achieved—a symbolic truth. Both realist and formalist directors know that the viewer tends to identify with the camera's lens. The realist wishes to make the audience forget that there's a camera at all. The formalist is constantly calling attention to it.

1–12.   *Bonnie and Clyde* (U.S.A., 1967), *with Faye Dunaway and Warren Beatty, directed by Arthur Penn.*
High angles tend to make people look powerless, trapped. The higher the angle, the more it tends to imply fatality. The camera's angle can be inferred by the background of a shot: High angles usually show the ground or floor; low angles the sky or ceiling. Because we tend to associate light with safety, high-key lighting is generally nonthreatening and reassuring. But not always. We have been socially conditioned to believe that danger lurks in darkness, so when a traumatic assault takes place in broad daylight, as in this scene, the effect is doubly scary because it's so unexpected.   *(Warner Bros.)*

1–13. *Halloween: The Curse of Michael Myers (U.S.A., 1995), with George Wilbur, directed by Joe Chappelle.*
Extreme low angles can make characters seem threatening and powerful, for they loom above the camera—and us—like towering giants. We are collapsed in a position of maximum vulnerability—pinned to the ground, dominated. *(Dimension Films)*

There are five basic angles in the cinema: **(1)** the bird's-eye view, **(2)** the high angle, **(3)** the eye-level shot, **(4)** the low angle, and **(5)** the oblique angle. As in the case of shot designations, there are many intermediate kinds of angles. For example, there can be a considerable difference between a low and extreme low angle—although usually, of course, such differences tend to be matters of degree. Generally speaking, the more extreme the angle, the more distracting and conspicuous it is in terms of the subject matter being photographed.

The *bird's-eye view* is perhaps the most disorienting angle of all, for it involves photographing a scene from directly overhead (**1–1b**). Because we seldom view events from this perspective, the subject matter of such shots might initially seem unrecognizable and abstract. For this reason, filmmakers tend to avoid this type of camera **setup.** In certain contexts, however, this angle can be highly expressive. In effect, bird's-eye shots permit us to hover above a scene like all-powerful gods. The people photographed seem antlike and insignificant.

Ordinary *high-angle shots* are not so extreme, and therefore not so disorienting. The camera is placed on a **crane,** or some natural high promontory, but the sense of audience omnipotence is not overwhelming. High angles give a viewer a sense of a general overview, but not necessarily one implying destiny or fate. High angles reduce the height of the objects photographed and usually include the ground or floor as background. Movement is slowed down: This angle tends to be ineffective for conveying a sense of

1 5

speed, useful for suggesting tediousness. The importance of setting or environment is increased: The locale often seems to swallow people. High angles reduce the importance of a subject. A person seems harmless and insignificant photographed from above. This angle is also effective for conveying a character's self-contempt.

Some filmmakers avoid angles because they're too manipulative and judgmental. In the movies of the Japanese master Yasujiro Ozu, the camera is usually placed four feet from the floor—as if an observer were viewing the events seated Japanese style. Ozu treated his characters as equals; his approach discourages us from viewing them either condescendingly or sentimentally. For the most part, they are ordinary people, decent and conscientious. But Ozu lets them reveal themselves. He believed that value judgments are implied through the use of angles, and he kept his camera neutral and dispassionate. Eye-level

1–14.   *How Green Was My Valley* (U.S.A., 1941), *cinematography by Arthur Miller, directed by John Ford.*
Lyricism is a vague but indispensable critical term suggesting subjective emotions and a sensuous richness of expression. Derived from the word *lyre,* a harplike stringed instrument, lyricism is most often associated with music and poetry. Lyricism in movies also suggests a rhapsodic exuberance. Though lyrical qualities can be independent of subject matter, at its best, lyricism is a stylistic externalization of a film's basic concept. John Ford was one of the supreme masters of the big studio era, a visual lyricist of the first rank. He disliked overt emotions in his movies. He preferred conveying feelings through forms. Stylized lighting effects and formal compositions such as this invariably embody intense emotions. "Pictures, not words, should tell the story," Ford insisted.   *(Twentieth Century–Fox)*

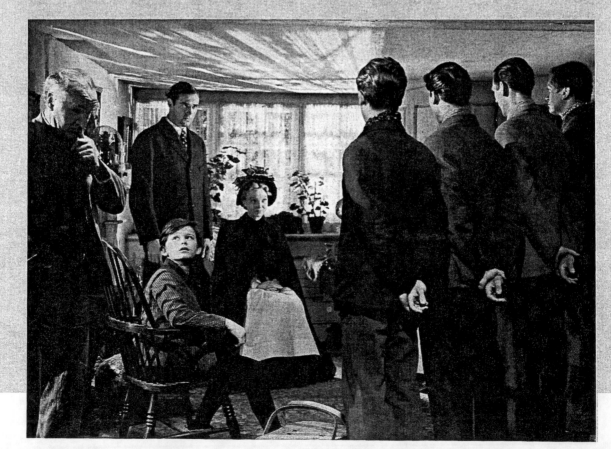

shots permit us to make up our own minds about what kind of people are being presented.

  Low angles have the opposite effect of high. They increase height and thus are useful for suggesting verticality. More practically, they increase a short actor's height. Motion is speeded up, and in scenes of violence especially, low angles capture a sense of confusion. Environment is usually minimized in low angles, and often the sky or a ceiling is the only background. Psychologically, low angles heighten the importance of a subject. The figure looms threateningly over the spectator, who is made to feel insecure and dominated. A person photographed from below inspires fear and awe (**1–13**). For this reason, low angles are often used in propaganda films or in scenes depicting heroism.

  An *oblique angle* involves a lateral tilt of the camera. When the image is projected, the horizon is skewed (**1–15**). People photographed at an oblique angle will look as though they're about to fall to one side. This angle is sometimes used for **point-of-view shots**—to suggest the imbalance of a drunk, for example. Psychologically, oblique angles suggest tension, transition, and impending movement. The natural horizontal and vertical lines of a scene are converted into unstable diagonals. Oblique angles are not used often, for they can disorient a viewer. In scenes depicting violence, however, they can be effective in capturing precisely this sense of visual anxiety.

1–15. *Shallow Grave* (Great Britain, 1994), *with Kerry Fox, Ewan McGregor, and Christopher Eccleston; directed by Danny Boyle.*
Oblique angles, sometimes known as "Dutch tilt" shots, produce a sense of irresolution, of visual anxiety. The scene's normal horizontal and vertical lines are tilted into tense, unresolved diagonals. Such shots are generally employed in thrillers, especially in scenes such as this that are meant to throw the spectator off balance with a shocking revelation. *(Gramercy Pictures)*

Light and Dark

Generally speaking, the **cinematographer** (who is also known as the director of photography, or D.P.) is responsible for arranging and controlling the lighting of a film and the quality of the photography. Usually the cinematographer executes the specific or general instructions of the director. The illumination of most movies is seldom a casual matter, for lights can be used with pinpoint accuracy. Through the use of spotlights, which are highly selective in their focus and intensity, a director can guide the viewer's eyes to any area of the photographed image. Motion picture lighting is seldom static, for even the slightest movement of the camera or the subject can cause the lighting to shift. Movies take so long to complete, primarily because of the enormous complexities involved in lighting each new shot. The cinematographer must make allowances for every movement within a continuous **take.** Each different color, shape, and texture reflects or absorbs differing amounts of light. If an image is photographed in depth, an even greater complication is involved, for the lighting must also be in depth. Furthermore, cinematographers don't have at their disposal most of the darkroom techniques of a still photographer: variable paper, dodging, airbrushing, choice of development, enlarger filters, etc. In a color film, the subtle effects of lights and darks are often obscured, for color tends to obliterate shadings and flatten images: Depth is negated.

There are a number of different styles of lighting. Usually designated as a lighting *key,* the style is geared to the theme and mood of a film, as well as its **genre.** Comedies and musicals, for example, tend to be lit in **high key,** with bright, even illumination and few conspicuous shadows. Tragedies and melodramas are usually lit in **high contrast,** with harsh shafts of lights and dramatic streaks of blackness. Mysteries, thrillers, and gangster films are generally in **low key,** with diffused shadows and atmospheric pools of light **(1–16).** Each lighting key is only an approximation, and some images consist of a combination of lighting styles—a low-key background with a few high-contrast elements in the foreground, for example. Movies shot in studios are generally more stylized and theatrical, whereas location photography tends to use available illumination, with a more natural style of lighting.

Lights and darks have had symbolic connotations since the dawn of humanity. The Bible is filled with light–dark symbolism. Rembrandt and Caravaggio used light–dark contrasts for psychological purposes as well. In general, artists have used darkness to suggest fear, evil, the unknown. Light usually suggests security, virtue, truth, joy. Because of these conventional symbolic associations, some filmmakers deliberately reverse light–dark expectations **(1–12).** Hitchcock's movies attempt to jolt viewers by exposing their shallow sense of security. He staged many of his most violent scenes in the glaring light.

Lighting can also be used to subvert subject matter. Paul Brickman's *Risky Business* is a coming-of-age comedy, and like most examples of its genre, the adolescent hero (Tom Cruise) triumphs over the System and its hypocritical morality. But in this movie, the naive hero learns to play the game and becomes a winner by being even more hypocritical than the upholders of the System.

1–16. *Red* **(France/Poland/Switzerland, 1994),** *with Irene Jacob and Jean-Louis Trintignant, cinematography by Piotr Sobocinski, directed by Krzysztof Kieslowski.*

During the Hollywood big studio era, cinematographers developed the technique of **three-point lighting,** which is still widely practiced throughout the world. With three-point lighting, the **key light** is the primary source of illumination. This light creates the **dominant** of an image—that area that first attracts our eye because it contains the most compelling contrast, usually of light and shadow. Generally, the dominant is also the area of greatest dramatic interest, the shot's focal point of action, either physical or psychological. **Fill lights,** which are less intense than the key, soften the harshness of the main light source, revealing subsidiary details that would otherwise be hidden by shadow. The **backlights** separate the foreground figures from their setting, heightening the illusion of three-dimensional depth in the image. Three-point methods tend to be most expressive with low-key lighting such as this. When a shot is bathed with high-key illumination, the three sources of light are more equally distributed over the surface of the image, and hence are more bland photographically. *(Miramax Films)*

19

1–17. *Double Indemnity* (U.S.A., 1944), *with Barbara Stanwyck and Fred MacMurray, directed by Billy Wilder.*

Film noir (literally, black cinema) is a style defined primarily in terms of light—or the lack of it. This style typified a variety of American genres in the 1940s and early 1950s. Noir is a world of night and shadows. Its milieu is almost exclusively urban. The style is profuse in images of dark streets, cigarette smoke swirling in dimly lit cocktail lounges, and symbols of fragility, such as windowpanes, sheer clothing, glasses, and mirrors. Motifs of entrapment abound: alleys, tunnels, subways, elevators, and train cars. Often the settings are locations of transience, like cheap rented rooms, piers, bus terminals, and railroad yards. The images are rich in sensuous textures, like neon-lit streets, windshields streaked with mud, and shafts of light streaming through windows of lonely rooms. Characters are imprisoned behind ornate lattices, grillwork, drifting fog and smoke. Visual designs emphasize harsh lighting contrasts, jagged shapes, and violated surfaces. The tone of film noir is fatalistic and paranoid. It's suffused with pessimism, emphasizing the darker aspects of the human condition. Its themes characteristically revolve around violence, lust, greed, betrayal, and depravity. *(Paramount Pictures)*

Most of the film is shot in low-key lighting—unusual for any comedy—which darkens the tone of the comic scenes. By the conclusion of the film, we're not entirely sure if the hero's "success" is ironic or straight. The movie would probably have been funnier if it had been shot in the usual high key, but the low-key photography makes it a more serious comedy—ironic and paradoxical.

Lighting can be used realistically or expressionistically. The realist tends to favor available lighting, at least in exterior scenes. Even out of doors, however, most filmmakers use some lamps and reflectors, either to augment the natural light or, on bright days, to soften the harsh contrasts produced by the sun. With the aid of special **lenses** and more light-sensitive film stocks, some directors have managed to dispense with artificial lighting completely. Available lighting tends to produce a documentary look in the film image, a hard-edged quality and an absence of smooth modeling. For interior shots, realists tend to prefer images with an obvious light source—a window or a lamp. Or they often use a diffused kind of lighting with no artificial, strong contrasts. In short, the realist doesn't use conspicuous lighting unless its source is dictated by the context.

20

1–18. *The Empire Strikes Back Special Edition* (U.S.A., 1997), *directed by Irvin Kershner.* High-contrast lighting is aggressively theatrical, infusing the photographed materials with a sense of tension and visual anguish. This dueling sequence is rendered more dynamic by the jagged knife blades of light that pierce the pervasive darkness. In the background, a desperate cosmic search is tearing up the sky. High-contrast lighting is typical of such genres as crime films, melodramas, thrillers, and mysteries. The lack of light in such movies symbolizes the unknown, deceptive surfaces, evil itself. *(Twentieth Century Fox)*

Formalists use light less literally. They are guided by its symbolic implications and will often stress these qualities by deliberately distorting natural light patterns. A face lighted from below almost always appears sinister, even if the actor assumes a totally neutral expression. Similarly, an obstruction placed in front of a light source can assume frightening implications, for it tends to threaten our sense of safety. On the other hand, in some contexts, especially in exterior shots, a silhouette effect can be soft and romantic (**1–34c**).

When a face is obviously lighted from above, a certain angelic quality, known as the halo effect, is the result. "Spiritual" lighting of this type tends to border on the cliché, however. **Backlighting,** which is a kind of semisilhouetting, is soft and ethereal. Love scenes are often photographed with a halo effect around the heads of the lovers to give them a romantic aura. Backlighting is especially evocative when used to highlight blonde hair (**1–20a**).

Through the use of spotlights, an image can be composed of violent contrasts of lights and darks. The surface of such images seems disfigured, torn up. The formalist director uses such severe contrasts for psychological and thematic purposes (**1–18**).

By deliberately permitting too much light to enter the aperture of the camera, a filmmaker can overexpose an image—producing a blanching flood of

21

a   b

1–19. *Leatherface: The Texas Chainsaw Massacre III* (U.S.A., 1990), *with R. A. Mihailoff, directed by Jeff Burr.*
Many people would argue that the backlit low-key lighting of **(a)** is more frightening than frontal lighting of **(b)**. Horrific as Leatherface's features are, at least we know what we have to deal with, whereas the faceless killer **(a)** conjures unspeakable unseen terrors. *(New Line Cinema)*

light over the entire surface of the picture. **Overexposure** has been most effectively used in nightmare and fantasy sequences. Sometimes this technique can suggest a kind of horrible glaring publicity, a sense of emotional exaggeration.

Color

Color in film didn't become commercially widespread until the 1940s. There were many experiments in color before this period, however. Some of Méliès's movies, for example, were painted by hand in assembly line fashion, with each painter responsible for coloring a minute area of the filmstrip. The original version of *The Birth of a Nation* (1915) was printed on various tinted stocks to suggest different moods: The burning of Atlanta was tinted red, the night scenes blue, the exterior love scenes pale yellow. Many silent filmmakers used this tinting technique to suggest different moods.

Sophisticated film color was developed in the 1930s, but for many years a major problem was its tendency to prettify everything. If color enhanced a sense of beauty—in a musical or a historical extravaganza—the effects were often appropriate. Thus, the best feature films of the early years of color were usually those with artificial or exotic settings. Realistic dramas were thought to be unsuitable vehicles for color. The earliest color processes tended also to emphasize garishness, and often special consultants had to be called in to harmonize the color schemes of costumes, makeup, and decor.

22

1–20a. *Braveheart* **(U.S.A., 1995),** *with Sophie Marceau and Mel Gibson, directed by Gibson.* (Paramount Pictures)

Art historians often distinguish between a "painterly" and a "linear" style, a distinction that's also useful in the photographic arts. A **painterly** style is soft-edged, sensuous, and romantic, best typified by the Impressionist landscapes of Claude Monet and the voluptuous figure paintings of Pierre Auguste Renoir. Line is deemphasized: Colors and textures shimmer in a hazily defined, radiantly illuminated environment. On the other hand, a **linear** style emphasizes drawing, sharply defined edges, and the supremacy of line over color and texture. In the field of painting, a linear style typifies such artists as Leonardo Da Vinci and the French classicist Jean-Auguste-Dominique Ingres.

Movies can also be photographed in a painterly or linear style, depending on the lighting, the lenses, and filters. The shot from *Braveheart* might almost have been painted by Renoir. Cinematographer John Toll used soft focus lenses and warm "natural" backlighting (creating a halo effect around the characters' heads) to produce an intensely romantic lyricism. Wyler's post-World War II masterpiece, *The Best Years of Our Lives,* was photographed by the great Gregg Toland. Its linear style is austere, deglamourized, shot in razor-sharp deep-focus. It was a style suited to the times. The postwar era was a period of disillusionment, sober reevaluations, and very few sentimental illusions. The high-key cinematography is polished, to be sure, but it's also simple, matter-of-fact, the invisible servant of a serious subject matter.

1–20b. *The Best Years of Our Lives* **(U.S.A., 1946),** *with Harold Russell, Teresa Wright, Dana Andrews, Myrna Loy, Hoagy Carmichael (standing), and Fredric March; directed by William Wyler.* (RKO).

Furthermore, each color process tended to specialize in a certain base hue—red, blue, or yellow, usually—whereas other colors of the spectrum were somewhat distorted. It was well into the 1950s before these problems were resolved. Compared with the subtle color perceptions of the human eye, however, and despite the apparent precision of most present-day color processing, cinematic color is still a relatively crude approximation.

The most famous color films tend to be expressionistic. Michelangelo Antonioni's attitude was fairly typical: "It is necessary to intervene in a color film, to take away the usual reality and replace it with the reality of the moment." In *Red Desert* (photographed by Carlo Di Palma), Antonioni spray-painted natural locales to emphasize internal psychological states. Industrial wastes, river pollution, marshes, and large stretches of terrain were painted gray to suggest the ugliness of contemporary industrial society and the heroine's drab, wasted existence. Whenever red appears in the movie, it suggests sexual passion. Yet the red—like the loveless sexuality—is an ineffective coverup of the pervasive gray.

1-21. *This Is Elvis* (U.S.A., 1981), *with Elvis Presley, directed by Malcolm Leo and others.* Documentaries are often photographed on the run. Cinematographers don't usually have a chance to augment the lighting, but have to capture the images as best they can under conditions that are almost totally uncontrolled. Many documentaries are photographed with hand-held cameras for maximum portability and with fast film stocks, which can register images using only ambient light. The images are valued not for their formal beauty, which is usually negligible (or nonexistent), but for their authenticity and spontaneity. Such images offer us privileged moments of intimacy that are all the more powerful because they're not simulated. They're the real thing.   *(Warner Bros.)*

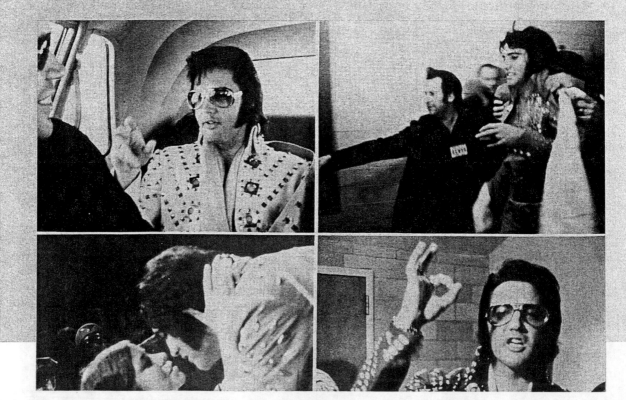

1–22. *From Here to Eternity* **(U.S.A., 1953),** *with Montgomery Clift and Burt Lancaster, directed by Fred Zinnemann.*
The expert cinematographers of the big-studio era were adept in revealing a surprising amount of detail even in scenes that take place at night, as in this photo. The preponderance of shadow in this shot clearly establishes the nighttime milieu, but note how an offscreen street lamp conveniently manages to illuminate the characters' facial expressions and body language. (They're both very drunk, sitting in the middle of a dirt road.) Sometimes studio-era D.P.s preferred to use the day-for-night filter, which gives the illusion of an evening setting even though the scene was originally photographed in daylight. To many present-day audiences, however, day-for-night shots look artificial, too bright and crisp to be convincing. *(Columbia Pictures)*

Color tends to be a subconscious element in film. It's strongly emotional in its appeal, expressive and atmospheric rather than intellectual. Psychologists have discovered that most people actively attempt to interpret the lines of a composition, but they tend to accept color passively, permitting it to suggest moods rather than objects. Lines are associated with nouns; color with adjectives. Line is sometimes thought to be masculine; color feminine. Both lines and colors suggest meanings, then, but in somewhat different ways.

Since earliest times, visual artists have used color for symbolic purposes. Color symbolism is probably culturally acquired, though its implications are surprisingly similar in otherwise differing societies. In general, cool colors (blue, green, violet) tend to suggest tranquility, aloofness, and serenity. Cool colors also have a tendency to recede in an image. Warm colors (red, yellow, orange) suggest aggressiveness, violence, and stimulation. They tend to come forward in most images.

25

1–23. *Crime and Punishment* (U.S.A., 1935), *with Peter Lorre (center), cinematography by Lucien Ballard, directed by Josef von Sternberg.*
Sternberg was a master of atmospheric lighting effects and closely supervised the photography of his films. His stories are unfolded primarily in terms of light and shade, rather than conventional dramatic means. "Every light has a point where it is brightest, and a point toward which it wanders to lose itself completely," he explained. "The journey of rays from that central core to the outposts of blackness is the adventure and drama of light." Note how the closed form of the **mise en scène** and the light encircling the protagonist (Lorre) produce an accusatory effect, a sense of entrapment. *(Paramount Pictures)*

Some filmmakers deliberately exploit color's natural tendency to garishness. Fellini's *Juliet of the Spirits* features many bizarre costumes and settings to suggest the tawdry but fascinating glamour of the world of show business. Bob Fosse's *Cabaret* is set in Germany and shows the early rise of the Nazi party. The colors are somewhat neurotic, with emphasis on such 1930s favorites as plum, acid green, purple, and florid combinations, like gold, black, and pink.

Black-and-white photography in a color film is sometimes used for symbolic purposes. Some filmmakers alternate whole episodes in black and white with entire sequences in color. The problem with this technique is its facile symbolism. The jolting black-and-white sequences are too obviously "significant" in the most arty sense. A more effective variation is simply not to use too much color, to let black and white predominate. In De Sica's *The Garden of the Finzi-Continis*, which is set in Fascist Italy, the early portions of the movie are

26

1–24. *Starman* (U.S.A., 1984), *with Karen Allen and Jeff Bridges, directed by John Carpenter.* Not every shot in a movie is photographed in the same style. Many of the earlier portions of this sci-fi film are photographed in a plain, functional style. After the earthling protagonist (Allen) falls in love with an appealing and hunky alien (Bridges), the photographic style becomes more romantic. The city's lights are etherealized by the shimmering soft-focus photography. The halo effect around the lovers' heads reinforces the air of enchantment. The gently falling snowflakes conspire to enhance the magical moment. These aren't just lovers, these are soul mates.   *(Columbia Pictures)*

richly resplendent in shimmering golds, reds, and almost every shade of green. As political repression becomes more brutal, these colors almost imperceptibly begin to wash out, until near the end of the film the images are dominated by whites, blacks, and blue-grays (see also **Color Plate 6**).

In the 1980s, a new computer technology was developed, allowing black-and-white movies to be "colorized"—a process that provoked a howl of protest from most film artists and critics. The colorized versions of some genres, like period films, musicals, and other forms of light entertainment, are not damaged too seriously by this process, but the technique is a disaster in carefully photographed black-and-white films, like *Citizen Kane*, with its **film noir** lighting style and brilliant deep-focus photography (see Chapter 12, "Synthesis: *Citizen Kane*").

Colorization also throws off the compositional balance of some shots, creating new **dominants**. In the shot from *Dark Victory* (**C.P. 18**), for example, the dominant is Brent's blue suit, which is irrelevant to the dramatic context. In the original black-and-white version, Davis is the dominant, her dark outfit contrasting with the white fireplace that frames her figure. Distracting visual dominants undercut the dramatic impact of such scenes. We keep thinking Brent's suit *must* be important. It is, but only to the computer.

Lenses, Filters, Stocks, Opticals, and Gauges

Because the camera's lens is a crude mechanism compared to the human eye, some of the most striking effects in a movie image can be achieved through the distortions of the photographic process itself. Particularly with regard to size and distance, the camera lens doesn't make mental adjustments but records things literally. For example, whatever is placed closest to the camera's lens will appear larger than an object at a greater distance. Hence, a coffee cup can totally obliterate a human being if the cup is in front of the lens and the human is standing at long-shot range.

Realist filmmakers tend to use normal, or standard, lenses to produce a minimum of distortion. These lenses photograph subjects more or less as they are perceived by the human eye. Formalist filmmakers often prefer lenses and **filters** that intensify given qualities and suppress others. Cloud formations, for example, can be exaggerated threateningly or softly diffused, depending on what kind of lens or filter is used. Different shapes, colors, and lighting intensities can be radically altered through the use of specific optical modifiers. There are literally dozens of different lenses, but most of them are subsumed under three major categories: those in the standard (nondistorted) range, the telephoto lenses, and the wide angles.

The *telephoto lens* is often used to get close-ups of objects from extreme distances. For example, no cinematographer is likely to want to get close enough to a lion to photograph a close-up with a standard lens. In cases such as these, the telephoto is used, thus guaranteeing the safety of the cinematographer while still producing the necessary close-up. Telephotos also allow cinematographers to work discreetly. In crowded city locations, for example, passersby are likely to stare at a movie camera. The telephoto permits the cinematographer to remain hidden—in a truck, for example—while he or she shoots close shots through a windshield or window. In effect, the lens works like a telescope, and because of its long focal length, it is sometimes called a *long lens*.

Telephoto lenses produce a number of side effects that are sometimes exploited by directors for symbolic use. Most long lenses are in sharp focus on one distance plane only. Objects placed before or beyond that distance blur, go out of focus—an expressive technique, especially to the formalist filmmaker **(1–25)**. The longer the lens, the more sensitive it is to distances; in the case of extremely long lenses, objects placed a mere few inches away from the selected focal plane can be out of focus. This deliberate blurring of planes in the background, foreground, or both can produce some striking photographic and atmospheric effects.

The focal distance of long lenses can usually be adjusted while shooting, and thus, the director is able to neutralize planes and guide the viewer's eye to various distances in a sequence—a technique called **rack focusing,** or selective focusing. In *The Graduate,* director Mike Nichols used a slight focus shift instead of a cut when he wanted the viewer to look first at the young heroine, who then blurs out of focus, then at her mother, who is standing a few feet

off in a doorway. The focus-shifting technique suggests a cause–effect relationship and parallels the heroine's sudden realization that her boyfriend's secret mistress is her own mother. In *The French Connection*, William Friedkin used selective focus in a sequence showing a criminal under surveillance. He remains in sharp focus while the city crowds of his environment are an undifferentiated blur. At strategic moments in the sequence, Friedkin shifted the focus plane from the criminal to the dogged detective who is tailing him in the crowd.

Long lenses also flatten images, decreasing the sense of distance between depth planes. Two people standing yards apart might look inches away when photographed with a telephoto lens. With very long lenses, distance planes are so compressed that the image can resemble a flat surface of abstract patterns. When anything moves toward or away from the camera in such shots, the mobile object doesn't seem to be moving at all. In *Marathon Man*, the hero (Dustin Hoffman) runs desperately toward the camera, but because of the flattening of the long lens, he seems almost to be running in place rather than moving toward his destination.

The *wide-angle lenses*, also called "short lenses," have short focal lengths and wide angles of view. These are the lenses used in deep-focus shots, for they preserve a sharpness of focus on virtually all distance planes. The distortions involved in short lenses are both linear and spatial. The wider the angle, the more lines and shapes tend to warp, especially at the edges of the image. Distances between various depth planes are also exaggerated with these lenses: Two people standing a foot away from each other can appear yards apart in a wide-angle image.

1–27.   Filmstrips of the four principal gauges used in movies, expressed in millimeters wide.
Photographic quality depends in part on the gauge of the film used to photograph and project the images. **(1)** Suitable for projecting in an average-sized room, 8 mm and Super 8 mm are primarily for home use. **(2)** The gauge ordinarily used in schools and museums is 16 mm; if projected in extremely large halls, 16-mm images tend to grow fuzzy and the color tends to fade. **(3)** The standard gauge for the vast majority of movie theaters is 35 mm. **(4)** For epic subjects requiring a huge screen, 70 mm is generally used; the images retain their linear sharpness and color saturation even in enormous theaters.

(1)   (2)   (3)   (4)

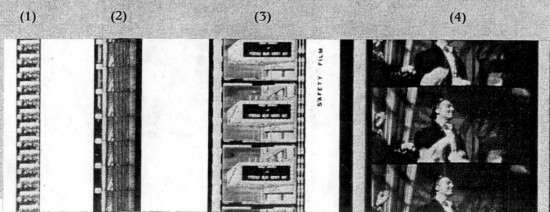

Movement toward or away from the camera is exaggerated when photographed with a short lens. Two or three ordinary steps can seem like unhumanly lengthy strides—an effective technique when a director wants to emphasize a character's strength, dominance, or ruthlessness. The fish-eye lens is the most extreme wide-angle modifier; it creates such severe distortions that the lateral portions of the screen seem reflected in a sphere, as though we were looking through a crystal ball.

Lenses and filters can be used for purely cosmetic purposes—to make an actor or actress taller, slimmer, younger, or older. Josef von Sternberg sometimes covered his lens with a translucent silk stocking to give his images a gauzy, romantic aura. A few glamour actresses beyond a certain age even had clauses in their contracts stipulating that only beautifying soft-focus lenses could be used for their close-ups. These optical modifiers eliminate small facial wrinkles and skin blemishes.

There are even more filters than there are lenses. Some trap light and refract it in such a way as to produce a diamondlike sparkle in the image. Many filters are used to suppress or heighten certain colors. Color filters can be espe-

1-28. *Kids* (U.S.A., 1995), *with Yakira Peguero and Leo Fitzpatrick, directed by Larry Clark.*

Fast film stocks are highly sensitive to light and can record images with no additional illumination except what's available on a set or location—even at night. These stocks tend to produce harsh light–dark contrasts, an absence of details, and images so grainy that they can appear more painterly than linear. Fast stocks are especially effective in fiction films that purport to be realistic and documentarylike, such as this controversial depiction of some urban teenagers and their high-risk sexual practices. *(Excalibur Films)*

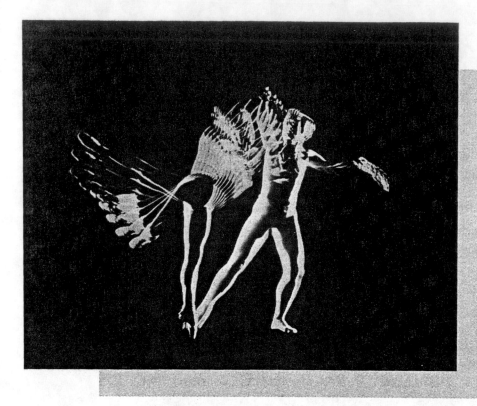

1–29. *Pas De Deux* (Canada, 1968), *directed by Norman McLaren.* The optical printer is an invaluable piece of equipment, particularly to the formalist filmmaker, because, among other things, it allows the superimposition of two or more realities within a unified space. This film uses a technique called chronophotography, in which the movements of two dancers are staggered and overlayed by the optical printer to produce a stroboscopic effect: As the dancers move, they leave a ghostly imprint on the screen. *(National Film Board of Canada)*

cially striking in exterior scenes. Robert Altman's *McCabe and Mrs. Miller* (photographed by Vilmos Zsigmond) uses green and blue filters for many of the exterior scenes, yellow and orange for interiors. These filters emphasize the bitter cold of the winter setting and the communal warmth of the rooms inside the primitive buildings.

Though there are a number of different kinds of film stocks, most of them fall within the two basic categories: fast and slow. **Fast stock** is highly sensitive to light and in some cases can register images with no illumination except what's available on location, even in nighttime sequences **(1–28)**. **Slow stock** is relatively insensitive to light and requires as much as ten times more illumination than fast stocks. Traditionally, slow stocks are capable of capturing colors precisely, without washing them out.

Fast stocks are commonly associated with documentary movies, for with their great sensitivity to light, these stocks can reproduce images of events while they're actually occurring. The documentarist is able to photograph people and places without having to set up cumbersome lights. Because of this light sensitivity, fast stocks produce a grainy image in which lines tend to be fuzzy and colors tend to wash out. In a black-and-white film, lights and darks contrast sharply and many variations of gray can be lost.

Ordinarily, technical considerations such as these would have no place in a book of this sort, but the choice of stock can produce considerable psychological and aesthetic differences in a movie. Since the early 1960s, many fiction filmmakers have switched to fast stocks to give their images a documentary sense of urgency.

The **optical printer** is an elaborate machine that produces many special effects in the cinema. It includes a camera and projector precisely aligned, and

3 4

1–30. *Multiplicity* (U.S.A., 1996), *with (from left to right) Michael Keaton, Michael Keaton, Michael Keaton, and Michael Keaton; directed by Harold Ramis.*
The American cinema has always been on the cutting edge of film technology, especially in the area of special effects. Computer-generated images have allowed filmmakers to create fantasy worlds of the utmost realism. In this movie, for example, Keaton plays a man who has lost his wife and his job, and must clone himself in order to function effectively. Computer artist Dan Madsen created a film reality that obviously has no counterpart in the outside physical world. Critic Stephen Prince has observed that such technological advancements as computer-generated images have radically undermined the traditional distinctions between realism and formalism in film theory. See Stephen Prince, "True Lies: Perceptual Realism, Digital Images, and Film Theory," in *Film Quarterly* (Spring, 1996). *(Columbia Pictures)*

it permits the operator to rephotograph all or a portion of an existing frame of a film. **Double exposure,** or the superimposition of two images, is one of the most important of these effects, for it permits the director to portray two levels of reality simultaneously. For this reason, the technique is often used in fantasy and dream sequences, as well as in scenes dealing with the supernatural. The optical printer can also produce **multiple exposures,** or the superimposition of many images simultaneously. Multiple exposures are useful for suggesting mood, time lapses, and any sense of mixture—of time, places, objects, events. The optical printer can combine one actor with moving images of others in a different time and place.

1–31. Twentieth Century–Fox publicity photo of Marilyn Monroe (1953). Cinematographers often comment that the camera "likes" certain individuals and "doesn't like" others, even though these others might be good-looking people in real life. Highly photogenic performers like Marilyn Monroe are rarely uncomfortable in front of the camera. Indeed, they often play to it, ensnaring our attention. Photographer Richard Avedon said of Marilyn, "She understood photography, and she also understood what makes a great photograph—not the technique, but the content. She was more comfortable in front of the camera than away from it." Philippe Halsman went even further, pointing out that her open mouth and frequently open décolletage were frankly invitational: "She would try to seduce the camera as if it were a human being. . . . She knew that the camera lens was not just a glass eye but a symbol of the eyes of millions of men, so the camera stimulated her strongly." *(Twentieth Century–Fox)*

The Cinematographer

The cinema is a collaborative enterprise, the result of the combined efforts of many artists, technicians, and businesspeople. Because the contributions of these individuals vary from film to film, it's hard to determine who's responsible for what in a movie. Most sophisticated viewers agree that the director is generally the dominant artist in the best movies. The principal collaborators—actors, writers, cinematographers—perform according to the director's unifying sensibility. But directorial dominance is an act of faith. Many films are stamped by the personalities of others—a prestigious **star,** for example, or a skillful editor who manages to make sense out of a director's botched **footage.**

Cinematographers sometimes chuckle sardonically when a director's visual style is praised by critics. Some directors don't even bother looking through the viewfinder and leave such matters as composition, angles, and lenses up to the cinematographer. When directors ignore these important formal elements, they throw away some of their most expressive pictorial opportunities and function more like stage directors, who are concerned with dramatic

1–32. *The Emigrants* **(Sweden, 1972),** *with Liv Ullmann and Max von Sydow, photographed and directed by Jan Troell.*
If we were to view a scene similar to this in real life, we would probably concentrate most of our attention on the people in the wagon. But there are considerable differences between reality and cinematic realism. Realism is an artistic style. In selecting materials from the chaotic sprawl of reality, the realist filmmaker necessarily eliminates some details and emphasizes others into a structured hierarchy of visual significance. For example, the stone wall in the foreground of this shot occupies more space than the humans. Visually, this dominance suggests that the rocks are more important than the people. The unyielding stone wall symbolizes divisiveness and exclusion—ideas that are appropriate to the dramatic context. If the wall were irrelevant to the theme, Troell would have eliminated it and selected other details from the copiousness of reality—details that would be more pertinent to the dramatic context. *(Warner Bros.)*

rather than visual values—that is, with the script and the acting rather than the photographic quality of the image itself.

On the other hand, a few cinematographers have been praised for their artistry when in fact the effectiveness of a film's images is largely due to the director's pictorial skills. Hitchcock provided individual frame drawings for most of the shots in his films, a technique called **storyboarding.** His cinematographers framed up according to Hitchcock's precise sketches. Hence, when Hitchcock claimed that he never looked through the viewfinder, he meant that he assumed his cinematographer had followed instructions.

Sweeping statements about the role of the cinematographer are impossible to make, for it varies widely from film to film and from director to direc-

37

tor. In actual practice, virtually all cinematographers agree that the style of the photography should be geared to the story, theme, and mood of the film. William Daniels had a prestigious reputation as a glamour photographer at MGM and for many years was known as "Greta Garbo's cameraman." Yet Daniels also shot Erich von Stroheim's harshly realistic *Greed*, and the cinematographer won an Academy Award for his work in Jules Dassin's *Naked City*, which is virtually a semidocumentary.

During the big-studio era, most cinematographers believed that the aesthetic elements of a film should be maximized—beautiful pictures with beautiful people was the goal. Today such views are considered rigid and doctrinaire. Sometimes images are even coarsened if such a technique is considered appropriate to the dramatic materials. For example, Vilmos Zsigmond, who photographed *Deliverance*, didn't want the rugged forest setting to appear too pretty

1–33.   *Women on the Verge of a Nervous Breakdown* (Spain, 1988), *with Carmen Maura, directed by Pedro Almodóvar.*

What's wrong with this photo? For one thing, the character is not centered in the composition. The image is asymmetrical, apparently off balance because the "empty" space on the right takes up over half the viewing area. Visual artists often use "negative space" such as this to create a vacuum in the image, a sense of something missing, something left unsaid. In this case, the pregnant protagonist (Maura) has just been dumped by her lover. He is an unworthy swine, but inexplicably, perversely, she still loves him. His abandonment has left a painful empty place in her life.   *(Orion Pictures)*

because beautiful visuals would contradict the Darwinian theme of the film. He wanted to capture what Tennyson described as "nature red in tooth and claw." Accordingly, Zsigmond shot on overcast days as much as possible to eliminate the bright blue skies. He also avoided reflections in the water because they tend to make nature look cheerful and inviting. "You don't make beautiful compositions just for the sake of making compositions," cinematographer Laszlo Kovacs has insisted. Content always determines form; form should be the embodiment of content.

"Many times, what you don't see is much more effective than what you do see," Gordon Willis has noted. Willis is arguably the most respected of all American cinematographers, a specialist in low-key lighting styles. He photographed all three of Francis Ford Coppola's *Godfather* films—which many traditionalists consider too dark. But Willis was aiming for poetry, not realism. Most of the interior scenes were very dark to suggest an atmosphere of evil and secrecy **(C.P.8).**

Willis's preference for low levels of light has been enormously influential in the contemporary cinema. Unfortunately, many filmmakers today regard low-key lighting as intrinsically more "serious" and "artistic," whatever the subject matter. These needlessly dark movies are often impenetrably obscure when shown on the television screen in VCR or DVD formats. Conscientious filmmakers often supervise the transfer from film to video because each medium requires different lighting intensities. Generally, low-key images must be lightened for video and DVD.

Some film directors are totally ignorant of the technology of the camera and leave such matters entirely to the cinematographer. Other filmmakers are very sophisticated in the art of the camera. For example, Sidney Lumet, who is best known for directing such realistic New York City dramas as *The Pawnbroker, Dog Day Afternoon,* and *Serpico,* always makes what he calls a "lens chart" or a "lens plot." In Lumet's *Prince of the City,* for instance, the story centers on a Serpicolike undercover cop who is gathering information on police corruption. Lumet used no "normal" lenses in the movie, only extreme telephotos and wide-angle lenses, because he wanted to create an atmosphere of distrust and paranoia. He wanted the space to be distorted, untrustworthy. "The lens tells the story," Lumet explained, even though superficially the film's style is gritty and realistic.

There are some great movies that are photographed competently, but without distinction. Realist directors are especially likely to prefer an unobtrusive style. Many of the works of Luis Buñuel, for example, can only be described as "professional" in their cinematography. Buñuel was rarely interested in formal beauty—except occasionally to mock it. Rollie Totheroh, who photographed most of Chaplin's works, merely set up his camera and let Chaplin the actor take over. Photographically speaking, there are few memorable shots in his films. What makes the images compelling is the genius of Chaplin's acting. This photographic austerity—some would consider it poverty—is especially apparent in those rare scenes when Chaplin is off camera.

1–34a. *Muriel's Wedding* (Australia, 1995), *with Toni Collette (with flowers), directed by P. J. Hogan.* (Miramax Films)

1–34b. *Kafka* (U.S.A., 1991), *with Jeremy Irons (left), directed by Steven Soderbergh.* (Miramax Films)

Cinematography is very important, but it usually can't make or break a movie—only make it better or worse. For example, the low-budget *Muriel's Wedding* was shot mostly on location using available lighting. The photography is adequate, but nothing more. In this shot, for instance, the protagonist (Collette) has the key light on her, but the background is too busy and the depth layers of the image are compressed into an undifferentiated messy blur. Nonetheless, the movie was an international hit and was widely praised by critics, thanks mostly to Collette's endearing performance, a funny script, and Hogan's exuberant direction. No one complained about the lackluster photography.

On the other hand, the cinematography of *Kafka* is ravishing—bold, theatrical, richly textured. This shot alone must have taken many hours to set up. But the movie was a failure, both with the public and with most critics. In short, not all beautifully photographed movies

continued ▶

40

1–34c. Days of Heaven (U.S.A., 1978), written and directed by Terrence Malick.
(A Paramount Picture)

are great. And not all great movies are beautifully photographed. Many of them—especially realistic films—are plain and straightforward. Realists often don't *want* you to notice the photography. They want you to concentrate on *what's* being photographed, not on how it's being photographed.

Perhaps an ideal synthesis is found in a movie like *Days of Heaven*. Malick's powerful allegory of human frailty and corruption is written in a spare, poetic idiom. The actors are also first-rate, needy, and touching in their doomed vulnerability. The film was photographed by Nestor Almendros, who won a well-deserved Oscar for his cinematography. The story is set in the early twentieth century in a lonely wheat-growing region of the American midwest. Malick wanted the setting to suggest a lush Garden of Eden, a lost paradise. Almendros suggested that virtually the entire movie could be shot during the "magic hour." This is a term used by photographers to denote dusk, roughly the last hour of the day before the sun yields to night. During this fleeting interlude, shadows are soft and elongated, figures are lit from the side rather than from above, rimmed with a golden halo, and the entire landscape is bathed in a luminous glow. Naturally, shooting one hour a day was expensive and time-consuming. But they got what they wanted: Whether focusing on a close-up of a locust munching on a stalk of wheat, or an extreme long shot of a rural sunset, the images are rapturous in their lyricism. We feel a sense of poignant loss when the characters must leave this land of milk and honey.

But there are far more films in which the *only* interesting or artistic quality is the cinematography. For every great work like Fritz Lang's *You Only Live Once*, Leon Shamroy had to photograph four or five bombs of the ilk of *Snow White and the Three Stooges*. Lee Garmes photographed several of von Sternberg's visually opulent films, but he also was required to shoot *My Friend Irma Goes West*, a piece of garbage.

In this chapter, we've been concerned with visual images largely as they relate to the art and technology of cinematography. But the camera must have materials to photograph—objects, people, settings. Through the manipulation of these materials, the director is able to convey a multitude of ideas and emotions spatially. This arrangement of objects in space is referred to as a director's *mise en scène*—the subject of the following chapter.

FURTHER READING

ALTON, JOHN, *Painting with Light* (Berkeley: University of California Press, 1995). Reprint of a classic work.

COE, BRIAN, *The History of Movie Photography* (London: Ash & Grant, 1981).

COPJEC, JOAN, ed. *Shades of Noir* (London and New York: Routledge, 1994). Essays on the origins and persistence of film noir.

EYMAN, SCOTT, *Five American Cinematographers* (Metuchen, N.J., and London: Scarecrow Press, 1987). Interviews with Karl Struss, Joseph Ruttenberg, James Wong Howe, Linwood Dunn, and William Clothier.

FIELDING, RAYMOND, *The Techniques of Special Effects Cinematography* (New York: Hastings House, 1965). Somewhat dated, but still valuable.

FINCH, CHRISTOPHER, *Special Effects: Creating Movie Magic* (New York: Abbeville, 1984). Lavishly illustrated.

MASCELLI, JOSEPH, *The Five C's of Cinematography* (Hollywood: Cine/Graphics, 1965). A practical manual.

SCHAEFER, DENNIS, and LARRY SALVATO, eds., *Masters of Light* (Berkeley: University of California Press, 1984). Excellent collection of interviews with contemporary cinematographers.

SCHECHTER, HAROLD, AND DAVID EVERITT, *Film Tricks: Special Effects in Movies* (New York: Dial, 1980).

YOUNG, FREDDIE, *The Work of the Motion Picture Cameraman* (New York: Hastings House, 1972). Technical emphasis.

Mise en Scène

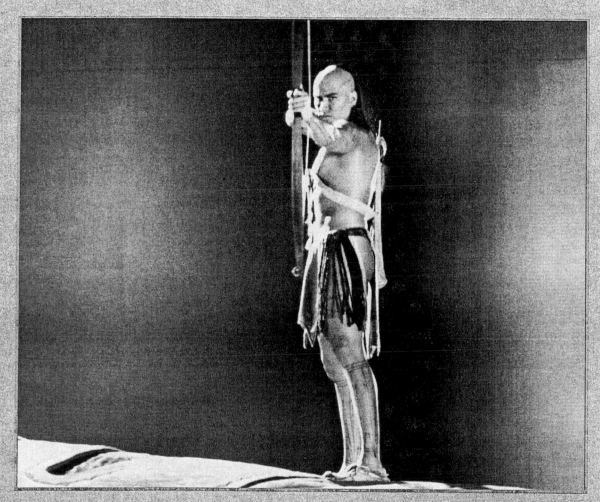

One must compose images as the old masters did their canvases, with the same preoccupation with effect and expression.

—MARCEL CARNÉ, FILMMAKER

a

2-38. *Full Metal Jacket* (Great Britain/U.S.A., 1987), *directed by Stanley Kubrick.*
Even within a single scene, filmmakers will switch from open to closed forms, depending on the feelings or ideas that are being stressed in each individual shot. For example, both of these shots take place during a battle scene in the Vietnamese city of Hue. In **(a),** the characters are under fire, and the wounded soldier's head is not even in the frame. The form is appropriately open. The frame functions as a temporary masking device that's too narrow in its scope to include all the relevant information. Often, the frame seems to cut figures off in an arbitrary manner in open form, suggesting that the action is continued off screen, like newsreel footage that was fortuitously photographed by a camera operator who was unable to superimpose an artistic form on the runaway materials. In **(b),** the form is closed, as four soldiers rush to their wounded comrade, providing a protective buffer from the outside world. Open and closed forms aren't intrinsically meaningful, then, but derive their significance from the dramatic context. In some cases, closed forms can suggest entrapment **(2-37);** in other cases, such as **(b),** closed form implies security, camaraderie. *(Warner Bros.)*

b

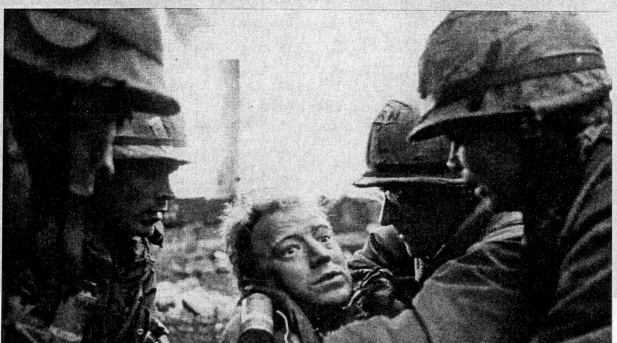

A systematic mise en scène analysis of any given shot includes the following fifteen elements:

1. *Dominant.* Where is our eye attracted first? Why?

2. *Lighting key.* High key? Low key? High contrast? Some combination of these?

3. *Shot and camera proxemics.* What type of shot? How far away is the camera from the action?

4. *Angle.* Are we (and the camera) looking up or down on the subject? Or is the camera neutral (eye level)?

5. *Color values.* What is the dominant color? Are there contrasting foils? Is there color symbolism?

6. *Lens/filter/stock.* How do these distort or comment on the photographed materials?

7. *Subsidiary contrasts.* What are the main eye-stops after taking in the dominant?

8. *Density.* How much visual information is packed into the image? Is the texture stark, moderate, or highly detailed?

9. *Composition.* How is the two-dimensional space segmented and organized? What is the underlying design?

10. *Form.* Open or closed? Does the image suggest a window that arbitrarily isolates a fragment of the scene? Or a proscenium arch, in which the visual elements are carefully arranged and held in balance?

11. *Framing.* Tight or loose? Do the characters have no room to move around, or can they move freely without impediments?

12. *Depth.* On how many planes is the image composed? Does the background or foreground comment in any way on the midground?

13. *Character placement.* What part of the framed space do the characters occupy? Center? Top? Bottom? Edges? Why?

14. *Staging positions.* Which way do the characters look vis-à-vis the camera?

15. *Character proxemics.* How much space is there between the characters?

These visual principles, with appropriate modifications, can be applied to any image analysis. Of course, while we're actually watching a movie, most of us don't have the time or inclination to explore all fifteen elements of mise en scène in each shot. Nonetheless, by applying these principles to a still photo, we can train our eyes to "read" a movie image with more critical sophistication.

For example, the image from *M* **(2–40)** is a good instance of how form (mise en scène) is actually content. The shot takes place near the end of the movie. A psychotic child-killer (Lorre) has been hunted down by the members of the underworld. These "normal" criminals have taken him to an abandoned warehouse where they intend to prosecute and execute the psychopath for his heinous crimes and in doing so take the police heat off themselves. In this scene, the killer is confronted by a witness (center) who holds an incriminating piece of evidence—a balloon. The components of the shot include the following:

Many filmmakers insist on using a video assist monitor on their sets as a quick-check device before actually shooting a scene on film stock. Stock is more expensive and not nearly so immediate in terms of feedback. By photographing a scene with a video camera, the director can correct any problems in the staging and mise en scène. The actors can check to see if their performances are too subdued or too broad or too whatever. The cinematographer can preview the lighting and camerawork. And the producers can see if their money is going down the drain. When everyone is satisfied, they can then proceed to shoot the scene on movie stock. The video run-through is like a preliminary sketch for a finished painting or a dress rehearsal for a stage play. *(Columbia Pictures)*

1. *Dominant.* The balloon, the brightest object in the frame. When the photo is turned upside down and converted to a pattern of abstract shapes, its dominance is more readily discernible.

2. *Lighting key.* Murky low key, with high-contrast spotlights on the balloon and the four main figures.

3. *Shot and camera proxemics.* The shot is slightly more distant than a full shot. The camera proxemic range is social, perhaps about ten feet from the dominant.

4. *Angle.* Slightly high, suggesting an air of fatality.

5. *Color values.* The movie is in black and white.

6. *Lens/filter/stock.* A standard lens is used, with no apparent filter. Standard slow stock.

7. *Subsidiary contrasts.* The figures of the killer, the witness, and the two criminals in the upper left.

8. *Density.* The shot has a high degree of density, especially considering the shadowy lighting. Such details as the texture of the brick walls, the creases in the clothing, and the expressive faces of the actors are highlighted.

9. *Composition.* The image is divided into three general areas—left, center, and right—suggesting instability and tension.

10. *Form.* Definitely closed: The frame suggests a constricting cell, with no exit for the prisoner.

11. *Framing.* Tight: The killer is trapped in the same territory with his threatening accusors.

12. *Depth.* The image is composed on three depth planes: the two figures in the foreground, the two figures on the stairs in the midground, and the brick wall of the background.

13. *Character placement.* The accusers and balloon tower above the killer, sealing off any avenue of escape, while he cowers below at the extreme right edge, almost falling into the symbolic blackness outside the frame.

14. *Staging positions.* The accusers stand in a quarter-turn position, implying a greater intimacy with us than the main character, who is in the profile position, totally unaware of anything but his own terror.

15. *Character proxemics.* Proxemics are personal between the foreground characters, the killer's immediate problem, and intimate between the men on the stairs, who function as a double threat. The range between the two pairs is social.

Actually, a complete mise en scène analysis of a given shot is even more complex. Ordinarily, any **iconographical** elements, in addition to a costume and set analysis, are considered part of the mise en scène. But since these elements are discussed in Chapters 6 and 7, respectively, we confine ourselves only to these fifteen formal characteristics.

In these first two chapters, we've been concerned with the most important source of meaning in the movies—the visual image. But of course movies exist in time and have many other ways of communicating information. Photography and mise en scène are merely two language systems of many. For this rea-

2-40. *M (Germany, 1931), with Peter Lorre (extreme right), directed by Fritz Lang.* (Janus Films)

BU-45

son, a film image must sometimes be restrained or less saturated with meanings than a painting or still photo, in which all the necessary information is contained within a single image. The principles of variation and restraint exist in all temporal arts. In movies, these principles can be seen in those images that seem rather uninteresting, usually because the dominant is found elsewhere—in the music, for example, or the **editing.** In a sense, these images are visual rest areas.

A filmmaker has literally hundreds of different ways to convey meanings. Like the painter or still photographer, the movie director can emphasize visual dominants. In a scene portraying violence, for example, he or she can use diagonal and zigzagging lines, aggressive colors, close-ups, extreme angles, harsh lighting contrasts, unbalanced compositions, large shapes, and so on. Unlike most other visual artists, the filmmaker can also suggest violence through movement, either of the subject itself, the camera, or both. The film artist can suggest violence through editing, by having one shot collide with another in a kaleidoscopic explosion of different perspectives. Furthermore, through the use of the soundtrack, violence can be conveyed by loud or rapid dialogue, harsh sound effects, or strident music. Precisely because there are so many ways to convey a given effect, the filmmaker will vary the emphasis, sometimes stressing image, sometimes movement, other times sound. Occasionally, especially in climactic scenes, all three are used at the same time.

FURTHER READING

ARNHEIM, RUDOLF, *Art and Visual Perception: A Psychology of the Creative Eye* (Berkeley: University of California Press, 1954). Primarily about paintings and drawings.

BORDWELL, DAVID, JANET STAIGER, and KRISTIN THOMPSON, *The Classical Hollywood Cinema: Film Style and Mode of Production to 1960* (New York: Columbia University Press, 1985). A fine scholarly study.

BRAUDY, LEO, *The World in a Frame* (Garden City, N.Y.: Doubleday, 1976). Filled with intelligent insights.

DONDIS, DONIS A., *A Primer of Visual Literacy* (Cambridge, Mass., and London, England: The M.I.T. Press, 1974). Primarily on design and composition.

DYER, RICHARD. *The Matter of Images* (London and New York: Routledge, 1993). The ideological implications of images.

FREEBURG, VICTOR O., *Pictorial Beauty on the Screen* (New York: Macmillan, 1923). A discussion of the conventions of classical composition.

HALL, EDWARD T., *The Hidden Dimension* (Garden City, N.Y.: Doubleday, 1969). How humans and other animals use space.

NILSEN, VLADIMIR, *The Cinema As a Graphic Art* (New York: Hill and Wang, 1959). How reality is shaped by form, with major emphasis on classical composition.

RUESCH, JURGEN, and WELDON KEES, *Nonverbal Communication* (Berkeley: University of California Press, 1966).

SOMMERS, ROBERT, *Personal Space* (Englewood Cliffs, N.J.: Prentice-Hall, 1969). How individuals use and abuse space.

3

Movement

Warner Bros.

*The opening of a door, a hand, or an eye can bring about a
climax as thrilling as a crash of locomotives on the screen.*
—RICHARD DYER MACCANN

93

BU-47

The Moving Camera

Before the 1920s, filmmakers tended to confine movements to the subject photographed. There were relatively few who moved their cameras during a shot, and then usually to keep a moving figure within the frame. In the 1920s, such German filmmakers as F. W. Murnau and E. A. Dupont moved the camera within the shot not only for physical reasons but for psychological and thematic reasons as well. The German experiments permitted subsequent filmmakers to use the mobile camera to communicate subtleties previously considered impossible. True, **editing**—that is, moving the camera *between* shots—is faster, cheaper, and less distracting. But cutting is also abrupt, disconnected, and unpredictable compared to the fluid lyricism of a moving camera.

A major problem of the moving camera involves time. Films that use this technique extensively tend to seem slow-moving, since moving in or out of

3-16. *Circle of Friends* (Ireland, 1994), *with Minnie Driver and Chris O'Donnell, directed by Pat O'Connor.*
Movement is not always an automatic dominant. In this scene, for example, unimportant characters dance in and out of the frame, occasionally obscuring our view of the two central characters, who are not moving much as they dance and talk. Note how O'Connor shoots the scene with a telephoto lens, with the romantic couple in focus and the other dancers blurred into an undulating sea of irrelevance. What matters for these two is here and now in each other's arms. The rest of the world seems very far away.   *(Savoy Pictures)*

3–17. *Forrest Gump* (U.S.A., 1994), *with Tom Hanks, directed by Robert Zemeckis.*
Reverse dolly shots such as this are more unsettling than conventional traveling shots. When we dolly *into* a scene, we can usually see where we're headed, to a geographical goal of some sort. But when the camera moves in reverse, sweeping backwards as it keeps the running protagonist in frame, we have no sense of a final destination, just the urgent, desperate need to flee. *(Paramount Pictures)*

a scene is more time-consuming than a straight cut. A director must decide whether moving the camera is worth the film time involved and whether the movement warrants the additional technical and budgetary complications. If a filmmaker decides to move the camera, he or she must then decide how. Should it be mounted on a vehicle or simply moved around the axis of a stationary tripod? Each major type of camera movement implies different meanings, some obvious, others subtle. There are seven basic moving camera shots: **(1) pans, (2) tilts, (3) crane shots, (4) dolly shots, (5) zoom shots, (6) hand-held shots,** and **(7) aerial shots.**

Panning shots—those movements of the camera that scan a scene horizontally—are taken from a stationary axis point, with the camera mounted on a tripod. Such shots are time-consuming because the camera's movement must ordinarily be smooth and slow to permit the images to be recorded clearly. Pans are also unnatural in a sense, for when the human eye pans a scene, it jumps from one point to another, skipping over the intervals between points. The most common use of a pan is to keep the subject within frame. If a person moves from one position to another, the camera moves horizontally to keep the person in the center of the composition. Pans in extreme long shots are especially effective in epic films where an audience can experience the vastness of a locale. But pans can be just as effective at medium and close ranges. The so-called **reaction shot,** for instance, is a movement of the camera away from the central attraction—usually a speaker—to capture the reaction of an onlooker

113

or listener. In such cases, the pan is an effective way of preserving the cause–effect relationship between the two subjects and of emphasizing the solidarity and connectedness of people.

The **swish pan** (also known as a flash pan and a zip pan) is a variation of this technique and is often used for transitions between shots—as a substitute cut. The swish pan involves a whirling of the camera at a speed so rapid that only blurred images are recorded (**3–2b**). Although they actually take more time than cuts, swish pans connect one scene to another with a greater sense of simultaneity than cuts can suggest. For this reason, flash pans are often used to connect events at different locales that might otherwise appear remote from each other.

Pan shots tend to emphasize the unity of space and the connectedness of people and objects within that space. Precisely because we expect a panning shot to emphasize the literal contiguity of people sharing the same space, these shots can surprise us when their realistic integrity is violated. In Robert Benton's *Places in the Heart,* for example, the final shot of the movie connects the

3–18.   *Cabaret* (U.S.A., 1972), *with Joel Grey, choreographed and directed by Bob Fosse.*
A former dancer, Fosse was the foremost stage choreographer–director of his generation, winning many Tony Awards for his Broadway musicals. He also directed a half dozen or so movies, including this classic musical, his greatest work on film. Fosse's dancers are rarely elegant or lyrical. Rather, they are more likely to scrunch their shoulders, hunch up their back, or thrust out their pelvis. Fosse also loved glitzy/tacky costumes—usually accompanied by hats, which were integrated into his dance numbers. He is also the most witty of choreographers, with his dancers snapping their fingers in unison, mincing to a percussive beat like cartoon characters, or locking their knees and pointing their toes inwardly. Above all, Fosse's dance numbers are sexy—not the wholesome athletic sex appeal of a Gene Kelly choreography, but something funkier, more raffish, and down-and-dirty. His mature style is uniquely cinematic, not merely an objective recording of a stage choreography. In *Cabaret,* for example, he intercuts shots from the musical numbers with shots of the dramatic action and vice versa. In some numbers, he cuts to an avalanche of colliding shots to create a choreography that could not exist in the literal space of a theatrical stage.   *(Allied Artists)*

world of the living with the dead. The film is a celebration of the simple Christian values that bind a small Texas community together during the troubled times of the 1930s depression. The final shot takes place in church. The camera begins to pan the congregation in a long sweeping motion down each row of pews. Interspersed among the surviving characters are several that we know to be dead, including a murderer and his victim, worshipping side by side. Though the rest of the movie is realistically presented, this final shot leaps to a symbolic level, suggesting that the unified spirit of the community includes all its members, deceased as well as living.

   Tilt shots are vertical movements of the camera around a stationary horizontal axis. Many of the same principles that apply to pans apply to tilts: They can be used to keep subjects within frame, to emphasize spatial and psychological interrelationships, to suggest simultaneity, and to emphasize cause–effect relationships. Tilts, like pans, can also be used subjectively in **point-of-view shots:** The camera can simulate a character's looking up or down a scene, for instance. Since a tilt is a change in angle, it is often used to suggest a psychological shift within a character. When an eye-level camera tilts downward, for example, the person photographed suddenly appears more vulnerable.

   Dolly shots, sometimes called trucking or tracking shots, are taken from a moving vehicle (dolly). The vehicle literally moves in, out, or alongside a moving figure or object while the action is being photographed. Tracks are

3–19.   Production photo from the set of *Broken Arrow* (U.S.A., 1996), *with Christian Slater, director John Woo (in white shirt), and John Travolta.*
Action and adventure films are among the most kinetic of genres, stressing physical movement above all other qualities. Action films also tend to be violent, fast-paced, and steeped in machismo values. The genre is dominated by Americans, though it has attracted such international talent as Hong Kong's John Woo. Asian films in general tend to be slow-paced, but action films made in the East (and especially Hong Kong) are often frenzied, with one brawl spilling over into the next, driving toward an orgiastic explosion of violence at the climax. Woo's American movies have been somewhat less frantic, though still energetically and stylishly directed.   *(Twentieth Century–Fox)*

3-20. *Singin' in the Rain* (U.S.A., 1952), *with Gene Kelly and Cyd Charisse, choreographed by Kelly, directed by Kelly and Stanley Donen.*
Cyd Charisse, tall, elegant, and gorgeous, was the foremost female dancer during MGM's golden age of musicals, the 1950s. Trained in ballet rather than tap, she was usually at her best in classy numbers such as this balletic dream sequence. However, she could also convey a sizzling eroticism in such torrid dance numbers as those from *It's Always Fair Weather* and *The Band Wagon.* Stage choreography is always viewed from a stationary position. Film choreography can be more complex. In movies, the camera can be choreographed as well as the dancers. Kelly's choreographies often feature lyrical crane shots in which the camera's swirling motions are dreamily counterpointed by the motions of the dancers, a virtual *pas de trois.* (MGM)

sometimes laid on the set to permit the vehicle to move smoothly—hence the term *tracking shot.* If these shots involve long distances, the tracks have to be laid or withdrawn while the camera is moving in or out. Today, any vehicular movement of the camera can be referred to as a dolly shot. The camera can be mounted on a car, a train, even a bicycle.

Tracking is a useful technique in point-of-view shots to capture a sense of movement in or out of a scene. If a filmmaker wants to emphasize the *destination* of a character's movement, the director is more likely to use a straight cut between the initiation of the movement and its conclusion. If the experience of the movement itself is important, the director is more likely to dolly. Thus, if a character is searching for something, the time-consuming point-of-view dolly helps to elongate the suspense of the search. Similarly, the reverse dolly and the **pull-back dolly** are effective techniques for surprising the audience with a revelation **(3–17, 3–21).** By moving back, the camera reveals something startling, something previously off frame.

A common function of traveling shots is to provide an ironic contrast with dialogue. In Jack Clayton's *The Pumpkin Eater,* a distraught wife (Anne Bancroft) returns to an ex-husband's house, where she has an adulterous liaison

116

3–21. *Gone With the Wind* (U.S.A., 1939), *with Vivien Leigh (left, in front of boiling cauldron), directed by Victor Fleming.*

The pull-back dolly or crane shot begins with a close view of a subject, then withdraws to reveal the larger context. The contrast between the close and distant views can be funny, shocking, or sadly ironic. In this famous scene, the camera begins with a close shot of the heroine (Leigh), then slowly pulls back, revealing the wounded bodies of hundreds of soldiers, and stopping finally at a distant long-shot range, in front of a high flagpole, the tattered Confederate flag blowing in the wind like a shredded remnant. *(MGM)*

with him. As the two lie in bed, she asks him if he had been upset over their divorce and whether or not he missed her. He assures her that he wasn't upset, but while their voices continue on the soundtrack, the camera belies his words by slowly dollying through his living room, revealing pictures and mementos of the ex-wife. The shot is a kind of direct communication between the director and audience, bypassing the characters. These techniques are deliberate authorial intrusions. They are favored by filmmakers who view their characters with skepticism or irony—Lubitsch and Hitchcock, for example.

One of the most common uses of dolly shots is to emphasize psychological rather than literal revelations. By slowly tracking in on a character, the filmmaker is getting close to something crucial. The movement acts as a signal to the audience, suggesting, in effect, that we are about to witness something important. A cut to a close-up would tend to emphasize the rapidity of the discovery, but slow dolly shots suggest a more gradual revelation. For example, in Clive Donner's *The Caretaker* (also known as *The Guest*), this technique is used several times. Based on Harold Pinter's play, the movie concerns two brothers and an old tramp who tries to set one brother against the other. The dialogue, as is often the case in a Pinter script, is evasive and not very helpful in providing

1 1 7

3–22a. *Strictly Ballroom* (Australia, 1992), with Tara Morice and Paul Mercurio, directed by Baz Lurhmann. *(Miramax Films)*

3–22b. *Dance with Me* (U.S.A., 1998), with Chayanne and Jane Krakowski, directed by Randa Haines. *(Mandalay Entertainment)*

"Dance is the activity where the sexual connection is most explicit," Michael Malone has pointed out, "which is why movies use it to symbolize sex and why skillful dancing is an invariable movie clue to erotic sophistication, a prerequisite for the lover." Eroticism underlies virtually all dances centered on the couple, whether the style is a sizzling flamenco with bodies literally pressed together as in *Strictly Ballroom*; or an edgy, pulsating Latin-American number as in *Dance with Me*; or even a stately, formalized eighteenth century English gavotte as in the Jane Austen adaptation, *Mansfield Park*. In each, the male courts his partner with sinuously seductive urgency. See Michael Malone, *Heroes of Eros: Male Sexuality in the Movies* (New York: E.P. Dutton, 1979).

3–22c. *Mansfield Park* (Great Britain, 1999), with Frances O'Connor and Alessandro Nivola, directed by Patricia Rozema. *(Miramax Films)*

an understanding of the characters. The brothers are different in most respects. Mick (Alan Bates) is materialistic and aggressive. Aston (Robert Shaw) is gentle and withdrawn. Each brother has a crucial speech in which the camera slowly tracks from a long range to a close-up. Neither of the speeches is really very informative, at least not on a literal level. However, the juxtaposition of the dialogue with the implications of the dolly shot helps the audience to feel that it has finally "arrived" at an understanding of each character.

A stationary camera tends to convey a sense of stability and order, unless there is a great deal of movement within the frame. The moving camera—by its very instability—can create ideas of vitality, flux, and sometimes disorder. Orson Welles exploited the mobile camera to suggest the title character's dynamic energy in *Othello.* Early in the movie, the confident Moor is often photographed in traveling shots. In the ramparts scene, he and Iago walk with military briskness as the camera moves with them at an equally energetic pace. When Iago tells him of his suspicions, the camera slows down, then comes to a halt. Once Othello's mind has been poisoned, he is photographed mostly from stationary setups. Not only has his confident energy drained away, but a spiritual paralysis invades his soul. In the final shots of the movie, he barely moves, even within the still frame. This paralysis motif is completed when Othello kills himself.

When the camera literally follows a character, the audience assumes that it will discover something along the way. A journey, after all, usually has a destination. But traveling shots are often symbolic rather than literal. In Federico Fellini's *8½*, for example, the moving camera is used to suggest a variety of thematic ideas. The protagonist, Guido (Marcello Mastroianni), is a film director who's trying to put together a movie near a bizarre health spa. Everywhere he turns, he's confronted by memories, fantasies, and realities more fantastic than anything he can imagine. But he is paralyzed by indecision. What, if anything, from all this copious flux will he select for his movie? He can't use it all, for it won't fit together—the materials are too sprawling. Throughout the film, the camera wanders restlessly, prowling over the fantastic locale, compulsively hoarding images of faces, textures, and shapes. All are absorbed by Guido, but he is unable to detach them from their contexts to form a meaningful artistic structure.

A number of film theorists have discussed the unique capacity of cinema to convert space into time and time into space. The amount of time it takes to photograph a concrete object can be the main purpose of a shot, especially a traveling shot. The acknowledged master of these types of dolly shots was Max Ophüls. In movies such as *Letter From an Unknown Woman* and *The Earrings of Madame De . . .* , the heroines throw themselves into imprudent but glorious love affairs. The camera tracks relentlessly as the women become more irrevocably involved with their lovers. As critic Andrew Sarris pointed out, Ophüls uses his dolly shots as metaphors of time's cruel prodigality. His world is one of tragic flux and instability in which love is destined to run its eventually bitter course. These lengthy tracking shots preserve the continuity of time by preserving the continuity of space. There is no time for pause and reflection "between shots" in these films. This symbolic technique can be overlooked by the casual viewer because the dolly shots are to some degree functional: They follow characters in their daily round of activities. But a stationary camera would be just as functional (not to mention less expensive), for the characters could move toward or away from a fixed setup.

Hand-held shots are generally less lyrical, more noticeable than vehicular shots. Hand-held cameras, which are usually mounted with a harness on the

3-23. Born on the Fourth of July (U.S.A., 1989), *with Tom Cruise, directed by Oliver Stone.* In film as in the other arts, subject matter usually determines technique. This scene portrays an antiwar protest rally during the Vietnam War era. The scene is deliberately shot in a ragged manner, with shaky hand-held shots, fragmentary editing, and open-form asymmetrical compositions that look like newsreel footage captured in the midst of the chaos. A stable, aesthetically balanced shot would be more beautiful, but such a composition would be completely at odds with the essence of the subject matter. *(Universal City Studios)*

cinematographer's shoulder, were perfected in the 1950s to allow camera operators to move in or out of scenes with greater flexibility and speed. Originally used by documentarists to permit them to shoot in nearly every kind of location, these cameras were quickly adopted by many fiction film directors as well. Hand-held shots are often jumpy and ragged. The camera's rocking is hard to ignore, for the screen exaggerates these movements, especially if the shots are taken from close ranges. For this reason, filmmakers often use the hand-held camera for point-of-view shots. In Mike Nichols's *The Graduate,* for example, a hand-held shot is used to simulate the hero's attempts to maneuver through a crowded room of people.

Crane shots are essentially airborne dolly shots. A crane is a kind of mechanical arm, often more than twenty feet in length. In many respects, it resembles the cranes used by the telephone company to repair lines. It can lift a cinematographer and camera in or out of a scene. It can move in virtually any direction: up, down, diagonally, in, out, or any combination of these. In Hitchcock's *Notorious,* the camera sweeps from an extreme high-angle long shot of a ballroom to an extreme close-up of the hand of the heroine (Ingrid Bergman) clasping a small key.

The Steadicam is a camera stabilizing device that was perfected in the 1970s. It allows cinematographers to move smoothly through a set or location without shaking or bobbing. The Steadicam enables filmmakers to eliminate the need for such expensive devices as cranes and dollies, which can restrict

120

camera movements considerably. The Stedicam also reduced the need for extra crew members to activate the cumbersome old technology of tracks, hand-operated dollies, and many types of cranes. Perhaps the most impressive use of the Steadicam during the 1970s was in Kubrick's horror classic, *The Shining,* where the camera was able to follow a young boy's tricycle as he eerily peddled down empty hotel corridors.

Zoom lenses don't usually involve the actual movement of the camera, but on the screen their effect is very much like an extremely fast tracking or crane shot. The zoom is a combination of lenses, which are continuously variable, permitting the camera to change from close wide-angle distances to extreme telephoto positions (and vice versa) almost simultaneously. The effect of the zoom is a breathtaking sense of being plunged into a scene, or an equally jolting sense of being plucked out of it. Zoom shots are used instead of dolly or crane shots for a number of reasons. They can zip in or out of a scene much faster than any vehicle. From the point of view of economy, they are cheaper than dolly or crane shots since no vehicle is necessary. In crowded locations, zoom lenses can be useful for photographing from long distances, away from the curious eyes of passersby.

3-24.   *The Crucible* (U.S.A., 1996), *with Winona Ryder (behind smoking cauldron), directed by Nicholas Hytner.*

When adapting a play—especially a famous stage drama like Arthur Miller's *The Crucible*—the film director must decide whether or not to "open it up." That is, whether the confined interiors of most stage sets ought to be transferred to the wide open spaces afforded by natural locations. To do so risks dissipating the spatial tension of the original, which is usually conceived by the playwright as a kind of No Exit situation. Nicholas Hytner, who is one of Britain's most famous stage directors, decided to open up Miller's tale of witch-hunt hysteria in seventeenth-century Puritan Salem. Hytner also decided to use movement as metaphor: "I had a feeling that the whole hysteria should work like an infection, like a virus, which immediately suggested that the thing should be moving around. You should not only see the hysterics, but you should actually feel the hysterics traveling from one place to another, which means traveling people and traveling cameras." This technique resulted in a brilliant movie, which heightened rather than lessened the impact of Miller's stagebound drama. (Miller wrote the screenplay of the movie and was very pleased with Hytner's concept.)   *(Twentieth Century-Fox)*

3-25. *The Blair Witch Project* (U.S.A., 1999), *with Heather Donahue, directed by Dan Myrick and Eduardo Sanchez.*
A rocking, turbulently roiling camera can produce a sense of nausea in some people, almost like sea-sickness aboard a violently swaying boat on rough waters. This low-budget thriller had its audiences literally hurling in the aisles—sometimes even before they reached the aisles. Virtually the entire movie was shot with an unstable hand-held camera, to suggest an on-the-spot documentary recording of events while they're actually taking place. The film is a good example of how budgetary liabilities can be converted into aesthetic virtues. The story centers on three college students who go to an isolated forest to explore a local myth about witchcraft. They plan to videotape the entire project. There was no set to build, no lights to set up, no costumes to sew, and no costly special effects to drain the budget. The cast consisted of only three nonprofessional actors. The movie cost a piddling $35,000 and grossed an astonishing $150 million. *(Artisan Entertainment)*

There are certain psychological differences between zoom shots and those involving an actual moving camera. Dolly and crane shots tend to give the viewer a sense of entering into or withdrawing from a set: Furniture and people seem to stream by the sides of the screen as the camera penetrates a three-dimensional space. Zoom lenses foreshorten people and flatten space. The edges of the image simply disappear at all sides. The effect is one of sudden magnification. Instead of feeling as though we are entering a scene, we feel as though a small portion of it has been thrust toward us. In shots of brief duration, these differences are not significant, but in more lengthy shots, the psychological differences can be pronounced.

Aerial shots, usually taken from a helicopter, are really variations of the crane shot. Like a crane, the helicopter can move in virtually any direction. When a crane is impractical—usually on exterior locations—an aerial shot can duplicate the effect. The helicopter shot can be much more extravagant, of course, and for this reason is occasionally used to suggest a swooping sense of freedom. In *Apocalypse Now,* Francis Coppola used aerial shots to produce a godlike sense of inexorability, as swirling American helicopters annihilate a Vietnamese village. The sequence is a kinetic tour de force, suffusing the action

122

with a sense of exhilaration—and horror. Virtually every shot in this brilliantly edited sequence contains a forward rush, a sense of being swept up by events that are out of control.

Mechanical Distortions of Movement

Movement in film is not a literal phenomenon but an optical illusion. Present-day cameras record movement at twenty-four frames per second (fps).

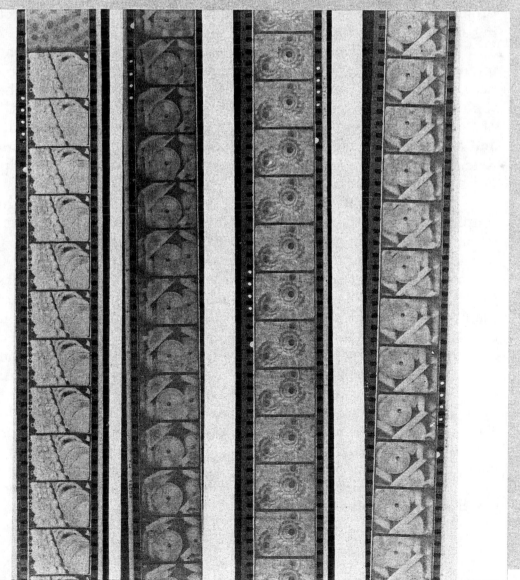

3–26. *Ballet Mécanique* **(France, 1924),** *directed by Fernand Léger.*
Best known for his cubist paintings, Léger was also an avant-garde filmmaker. One of the first to explore abstraction in the cinema, he created many striking kinetic effects by animating and choreographing ordinary objects like crockery, dishes, and machine gears.   *(Museum of Modern Art)*

That is, in each second, twenty-four separate still pictures are photographed. When the film is shown in a projector at the same speed, these still photographs are mixed instantaneously by the human eye, giving the illusion of movement. This phenomenon is called the *persistence of vision*. By simply manipulating the timing mechanism of the camera and/or projector, a filmmaker can distort movement on the screen. There are five basic distortions of this kind: **(1) animation, (2) fast motion, (3) slow motion, (4) reverse motion,** and **(5) freeze frames.**

There are two fundamental differences between animation and live-action movies. In animation sequences, each frame is photographed separately, rather than continuously at the rate of twenty-four frames per second. Another difference is that animation, as the word implies, doesn't ordinarily involve the photographing of subjects that move by themselves. The subjects photographed are generally drawings or static objects. Thus, in an animated movie, thousands of frames are separately photographed. Each frame differs from its neighbor only to an infinitesimal degree. When a sequence of these frames is projected at twenty-four fps, the illusion is that the drawings or objects are moving and, hence, are "animated."

A popular misconception about animated movies is that they are intended primarily for the entertainment of children—perhaps because the field was dominated for so many years by Walt Disney. In actuality, the gamut of sophistication in the genre is as broad as in live-action fiction films. The works of Disney and the puppet films of the Czech Jiri Trnka appeal to both children and adults. A few of these films are as sophisticated as the drawings of Paul Klee. There are even some X-rated animated films, most notably Ralph Bakshi's *Fritz the Cat* and *Heavy Traffic*.

Another popular misconception about animated movies is that they are simpler than live-action films. The contrary is more often the case. For every second of screen time, twenty-four separate drawings usually have to be photographed. Thus, in an average ninety-minute feature, over 129,600 drawings are necessary. Furthermore, some animators use transparent plastic sheets (called **cels**), which they layer over each other to give the illusion of depth to their drawings. Some single frames consist of as many as three or four layers of cels. Most animated films are short precisely because of the overwhelming difficulty of producing all the necessary drawings for a longer movie. Feature-length animated movies are usually produced in assembly line fashion, with dozens of artists drawing thousands of separate frames.

Technically, animated films can be as complex as live-action movies. The same techniques can be used in both forms: traveling shots, zooms, angles, various lenses, editing, **dissolves,** etc. The only difference is that animators *draw* these elements into their images. Furthermore, animators also can use most of the techniques of the painter: different kinds of paints, pens, pencils, pastels, washes, acrylics, and so on.

In watching a movie, we ought to ask ourselves why a director is moving the camera during a scene. Or why the camera *doesn't* move. Does the director keep the camera close in to the action, thus emphasizing motion? Or does he or she deemphasize movement through the use of longer shots, high angles, and slow-paced action? Are the movements in a scene naturalistic or stylized? Literal or symbolic? Are the camera's movements smooth or choppy? Lyrical or disorienting? What are the symbolic implications of such mechanical distortions as fast and slow motion, freeze frames, and animation?

Movement in film is not simply a matter of "what happens." The director has dozens of ways to convey motion, and what differentiates a great director from a merely competent one is not so much a matter of what happens, but *how* things happen—how suggestive and resonant are the movements in a given dramatic context? Or, how effectively does the form of the movement embody its content?

FURTHER READING

BACHER, LUTZ, *The Mobile Mise en Scène* (New York: Arno Press, 1978). Primarily on lengthy takes and camera movements.

DEREN, MAYA, "Cinematography: The Creative Use of Reality," in *The Visual Arts Today,* Gyorgy Kepes, ed. (Middletown, Conn.: Wesleyan University Press, 1960). A discussion of dance and documentary in film.

GEUENS, JEAN-PIERRE, "Visuality and Power: The Work of the Steadicam," *Film Quarterly* (Winter 1994–1995).

GIANNETTI, LOUIS D., "The Aesthetic of the Mobile Camera," in *Godard and Others: Essays in Film Form* (Cranbury, N.J.: Fairleigh Dickinson University Press, 1975). Symbolism and the moving camera.

HALAS, JOHN, and ROGER MANVELL, *Design in Motion* (New York: Focal Press, 1962). Movement and mise en scène.

HOLMAN, BRUCE L., *Puppet Animation in the Cinema* (San Diego, Cal.: A. S. Barnes, 1975). Emphasis on Czech and Canadian animators.

JACOBS, LEWIS, et al., "Movement" in *The Movies as Medium,* Lewis Jacobs, ed. (New York: Farrar, Straus & Giroux, 1970). A collection of essays.

KNIGHT, ARTHUR, "The Street Films: Murnau and the Moving Camera," in *The Liveliest Art,* rev. ed. (New York: Mentor, 1979). The German school of the 1920s.

LINDSAY, VACHEL, *The Art of the Moving Picture* (New York: Liveright, 1970). Reprint of an early classic study.

STEPHENSON, RALPH, *The Animated Film* (San Diego, Cal.: A. S. Barnes, 1973). Historical survey.

Editing

The foundation of film art is editing.
—V. I. PUDOVKIN

133

Overview

Real time versus reel time: the problem of continuity. Cutting to continuity: condensing unobtrusively. D. W. Griffith and the development of a universal cutting style. The invisible manipulation of classical cutting: editing for emphasis and nuance. The problem of time. Subjective editing: thematic montage and the Soviet school. Pudovkin and Eisenstein: two early masters of thematic cutting. The famous Odessa Steps sequence of *Potemkin*. The countertradition: the realism of André Bazin. How editing lies. When not to cut and why. Real time and space and how to preserve them. The realist arsenal: sound, deep focus, sequence shots, widescreen. Alfred Hitchcock, supreme master of editing: storyboard sequence from *North by Northwest*.

So far, we've been concerned with cinematic communication as it relates to the single shot, the basic unit of construction in movies. Except for traveling shots and **lengthy takes,** however, shots in film tend to acquire meaning when they are juxtaposed with other shots and structured into an **edited** sequence. Physically, editing is simply joining one strip of film (**shot**) with another. Shots are joined into scenes. On the most mechanical level, editing eliminates unnecessary time and space. Through the association of ideas, editing connects one shot with another, one scene with another, and so on. Simple as this may now seem, the convention of editing represents what critic Terry Ramsaye referred to as the "syntax" of cinema, its grammatical language. Like linguistic syntax, the syntax of editing must be learned. We don't possess it innately.

Continuity

In the earliest years of cinema, the late 1890s, movies were brief, consisting of short events photographed in **long shot** in a single **take.** The duration of the shot and the event were equal. Soon, filmmakers began to tell stories—simple ones, it's true, but requiring more than a single shot. Scholars have traced the development of narrative to filmmakers in France, Great Britain, and the United States.

By the early twentieth century, filmmakers had already devised a functional style of editing we now call *cutting to continuity*. This type of cutting is a technique used in most fiction films even today, if only for exposition scenes. Essentially, this style of editing is a kind of shorthand, consisting of time-honored conventions. Continuity cutting tries to preserve the fluidity of an event without literally showing all of it.

For example, a continuous shot of a woman leaving work and going home might take forty-five minutes. Cutting to continuity condenses the action into five brief shots, each of which leads by association to the next: **(1)** She enters a corridor as she closes the door to her office. **(2)** She leaves the office

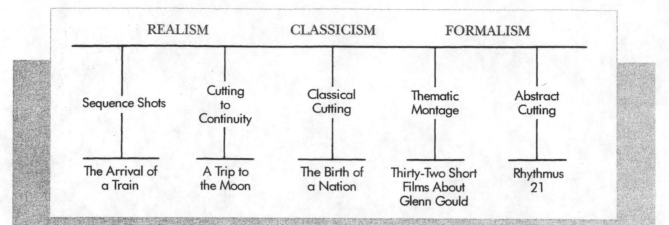

REALISM		CLASSICISM	FORMALISM	
Sequence Shots	Cutting to Continuity	Classical Cutting	Thematic Montage	Abstract Cutting
The Arrival of a Train	A Trip to the Moon	The Birth of a Nation	Thirty-Two Short Films About Glenn Gould	Rhythmus 21

4–2. Editing styles can be classified according to how intrusive or interpretive the cutting is. The least manipulative style is found in a sequence shot, which contains no editing at all. Cutting to continuity merely condenses the time and space of a completed action. Classical cutting interprets an action by emphasizing certain details over others. Thematic montage argues a thesis—the shots are connected in a relatively subjective manner. Abstract cutting is a purely formalistic style of editing, totally divorced from any recognizable subject matter.

building. **(3)** She enters and starts her car. **(4)** She drives her car along a highway. **(5)** Her car turns into her driveway at home. The entire forty-five-minute action might take ten seconds of screen time, yet nothing essential is left out. It's an unobtrusive condensation.

To keep the action logical and continuous, there must be no confusing breaks in an edited sequence of this sort. Often, all the movement is carried out in the same direction on the screen to avoid confusion. For example, if the woman moves from right to left in one shot and her movements are from left to right in the other shots, we might think that she is returning to her office. Cause–effect relationships must be clearly set forth. If the woman slams on her brakes, the director is generally obliged to offer us a shot of what prompted the driver to stop so suddenly.

The continuity of actual space and time is fragmented as smoothly as possible in this type of editing. Unless the audience has a clear sense of a continuous action, an editing transition can be disorienting. Hence, the term **jump cut,** which means an editing transition that's confusing in terms of space and time. To make their transitions smooth, filmmakers generally use **establishing shots** at the beginning of their stories or at the beginning of any new scene within the narrative.

Once the location is established, filmmakers then can cut to closer shots of the action. If the events require a considerable number of cuts, the filmmaker might cut back to a **reestablishing shot**—a return to the opening long shot. In this way, the viewer is reminded of the spatial context of the closer shots. "Between" these various shots, time and space can be expanded or contracted with considerable subtlety.

136

4–3. *The Arrival of a Train* (France, 1895), *directed by Louis and Auguste Lumière*.
The Lumière brothers might be regarded as the godfathers of the documentary movement.
Their brief *actualités* (as they called them) are primitive documentaries shot for the most part
in single takes. These early newsreels often contained several different sequences, but rarely
is there much cutting within a sequence—hence the term *sequence shot* (that is, a complex
action photographed in a continuous take, without cuts). Audiences of this era were so aston-
ished by the novelty of a moving picture that this alone was enough to hold their attention.
See also Bill Nichols, *Representing Reality: Issues and Concepts in Documentary* (Bloomington:
Indiana University Press, 1991).   *(Museum of Modern Art)*

By 1908, when the American genius D. W. Griffith entered the field of
filmmaking, movies had already learned how to tell stories thanks to the technique of cutting to continuity. But the stories were simple and crude compared
to those in more sophisticated narrative mediums like literature and drama.
Nonetheless, movie storytellers already knew that by breaking up an action into
different shots, the event can be contracted or expanded, depending on the
number of shots. In other words, the shot, not the scene, was the basic unit of
film construction.

4-4. *A Trip to the Moon* (France, 1902), *directed by Georges Méliès.*
Around 1900, in America, England, and France, filmmakers began to tell stories. Their narratives were crude, but they required more than just one shot to complete. Méliès was one of the first to devise the style of cutting to continuity. The narrative segments are connected by a fade-out. The next scene then fades in, often in a different location and at a different time, though usually with the same characters. Méliès advertised these films as stories in "arranged scenes." *(Museum of Modern Art)*

Movies before Griffith were usually photographed in stationary long shot—roughly the position of a close observer in the live theater. Because film time doesn't depend on the duration of the literal event, filmmakers of this era introduced a more subjective time, one that's determined by the duration of the shots (and the elapsed time implied between them), not by the actual occurrence.

D. W. Griffith and Classical Cutting

The basic elements of editing syntax were already in place when Griffith entered the field, but it was he more than any other individual who molded these elements into a language of power and subtlety. Film scholars have called this language *classical cutting.* Griffith has been called the Father of Film because he consolidated and expanded many of the techniques invented by his predecessors and was the first to go beyond gimmickry into the realm of art. By 1915, the year of his masterpiece *The Birth of a Nation,* classical cutting was already an editing style of great sophistication and expressiveness. Griffith had seized on the principle of the association of ideas in the concept of editing and expanded it in a variety of ways.

Classical cutting involves editing for dramatic intensity and emotional emphasis rather than for purely physical reasons. Through the use of the

138

4–5. *The Birth of a Nation* (U.S.A., 1915), *directed by D. W. Griffith.*
Griffith's greatest gift to the cinema was classical cutting—a style of editing that still characterizes most of the fiction films around the world. Classical cutting allows filmmakers to inflect their narratives, to add nuances and emphasis. It also subjectivizes time. For example, in this famous last-minute rescue finale, Griffith cross-cuts to four different groups. Despite the sense of speed suggested by the brevity of the shots, the sequence actually expands time. Griffith used 255 separate shots for about twenty minutes of screen time.
(Museum of Modern Art)

close-up within the scene, Griffith managed to achieve a dramatic impact that was unprecedented. Close-ups had been used earlier, but Griffith was the first to use them for psychological rather than physical reasons alone. Audiences were now permitted to see the smallest details of an actor's face. No longer were performers required to flail their arms and tear their hair. The slightest arch of an eyebrow could convey a multitude of subtleties.

By splitting the action into a series of fragmentary shots, Griffith achieved not only a greater sense of detail, but a far greater degree of control over his audience's reactions. In carefully selecting and juxtaposing long, **medium,** and close shots, he constantly shifted the spectator's point of view within a scene—expanding here, excluding there, emphasizing, consolidating, connecting, contrasting, paralleling, and so on. The possibilities were far ranging. The space and time continuum of the real scene was radically altered. It

139

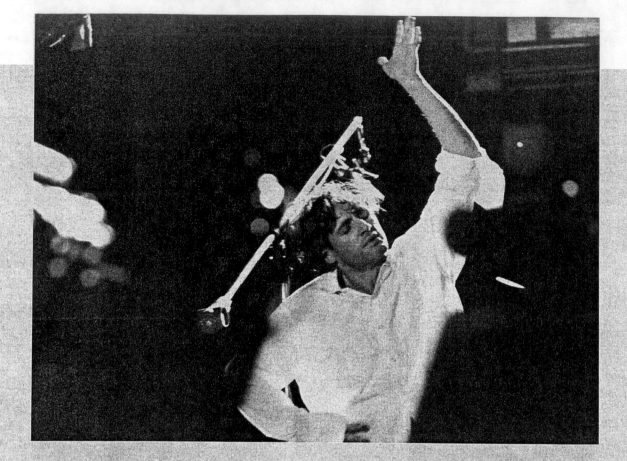

4–6. *Thirty-Two Short Films About Glenn Gould* (Canada, 1994), *with Colm Feore, directed by François Girard.*
This movie combines elements from documentary filmmaking, fiction films, and the avant-garde. Its editing style is radically subjective. The movie features documentary footage of the late Glenn Gould, a controversial and eccentric Canadian pianist considered to be one of the great musicians of the twentieth century. There are also many re-created scenes with the brilliant Colm Feore playing the quirky and obsessive artist. The movie's structure is not a straightforward narrative, but a series of fragments, loosely based on the thirty-two-part *Goldberg Variations* of Johann Sebastian Bach—one of Gould's most celebrated virtuoso performances. The film is structured around ideas rather than a linear story, and for this reason, thematic montage is its style of editing. *(The Samuel Goldwyn Company)*

was replaced by a subjective continuity—the association of ideas implicit in the connected shots.

In its most refined form, classical cutting presents a series of psychologically connected shots—shots that aren't necessarily separated by real time and space **(4–12).** For example, if four characters are seated in a room, a director might cut from one speaker to a second with a dialogue exchange, then cut to a **reaction shot** of one of the listeners, then to a **two-shot** of the original speakers, and finally to a close-up of the fourth person. The sequence of shots represents a kind of psychological cause–effect pattern. In other words, the breakup of shots is justified on the basis of dramatic rather than literal necessity. The scene

140

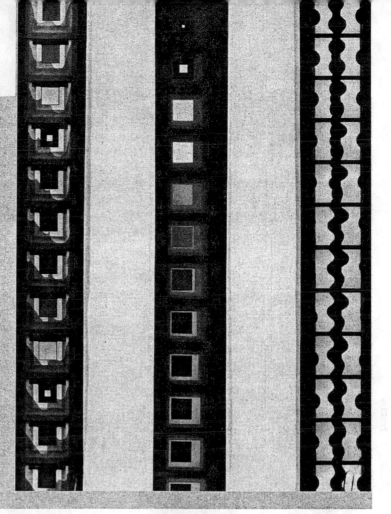

4–7. *Rhythmus 21* (Germany, 1921), *directed by Hans Richter.*
In the avant-garde cinema, subject matter is often suppressed or exploited primarily as abstract data. The continuity between shots has nothing to do with a story but is determined by purely subjective or formal considerations. Along with many other European abstract artists of his generation, Richter was a champion of the "absolute film," which consists solely of nonrepresentational forms and designs.
(Museum of Modern Art)

could be photographed just as functionally in a single shot, with the camera at long-shot range. This type of setup is known as a **master shot** or a **sequence shot.** Classical cutting is more nuanced and more intrusive. It breaks down the unity of space, analyzes its components, and refocuses our attention to a series of details. The action is mental and emotional rather than literal.

During the golden years of the American studio system—roughly the 1930s and 1940s—directors were often urged (or forced) to adopt the master-shot technique of shooting. This method involved shooting an entire scene in long shot without cuts. This take contained all the dramatic variables and hence served as the basic or "master" shot for the scene. The action was then repeated a number of times, with the camera photographing medium shots and close-ups of the principals in the scene. When all this footage was gathered together, the editor had a number of choices in constructing a story continuity. Often, disagreements arose over the proper sequence of shots. Usually, the studio director was permitted a **first cut**—that is, the sequence of shots representing his or her interpretation of the materials. Under this system, the studios usually had the right to a **final cut.** Many directors disliked master-shot techniques precisely because, with so much footage available, a meddling producer could construct a radically different continuity.

Master shots are still used by many directors. Without a master, editors often complain of inadequate footage—that the available shots won't cut

4–8. *Fat City* (U.S.A., 1972), *directed by John Huston*.
Classical cutting involves editing for dramatic emphasis, to highlight details that might otherwise be overlooked. In Huston's fight scene, for example, the entire boxing match could have been presented in a single setup **(a)**. Such a presentation would probably strike us as underwhelming. Instead, Huston breaks up his shots according to the psychological actions and reactions within the fighter protagonist (Stacy Keach), his manager (Nicholas Colosanto), and two friends in the auditorium (Candy Clark and Jeff Bridges).   *(Columbia Pictures)*

smoothly. In complex battle scenes, most directors are likely to shoot many **cover shots**—that is, general shots that can be used to reestablish a sequence if the other shots won't cut. In *The Birth of a Nation*, Griffith used multiple cameras to photograph many of the battle scenes, a technique also used by Akira Kurosawa in some sequences of *The Seven Samurai*.

Griffith and other classical filmmakers developed a variety of editing conventions that they thought made the cutting "invisible," or at least didn't call attention to itself. One of these techniques is the *eyeline match*. We see character A look off frame left. Cut to a shot—from his point of view—of character B. We assume B is to A's left. Cause–effect.

142

Another convention of classical cutting is *matching action*. Character A is seated but begins to rise. Cut to another shot of character A concluding the rising action and then moving away. The idea is to keep the action fluid, to mask the cut with a smooth linkage that's not noticed because the motion of the character takes precedence. The continuity of the movement conceals the suture.

The so-called *180° rule* is still observed by filmmakers, though even during the big-studio era there was nothing sacred about it. (For example, John Ford loved violating the 180° rule. He loved violating almost any rule.) This convention involves **mise en scène** as well as editing. The purpose is to stabilize the space of the playing area so the spectator isn't confused or disoriented. An imaginary "axis of action" line is drawn through the middle of a scene, viewed from the **bird's-eye** angle **(4–9).** Character A is on the left; character B is on the right. If the director wanted a two-shot, he or she would use camera 1. If we then go to a close-up of A (camera 2), the camera must stay on the same side of the 180° line to keep the same background—a continuity aid for the spectator. Similarly, a close-up of character B (camera 3) would be shot on the same side of the axis of action.

In shot **reverse angle** exchanges—common for dialogue sequences—the director takes care to fix the placement of the characters from shot to shot.

4–9.   Bird's-eye view of the 180° rule.

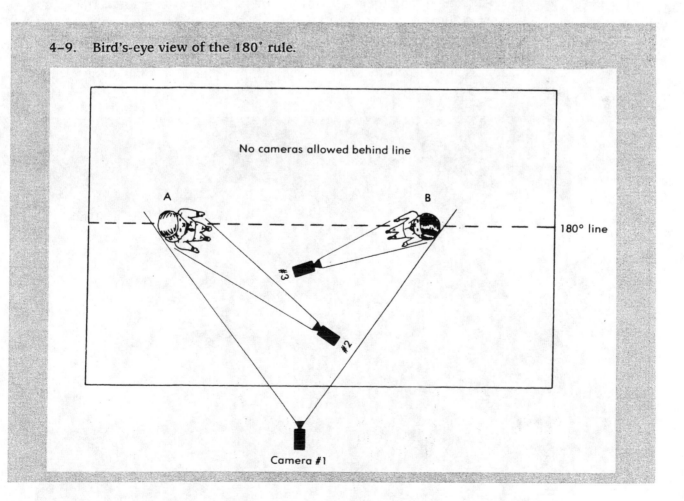

If character A is on the left and character B is on the right in the first shot, they must remain that way in the reverse angle taken from over the shoulder of character B. Usually the reverse angle is not literally 180° opposite, but we agree to accept it as such.

Even today, filmmakers rarely take the camera behind the imaginary axis line, unless their deliberate intention is to confuse the spectator. During fight scenes and other types of chaotic clashes, the filmmaker often wants the spectator to feel threatened, disoriented, anxious. This can be accomplished by deliberately violating the 180° rule.

Griffith also perfected the conventions of the chase—still very much with us. Many of his movies ended with a chase and last-minute rescue sequence. Most of them feature **parallel editing**—the alternation of shots of

4–10.   *It's a Wonderful Life* (U.S.A., 1946), *with James Stewart, directed by Frank Capra.* Capra was a master of classical editing. His cutting style was fast, light, seamless. But he never displayed his editing virtuosity for its own sake. Like every other technique, editing is subordinated to the needs of the characters in action—the cardinal commandment of classical cutting. In this and other scenes, Capra included a "reactive character" who guides the viewer's response to the action. This character represents a kind of norm, the way an average person would respond to a given situation. In this scene, for example, Capra's charming fantasy takes a whimsical turn. The forlorn hero (Stewart) listens to his guardian angel (Henry Travers, left) explain why he isn't a very *distinguished* angel (he has yet to earn his wings). A casual bystander (Tom Fadden, center) happens to overhear and is totally spooked by their conversation. Capra is able to punctuate the comedy of the scene by cutting to this character's response whenever the angel says something weird.   *(RKO)*

one scene with another at a different location. By **cross-cutting** back and forth between the two (or three or four) scenes, Griffith conveyed the idea of simultaneous time. For example, near the end of *The Birth of a Nation,* Griffith cross-cuts between four groups. In juxtaposing shots from these separate scenes, he manages to intensify the suspense by reducing the duration of the shots as the sequence reaches its climax. The sequence itself lasts twenty minutes of film time, but the psychological effect of the cross-cutting (the shots average about five seconds each) suggests speed and tension. Generally speaking, the greater the number of cuts within a scene, the greater its sense of speed. To avoid the risk of monotony during this sequence, Griffith changed his **setups** many times. There are **extreme long,** long, medium, and close shots, varied angles, lighting contrasts, even a moving camera (it was mounted on a truck).

If the continuity of a sequence is reasonably logical, the fragmentation of space presents no great difficulties. But the problem of time is more complex. Its treatment in film is more subjective than the treatment of space. Movies can compress years into two hours of projection time. They can also stretch a split second into many minutes. Most films condense time. There are only a handful that attempt to make screen time conform to real time: Agnès Varda's *Cleo From Five to Seven* and Fred Zinnemann's *High Noon* (**1–22**) are perhaps the best-known examples. Both deal with about 90 minutes of time—also the approximate length of the films. Even these movies cheat by compressing time in the expository opening sequences and expanding it in the climactic scenes. In actual practice, time exists in a kind of limbo: As long as the audience is absorbed by the screen action, time is what the film says it is. The problem, then, is to absorb the viewer.

On the most mechanical level, screen time is determined by the physical length of the filmstrip containing the shot. This length is governed generally by the complexity of the image subject matter. Usually, longer shots are more densely saturated with visual information than close-ups and need to be held longer on the screen. Raymond Spottiswoode, an early film theorist, claimed that a cut must be made at the peak of the "content curve"—that is, the point in a shot at which the audience has been able to assimilate most of its information. Cutting after the peak of the content curve produces boredom and a sense of dragging time. Cutting before the peak doesn't give the audience enough time to assimilate the visual action. An image with a complex mise en scène requires more time to assimilate than a simple one. Once an image has been established, however, a return to it during the sequence can be considerably shorter, because it works as a reminder.

But the sensitive treatment of time in editing is largely an instinctive matter that defies mechanical rules. Most great directors have edited their own films, or at least worked in close collaboration with their editors, so crucial is this art to the success of films. The best-edited sequences are determined by mood as well as subject matter. Griffith, for example, generally edited love scenes in long **lyrical** takes, with relatively few setups. His chase and battle scenes were composed of brief shots, jammed together. Paradoxically, the love scenes actually compress real time, whereas the rapidly cut sequences elongate it.

There are no fixed rules concerning rhythm in films. Some editors cut according to musical rhythms **(see 5–12)**. The march of soldiers, for example, could be edited to the beat of a military tune, as can be seen in several marching sequences in King Vidor's *The Big Parade*. This technique is also common with American avant-garde filmmakers, who feature rock music soundtracks or cut according to a mathematical or structural formula. In some cases, a director will cut before the peak of the content curve, especially in highly suspenseful sequences. In a number of movies, Hitchcock teases the audience by not providing enough time to assimilate all the meanings of a shot. Violent scenes are con-

4–12.   *The Last Picture Show* (U.S.A., 1971), *with Cybill Shepherd and Ellen Burstyn, directed by Peter Bogdanovich.*

In its subtlest form, classical cutting can break up even a confined action into smaller units of meaning. François Truffaut once observed that movies in which people tell lies require more shots than those in which they tell the truth. For example, if a young daughter tells her mother that she thinks she is in love with a boy, and the mother responds by warning the girl of some of the emotional dangers involved, there is no reason why the scene shouldn't be photographed in a single setup with both females in the same frame. Essentially, this is how Bogdanovich presents a similar scene **(a)**. However, if the mother were a lying hypocrite, and the daughter suspected that the older woman might be in love with the boy herself, a director would be forced to break the scene down into five or six shots **(b–g)** to give viewers emotional information they wouldn't receive from the characters themselves.   *(Columbia Pictures)*

a

continued ▶

4-13. ***The Deer Hunter*** (U.S.A., 1978), *directed by Michael Cimino.*
Editing is an art as well as a craft. Like all art, it often defies mechanical formulations, taking on a life of its own. For example, when sneak preview audiences were asked for their reactions to this three-hour movie, most viewers responded enthusiastically but felt that the hour-long wedding sequence of the opening could have been cut down. In terms of its plot, nothing much "happens" in this sequence. Its purpose is primarily *lyrical*—a loving celebration of the social rituals that bind the community together. The story content of the sequence could be condensed to a few minutes of screen time—which is exactly what its makers did. When the shortened version was shown to audiences, reactions were negative. Cimino and his editor, Peter Zinner, restored the cut footage. The long wedding sequence is necessary not for its story content so much as for its experiential value. It provides the movie with a sense of balance: The community solidarity of the sequence is what the characters fight *for* in the subsequent battle footage of the film. *(Universal Pictures)*

ventionally cut in a highly fragmented manner. On the other hand, Antonioni usually cuts long after the content curve has peaked. In *La Notte,* for example, the rhythm is languorous and even monotonous: The director attempts to create a sense of weariness in the audience, paralleling that of the characters. Antonioni's characters are usually tired people—in every sense of the term **(see 3–7).**

Tact is another editing principle that's difficult to generalize about, because it too depends on context. No one likes to have the obvious pointed out to us, whether in real life or while watching a movie. Like personal tact, directorial tact is a matter of restraint, taste, and respect for the intelligence of others. Hack directors often present us with emotionally gratuitous shots, falling over themselves to make sure we haven't missed the point.

150

Soviet Montage and the Formalist Tradition

Griffith was a practical artist, concerned with communicating ideas and emotions in the most effective manner possible. In the 1920s, the Soviet filmmakers expanded his associational principles and established the theoretical premises for thematic editing, or *montage* as they called it (from the French, *monter,* to assemble). V. I. Pudovkin wrote the first important theoretical treatises on what he called constructive editing. Most of his statements are explanations of Griffith's practices, but he differed with the American (whom he praises lavishly) on several points. Griffith's use of the close-up, Pudovkin claimed, is too limited. It's used simply as a clarification of the long shot, which carries most of the meaning. The close-up, in effect, is merely an interruption, offering no meanings of its own. Pudovkin insisted that each shot should make a new point. Through the juxtaposition of shots, new meanings can be created. The meanings, then, are in the juxtapositions, not in one shot alone.

Filmmakers in the Soviet Union were strongly influenced by the psychological theories of Pavlov, whose experiments in the association of ideas served as a basis for the editing experiments of Lev Kuleshov, Pudovkin's mentor. Kuleshov believed that ideas in cinema are created by linking together fragmentary details to produce a unified action. These details can be totally unrelated in real life. For example, he linked together a shot of Moscow's Red Square with a

4–18.   *Dead Men Don't Wear Plaid* (U.S.A., 1982), *with Steve Martin and Carl Reiner (bald pate), directed by Reiner.*
Reiner's comic parody of Nazi films and other noir genres of the 1940s is a tour de force of editing. A silly spy plot involving Martin is intercut with footage from such vintage 1940s movies as *Double Indemnity, Suspicion, The Bribe, Out of the Past,* and *Sorry, Wrong Number.* Pudovkin and Kuleshov would have understood perfectly.   *(University City Studios)*

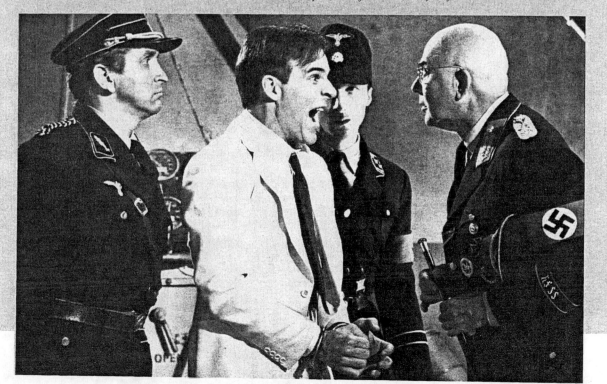

shot of the American White House, close-ups of two men climbing stairs with another close-up of two hands shaking. Projected as a continuous scene, the linked shots suggest that the two men are in the same place at the same time.

Kuleshov conducted another famous experiment that provided a theoretical foundation for the use of nonprofessional actors in movies. Kuleshov and many of his colleagues believed that traditional acting skills were quite unnecessary in the cinema. First, he shot a close-up of an actor with a neutral expression. He juxtaposed this with a close-up of a bowl of soup. Then he joined the close-up of the actor with a shot of a coffin containing a female corpse. Finally, he linked the actor's neutral expression with a shot of a little girl playing. When these combinations were shown to audiences, they exclaimed at the actor's expressiveness in portraying hunger, deep sorrow, and paternal pride. In each case, the meaning was conveyed by juxtaposing two shots, not by one alone. Actors can be used as raw material, as objects juxtaposed with other objects. The emotion is produced not by the actor's performance, but by associations brought about by the juxtapositions. In a sense, the *viewer* creates the emotional meanings, once the appropriate objects have been linked together by the filmmaker (**4–20**).

4-19. *Lifeboat* (U.S.A., 1944), *with Tullulah Bankhead (center), directed by Alfred Hitchcock.* Hitchcock was one of Pudovkin's most articulate champions. "Cinema is form," Hitchcock insisted. "The screen ought to speak its own language, freshly coined, and it can't do that unless it treats an acted scene as a piece of raw material which must be broken up, taken to bits, before it can be woven into an expressive visual pattern." He referred to the piecing together of fragmentary shots as "pure cinema," like individual notes of music that combine to produce a melody. In this movie, he confined himself entirely to nine characters adrift at sea in a small boat. In other words, this photo contains the raw material for every shot in the film. Formalists insist that the artistry lies not in the materials per se, but in the way they are taken apart and reconstructed expressively. *(Twentieth Century–Fox)*

For Kuleshov and Pudovkin, a sequence was not filmed; it was constructed. Using far more close-ups than Griffith, Pudovkin built a scene from many separate shots, all juxtaposed for a unified effect. The environment of the scene is the source of the images. Long shots are rare. Instead, a barrage of close-ups (often of objects) provides the audience with the necessary associations to link together the meaning. These juxtapositions can suggest emotional and psychological states, even abstract ideas.

The Soviet theorists of this generation were criticized on several counts. This technique detracts from a scene's sense of realism, some critics complained, for the continuity of actual time and place is totally restructured. But Pudovkin and the other Soviet formalists claimed that realism captured in long shot is *too* near reality: It's theatrical rather than cinematic. Movies must capture the essence, not merely the surface, of reality, which is filled with irrelevancies. Only by juxtaposing close-ups of objects, textures, symbols, and other selected details can a filmmaker convey *expressively* the idea underlying the undifferentiated jumble of real life.

Some critics also believe that this manipulative style of editing guides the spectator too much—the choices are already made. The audience must sit back passively and accept the inevitable linking of associations presented on the screen. Political considerations are involved here, for the Soviets tended to link film with propaganda. Propaganda, no matter how artistic, doesn't usually involve free and balanced evaluations.

Like many Soviet formalists, Sergei Eisenstein was interested in exploring general principles that could be applied to a variety of apparently different forms of creative activity. He believed that these artistic principles were organically related to the basic nature of all human activity and, ultimately, to the nature of the universe itself. Like the ancient Greek philosopher Heraclitus, Eisenstein believed that the essence of existence is constant change. He believed that nature's eternal fluctuation is **dialectical**—the result of the conflict and synthesis of opposites. What appears to be stationary or unified in nature is only temporary, for all phenomena are in various states of becoming. Only energy is permanent, and energy is constantly in a state of transition to other forms. Every opposite contains the seed of its own destruction in time, Eisenstein believed, and this conflict of opposites is the mother of motion and change.

The function of all artists is to capture this dynamic collision of opposites, to incorporate dialectical conflicts not only in the subject matter of art but in its techniques and forms as well. Conflict is universal in all the arts, according to Eisenstein, and therefore all art aspires to motion. Potentially, at least, the cinema is the most comprehensive of the arts because it can incorporate the visual conflicts of painting and photography, the kinetic conflicts of dance, the tonal conflicts of music, the verbal conflicts of language, and the character and action conflicts of fiction and drama.

Eisenstein placed special emphasis on the art of editing. Like Kuleshov and Pudovkin, he believed that montage was the foundation of film art. He agreed with them that each shot of a sequence ought to be incomplete, con-

a   b

4–20a, b, c, d.   An "edited sequence" from *Rear Window* **(U.S.A., 1954),** *directed by Alfred Hitchcock.*

Hitchcock's thriller centers on a photographic journalist (James Stewart) who is confined to his apartment because of a broken leg. Out of boredom, he begins to observe the lives of his neighbors, who live in the apartment building just behind his own. His high-society girlfriend (Grace Kelly, **4–20a**) wants to get married and sees no reason why marriage should interfere with his work. But he puts her off, filling in his idle hours by speculating on the various problems of his neighbors. Each neighbor's window symbolizes a fragment of Stewart's divided sentiments: They are projections of his own anxieties and desires, which center on love, career, and marriage. Each window suggests a different option for the hero. One neighbor is a desperately lonely woman. Another apartment is occupied by lusty newlyweds. A friendless bachelor musician occupies a third apartment. A shallow and promiscuous dancer lives in another. In still another is a childless married couple, who fawn pathetically over their dog

continued   ▶

tributory rather than self-contained. However, Eisenstein criticized the concept of linked shots for being mechanical and inorganic. He believed that editing ought to be dialectical: The conflict of two shots (thesis and antithesis) produces a wholly new idea (synthesis). Thus, in film terms, the conflict between shot A and shot B is not AB (Kuleshov and Pudovkin), but a qualitatively new factor—C (Eisenstein). Transitions between shots should not be smooth, as Pudovkin suggested, but sharp, jolting, even violent. For Eisenstein, editing

c   d

to fill in the vacuum of their lives. In the most sinister apartment is a tormented middle-aged man (Raymond Burr, **4–20c**), who is so harassed by his wife that he eventually murders her. By cutting from shots of the spying hero to shots of the neighbors' windows, Hitchcock dramatizes the thoughts going through Stewart's mind. The audience is moved by the editing style rather than by the material per se or even by the actors' performances. Somewhat like the early experiments of Pudovkin and Kuleshov, who edited together unrelated bits of film to create a new concept, this phony "edited sequence" is composed of totally random publicity photos, and might be viewed as a kind of guilt by associational montage. Such editing techniques represent a form of characterization. Actors sometimes complained that Hitchcock didn't allow them to *act*. But he believed that people don't always express what they're thinking or feeling, and hence the director must communicate these ideas through the editing. The actor, in short, provides only a part of the characterization. The rest is provided by Hitchcock's montage.   *(Paramount Pictures)*

produces harsh collisions, not subtle linkages. A smooth transition, he claimed, was an opportunity lost.

Editing for Eisenstein was an almost mystical process. He likened it to the growth of organic cells. If each shot represents a developing cell, the cinematic cut is like the rupturing of the cell when it splits into two. Editing is done at the point that a shot "bursts"—that is, when its tensions have reached their maximum expansion. The rhythm of editing in a movie should be like the explosions of an internal combustion engine, Eisenstein claimed. A master of dynamic rhythms, his films are almost mesmerizing in this respect: Shots of contrasting volumes, durations, shapes, designs, and lighting intensities collide against each other like objects in a torrential river plunging toward their inevitable destination.

The differences between Pudovkin and Eisenstein may seem academic. In actual practice, however, the two approaches produced sharply contrasting results. Pudovkin's movies are essentially in the classical mold. The shots tend to be additive and are directed toward an overall emotional effect, which is guided by the story. In Eisenstein's movies, the jolting images represent a series of essentially intellectual thrusts and parries, directed toward an ideological argument. The directors' narrative structures also differed. Pudovkin's stories didn't differ much from the kind Griffith used. On the other hand, Eisenstein's stories were much more loosely structured, usually a series of documentarylike episodes used as convenient vehicles for exploring ideas.

When Pudovkin wanted to express an emotion, he conveyed it in terms of physical images—objective correlatives—taken from the actual locale. Thus, the sense of anguished drudgery is conveyed through a series of shots showing details of a cart mired in the mud: close-ups of the wheel, the mud, hands coaxing the wheel, straining faces, the muscles of an arm pulling the wheel, and so on. Eisenstein, on the other hand, wanted film to be totally free of literal continuity and context. Pudovkin's correlatives, he felt, were too restricted by realism.

Eisenstein wanted movies to be as flexible as literature, especially to make figurative comparisons without respect to time and place. Movies should

include images that are thematically or metaphorically relevant, Eisenstein claimed, regardless of whether they can be found in the locale or not. Even in his first feature, *Strike* (1925), Eisenstein intercut shots of workmen being machine-gunned with images of oxen being slaughtered. The oxen are not literally on location, but are intercut purely for metaphorical purposes. A famous sequence from *Potemkin* links three shots of stone lions: one asleep, a second aroused and on the verge of rising, and a third on its feet and ready to pounce. Eisenstein considered the sequence an embodiment of a metaphor: "The very stones roar."

Ingenious as these metaphorical comparisons can be, the major problem with this kind of editing is its tendency to be obvious—or impenetrably obscure. Eisenstein saw no difficulty in overcoming the space and time differences between film and literature. But the two mediums use metaphors in different ways. We have no difficulty in understanding what's meant by the comparison "he's timid as a sheep," or even the more abstract metaphor, "whorish time undoes us all." Both statements exist outside of time and place. The simile isn't set in a pasture, nor is the metaphor set in a brothel. Such comparisons are not meant to be understood literally, of course. In movies, figurative devices of this kind are more difficult. Editing can produce a number of figurative comparisons, but they don't work in quite the same way that they do in literature. Eisenstein's theories of collision montage have been explored primarily in the avant-garde cinema, music videos, and TV commercials. Most fiction filmmakers have found them too intrusive and heavy-handed.

André Bazin and the Tradition of Realism

André Bazin was not a filmmaker, but solely a critic and theorist. For a number of years, he was the editor of the influential French journal *Cahiers du Cinéma,* in which he set forth an aesthetic of film that was in sharp opposition to such formalists as Pudovkin and Eisenstein. Bazin was untainted by dogmatism. Although he emphasized the realistic nature of the cinema, he was generous in his praise of movies that exploited editing effectively. Throughout his writings, however, Bazin maintained that montage was merely one of many techniques a director could use in making movies. Furthermore, he believed that in many cases editing could actually destroy the effectiveness of a scene (**4–24** and **4–26**).

Bazin's realist aesthetic was based on his belief that photography, TV, and cinema, unlike the traditional arts, produce images of reality automatically, with a minimum of human interference. This technological objectivity connects the moving image with the observable physical world. A novelist or a painter must represent reality by re-presenting it in another medium—through language and color pigments. The filmmaker's image, on the other hand, is essentially an objective recording of what actually exists. No other art, Bazin felt, can be as comprehensive in the presentation of the physical world. No other art can be as realistic, in the most elementary sense of that word.

Bazin's aesthetic had a moral as well as technological bias. He was influenced by the philosophical movement called Personalism. This school of thought emphasized the individualistic and pluralistic nature of truth. Just as most Personalists agreed that there are many truths, Bazin felt that in the cinema there are many ways of portraying the real. The essence of reality, he believed, lies in its ambiguity. Reality can even be interpreted in opposing, and equally valid, ways, depending on the sensitivities of the artist. To capture this ambiguity, the filmmaker must be modest and self-effacing, a patient observer willing to follow where reality leads. The film artists that Bazin admired most—Flaherty, Renoir, and De Sica, for example—are those whose movies reflect a sense of wonder before the ambiguous mysteries of reality.

4–22. *High Noon* (U.S.A., 1952), *with Gary Cooper and Lloyd Bridges, directed by Fred Zinnemann.*
Almost all movies compress time, condensing many months or even years into a running time of roughly two hours, the average length of most films. Zinnemann's movie is a rare example of a literal adherence to the unities of time, place, and action, for the entire story takes place in a breathless 84 minutes—the film's running time.   *(United Artists)*

Bazin believed that the distortions involved in using formalist techniques—especially thematic editing—often violate the complexities of reality. Montage superimposes a simplistic ideology over the infinite variability of actual life. Formalists tend to be too egocentric and manipulative, he felt. They are concerned with imposing their narrow view of reality, rather than allowing reality to exist in its awesome complexity. He was one of the first to point out that such great filmmakers as Chaplin, Mizoguchi, and Murnau preserved the ambiguities of reality by minimizing editing.

Bazin even viewed classical cutting as potentially corrupting. Classical cutting breaks down a unified scene into a certain number of closer shots that correspond implicitly to a mental process. But the technique encourages us to follow the shot sequence without our being conscious of its arbitrariness. "The editor who cuts for us makes in our stead the choice which we would make in real life," Bazin pointed out. "Without thinking, we accept his analysis because it conforms to the laws of attention, but we are deprived of a privilege." He believed that classical cutting subjectivizes an event because each shot represents what the filmmaker thinks is important, not necessarily what we would think.

One of Bazin's favorite directors, the American William Wyler, reduced editing to a minimum in many of his films, substituting the use of **deep-focus** photography and lengthy takes. "His perfect clarity contributes enormously to

4–23.   *Dog Day Afternoon* (U.S.A., 1975), *with Al Pacino, directed by Sidney Lumet.*
Not all realists use an unobtrusive style of editing. Most of Lumet's gritty New York City dramas like *The Pawnbroker, Serpico, Prince of the City,* and *Dog Day Afternoon* are based on actual events and were shot mostly in the streets of the city. All are considered masterpieces of realism, yet all of them are edited in a nervous, jumpy style that connects a wide assortment of characters and explosive events. As early as 1910, the great Russian novelist Leo Tolstoy realized that this fledgling new art form would surpass the magnificent achievements of 19th century literary realism: "This little clinking contraption with the revolving handle will make a revolution in our life—in the life of writers. It is a direct attack on the old methods of literary art. This swift change of scene, this blending of emotion and experience—it is much better than the heavy, long-drawn-out kind of writing to which we are accustomed. It is closer to life." *(Warner Bros.)*

4–24. *Jurassic Park* (U.S.A., 1993), *with Joseph Mazzello, Sam Neill, Ariana Richards, and a friendly brachiosaurus; directed by Steven Spielberg.*
Cheap science-fiction films and low-budget adventure movies often combine realistic elements with the supernatural or the very dangerous, but seldom in the same frame. It's cheaper and easier to keep the terrified people in one shot, then cut to the object of their terror (or fascination) in another shot. Kuleshov would have applauded such a solution. But Bazin claimed that a realistic presentation—that is, *not* cutting, but keeping them both in the same frame—is far more effective, for audiences instinctively sense when a scene of this type is being faked with manipulative editing techniques. The most magical scenes in this movie are those that feature startlingly realistic dinosaurs—never so realistic as when they are combined in the same frame with humans. Bazin would have applauded. *(Universal Pictures/Amblin Entertainment)*

the spectator's reassurance and leaves to him the means to observe, to choose, and form an opinion," Bazin said of Wyler's austere cutting style. In such movies as *The Little Foxes, The Best Years of Our Lives* **(1–20b),** and *The Heiress,* Wyler achieved an unparalleled neutrality and transparency. It would be naive to confuse this neutrality with an absence of art, Bazin insisted, for all of Wyler's effort tends to hide itself.

Unlike some of his followers, Bazin did not advocate a simpleminded theory of realism. He was perfectly aware, for example, that cinema—like all art—involves a certain amount of selectivity, organization, and interpretation. In short, a certain amount of distortion. He also recognized that the values of the filmmaker will inevitably influence the manner in which reality is perceived. These distortions are not only inevitable, but in most cases desirable. For Bazin, the best films were those in which the artist's personal vision is held in delicate balance with the objective nature of the medium. Certain aspects of reality must be sacrificed for the sake of artistic coherence, then, but Bazin felt that abstraction and artifice ought to be kept to a minimum. The materials

171

4–25a. *The Sorrow and the Pity* (France/ Switzerland/W. Germany, 1970), *directed by Marcel Ophüls.*

Even in the world of documentary films, editing styles can range from ultrarealistic to ultraformalistic. Like most **cinéma-vérité** documentarists, Marcel Ophüls keeps editing to an absolute minimum. Implicit in the art of editing is artifice—that is, the manipulation of formal elements to produce a seductive aesthetic effect. Many documentarists believe that an edited analysis of a scene shapes and aestheticizes it—compromising its authenticity. A selected sequence of shots, however factually based, extrapolates one person's truth from an event and, in so doing, infuses it with an ideology. An unedited presentation, on the other hand, preserves a multiplicity of truths. *(Cinema 5)*

4–25b. *Looking for Richard* (U.S.A., 1996), *with Al Pacino, directed by Pacino.*

The editing style of this documentary is subjective and personal. The movie itself is almost like an intimate diary by a famous actor exploring one of his most celebrated stage roles, Shakespeare's fascinating disciple of evil, Richard III. Pacino's **voice-over** connects many of the shots, which include interviews with other actors, historical artifacts, views of Shakespeare's Old Globe Theatre, and snippets of scenes from the play in rehearsal and performance. The movie is like a dazzling lecture/presentation by someone who is both an artist and an educator. *(Twentieth Century–Fox)*

Most documentaries fall between these two extremes, as Albert Maysles has pointed out: "We can see two kinds of truth here. One is the raw material, which is the footage, the kind of truth that you get in literature in the diary form—it's immediate, no one has tampered with it. Then there's the other kind of truth that comes in extracting and juxtaposing the raw material into a more meaningful and coherent storytelling form which finally can be said to be more than just raw data. In a way, the interests of the people in shooting and the people in editing (even if it's the same individual) are in conflict with one another, because the raw material doesn't want to be shaped. It wants to maintain its truthfulness. One discipline says that if you begin to put it into another form, you're going to lose some of the veracity. The other discipline says if you don't let me put this into a form, no one is going to see it and the elements of truth in the raw material will never reach the audience with any impact, with any artistry, or whatever. So there are these things which are in conflict with one another and the thing is to put it all together, deriving the best from both. It comes almost to an argument of content and form, and you can't do one without the other."

should be allowed to speak for themselves. Bazinian realism is not mere news-reel objectivity—even if there were such a thing. He believed that reality must be heightened somewhat in the cinema, that the director must reveal the poetic implications of ordinary people, events, and places. By poeticizing the commonplace, the cinema is neither a totally objective recording of the physical world nor a symbolic abstraction of it. Rather, the cinema occupies a unique middle position between the sprawl of raw life and the artificially re-created worlds of the traditional arts.

Bazin wrote many articles overtly or implicitly criticizing the art of editing, or at least pointing out its limitations. If the essence of a scene is based on the idea of division, separation, or isolation, editing can be an effective technique in conveying these ideas. But if the essence of a scene demands the simultaneous presence of two or more related elements, the filmmaker ought to preserve the continuity of real time and space **(4–26).** He or she can do this by including all the dramatic variables within the same mise en scène—that is, by exploiting the resources of the long shot, the lengthy take, deep focus, and **widescreen.** The filmmaker can also preserve actual time and space by **panning, craning, tilting,** or **tracking** rather than cutting to individual shots.

John Huston's *The African Queen* contains a shot illustrating Bazin's principle. In attempting to take their boat down river to a large lake, the two protagonists (Humphrey Bogart and Katharine Hepburn) get sidetracked on a tributary of the main river. The tributary dwindles down to a stream and finally trickles into a tangle of reeds and mud, where the dilapidated boat gets hope-

4–26. *Safety Last* (U.S.A., 1923), *with Harold Lloyd, directed by Fred Newmeyer and Sam Taylor.*
In direct opposition to Pudovkin, Bazin believed that when the essence of a scene lies in the simultaneous presence of two or more elements, editing is ruled out. Such scenes gain their emotional impact through the unity of space, not through the juxtaposition of separate shots. In this famous sequence, for example, Lloyd's comedy of thrills is made more comic and more thrilling by the scene's realistic presentation: The dangling hero and the street below are kept in the same frame. Actually, the distance between the two is exaggerated by the cunning placement of the camera, and there was always at least a platform about three stories below him—"but who wants to fall three stories?" Lloyd asked. *(Museum of Modern Art)*

lessly mired. The exhausted travelers resign themselves to a slow death in the suffocating reeds, and eventually fall asleep on the floor of the boat. The camera then moves upward, over the reeds, where—just a few hundred yards away—is the lake. The bitter irony of the scene is conveyed by the continuous movement of the camera, which preserves the physical proximity of the boat, the intervening reeds, and the lake. If Huston had cut to three separate shots, we wouldn't understand these spatial interrelationships, and therefore the irony would be lost.

Bazin pointed out that in the evolution of movies, virtually every technical innovation pushed the medium closer to a realistic ideal: in the late 1920s, sound; in the 1930s and 1940s, color and deep-focus photography; in the 1950s, widescreen. In short, technology, not critics and theorists, usually alters technique. For example, when *The Jazz Singer* ushered in the talkie revolution in 1927, sound eclipsed virtually every advance made in the art of editing since Griffith's day. With the coming of sound, films *had* to be more realistically edited, whether their directors wished them so or not. Microphones were placed on the set itself, and sound had to be recorded while the scene was being photographed. Usually the microphones were hidden—in a vase of flowers, a wall sconce, etc. Thus, in the earliest sound movies, not only was the camera restricted, but the actors were as well. If they strayed too far from the microphone, the dialogue couldn't be recorded properly.

The effects on editing of these early talkies were disastrous. **Synchronized sound** anchored the images, so whole scenes were played with no cuts—a return to the "primitive" **sequence shot.** Most of the dramatic values were aural.

4–27. *Utamaro and His Five Women* (Japan, 1955), *directed by Kenji Mizoguchi.*
Bazin and his disciples were enthusiastic champions of the films of Mizoguchi. The Japanese master favored the use of lengthy takes rather than editing. He generally cut within a continuous take only when there was a sharp psychological shift within the scene. Used sparingly in this way, the cut acquires a greater dramatic impact than can be found in most conventionally edited movies. *(New Yorker Films)*

Even commonplace sequences held a fascination for audiences. If someone entered a room, the camera recorded the fact, whether it was dramatically important or not, and millions of spectators thrilled to the sound of the door opening and slamming shut. Critics and filmmakers despaired: The days of the recorded stage play had apparently returned. Later these problems were solved by the invention of the **blimp,** a soundproof camera housing that permits the camera to move with relative ease, and by the practice of **dubbing** sound after the shooting is completed (see Chapter 5).

But sound also provided some distinct advantages. In fact, Bazin believed that it represented a giant leap in the evolution toward a totally realistic medium. Spoken dialogue and sound effects heightened the sense of reality. Acting styles became more sophisticated as a result of sound. No longer did performers have to exaggerate visually to compensate for the absence of

4–28.   *Clerks* (U.S.A., 1994), *with Jeff Anderson and Brian O'Halloran; written, edited, and directed by Kevin Smith.*
Sometimes economics dictates style, as with this witty low-budget feature. Everyone worked for free. Smith shot the movie in the same convenience store he worked at (for $5 an hour) during the day. He also used lengthy takes in a number of scenes. The actors were required to memorize pages of dialogue (often very funny) so that the entire sequence could be shot without a cut. Why? Because Smith didn't need to worry about such costly decisions as where to put the camera with each new cut or how to light each new shot or whether he could afford to rent editing equipment to cut the sequence properly. Lengthy takes require one setup: The lights and camera usually remain stationary for the duration of the scene. The movie's final cost: a piddling $27,575. He charged it. It went on to win awards at the Sundance and Cannes Film Festivals. *(Miramax Films)*

voices. Talkies also permitted filmmakers to tell their stories more economically, without the intrusive titles that interspersed the visuals of silent movies. Tedious expository scenes could also be dispensed with. A few lines of dialogue easily conveyed what an audience needed to know about the premise of the story.

The use of deep-focus photography also exerted a modifying influence on editing practices. Prior to the 1930s, most cameras photographed interiors on one focal plane at a time. These cameras could capture a sharp image of an object from virtually any distance, but unless an enormous number of extra lights were set up, other elements of the picture that weren't at the same distance from the camera remained blurred, out of focus. One justification for editing, then, was purely technical: clarity of image.

The aesthetic qualities of deep-focus photography permitted composition in depth: Whole scenes could be shot in one setup, with no sacrifice of detail, for every distance appeared with equal clarity on the screen. Deep focus tends to be most effective when it adheres to the real time–space continuum. For this reason, the technique is sometimes thought to be more theatrical than cinematic, for the effects are achieved primarily through a spatially unified mise en scène rather than a fragmented juxtaposition of shots.

Bazin liked the objectivity and tact of deep focus. Details within a shot can be presented more democratically, as it were, without the special attention that a close-up inevitably confers. Thus, realist critics like Bazin felt that audiences would be more creative—less passive—in understanding the relationships between people and things. Unified space also preserves the ambiguity of life. Audiences aren't led to an inevitable conclusion but are forced to evaluate, sort out, and eliminate "irrelevancies" on their own.

In 1945, immediately following World War II, a movement called **neorealism** sprang up in Italy and gradually influenced directors all over the world. Spearheaded by Roberto Rossellini and Vittorio De Sica, two of Bazin's favorite filmmakers, neorealism deemphasized editing. The directors favored deep-focus photography, long shots, lengthy takes, and an austere restraint in the use of close-ups. Rossellini's *Paisan* features a sequence shot that was much admired by realistic critics. An American G.I. talks to a Sicilian young woman about his family, his life, and his dreams. Neither character understands the other's language, but they try to communicate in spite of this considerable obstacle. By refusing to condense time through the use of separate shots, Rossellini emphasizes the awkward pauses and hesitations between the two characters. Through its preservation of real time, the lengthy take forces us to experience the increasing, then relaxing, tensions that exist between them. An abridgement of time through the use of a cut would have dissipated these tensions.

When asked why he deemphasized editing, Rossellini replied: "Things are there, why manipulate them?" This statement might well serve as Bazin's theoretical credo. He deeply admired Rossellini's openness to multiple interpretations, his refusal to diminish reality by making it serve an a priori thesis. "Neorealism by definition rejects analysis, whether political, moral, psychological, logical, or social, of the characters and their actions," Bazin pointed out. "It looks on reality as a whole, not incomprehensible, certainly, but inescapably one."

Sequence shots tend to produce (often unconsciously) a sense of mounting anxiety in the viewer. We expect setups to change during a scene. When they don't, we often grow restless, hardly conscious of what's producing our uneasiness. Jim Jarmusch's bizarre comedy, *Stranger Than Paradise*, uses sequence shots throughout (4–29). The camera inexorably waits at a predetermined location. The young characters enter the scene and play out their tawdry, comic lives, complete with boring stretches of silence, glazed expressions of torpor, and random ticks. Finally, they leave. Or they just sit there. The camera sits with them. Fade out. Very weird.

Like many technological innovations, widescreen provoked a wail of protest from many critics and directors. The new screen shape would destroy the

4–29.   *Stranger Than Paradise* (U.S.A., 1984), *directed by Jim Jarmusch.*
Each scene in this movie is a sequence shot—a lengthy take without cuts. Far from being "primitive," the sequence-shot technique produces a sophisticated, wry effect, bizarre and funny. In this scene, the two protagonists (John Lurie and Richard Edson) eat yet another goulash dinner while Lurie berates his stout, outspoken aunt (Cecillia Stark) for still speaking Hungarian after years of living in America. The scene's comic rhythms are accented by the staging: The bickering relatives must bend forward to see each other, while the visitor, caught in the crossfire, tries unsuccessfully to stay neutral.   *(Samuel Goldwyn)*

4–30. *The Straight Story* **(U.S.A., 1999),** *with Richard Farnsworth, directed by David Lynch.*
American movies are usually edited at a fast pace without any slackness or "dead spots" between the shots. *The Straight Story* is a conspicuous exception. Based on true life events, the movie is a road picture, but instead of the usual vroom-vrooming vehicles racing down streets and screeching 'round corners, the vehicle of choice is a '66 John Deere tractor that the elderly hero (Farnsworth) drives from Iowa to Wisconsin where his estranged and ailing brother lives. The movie is cut at a very, very slow pace—to approximate the chugging progress of his antiquated transport. *(The Straight Story, Inc. and Disney Enterprises, Inc.)*

close-up, many feared, especially of the human face. There simply was too much space to fill, even in long shots, others complained. Audiences would never be able to assimilate all the action, for they wouldn't know where to look. It was suitable only for horizontal compositions, some argued, useful for epic films, but too spacious for interior scenes and small subjects. Editing would be further minimized, the formalists complained, for there would be no need to cut to something if everything was already there, arranged in a long horizontal series.

At first, the most effective widescreen films were, in fact, westerns and historical extravaganzas. But before long, directors began to use the new screen with more sensitivity. Like deep-focus photography, scope meant that they had to be more conscious of their mise en scène. More relevant details had to be included within the frame, even at its edges. Films could be more densely saturated and—potentially, at least—more effective artistically. Filmmakers discovered that the most expressive parts of a person's face were the eyes and mouth, and consequently close-ups that chopped off the tops and bottoms of actors' faces weren't as disastrous as had been predicted.

Not surprisingly, the realist critics were the first to reconsider the advantages of widescreen. Bazin liked its authenticity and objectivity. Here was yet another step away from the distorting effects of editing, he pointed out. As with deep focus, widescreen helped to preserve spatial and temporal continuity. Close shots containing two or more people could now be photographed in one setup without suggesting inequality, as deep focus often did in its variety of depth planes. Nor were the relations between people and things fragmented as they were with edited sequences. Scope was also more realistic because the widescreen enveloped the viewer in a sense of an experience, even with its edges—a cinematic counterpart to the eye's peripheral vision. All the same advantages that had been applied to sound and deep focus were now applied to widescreen: its greater fidelity to real time and space; its detail, complexity, and density; its more objective presentation; its more coherent continuity; its greater ambiguity; and its encouragement of creative audience participation.

Interestingly, several of Bazin's protégés were responsible for a return to more flamboyant editing techniques in the following decades. Throughout the 1950s, Godard, Truffaut, and Chabrol wrote criticism for *Cahiers du Cinéma*. By the end of the decade, they turned to making their own movies. The *nouvelle vague*, or **New Wave** as this movement was called in English, was

4–31.   *The Hidden Fortress* (Japan, 1958), *directed by Akira Kurosawa*.
Most filmmakers bemoaned the advent of widescreen in the 1950s almost as much as they bemoaned sound in the late 1920s. Bazin and other realists embraced the innovation as yet another step away from the distorting effects of montage. Widescreen *tends to deemphasize depth in favor of breadth, but Bazin believed that a horizontal presentation of the visual materials could be more democratic—less distorting even than deep focus, which tends to emphasize visual importance in terms of an object's closeness to the camera's lens.   *(Toho Films)*

4–32. *The Innocents* (Great Britain, 1961), *with Deborah Kerr, directed by Jack Clayton.* Throughout most of this psychological thriller (which is based on Henry James's novelette *The Turn of the Screw*), we are not sure if the ghost is "real" or simply the hysterical projection of a repressed governess (Kerr), because we usually see the apparition through her eyes. That is, the camera represents her point of view, which may or may not be reliable. But when an objective camera is used, as in this photo, both the governess and the ghost are included in the same space, with no cutting between separate shots. Hence, we conclude that the spirit figure has an independent existence outside of the governess's imagination.   *(Twentieth Century–Fox)*

eclectic in its theory and practice. The members of this group, who were not very tightly knit, were unified by an almost obsessional enthusiasm for film culture, especially American film culture. Unlike that of most previous movements, the range of enthusiasms of these critic/filmmakers was extraordinarily broad: Hitchcock, Renoir, Eisenstein, Hawks, Bergman, Ford, and many more. Although rather dogmatic in their personal tastes, the New Wave critics tended to avoid theoretical dogmatism. They believed that technique was meaningful only in terms of subject matter. In fact, it was the New Wave that popularized the idea that *what* a movie says is inextricably bound up with *how* it's said. They insisted that editing styles ought to be determined not by fashion, the limitations of technology, or dogmatic pronouncements, but by the essence of the subject matter itself.

Some questions we ought to ask ourselves about a movie's editing style include: How much cutting is there and why? Are the shots highly fragmented or relatively lengthy? What is the point of the cutting in each scene? To clarify? To stimulate? To lyricize? To create suspense? To explore an idea or emotion in depth? Does the cutting seem manipulative or are we left to interpret the images on our own? What kind of rhythm does the editing establish with each scene? Is the personality of the filmmaker apparent in the cutting or is the presentation of shots relatively objective and functional? Is editing a major language system of the movie or does the film artist relegate cutting to a relatively minor function?

FURTHER READING

BALMUTH, BERNARD, *Introduction to Film Editing* (Boston: Focal Press, 1989). Technical emphasis.

BAZIN, ANDRÉ, *What Is Cinema?* Hugh Gray, ed. and trans. (Berkeley: University of California Press, vol. I, 1967, vol. II, 1971). A collection of essays emphasizing the realistic nature of the film medium.

CHRISTIE, IAN, AND RICHARD TAYLOR, eds. *Eisenstein Rediscovered* (New York and London: Routledge, 1993). A collection of scholarly essays on Eisenstein and his legacy.

DMYTRYK, EDWARD, *On Film Editing* (Boston: Focal Press, 1984). A practical handbook by a former editor turned director.

GRAHAM, PETER, ed., *The New Wave* (London: Secker & Warburg, 1968). A collection of essays by and about Bazin, Truffaut, Godard, and others.

LA VALLEY, ALBERT J., ed., *Focus on Hitchcock* (Englewood Cliffs: N. J.: Prentice-Hall, 1972).

LOBRUTTO, VINCENT, ed., *Selected Takes: Film Editors on Film Editing* (New York: Praeger, 1991).

OLDHAM, GABRIELLA, ed., *First Cut* (Berkeley: University of California Press, 1992). Interviews with twenty-three award-winning film editors.

PUDOVKIN, V. I., *Film Technique and Film Acting.* Ivor Montague, ed. and trans. (New York: Grove Press, 1960). See also *Kuleschov on Film,* Ronald Levaco, ed. and trans. (Berkeley: University of California Press, 1974).

REISZ, KAREL, *The Technique of Film Editing* (New York: Hastings House, 1968). The standard text on the history, practice, and theory of editing.

Story

Paramount Pictures

*Narratives are composed in order to reward, modify,
frustrate, or defeat the perceiver's search for coherence.*
—DAVID BORDWELL

The classical paradigm is a term invented by scholars to describe a certain
kind of narrative structure that has dominated fiction film production ever
since the 1910s. It's by far the most popular type of story organization, especially in the United States, where it reigns virtually unchallenged. The model is

called "classical" because it's a norm of actual practice, not necessarily because of a high degree of artistic excellence. In other words, bad movies as well as good ones use this narrative formula.

Derived from the live theater, the classical paradigm is a set of conventions, not rules. This narrative model is based on a conflict between a protagonist, who initiates the action, and an antagonist, who resists it. Most films in this form begin with an implied dramatic question. We want to know how the protagonist will get what he or she wants in the face of considerable opposition. The following scenes intensify this conflict in a rising pattern of action. This escalation is treated in terms of cause–effect, with each scene implying a link to the next.

The conflict builds to its maximum tension in the climax. Here, the protagonist and antagonist clash overtly. One wins, the other loses. After their confrontation, the dramatic intensity subsides in the resolution. The story ends with

8–10.   The classical paradigm.

Aristotle implicitly suggested the structure of classical drama in *The Poetics*, but it was not until the nineteenth century that the inverted V structure was diagrammed by the German scholar Gustav Freytag. This type of narrative structure begins with an overt conflict, which is increasingly intensified with the rising action of the following scenes. Details that don't relate to this conflict are eliminated or kept incidental. The battle between the main character and his or her antagonists reaches its highest pitch in the climax. In the resolution, the strands of the story are tied up and life returns to normal with a closing off of the action.

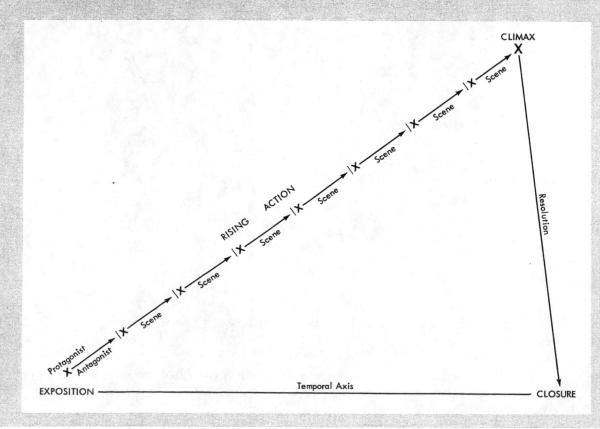

some kind of formal closure—traditionally a wedding or a dance in comedies, a death in tragedies, a reunion or return to normal in dramas. The final **shot**—because of its privileged position—is often meant to be a philosophical overview of some kind, a summing up of the significance of the previous material.

The classical paradigm emphasizes dramatic unity, plausible motivations, and coherence of its constituent parts. Each shot is seamlessly elided to the next in an effort to produce a smooth flow of action, and often a sense of inevitability. To add urgency to the conflict, filmmakers sometimes include some kind of deadline, thus intensifying the emotion. During the Hollywood studio era especially, classical structures often featured double plot lines, in which a romantic love story was developed to parallel the main line of action. In love stories, a comic second couple often paralleled the main lovers.

Classical plot structures are linear and often take the form of a journey, a chase, or a search. Even the characters are defined primarily in terms of what they do. "Action is character" insists Syd Field, the author of several handbooks on screenwriting. "What a person does is what he is, not what he says." Field and other advocates of the classical paradigm are not very interested in passive characters—people to whom things are done. (These types of characters are more typical in foreign films.) Classicists favor characters who are goal oriented so that we can take a rooting interest in their plans of action.

Field's conceptual model is expressed in traditional theatrical terms **(8–11)**. A screenplay is composed of three acts. Act I, "Setup," occupies the first quarter of the script. It establishes the dramatic premise: What is the main character's goal and what obstacles are likely to get in the way of its attainment? Act II, "Confrontation," consists of the middle two quarters of the story, with a major reversal of fortune at the midpoint. This portion of the screenplay complicates the conflict with plot twists and an increasing sense of urgency, showing the main character fighting against obstacles. Act III, "Resolution," constitutes

8–11. According to Syd Field, the narrative structure of a movie can be broken down into three acts. The story should contain about ten to twenty "plot points," major twists or key events in the action. At the midpoint of the second act, there is usually a big reversal of expectations, sending the action spinning in a new direction. Although the diagram might not be helpful in analyzing most realistic or formalistic narratives, it is surprisingly apt in movies using a classical structure.

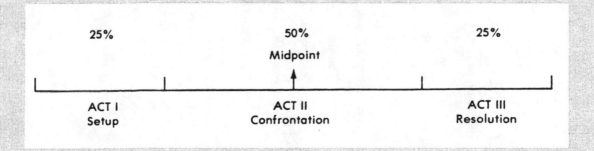

the final quarter of the story. This section dramatizes what happens as a result of the climactic confrontation.

One of the greatest plots in the history of cinema is found in Buster Keaton's *The General,* a textbook example of the classical paradigm. It fits Freytag's inverted V structure as well as Field's three-act play approach. As Daniel Moews has pointed out, all of Keaton's feature-length comedies use the same basic comic formula. Buster begins as a sincere but clumsy greenhorn who bungles every attempt to ingratiate himself with a person he holds in awe—usually a pretty girl. At the conclusion of the day, he falls asleep, lonely, depressed, and dispirited. When he awakens, he's a new man. He goes on to succeed, usually at the same or parallel activities of the earlier portions of the movie.

A Civil War comedy loosely based on an actual event, *The General* is laid out with the narrative elegance of a play by Congreve. The first act establishes the two loves in the hero's life: his train, *The General,* and Annabelle Lee, his somewhat flaky girlfriend. His only friends, apparently, are two prepubescent boys. (Among other things, the movie is a coming-of-age story.) When war is

8–12.   An outline of the plot structure of *The General.*
The plot moves forward with such smoothness and poise that we're hardly aware of its dazzling symmetry until the second chase, when most of the earlier gag clusters are triumphantly reprised.

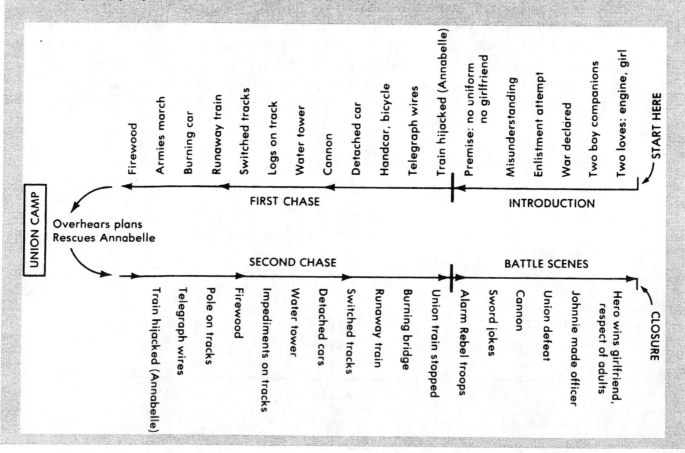

declared, our hero, Johnnie Gray, trying to impress his girl, attempts to enlist. But he's rejected by the authorities: He's more valuable to the South as an engineer. Through a misunderstanding, Annabelle thinks Johnnie is a coward. "I don't want you to speak to me again until you are in uniform," she haughtily informs him. End of Act I.

A full year is edited out of the story as we begin Act II. (The rest of the movie covers only about twenty-four hours.) We see the plans of the Union officers to hijack a Confederate train, thereby cutting off the supply lines of the Southern army. The Yankee leader's map shows the major stops and rivers along the railroad route. In fact, this map is a geographical outline of Act II.

On the day that the hijacking is to take place, Annabelle Lee boards Johnnie's train to visit her wounded father. She snubs her former suitor. The hijacking of the train sets off the rising action. The second quarter of the movie is a chase sequence: Johnnie pursues the stolen *General* (with Annabelle on board) as it flees northward. There are a series of gag clusters, each involving different props, such as telegraph wires, switched tracks, a water tower, a cannon **(8–13),** and so on. Johnnie is usually the butt of the jokes.

At the midpoint of the film, our hero sneaks into the enemy's camp, alone and exhausted. Nonetheless, he manages to rescue Annabelle. They fall asleep in the woods in a downpour, discouraged, almost wiped out.

8–13. *The General* (U.S.A., 1927), *with Buster Keaton, directed by Keaton and Clyde Bruckman.* Silent film comedians were masters of improvisation, capable of spinning off a profusion of gags with a single prop. For example, the gag cluster involving this cannon is a miniature drama, complete with exposition, variations on a theme that constitute the rising action, and a thrilling climax that serves as a topper to the sequence. Even more extraordinary, Keaton and his regular crew never used written scripts or shooting schedules. They knew only the premise of the film and its conclusion. The rest was improvised. They shot for about eight weeks, making due allowances for baseball games between scenes. Later, Keaton viewed all the footage, edited out the dull stuff, and created the narrative structure.   *(United Artists)*

The next day, a second chase begins, reversing the pattern of the previous day, and taking up the third quarter of the plot. Now the jokes are inflicted on the pursuing Yankees as Johnnie and Annabelle speed southward in the recaptured *General*. The gag clusters are also reversed. Most of them are parallels to those of the first chase: telegraph wires, logs on the tracks, a water tower, a burning bridge, and so on. Just in time, Johnnie and Annabelle arrive at the Confederate camp and warn the troops of an impending Union attack.

Act III is a battle sequence between the two great armies. Johnnie shows himself to be a doggedly perseverant soldier, though not always a successful one. He is rewarded for his heroism with a commission in the army. He also wins back the love of his girl. All ends happily.

Keaton's narrative structure follows an elaborately counterbalanced pattern, in which the earlier humiliations are triumphantly canceled out on the second day. Described thus schematically, Keaton's plots sound rather mechanical. But as his French admirers have pointed out, his architectural rigor can be likened to the works of the great neoclassical artists of the eighteenth century, with their intricately worked out parallels and neatly balanced symmetries.

Ordinarily, one would consider such an artificial plot structure as an example of a formalist narrative. However, the execution of each section is rigorously realistic. Keaton performed all his own gags (many of them dangerous), usually on the first **take.** He also insisted on absolute accuracy in the costuming, the sets, and even the trains, which are historically true to the period. This combination of realistic execution with a formally patterned narrative is typical of classical cinema. Classicism is an intermediate style that blends conventions from both stylistic extremes.

Realistic Narratives

Traditionally, critics have linked realism to "life," formalism with "pattern." Realism is defined as an absence of style, whereas style is a preeminent concern among formalists. Realists reject artifice to portray the material world "transparently," without distortion or even mediation. Conversely, formalists are concerned with fantasy materials or throwaway subject matter to emphasize the world of the imagination, of beauty for its own sake.

Today, these views are considered naive, at least so far as realism is concerned. Contemporary critics and scholars regard realism as a *style,* with an elaborate set of conventions that are less obvious perhaps, but just as artificial as those used by expressionists.

Both realistic and formalistic narratives are patterned and manipulated, but the realistic storyteller attempts to submerge the pattern, to bury it beneath the surface "clutter" and apparent randomness of the dramatic events. In other words, the pretense that a realistic narrative is "unmanipulated" or "like life" is precisely that—a pretense, an aesthetic deception.

8–14a. *Chinatown* (U.S.A., 1974), with Faye Dunaway and Jack Nicholson, directed by Roman Polanski. (Paramount Pictures)

8–14b. *A Simple Plan* (U.S.A., 1998), with Bill Paxton and Billy Bob Thornton, directed by Sam Raimi. (Paramount Pictures)

In genres that depend on mystery and suspense for their effects, the narrative often withholds information, forcing us to fill in the gaps, teasing and tantalizing us with possible solutions to mysteries that aren't totally resolved until the end of the movie. On the other hand, some thrillers provide the viewer with all the necessary information as it's needed. In *A Simple Plan*, for example, the emphasis is as much on character development as it is on action. Scott Smith wrote both the screenplay and the best-selling novel it was based on: "I wanted to portray a group of people who begin digging a deeper and deeper hole for themselves trying to hide something they've done," Smith explained. "They become driven, and then panicked, by the fear of getting caught. Desperate people have now turned into dangerous people."

8–15a. *Late Spring* **(Japan, 1949),** *with Chishu Ryu (seated) and Setsuko Hara (center), directed by Yasujiro Ozu.* (New Yorker Films)

Love and Marriage from a realist perspective. One of the most common genres in Japan is the home drama. It was the only genre Ozu worked in, and he was one of its most popular practitioners. This type of film deals with the day-to-day routines of domestic life. Although Ozu was a profoundly philosophical artist, his movies consist almost entirely of "little things"—the bitter pills of self-denial that ultimately render life disappointing. Many of Ozu's films have seasonal titles that symbolically evoke appropriate human analogues. *Late Spring,* for example, deals with the attempts of a decent widower (Ryu) to marry off his only daughter (Hara) before she wilts into spinsterhood.

    True Love is a wry exploration of male–female tensions in an Italian-American working-class community shortly before the marriage of the two main characters. Like most realistic movies, the plot line is loose. The scenes are arranged in apparently random order, and the everyday events are presented matter-of-factly, with no "heightening" for dramatic effect. The dialogue is raw, the language of the streets rather than the genteel living rooms of middle America. The conclusion of the film is ambivalent and ambiguous, with no neat solutions to the complex problems that the movie addresses.

8–15b. *True Love* **(U.S.A., 1989),** *with Kelly Cinnante and Annabella Sciorra, directed by Nancy Savoca.* (United Artists)

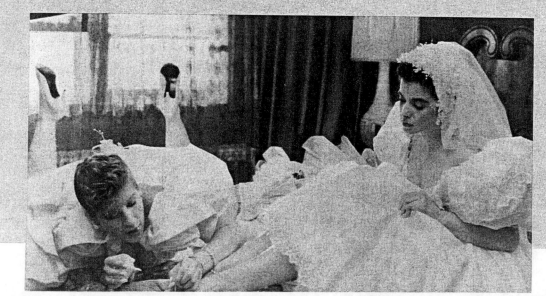

Realists prefer loose, discursive plots, with no clearly defined beginning, middle, or end. We dip into the story at an arbitrary point. Usually we aren't presented with a clear-cut conflict, as in classical narratives. Rather, the conflict emerges unobtrusively from the unforced events of the exposition. The story itself is presented as a "slice of life," as a poetic fragment, not a neatly structured tale. Rarely is reality neatly structured; realistic art must follow suit. Life goes on, even after the final reel.

Realists often borrow their structures from the cycles of nature. For example, many of the movies of Ozu are given seasonal titles that symbolize an appropriate human counterpart—*Early Summer, Late Autumn, Early Spring, The End of Summer, Late Spring* (8–15a). Other realistic films are structured around a limited period of time, like summer vacation or a school semester. Such movies sometimes center on **rites of passage,** such as birth, puberty, first love, first job, marriage, painful separations, death.

Often, we can't guess the principle of narrative coherence until the end of the movie, especially if it has a circular or cyclical structure, as many realistic films do. For example, Robert Altman's *M*A*S*H* opens with the fresh arrival of two soldier-surgeons, Hawkeye Pierce and Duke Forrest. The movie ends when their tour of duty is over. Yet the M*A*S*H unit will continue saving lives, even after these two excellent surgeons have left. (This same structural principle is used in a later military comedy, Barry Levinson's *Good Morning, Vietnam.*)

The episodic structure of *M*A*S*H* is what appealed to those who adapted it as a television series. Realistic film narratives frequently seem episodic, the sequence of events almost interchangeable. The plot doesn't "build" inexorably, but seems to drift into surprising scenes that don't necessarily propel the story forward. These are offered for their own sake, as examples of "real-life" oddities.

Spectators who like fast-moving stories are often impatient with realistic films, which frequently move slowly. This is especially true in the earlier scenes, while we wait for the main narrative strand to emerge. "Digressions" often turn out to be parallels to the central plotline. But this parallelism must be inferred; it's rarely pointed out explicitly. Other traits of realistic narratives include the following:

1. A nonintrusive implied author who "reports" objectively and avoids making judgments.

2. A rejection of clichés, stale conventions, stock situations and characters in favor of the unique, the concrete, the specific.

3. A fondness for exposé, with "shocking" or "low" subject matter that is often criticized for its grittiness and "bad taste."

4. An antisentimental point of view that rejects glib happy endings, wishful thinking, miraculous cures, and other forms of phony optimism.

5. An avoidance of melodrama and exaggeration in favor of understatement and dedramatization.

8-16. *Hate (La Haine),* **(France, 1996),** *with Vincent Cassel, Said Taghmaoui, and Hubert Kounde; directed by Mathieu Kassovitz.*
Ever since the late nineteenth century, when it became a dominant international style in the arts, realism has provoked controversy for its "sordid" or "shocking" subject matter, its pre-occupation with details that the conventional majority finds repulsive but fascinating. *La Haine* caused an uproar in France when it was released. Its uncompromising portrayal of three lower-class thugs (pictured) makes it hard to sympathize with their plight. They are vicious and violent, their language a steady torrent of filth, and their values cynically corrupt. The movie offers very little hope for this doomed underclass. Viewers are likely to ask themselves: How did the world get this way?   *(Gramercy Pictures)*

6. A scientific view of causality and motivation, with a corresponding rejection of such romantic concepts as Destiny and Fate.

7. An avoidance of the **lyrical** impulse in favor of a plain, straightforward presentation.

Formalistic Narratives

Formalistic narratives revel in their artificiality. Time is often scrambled and rearranged to hammer home a thematic point more forcefully. The design of the plot is not concealed but heightened. It's part of the show. Formalistic plots come in a wide assortment, but usually they are structured according to the filmmaker's theme. For example, Alfred Hitchcock was obsessed by themes dealing with "doubles" and "the wrong man"—a technically innocent man who is accused of a crime committed by an undetected counterpart.

8–17a. *The Lion King* (U.S.A., 1994), *directed by Roger Allers and Rob Minkoff.*
Movie plots often derive from the weirdest sources. This is a coming-of-age story of a lion cub named Simba, who is next in line to succeed his father, a benevolent and wise leader. But the king's evil brother brings about the monarch's death, and Simba's destiny is to avenge his father's death and return legitimate rule to the jungle. Sound familiar? The story is a shameless steal from *Hamlet*, with touches of *Oedipus Rex,* the story of Moses, *Bambi,* and *The Jungle Book.* Pretty classy stuff.   *(© The Walt Disney Company. All Rights Reserved.)*

8–17b. *Face/Off* (U.S.A., 1997), *with Nicolas Cage and John Travolta, directed by John Woo.*
The narrative structure of this sci-fi thriller is a riff on the symbolic implications of the title. Traditionally, a face-off is a ritualistic dual of some sort (pictured). But in this movie, the two main characters literally exchange facial features—a plot device every bit as artificial as Shakespeare's delight in doubles: twin protagonists, gender switches, and mistaken identities. By assuming each other's identities, the two central characters of *Face/Off* are able to explore their other selves, their secret selves. Could these men be mirror images? *(Paramount Pictures)*

Hitchcock's *The Wrong Man* is his most explicit treatment of these narrative motifs. The entire plot is doubled, structured in twos. There are two imprisonments, two handwriting tests, two conversations in the kitchen, two legal hearings, two visits to a clinic, two visits to the lawyer. The hero is arrested twice by two policemen. He is identified (wrongly) by two witnesses at two different shops. There are two transfers of guilt: The main character (Henry Fonda) is accused of a crime he didn't commit, and midway through the movie, his emotionally disturbed wife (Vera Miles) takes on the guilt, requiring her to be committed to an asylum. "People say that Hitchcock lets the wires show too often," Jean-Luc Godard noted. "But because he shows them, they are no longer wires. They are the pillars of a marvelous architectural design made to withstand our scrutiny."

Many formalistic narratives are intruded on by the author, whose personality is part of the show. For example, it's virtually impossible to ignore the personality of Buñuel in his films. He slyly interjects his sardonic black humor into his narratives. He loves to undermine his characters—their pomposity, their self-deception, their mean little souls (**8–18**). Godard's personality is also highly intrusive, especially in his nontraditional narratives, which he called "cinematic essays."

8–18.   *The Discreet Charm of the Bourgeoisie* (France, 1972), *directed by Luis Buñuel*. Most of Buñuel's movies feature bizarre scenes that are left unexplained, as though they were the most normal thing in the world. He delighted in satirizing middle-class hypocrisies, treating them with a kind of affectionate bemusement mingled with contempt. In this film, he presents us with a series of loosely connected episodes dealing with the inane rituals of a group of well-heeled semizombies. Interspersing these episodes are shots of the main characters walking on an empty road (pictured). No one questions why they are there. No one seems to know where they are going. Buñuel doesn't say.   *(Twentieth Century–Fox)*

8–19. *Mon Oncle d'Amerique* (France, 1980), *with Gerard Depardieu, directed by Alain Resnais.*
Depardieu portrays a hardworking idealist whose conservative values and faith in God are severely tested. The significance of the title? It's taken from European pop mythology—the proverbial adventurous uncle who left for America, made a fortune, and will someday return loaded with money to solve all their problems. Resnais was also thinking of Samuel Beckett's bitter stage comedy, *Waiting for Godot*, which revolves around an obscure figure (God?) who's constantly waited for, but never shows up. *(New World Pictures)*

Formalistic narratives are often interrupted by lyrical interludes, exercises in pure style—like the enchanting dance numbers in the Fred Astaire–Ginger Rogers RKO musicals of the 1930s. In fact, stylized genre films like musicals, science fiction, and fantasies offer the richest potential for displays of stylistic rapture and bravura effects. These lyrical interludes interrupt the forward momentum of the plot, which is often a mere pretext anyway.

An excellent example of a formalistic narrative is *Mon Oncle d'Amerique* (My Uncle in America), directed by Alain Resnais, with a script by Resnais and Jean Gruault (8–19). The film's structure is indebted to Godard's essay form, which can combine elements from the documentary and avant-garde film with fiction. The ideas in the movie are the stuff of Psychology 101. Resnais frames and intersperses his fictional episodes with footage of an actual medical doctor and behavioral scientist, Dr. Henri Laborit, who indulges in the French mania for dissection, analysis, and classification. He wittily discusses the relationship of human behavior to the makeup of the brain, the conscious and subconscious environment, social conditioning, the nervous system, zoology, and biology. He alludes to the behavior-modification theories of B. F. Skinner and other theories of human development.

The fictional episodes in the movie are concrete demonstrations of these theories. The characters are autonomous, not mechanized zombies. Nonetheless, they are victims of forces they hardly understand. Resnais focuses

355

on three appealing characters. Each is the product of a unique biological makeup and cultural environment. Their paths intersect by chance. "These people have everything to make them happy," Resnais observed, "yet they're not happy at all. Why?"

Resnais then shows us why through his dazzling editing and multiple narratives. In a kaleidoscope of shifting perspectives, Resnais juxtaposes snippets of the characters' lives, dreams, and memories with Dr. Laborit's abstract formulations, statistics, and wry observations. The three main characters are movie freaks, and at various points during the story, Resnais intercuts brief clips from the films of their childhood idols—Jean Marais, Danielle Darrieux, and Jean Gabin. Some of these movie clips bear a not-so-coincidental resemblance to the dramatic situations of the characters. Resnais is also paying homage to three great stars of the French cinema.

Nonfictional Narratives

There are three broad classifications of motion pictures: fiction, documentary, and **avant-garde.** Documentaries and avant-garde films usually don't tell stories, at least not in the conventional (that is, fictional) sense. Of course, documentaries and avant-garde movies are structured, but neither uses a plot. Rather, the story—if any—is structured according to a theme or an argument, especially in documentaries. In the avant-garde cinema, the structure is often a matter of the filmmaker's subjective instincts.

First, documentaries. Unlike most fiction films, documentaries deal with facts—real people, places, and events rather than invented ones. Documentarists believe that they're not creating a world so much as reporting on the one that already exists. They are not just recorders of external reality, however, for like fiction filmmakers they shape their raw materials through their selection of details. These details are organized into a coherent artistic pattern. Many documentaries deliberately keep the structure of their films simple and unobtrusive. They want their version of the facts to suggest the same apparent randomness of life itself.

Sound familiar? In fact, the concepts of realism and formalism are almost as useful in discussing documentaries as fiction films. However, the overwhelming majority of documentarists would insist that their main interest is with subject matter rather than style.

The realistic documentary is best illustrated by the **cinéma vérité** or "direct cinema" movement of the 1960s. Because of the need to be able to capture news stories quickly, efficiently, and with a minimal crew, television journalism was responsible for the development of a new technology, which in turn eventually led to a new philosophy of truth in documentary cinema. The technology included the following:

1. A lightweight 16-mm hand-held camera, allowing the cinematographer to roam virtually anywhere with ease.

8–20. *JFK* **(U.S.A., 1991),** *with Kevin Costner (center), written and directed by Oliver Stone.* History as narrative. As a number of historians have pointed out, "history" is actually a jumble of fragments, unsifted facts, random events, and details that no one thought were important enough to explain. This chaos is sorted out by a historian who superimposes a narrative over the sprawling materials. The historian excludes some data, heightens others. Effects are provided with causes; isolated events are connected with other superficially remote events. In short, many modern historians would insist that the past contains various histories, not just one. Each history is the product of a person who assembles, interprets, and shapes the facts into a narrative. Oliver Stone's controversial depiction of the assassination of President Kennedy is told from the point of view of New Orleans D.A. Jim Garrison (Costner). The movie does what a historian does: It offers a possible explanation for a traumatic national tragedy that was never adequately resolved in the minds of much of the American public. *JFK* is a dazzling display of bravura editing, encompassing dozens of characters, many years, thousands of miles, and hundreds of thousands of historical facts. *(Warner Bros.)*

2. Flexible **zoom lenses,** allowing the cinematographer to go from 12-mm **wide-angle** positions to 120-mm **telephoto** positions in one adjusting bar.

3. New **fast film stocks,** permitting scenes to be photographed without the necessity of setting up lights. So sensitive were these stocks to available lighting that even nighttime scenes with minimal illumination could be recorded with acceptable clarity.

4. A portable tape recorder, allowing a technician to record sound directly in automatic **synchronization** with the visuals. This equipment was so easy to use that only two people—one at the camera, the other with the sound system—were required to bring in a news story.

357

8–21. *Law and Order* (U.S.A., 1969), *directed by Frederick Wiseman.*
Cinéma vérité, or direct cinema, prided itself on its objectivity and straightforward presentation. Certainly, these documentarists realized that total neutrality is an impossible goal to achieve. Even Wiseman, among the most objective of documentarists, insists that his movies are a subjective *interpretation* of actual events, people, and places. He tries to be as "fair" as possible in presenting his materials. For example, he refuses to use off-frame narrators. The subjects of the film are allowed to speak for themselves, and the burden of interpretation is placed on the spectators, who must analyze the significance of the material on their own. Of course, most participants are aware of being photographed, and this surely influences their behavior. No one wants to look like a fool on camera. *(Zipporah Films)*

The flexibility of this hardware permitted documentarists to redefine the concept of authenticity. This new aesthetic amounted to a rejection of preplanning and carefully detailed scripts. A script involves preconceptions about reality and tends to cancel out any sense of spontaneity or ambiguity. Direct cinema rejected such preconceptions as fictional: Reality is not being observed but is being arranged to conform to what the script says it is. The documentarist is superimposing a *plot* over the materials. Re-creations of any kind were no longer necessary because, if the crew members are present while an event is actually taking place, they can capture it while it's happening.

The concept of minimal interference with reality became the dominating preoccupation of the American and Canadian schools of cinéma vérité. The filmmaker must not control events in any way. Re-creations—even with the people and places actually involved—were unacceptable. Editing was kept to a minimum, for otherwise it could lead to a false impression of the sequence of

358

8–22. *Harlan County, U.S.A.* (U.S.A., 1977), *directed by Barbara Kopple.*
Direct cinema is most effective with materials that are intrinsically dramatic, like crisis situations in which a conflict is about to reach its climax. For example, during the production of this documentary, which deals with a bitter coal-miners' strike for decent working conditions, Kopple and her crew were repeatedly plunged in the middle of violence. In one sequence, they are actually fired on by a trigger-happy yahoo. The camera recorded it all. Implicit in the concept of documentary is the verb *to document*—to verify, to provide an irrefutable record of an event. In a nonfiction film, these privileged moments of truth generally take precedence over considerations of narrative.   *(Museum of Modern Art)*

events. Actual time and space were preserved whenever possible by using **lengthy takes.**

Cinéma vérité also uses sound minimally. These filmmakers were—and still are—hostile to the "voice of God" commentaries that accompanied traditional documentaries. Off-screen narration tends to interpret images for the spectator, thus relieving us of the necessity of analyzing for ourselves. Some direct cinema advocates dispense with voice-over narration entirely (**8–21**).

The tradition of the formalistic or subjective documentary can be traced back to the Soviet filmmaker Dziga-Vertov. Like most Soviet artists of the 1920s, Vertov was a propagandist. He believed that the cinema should be a tool of the Revolution, a way of instructing workers about how to view events from an ideological perspective. "Art," he once wrote, "is not a *mirror* which reflects the historical struggle, but a *weapon* of that struggle."

Documentarists in this formalistic tradition tend to build their movies thematically, arranging and structuring the story materials to demonstrate a thesis, like the news stories on television's prestigious *60 Minutes*. In many cases, the sequence of shots and even entire scenes can be switched around with relatively

8–23. *Point of Order!* (U.S.A., 1964), *directed by Emile De Antonio.*
Materials that might seem politically neutral can acquire ideological significance when the footage is reedited expressively. Many documentaries in the Vertov mold—like this exposé of the political sleazebag Senator Joe McCarthy—were originally photographed by relatively impartial newsreel camera operators. The ideology is conveyed by the way in which this neutral material is restructured on the editing bench, a striking instance of how "plot" (or narrative structure) can radically alter "story." All montage films making use of newsreels descend from Vertov's theories. See also Jay Leyda, *Films Beget Films* (New York: Hill & Wang, 1964). *(Continental Distributing)*

little loss of sense or logic. The structure of the film is not based on chronology or narrative coherence, but on the documentarist's argument **(8–23).**

Avant-garde films are so variable that it's hard to generalize about their narrative structures. Most of these movies don't even try to tell a story. Autobiographical elements are common. Many avant-garde artists are primarily concerned with conveying their "inner impulses," their personal and subjective involvements with people, ideas, and experiences. For this reason, avant-garde movies are sometimes obscure and even incomprehensible. Many of these filmmakers create their own personal language and symbology.

With few exceptions, avant-garde films are not written out in advance. In part this is because the same artist usually shoots and edits the footage and is therefore able to control the material at these stages of the filmmaking process. Avant-garde filmmakers also value chance and spontaneity in their movies, and to exploit these elements, they avoid the inflexibility of a script.

Maya Deren, an American avant-garde filmmaker of the 1940s, differentiated her kind of movie (which she called "personal" or "poetic") from mainstream commercial films primarily in terms of structure. Like a lyric poem, personal films are "vertical" investigations of a theme or situation. The filmmaker is not concerned so much with what's happening as with what a situ-

360

ation feels like or what it means. The film artist is concerned with probing the depths and layers of meaning of a given moment.

Fiction movies, on the other hand, are like novels and plays, according to Deren. They're essentially "horizontal" in their development. Narrative filmmakers use linear structures that must progress from situation to situation, from feeling to feeling. Fiction directors don't have much time to explore the implications of a given idea or emotion, for they must keep the plot "moving along."

Other avant-garde filmmakers disdain any kind of recognizable subject matter. Hans Richter and other early avant-garde artists in Europe totally rejected narrative. Richter was a champion of the "absolute film," which consists solely of abstract shapes and designs (see **4–7**). Insisting that movies should have nothing to do with acting, stories, or literary themes, Richter believed that film—like music and abstract painting—should be concerned with pure nonrepresentational forms. Many contemporary avant-garde filmmakers share these biases (**8–24**).

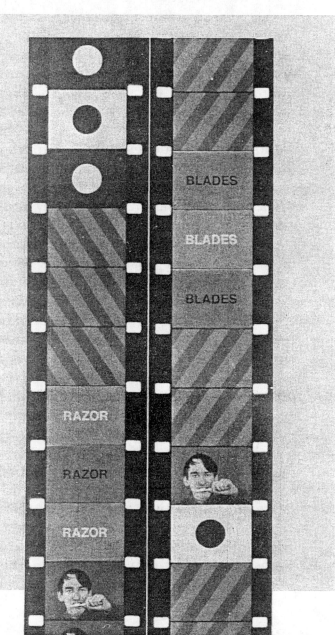

8–24. *Razor Blades* (U.S.A., 1968), *directed by Paul Sharits.*

Structuralism was an avant-garde movement that rejected narrative in favor of an abstract structure that owed nothing to subject matter. In the structuralist cinema, the codes of cognition are totally self-defined. They are structured according to the principles of recurrence, dialectical polarities, time and space increments, and so on. The process of deciphering these cognitive codes and their interrelationships is analogous to the film's working itself out, fulfilling its structural destiny. In Sharits's flicker film, two images (requiring separate screens and projectors) are simultaneously juxtaposed. Each filmstrip consists of irregularly recurring images—two or three frames in duration, interspersed by blank or color frames—or purely abstract designs, like colored stripes or circular shapes. The rapid flickering of images creates a mesmerizing stroboscopic effect, testing the audience's psychological and physiological tolerance. The content of the film is its structural form rather than the subject matter of the images as images. *(Anthology Film Archives)*

Genre and Myth

A genre film is a specific type of movie: a war picture, a gangster film, science fiction, and so on. There are literally hundreds of them, especially in the United States and Japan, where virtually all fiction movies can be classified according to genre. Genres are distinguished by a characteristic set of conventions in style, subject matter, and values. Genre is also a convenient way of focusing and organizing the story materials.

Many genre films are directed at a specific audience. Coming-of-age films are generally aimed at teenagers. Action-adventure genres tend to focus on all-male activities. Women are usually relegated to an incidental function, or they provide "romantic interest." The American **woman's picture** and Japanese mother films focus on domestic life. In these female-oriented genres, men are conventionalized in a similar manner—usually as breadwinners, sexual objects, or "the other man."

André Bazin once referred to the western as "a form in search of a content." The same could be said of all genre films. A genre is a loose set of expectations, then, not a divine injunction. That is, each example of a given story type is related to its predecessors, but not in ironclad bondage. Some genre films are good; others are terrible. It's not the genre that determines artistic excellence, but how well the artist exploits the conventions of its form.

The major shortcomings of genre pictures is that they're easy to imitate and have been debased by stale mechanical repetition. Genre conventions are mere clichés unless they're united with significant innovations in style or subject matter. But this is true of all the arts, not just movies. As Aristotle noted in *The Poetics,* genres are qualitatively neutral: The conventions of classical tragedy are basically the same whether they're used by a genius or a forgotten hack. Certain genres enjoy more cultural prestige because they have attracted the most gifted artists. Genres that haven't are widely regarded as innately inartistic, but in many cases, their déclassé status is due to neglect rather than intrinsic hopelessness. For example, the earliest film critics considered slapstick comedy an infantile genre—until such important comic artists as Chaplin and Keaton entered the field. Today, no critic would malign the genre, for it boasts a considerable number of masterpieces.

The most critically admired genre films strike a balance between the form's preestablished conventions and the artist's unique contributions. The artists of ancient Greece drew on a common body of mythology, and no one thought it strange when dramatists and poets returned to these tales again and again. Incompetent artists merely repeat. Serious artists reinterpret. By exploiting the broad outlines of a well-known tale or story type, the storyteller can play off its main features, creating provocative tensions between the genre's conventions and the artist's inventions, between the familiar and the original, the general and the particular. Myths embody the common ideals and aspirations of a civilization, and by returning to these communal tales the artist becomes, in a sense, a psychic explorer, bridging the chasm between the known and the unknown. The stylized conventions and **archetypal** story patterns of genres

8-25. *It Happened One Night* (U.S.A., 1934), *with Clark Gable and Claudette Colbert, written by Robert Riskin, directed by Frank Capra.*
Genres can be classified according to subject matter, style, period, national origin, and a variety of other criteria. In the 1930s, a new American genre was born: screwball comedy. Its heyday was roughly 1934–1945. Essentially love stories, these films feature zany but glamorous lovers, often from different social classes. More realistic than the slapstick of the silent era, screwball comedy is also more collaborative, requiring the sophisticated blending of talents of writers, actors, and directors. The snappy dialogue crackles with wit and speed. Sappy, sentimental speeches are often meant to deceive. The narrative premises are absurdly improbable, and the plots, which are intricate and filled with preposterous twists and turns, tend to snowball out of control. The movies center on a comic-romantic couple rather than a solitary protagonist. Often, they are initially hostile, with one trying to outwit or outmaneuver the other. Much of the comedy results from the utter seriousness of the characters, who are usually unaware that they're funny, even though they engage in the most loony masquerades and deceptions. Sometimes one of them is engaged to a sexless prude or a humorless bore: This lends an urgency to the attraction between the coprotagonists, who are clearly made for each other. The genre usually includes a menagerie of secondary characters who are as wacky as the lovers. *(Columbia Pictures)*

encourage viewers to participate ritualistically in the basic beliefs, fears, and anxieties of their age.

Filmmakers are attracted to genres because they automatically synthesize a vast amount of cultural information, freeing them to explore more personal concerns. A nongeneric movie must be more self-contained. The artist is forced to communicate virtually all the major ideas and emotions within the work itself—a task that preempts a lot of screen time. On the other hand, the genre artist never starts from scratch. He or she can build on the accomplish-

8–26a. *Unforgiven* (U.S.A., 1992), *with Gene Hackman and Clint Eastwood, directed by Eastwood.* (Warner Bros.)

8–26b. *The People VS. Larry Flynt* (U.S.A., 1996), *with Woody Harrelson and Courtney Love, directed by Milos Forman.* (Columbia Pictures)

8–26c. *Fargo* (U.S.A., 1996), *with Frances McDormand, written and directed by Joel and Ethan Coen.* (Gramercy Pictures)

Genres in their classical phase tend to portray a world where right and wrong are fairly clear-cut, where the moral values of the movie are widely shared by the audience, and where justice eventually triumphs over evil. Today's most respected film artists are likely to find such values out-of-touch and naive, if not out-and-out false. The contemporary cinema tends to favor genres that are revisionist—less idealistic, more ambiguous morally, and far from reassuring in their presentation of the human condition. For example, *Unforgiven* is a revisionist western whose grim protagonist, William Munny (Eastwood), is a hired killer, so lost in violence that he has doomed his soul. When a youthful crony remarks that their victim "had it coming," Munny replies, "We all got it coming, kid." *The People VS. Larry Flynt* is a biography film—not of an admirable role model or moral exemplar, but of a notorious pornographer and his zonked-out junkie wife. It's a love story. It's also a paradoxical defense of the First Amendment by a filmmaker who grew up in the communist police state of Czechoslovakia—where a Larry Flynt would never have been possible. *Fargo* is a revisionist detective film that's loosely based on an actual police case. The protagonist is Marge Gunderson (McDormand), the very pregnant police chief of Brainerd, Minnesota. The movie is often funny, interspersed with unsettling scenes of brutality and gore. Though the chief finally solves the case, the film's "happy ending" is considerably undercut by its tone of sadness and pessimism concerning our pathetic species.

8–27a.   *Rocky* (U.S.A., 1976), *with Sylvester Stallone, directed by John Avildsen.*

One of the most popular story patterns in America is the Horatio Alger myth—the inspiring tale of a social nobody who, through hard work and perseverance, and against all odds, manages to pull himself up by his bootstraps and achieve extraordinary success.   *(United Artists)*

8–27b.   *Don't Be a Menace to South Central While Drinking Your Juice in the Hood* (U.S.A., 1996), *with Marlon Wayans and Shawn Wayans, directed by Paris Barclay.*

The very title of this film suggests its parodic intent, its comic ridicule of conventional African American genres such as *Boyz N the Hood* **(10–20a)** and coming-of-age films. *Don't Be a Menace* features no less than six siblings of the talented, if slightly demented, Wayans family.   *(Miramax Films)*

8-28. *Risky Business* (U.S.A., 1983), *with Tom Cruise and Rebecca De Mornay, written and directed by Paul Brickman.*
Because 75 percent of the contemporary American film audience is composed of young people, rite-of-passage comedies—also known as coming-of-age films—appeal directly to this adolescent following. The worst of them pander shamelessly to this audience's sentimental and narcissistic view of itself, but a few—like *Risky Business*—are slyly revisionist. The protagonist's transition from childhood innocence to adult experience is subtly subverted by the film's increasingly low-key lighting style and its bittersweet tone of cynicism. Cruise's character begins as a straight, hardworking high school student, naive but likable. In his impatience for worldly success and status, he betrays his parents' trust by using their home as a bordello while they are away on a short trip. With the help of an enterprising hooker (De Mornay), he pimps for his friends, supplying them with the services of several ladies of the evening, who share his entrepreneurial spirit. They reap a profit of $8000 in a single night. By the end of the movie, he is a bona fide member in good standing of the world of adults, savoring the sweet smell of success. *(Warner Bros.)*

ments of predecessors, enriching their ideas or calling them into question, depending on his or her inclinations.

The most enduring genres tend to adapt to changing social conditions. Most of them begin as naive allegories of Good versus Evil. Over the years, they become more complex in both form and thematic range. Finally, they veer into an ironic mode, mocking many of the genre's original values and conventions. Some critics claim that this evolution is inevitable and doesn't necessarily represent an aesthetic improvement.

Film critics and scholars classify genre movies into four main cycles:

1. *Primitive.* This phase is usually naive, though powerful in its emotional impact, in part because of the novelty of the form. Many of the conventions of the genre are established in this phase.
2. *Classical.* This intermediate stage embodies such classical ideals as balance, richness, and poise. The genre's values are assured and widely shared by the audience.

366

8–29. *On the Town* (U.S.A., 1949), *with (clockwise, from one o'clock) Gene Kelly, Vera-Ellen, Ann Miller, Betty Garrett, Frank Sinatra, and Jules Munshin; directed by Kelly and Stanley Donen.*
Musicals were among the most popular genres throughout the big-studio era, appealing to men as well as women, to young audiences as well as adults. Most musicals heighten the artificiality of their narrative structures. For example, in this movie, everything comes in threes—three dashing sailor heroes and three spirited working-girl heroines. *(MGM)*

3. *Revisionist.* The genre is generally more symbolic, ambiguous, less certain in its values. This phase tends to be stylistically complex, appealing more to the intellect than to the emotions. Often, the genre's preestablished conventions are exploited as ironic foils to question or undermine popular beliefs.

4. *Parodic.* This phase of a genre's development is an outright mockery of its conventions, reducing them to howling clichés and presenting them in a comic manner.

For example, the western's primitive phase is exemplified by Edwin S. Porter's *The Great Train Robbery* (1903), the first western ever made, and an enormously popular movie with the public. It was imitated and embellished on for decades. The western's classical phase could be typified by many of the works of John Ford, especially *Stagecoach* (1939), one of the few westerns of that era to win wide critical approval as well as box-office success. *High Noon* (1952) was one of the first revisionist westerns, ironically questioning many of the populist values of the genre's classical phase. Throughout the following two decades, most westerns remained in this skeptical mode, including such major works as *The Wild Bunch* (1969) and *McCabe and Mrs. Miller* (1971). Some critics pointed to Mel Brooks's parodic *Blazing Saddles* (1973) as the genre's deathblow, for many of its conventions are mercilessly lampooned. However, genres have a way of springing back to life after being allowed to rest for a few years. For example, Clint Eastwood's popular *Pale Rider* (1985) is unabashedly classical. Many cultural theorists insist that questions of individual value in a genre's evolution are largely matters of taste and fashion, not the intrinsic merit of the phase per se.

Some of the most suggestive critical studies have explored the relation-

8–30. *Invasion of the Body Snatchers* (U.S.A., 1956), *directed by Don Siegel.*
Genre films often appeal to subconscious anxieties in the audience. For example, many Japanese science-fiction films of the 1950s dealt with hideous mutations that resulted from atomic radiation. A number of cultural commentators have remarked on the "paranoid style" of most American sci-fi movies of the 1950s, when the "Red Scare" intensified the Cold War atmosphere between the United States and the Soviet Union. Siegel's low-budget classic deals with how some alien pod-people insidiously invade human bodies, reducing their owners to anonymous zombies, incapable of feelings. The movie was produced during an era when many Americans were seriously discussing the possibility of building backyard bomb shelters to "protect" themselves from an expected nuclear attack by the U.S.S.R.   *(Allied Artists)*

ship of a genre to the society that nurtured it. This sociopsychic approach was pioneered by the French literary critic Hippolyte Taine in the nineteenth century. Taine claimed that the social and intellectual anxieties of a given era and nation will find expression in its art. The implicit function of an artist is to harmonize and reconcile cultural clashes of value. He believed that art must be analyzed for both its overt and covert meaning, that beneath its explicit content there exists a vast reservoir of latent social and psychic information (8–33).

This approach tends to work best with popular genres, which reflect the shared values and fears of a large audience. Such genres might be regarded as contemporary myths, lending philosophical meaning to the facts of everyday life. As social conditions change, genres often change with them, challenging some traditional customs and beliefs, reaffirming others. Gangster films, for example, are often covert critiques of American capitalism. They are often vehicles for exploring rebellion myths and are especially popular during periods of social breakdown. The protagonists—usually played by small men—are likened to ruthless businessmen, their climb to power a sardonic parody of the Horatio Alger myth. During the Jazz Age, gangster films like

368

8–31. *E.T.: The Extra-Terrestrial* **(U.S.A., 1982),** *with Henry Thomas and E.T., directed by Steven Spielberg.*
All narratives can be interpreted on a symbolic level. There is a principle of universality that can be inferred no matter how unique or strange a given story may be. In this scene from Spielberg's masterpiece, E.T. and his friend Eliot must say good-bye. But E.T. will live forever inside Eliot's mind. Symbolically, the boy will soon outgrow his childhood world of imaginary best friends, scary-looking creatures, and the vast Unknown. But he will never forget the beauty and innocence of that world. Nor will we. "A film is a ribbon of dreams," Orson Welles once stated. "The camera is much more than a recording apparatus; it is a medium via which messages reach us from another world that is not ours and that brings us to the heart of a great secret. Here magic begins." *(Universal Studios)*

Underworld (1927) dealt with the violence and glamour of the Prohibition era in an essentially apolitical manner. During the harshest years of the Depression in the early 1930s, the genre became subversively ideological. Movies like *Little Caesar* (1930) reflected the country's shaken confidence in authority and traditional social institutions. In the final years of the Depression, gangster films like *Dead End* (1937) were pleas for liberal reform, arguing that crime is the result of broken homes, lack of opportunity, and slum living. Gangsters of all periods tend to suffer from an inability to relate to women, but during the 1940s movies like *White Heat* (1949) featured protagonists who were outright sexual neurotics. In the 1950s, partly as a result of the highly publicized Kefauver Senate Crime Investigations, gangster movies like *The Phenix City Story* (1955) took the form of confidential exposés of syndicate crime. Francis Ford Coppola's *The Godfather* (1972) and *The Godfather, Part II* (1974) are a virtual recapitulation of the history of the genre, spanning three generations of

369

8–32. *Sweet Hours* (Spain, 1982), *with Inaki Aierra and Assumpta Serna, directed by Carlos Saura.*
Almost all civilizations have myths dealing with the rebellion of son against father, resulting in son and mother reunited in exclusive love. Sigmund Freud, the father of psychoanalysis, identified one such variant as the Oedipus complex (named for the Greek mythical hero), which he believed was the paradigm of prepubescent human sexuality. Its feminine form is known as the Electra complex, a name also derived from Greek myth. In most cases, this narrative motif is submerged beneath the surface details of a story, or sufficiently disguised to appeal primarily to the subconscious. Saura's *Sweet Hours* plays with this motif in an overt manner. The movie deals with the love affair between a filmmaker (Aierra) and an actress (Serna) who is playing his mother in an autobiographical film he is making about his childhood. *(New Yorker Films)*

characters and reflecting the weary cynicism of a nation still numbed by the hearts-and-minds hoax of Vietnam and the Watergate conspiracy. As Sergio Leone's fablelike title suggests, *Once Upon a Time in America* (1984) is frankly mythical, treating the traditional rise-and-fall structure of the genre in an almost ritualistic manner. Quentin Tarantino's *Pulp Fiction* (1994) is a witty send-up of the genre, parodying many of its conventions.

The ideas of Sigmund Freud and Carl Jung have also influenced many genre theorists. Like Taine, both psychiatrists believed that art is a reflection of underlying structures of meaning, that it satisfies certain subconscious needs in both the artist and audience. For Freud, art was a form of daydreaming and wish fulfillment, vicariously resolving urgent impulses and desires that can't be satisfied in reality. Pornographic films are perhaps the most obvious example of how anxieties can be assuaged in this surrogate manner, and in fact, Freud believed that most neuroses were sexually based. He thought that art was a by-product of neurosis, although essentially a socially beneficial one. Like neurosis, art is characterized by a repetition compulsion, the need to go over the same stories and rituals to reenact and temporarily resolve certain psychic conflicts **(8–32)**.

Jung began his career as a disciple of Freud but eventually broke away, believing that Freud's theories lacked a communal dimension. Jung was fascinated by myths, fairy tales, and folklore, which he believed contained symbols and story patterns that were universal to all individuals in all cultures and periods. According to Jung, unconscious complexes consist of archetypal symbols that are as deeply rooted and as inexplicable as instincts. He called this sub-

370

merged reservoir of symbols the *collective unconscious,* which he thought had a primordial foundation, traceable to primitive times. Many of these archetypal patterns are bipolar and embody the basic concepts of religion, art, and society: god–devil, active–passive, male–female, static–dynamic, and so on. Jung believed that the artist consciously or unconsciously draws on these archetypes as raw material, which must then be rendered into the generic forms favored by a given culture. For Jung, every work of art (and especially generic art) is an infinitesimal exploration of a universal experience—an instinctive groping toward an ancient wisdom. He also believed that popular culture offers the most unobstructed view of archetypes and myths, whereas elite culture tends to submerge them beneath a complex surface detail.

8–33. *Pinocchio* (U.S.A., 1940), *by Walt Disney.*
The French cultural anthropologist Claude Lévi-Strauss noted that myths have no author, no origin, no core axis—they allow "free play" in a variety of artistic forms. Disney's work draws heavily from fairy tales, myths, and folklore, which are profuse in archetypal elements. *Pinocchio* is a good example of how these elements can be emphasized rather than submerged beneath a surface realism. Early in the film, the boy/puppet Pinocchio is told that to be a "real boy," he must show that he is "brave, truthful, and unselfish." The three principal episodes of the movie represent ritualistic trials, testing the youth's moral fortitude. He dismally fails the first two, but redeems himself in the concluding whale episode, where he does indeed demonstrate courage, honesty, and unselfishness (pictured). Other archetypal elements include a monster (Monstro, the whale), magical transformations, a father's search for his lost son, supernatural creatures like a talking cricket (Jiminy Cricket, Pinocchio's "conscience"), a son's search for his imprisoned father, an anthropomorphized portrayal of nature, and a fairy godmother who rescues the improvident young hero when he fails to act responsibly. Like most of Disney's works of this era, the values in *Pinocchio* are traditional and conservative, an affirmation of the sanctity of the family unit; the importance of a Higher Power in guiding our destinies, and the need to play by society's rules.   *(Walt Disney Productions)*

A story can be many things. To a producer it's a property that has a box-office value. To a writer it's a screenplay. To a film star it's a vehicle. To a director it's an artistic medium. To a genre critic it's a classifiable narrative form. To a sociologist it's an index of public sentiment. To a psychiatrist it's an instinctive exploration of hidden fears or communal ideals. To a moviegoer it can be all of these, and more.

In analyzing a film's narrative structure, we ought to ask ourselves some basic questions. Who's telling the story? A voice-over narrator? Why him or her? Or does the story "tell itself," like most stage plays? Who is the implied narrator of such stories, the guiding hand in the arrangement of the narrative's constituent parts? What do we as spectators supply to the story? What information do we provide in order to fill in the narrative's gaps? How is time presented—chronologically or subjectively rearranged through flashbacks and other narrative disjunctions? Is the narrative realistic, classical, or formalistic? What genre, if any? What phase of the genre's evolution? What does the movie say about the social context and period that it was made in? How does the narrative embody mythical concepts or universal human traits?

FURTHER READING

ALTMAN, RICK. *Film/Genre* (Bloomington: Indiana University Press, 1999). The evolution of film genres.

BORDWELL, DAVID, *Narration in the Fiction Film* (Madison: University of Wisconsin Press, 1985). The fullest discussion of the role of the spectator.

BROOKS, PETER, *Reading for the Plot: Design and Intention in Narrative* (New York: Knopf, 1984). Primarily about literature.

CHATMAN, SEYMOUR, *Story and Discourse* (Ithaca, N.Y.: Cornell University Press, 1978). Well written, clear, and useful, covering literature as well as film.

FIELD, SYD, *The Screenwriter's Workbook* (New York: Dell, 1984). A practical handbook, emphasizing the classical paradigm.

MARTIN, WALLACE, *Recent Theories of Narrative* (Ithaca, N.Y.: Cornell University Press, 1986). Lucid and helpful, primarily about literature.

MITCHELL, W. J. T., ed., *On Narrative* (Chicago and London: University of Chicago Press, 1981). Collection of scholarly articles, mostly on literature.

MOEWS, DANIEL, *Keaton: The Silent Features Close Up* (Berkeley: University of California Press, 1977). An excellent critical study, especially strong on Keaton's plots.

NASH, CHRISTOPHER, ed., *Narrative in Culture* (London and New York: Routledge, 1990). Multidisciplinary essays.

THOMPSON, KRISTIN. *Storytelling in the New Hollywood* (Cambridge: Harvard University Press, 1999). Narrative strategies in mainstream American films.

Glossary

(C) predominantly critical terms   **(T)** predominantly technical terms

(I) predominantly industry terms   **(G)** terms in general usage

A

actor star. See *star.*

aerial shot (T). Essentially a variation of the *crane shot,* though restricted to exterior locations. Usually taken from a helicopter.

aesthetic distance (C). Viewers' ability to distinguish between an artistic reality and external reality—their realization that the events of a fiction film are simulated.

A-film (I). An American studio era term signifying a major production, usually with important stars and a generous budget. Shown as the main feature on double bills.

aleatory techniques (C). Techniques of filmmaking that depend on the element of chance. Images are not planned out in advance but must be composed on the spot by the camera operator. Usually used in documentary situations.

allegory (C). A symbolic technique in which stylized characters and situations represent rather obvious ideas, such as Justice, Death, Religion, Society, and so on.

allusion (C). A reference to an event, person, or work of art, usually well known.

angle (G). The camera's angle of view relative to the subject being photographed. A high-angle shot is photographed from above, a low angle from below the subject.

animation (G). A form of filmmaking characterized by photographing inanimate objects or individual drawings *frame* by frame, with each frame differing minutely from its predecessor. When such images are projected at the standard speed of twenty-four frames per second, the result is that the objects or drawings appear to move, and hence seem "animated."

anticipatory camera, anticipatory setup (C). The placement of the camera in such a manner as to anticipate the movement of an action before it occurs. Such setups often suggest predestination.

archetype (C). An original model or type after which similar things are patterned. Archetypes can be well-known story patterns, universal experiences, or personality types.

531

Myths, fairy tales, *genres,* and cultural heroes are generally archetypal, as are the basic cycles of life and nature.

art director (G). The individual responsible for designing and overseeing the construction of sets for a movie, and sometimes its interior decoration and overall visual style.

aspect ratio (T). The ratio between the horizontal and vertical dimensions of the screen.

auteur theory (C). A theory of film popularized by the critics of the French journal *Cahiers du Cinéma* in the 1950s. The theory emphasizes the director as the major creator of film art, stamping the material with his or her own personal vision, style, and thematic obsessions.

available lighting (G). The use of only that light which actually exists on location, either natural (the sun) or artificial (house lamps). When available lighting is used in interior locations, generally a sensitive *fast film stock* must also be used.

avant-garde (C). From the French, meaning "in the front ranks." Those minority artists whose works are characterized by an unconventional daring and by obscure, controversial, or highly personal ideas.

B

backlighting (G). When the lights for a shot derive from the rear of the set, thus throwing the foreground figures into semidarkness or silhouette.

back lot (I). During the studio era, standing exterior sets of such common locales as a turn-of-the-century city block, a frontier town, a European village, and so on.

B-film (G). A low-budget movie usually shown as the second feature during the big-studio era in America. B-films rarely included important stars and took the form of popular *genres,* such as thrillers, westerns, or horror films. The major studios used them as testing grounds for the raw talent under contract.

bird's-eye view (G). A shot in which the camera photographs a scene from directly overhead.

blimp (T). A soundproof camera housing that muffles the noise of the camera's motor so sound can be clearly recorded on the set.

blocking (T). The movements of the actors within a given playing area.

boom, mike boom (T). An overhead telescoping pole that carries a microphone, permitting the *synchronous* recording of sound without restricting the movement of the actors.

buddy film (G). A male-oriented action genre, especially popular in the 1970s, dealing with the adventures of two or more men, usually excluding any significant female roles.

C

camp, campy (C). An artistic sensibility typified by comic mockery, especially of the straight world and conventional morality. Campy movies are often ludicrously theatrical, stylistically gaudy, and gleefully subversive.

cels, also cells (T). Transparent plastic sheets that are superimposed in layers by *animators* to give the illusion of depth and volume to their drawings.

centrist (C). A political term signifying a moderate ideology, midway between the extremes of the *left* and *right* wings.

cinematographer, also director of photography or D.P. (G). The artist or technician responsible for the lighting of a shot and the quality of the photography.

cinéma vérité, also **direct cinema (C).** A method of documentary filming using *aleatory* methods that don't interfere with the way events take place in reality. Such movies are made with a minimum of equipment, usually a hand-held camera and portable sound apparatus.

classical cinema, classical paradigm (C). A vague but convenient term used to designate the style of mainstream fiction films produced in America, roughly from the midteens until the late 1960s. The classical paradigm is a movie strong in *story, star,* and *production values,* with a high level of technical achievement, and edited according to conventions of *classical cutting.* The visual style is functional and rarely distracts from the characters in action. Movies in this form are structured narratively, with a clearly defined conflict, complications that intensify to a rising climax, and a resolution that emphasizes formal closure.

classical cutting (C). A style of editing developed by D. W. Griffith, in which a sequence of shots is determined by a scene's dramatic and emotional emphasis rather than by physical action alone. The sequence of shots represents the breakdown of the event into its psychological as well as logical components.

closed forms (C). A visual style that inclines toward self-conscious designs and carefully harmonized compositions. The *frame* is exploited to suggest a self-sufficient universe that encloses all the necessary visual information, usually in an aesthetically appealing manner.

close-up, close shot (G). A detailed view of a person or object. A close-up of an actor usually includes only his or her head.

continuity (T). The kind of logic implied between edited shots, their principle of coherence. *Cutting to continuity* emphasizes smooth transitions between shots, in which time and space are unobtrusively condensed. More complex *classical cutting* is the linking of shots according to an event's psychological as well as logical breakdown. In *thematic montage,* the continuity is determined by the symbolic association of ideas between shots, rather than any literal connections in time and space.

convention (C). An implied agreement between the viewer and artist to accept certain artificialities as real in a work of art. In movies, editing (or the juxtaposition of shots) is accepted as "logical" even though a viewer's perception of reality is continuous and unfragmented.

coverage, covering shots, cover shots (T). Extra shots of a scene that can be used to bridge transitions in case the planned footage fails to edit as planned. Usually *long shots* that preserve the overall continuity of a scene.

crane shot (T). A shot taken from a special device called a crane, which resembles a huge mechanical arm. The crane carries the camera and the *cinematographer* and can move in virtually any direction.

creative producer (I). A producer who supervises the making of a movie in such detail that he or she is virtually its artistic director. During the studio era in America, the most famous creative producers were David O. Selznick and Walt Disney.

cross-cutting (G). The alternating of shots from two sequences, often in different locales, suggesting that they are taking place at the same time.

cutting to continuity (T). A type of *editing* in which the shots are arranged to preserve the fluidity of an action without showing all of it. An unobtrusive condensation of a continuous action.

D

day-for-night shooting (T). Scenes that are filmed in daytime with special *filters* to suggest nighttime settings in the movie image.

deep-focus shot (T). A technique of photography that permits all distance planes to remain clearly in focus, from close-up ranges to infinity.

dialectical, dialectics (C). An analytical methodology, derived from Hegel and Marx, that juxtaposes pairs of opposites—a thesis and antithesis—to arrive at a synthesis of ideas.

dissolve, lap dissolve (T). The slow fading out of one shot and the gradual fading in of its successor, with a superimposition of images, usually at the midpoint.

distributor (I). Those individuals who serve as go-betweens in the film industry, who arrange to book the product in theaters.

dolly shot, tracking shot, trucking shot (T). A shot taken from a moving vehicle. Originally, tracks were laid on the set to permit a smoother movement of the camera.

dominant contrast, dominant (C). That area of the film image that compels the viewer's most immediate attention, usually because of a prominent visual contrast.

double exposure (T). The superimposition of two literally unrelated images on film. See also *multiple exposure.*

dubbing (T). The addition of sound after the visuals have been photographed. Dubbing can be either *synchronous* with an image or *nonsynchronous.* Foreign language movies are often dubbed in English for release in this country.

E

editing (G). The joining of one shot (strip of film) with another. The shots can picture events and objects in different places at different times. In Europe, editing is called *montage.*

epic (C). A film *genre* characterized by bold and sweeping themes, usually in heroic proportions. The protagonist is an ideal representative of a culture—national, religious, or regional. The tone of most epics is dignified, the treatment larger than life. The western is the most popular epic genre in the United States.

establishing shot (T). Usually an *extreme long* or *long shot* offered at the beginning of a scene, providing the viewer with the context of the subsequent closer shots.

expressionism (C). A style of filmmaking emphasizing extreme distortion, *lyricism,* and artistic self-expression at the expense of objectivity.

extreme close-up (G). A minutely detailed view of an object or person. An extreme close-up of an actor generally includes only his or her eyes or mouth.

extreme long shot (G). A panoramic view of an exterior location, photographed from a great distance, often as far as a quarter-mile away.

eye-level shot (T). The placement of the camera approximately five to six feet from the ground, corresponding to the height of an observer on the scene.

F

fade (T). The fade-out is the snuffing of an image from normal brightness to a black screen. A fade-in is the opposite.

faithful adaptation (C). A film based on a literary original which captures the essence of the original, often by using cinematic equivalents for specific literary techniques.

fast motion (T). Shots of a subject photographed at a rate slower than twenty-four fps, which, when projected at the standard rate, convey motion that is jerky and slightly comical, seemingly out of control.

fast stock, fast film (T). Film stock that's highly sensitive to light and generally produces a grainy image. Often used by documentarists who wish to shoot only with *available lighting*.

fill light (T). Secondary lights that are used to augment the *key light*—the main source of illumination for a shot. Fill lights soften the harshness of the key light, revealing details that would otherwise be obscured in shadow.

film noir (C). A French term—literally, black cinema—referring to a kind of urban American *genre* that sprang up after World War II, emphasizing a fatalistic, despairing universe where there is no escape from mean city streets, loneliness, and death. Stylistically, *noir* emphasizes *low-key* and *high-contrast* lighting, complex compositions, and a strong atmosphere of dread and paranoia.

filters (T). Pieces of glass or plastic placed in front of the camera lens that distort the quality of light entering the camera and hence the movie image.

final cut, also **release print (I).** The sequence of shots in a movie as it will be released to the public.

first cut, also **rough cut (I).** The initial sequence of shots in a movie, often constructed by the director.

first-person point of view. See *point-of-view shot.*

flashback (G). An editing technique that suggests the interruption of the present by a shot or series of shots representing the past.

flash-forward (G). An editing technique that suggests the interruption of the present by a shot or series of shots representing the future.

focus (T). The degree of acceptable sharpness in a film image. "Out of focus" means the images are blurred and lack acceptable linear definition.

footage (T). Exposed film *stock.*

foregrounding (C). When a critic isolates and heightens one aspect of a work of art from its context to analyze that characteristic in greater depth.

formalist, formalism (C). A style of filmmaking in which aesthetic forms take precedence over the subject matter as content. Time and space as ordinarily perceived are often distorted. Emphasis is on the essential, symbolic characteristics of objects and people, not necessarily on their superficial appearance. Formalists are often *lyrical,* self-consciously heightening their style to call attention to it as a value for its own sake.

frame (T). The dividing line between the edges of the screen image and the enclosing darkness of the theater. Can also refer to a single photograph from the filmstrip.

freeze frame, freeze shot (T). A shot composed of a single *frame* that is reprinted a number of times on the filmstrip; when projected, it gives the illusion of a still photograph.

f-stop (T). The measurement of the size of the lens opening in the camera, indicating the amount of light that's admitted.

full shot (T). A type of *long shot* that includes the human body in full, with the head near the top of the *frame* and the feet near the bottom.

G

gauge (T). The width of the filmstrip, expressed in millimeters (mm). The wider the gauge, the better the quality of the image. The standard theatrical gauge is 35 mm.

genre (C). A recognizable type of movie, characterized by certain preestablished conventions. Some common American genres are westerns, thrillers, sci-fi movies, etc. A ready-made narrative form.

H

hand-held shot (G). A shot taken with a moving camera that is often deliberately shaky to suggest documentary footage in a uncontrolled setting.

high-angle shot (T). A shot in which the subject is photographed from above.

high contrast (T). A style of lighting emphasizing harsh shafts and dramatic streaks of lights and darks. Often used in thrillers and melodramas.

high key (T). A style of lighting emphasizing bright and even illumination, with few conspicuous shadows. Used mostly in comedies, musicals, and light entertainment films.

homage (C). A direct or indirect reference within a movie to another movie, filmmaker, or cinematic style. A respectful and affectionate tribute.

I

iconography (C). The use of a well-known cultural symbol or complex of symbols in an artistic representation. In movies, iconography can involve a star's *persona*, the preestablished conventions of a *genre* (like the shootout in a western), the use of *archetypal* characters and situations, and such stylistic features as lighting, settings, constuming, props, and so on.

independent producer (G). A producer not affiliated with a studio or large commercial firm. Many stars and directors have been independent producers to ensure their artistic control.

intercut (T). See *cross-cutting*.

intrinsic interest (C). An unobtrusive area of the film image that nonetheless compels our most immediate attention because of its dramatic or contextual importance.

iris (T). A *masking* device that blacks out portions of the screen, permitting only a part of the image to be seen. Usually, the iris is circular or oval in shape and can be expanded or contracted.

J

jump cut (T). An abrupt transition between shots, sometimes deliberate, which is disorienting in terms of the continuity of space and time.

K

key light (T). The main source of illumination for a *shot*.

kinetic (C). Pertaining to motion and movement.

L

leftist, left-wing (G). A set of ideological values, typically liberal in emphasis, stressing such traits as equality, the importance of environment in determining human behavior, relativism in moral matters, emphasis on the secular rather than religion, an optimistic view of the future and human nature, a belief in technology as the main propellant of progress, cooperation rather than competition, an identification with the poor and the oppressed, internationalism, and sexual and reproductive freedom.

lengthy take, long take (C). A shot of lengthy duration.

lens (T). A ground or molded piece of glass, plastic, or other transparent material through which light rays are refracted so they converge or diverge to form the photographic image within the camera.

linear (C). A visual style emphasizing sharply defined lines rather than colors or textures. *Deep-focus* lenses are generally used to produce this hard-edged style, which tends to be objective, matter-of-fact, and antiromantic.

literal adaptation (C). A movie based on a stage play, in which the dialogue and actions are preserved more or less intact.

long shot (G). A shot that includes an area within the image that roughly corresponds to the audience's view of the area within the proscenium arch in the live theater.

loose adaptation (C). A movie based on another medium in which only a superficial resemblance exists between the two versions.

loose framing (C). Usually in longer shots. The *mise en scène* is so spaciously distributed within the confines of the framed image that the people photographed have considerable freedom of movement.

low-angle shot (T). A shot in which the subject is photographed from below.

low key (T). A style of lighting that emphasizes diffused shadows and atmospheric pools of light. Often used in mysteries and thrillers.

lyrical (C). A stylistic exuberance and subjectivity, emphasizing the sensuous beauty of the medium and producing an intense outpouring of emotion.

M

majors (I). The principal production studios of a given era. In the golden age of the Hollywood studio system—roughly the 1930s and 1940s—the majors consisted of MGM, Warner Brothers, RKO, Paramount Pictures, and Twentieth Century–Fox.

Marxist (G). An ideological term used to describe any person or film that is biased in favor of *left-wing* values, particularly in their more extreme form.

masking (T). A technique whereby a portion of the movie image is blocked out, thus temporarily altering the dimensions of the screen's *aspect ratio*.

master shot (T). An uninterrupted shot, usually taken from a *long-* or *full-shot* range, that contains an entire scene. The closer shots are photographed later, and an *edited* sequence, composed of a variety of shots, is constructed on the editor's bench.

matte shot (T). A process of combining two separate shots on one print, resulting in an image that looks as though it had been photographed normally. Used mostly for special effects, such as combining a human figure with giant dinosaurs, etc.

medium shot (G). A relatively close shot, revealing the human figure from the knees or waist up.

metaphor (C). An implied comparison between two otherwise unlike elements, meaningful in a figurative rather than literal sense.

Method acting (C). A style of performance derived from the Russian stage director Stanislavsky, which has been the dominant acting style in America since the 1950s. Method actors emphasize psychological intensity, extensive rehearsals to explore a character, emotional believability rather than technical mastery, and "living" a role internally rather than merely imitating the external behavior of a character.

metteur en scène (C). The artist or technician who creates the *mise en scène*—that is, the director.

mickeymousing (T). A type of film music that is purely descriptive and attempts to mimic the visual action with musical equivalents. Often used in cartoons.

miniatures, also **model** or **miniature shots (T).** Small-scale models photographed to give the illusion that they are full-scale objects. For example, ships sinking at sea, giant dinosaurs, airplanes colliding, etc.

minimalism (C). A style of filmmaking characterized by austerity and restraint, in which cinematic elements are reduced to the barest minimum of information.

mise en scène (C). The arrangement of visual weights and movements within a given space. In the live theater, the space is usually defined by the proscenium arch; in movies, it is defined by the *frame* that encloses the images. Cinematic mise en scène encompasses both the staging of the action and the way that it's photographed.

mix (T). The process of combining separately recorded sounds from individual soundtracks onto a master track.

montage (T). Transitional sequences of rapidly edited images, used to suggest the lapse of time or the passing of events. Often uses *dissolves* and *multiple exposures*. In Europe, montage means the art of editing.

motif (C). Any unobtrusive technique, object, or thematic idea that's systematically repeated throughout a film.

multiple exposures (T). A special effect produced by the *optical printer*, which permits the superimposition of many images simultaneously.

N

negative image (T). The reversal of lights and darks of the subject photographed: blacks are white, whites are black.

negative space (C). Emply or unfilled space in the *mise en scène*, often acting as a foil to the more detailed elements in a shot.

neorealism (C). An Italian film movement that produced its best works between 1945 and 1955. Strongly *realistic* in its techniques, neorealism emphasized documentary aspects of film art, stressing loose episodic plots, unextraordinary events and characters, natural lighting, actual location settings, nonprofessional actors, a preoccupation with poverty and social problems, and an emphasis on humanistic and democratic ideals. The term has also been used to describe other films that reflect the technical and stylistic biases of Italian neorealism.

New Wave, nouvelle vague (C). A group of young French directors who came to prominence during the late 1950s. The most widely known are François Truffaut, Jean-Luc Godard, and Alain Resnais.

nonsynchronous sound (T). Sound and image that are not recorded simultaneously, or sound that is detached from its source in the film image. Music is usually nonsynchronous in a movie, providing background atmosphere.

O

oblique angle, tilt shot (T). A shot photographed by a tilted camera. When the image is projected on the screen, the subject itself seems to be tilted on a diagonal.

oeuvre (C). From the French, "work." The complete works of an artist, viewed as a whole.

omniscient point of view (C). An all-knowing narrator who provides the spectator with all the necessary information.

open forms (C). Used primarily by *realist* filmmakers, these techniques are likely to be unobtrusive, with an emphasis on informal compositions and apparently haphazard designs. The *frame* is exploited to suggest a temporary *masking*, a window that arbitrarily cuts off part of the action.

optical printer (T). An elaborate machine used to create special effects in movies. For example, *fades, dissolves, multiple exposures,* etc.

outtakes (I). Shots or pieces of shots that are not used in the final cut of a film. Leftover footage.

overexposure (T). Too much light enters the aperture of a camera lens, bleaching out the image. Useful for fantasy and nightmare scenes.

P

painterly (C). A visual style emphasizing soft edges, lush colors, and a radiantly illuminated environment, all producing a romantic lyricism.

pan, panning shot (T). Short for panorama, this is a revolving horizontal movement of the camera from left to right or vice versa.

parallel editing. See *cross-cutting*.

persona (C). From the Latin, "mask." An actor's public image, based on his or her previous roles, and often incorporating elements from their actual personalities as well.

personality star. See *star*.

pixillation, also **stop-motion photography (T).** An *animation* technique involving the photographing of live actors *frame* by frame. When the sequence is projected at the standard speed of twenty-four fps, the actors move abruptly and jerkily, like cartoon figures.

point-of-view shot, also **pov shot, first-person camera, subjective camera (T).** Any shot that is taken from the vantage point of a character in the film, showing what the character sees.

process shot, also **rear projection (T).** A technique in which a background scene is projected onto a translucent screen behind the actors so it appears that the actors are on location in the final image.

producer (G). An ambiguous term referring to the individual or company that controls the financing of a film, and often the way it's made. The producer can concern himself or herself solely with business matters, or with putting together a package deal (such as script, stars, and director), or the producer can function as an expeditor, smoothing over problems during production.

producer–director (I). A filmmaker who finances his or her projects independently, to allow maximum creative freedom.

production values (I). The box-office appeal of the physical mounting of a film, such as sets, costumes, props, etc.

prop (T). Any movable item that is included in a movie: tables, guns, books, etc.

property (I). Anything with a profit-making potential in movies, though generally used to describe a story of some kind: a screenplay, novel, short story, etc.

proxemic patterns (C). The spatial relationships among characters within the *mise en scène,* and the apparent distance of the camera from the subject photographed.

pull-back dolly (T). Withdrawing the camera from a scene to reveal an object or character that was previously out of *frame*.

R

rack focusing, selective focusing (T). The blurring of focal planes in sequence, forcing the viewer's eyes to travel with those areas of an image that remain in sharp focus.

reaction shot (T). A cut to a shot of a character's reaction to the contents of the preceding shot.

realism (G). A style of filmmaking that attempts to duplicate the look of objective reality as it's commonly perceived, with emphasis on authentic locations and details, *long shots, lengthy takes,* and a minimum of distorting techniques.

reestablishing shot (T). A return to an initial *establishing shot* within a scene, acting as a reminder of the physical context of the closer shots.

reprinting (T). A special effects technique in which two or more separately photographed images are rephotographed onto one strip of film.

reverse angle shot (T). A shot taken from an angle 180° opposed to the previous shot. That is, the camera is placed opposite its previous position.

reverse motion (T). A series of images are photographed with the film reversed. When projected normally, the effect is to suggest backward movement—an egg "returning" to its shell, for example.

rightist, right-wing (G). A set of ideological values, typically conservative in emphasis, stressing such traits as family values, patriarchy, heredity and caste, absolute moral and ethical standards, religion, veneration for tradition and the past, a tendency to be pessimistic about the future and human nature, the need for competition, an identification with leaders and elite classes, nationalism, open market economic principals, and marital monogamy.

rite of passage (C). Narratives that focus on key phases of a person's life, when an individual passes from one stage of development to another, such as adolescence to adulthood, innocence to experience, middle age to old age, and so on.

rough cut (T). The crudely edited footage of a movie before the editor has tightened up the slackness between shots. A kind of rough draft.

rushes, dailies (I). The selected footage of the previous day's shooting, which is usually evaluated by the director and *cinematographer* before the start of the next day's shooting.

S

scene (G). An imprecise unit of film, composed of a number of interrelated *shots*, unified usually by a central concern—a location, an incident, or a minor dramatic climax.

screwball comedy (C). A film *genre*, introduced in the 1930s in America and popular up to the 1950s, characterized by zany lovers, often from different social classes. The plots are often absurdly improbable and have a tendency to veer out of control. These movies usually feature slapstick comedy scenes, aggressive and charming heroines, and an assortment of outlandish secondary characters.

script, screenplay, scenario (G). A written description of a movie's dialogue and action, which occasionally includes camera directions.

selective focus. See *rack focusing.*

sequence shot, also *plan-séquence* (C). A single lengthy shot, usually involving complex staging and camera movements.

setup (T). The positioning of the camera and lights for a specific shot.

shooting ratio (I). The amount of film stock used in photographing a movie in relation to what's finally included in the finished product. A shooting ratio of 20:1 means that twenty feet of film were shot for every one used in the *final cut*.

shooting script (I). A written breakdown of a movie story into its individual shots, often containing technical instructions. Used by the director and his or her staff during the production.

short lens. See *wide-angle lens*.

shot (G). Those images that are recorded continuously from the time the camera starts to the time it stops. That is, an unedited strip of film.

slow motion (T). Shots of a subject photographed at a faster rate than twenty-four fps, which when projected at the standard rate produce a dreamy, dancelike slowness of action.

slow stock, slow film (T). Film stocks that are relatively insensitive to light and produce crisp images and a sharpness of detail. When used in interior settings, these stocks generally require considerable artificial illumination.

soft focus (T). The blurring out of focus of all except one desired distance range. Can also refer to a glamorizing technique that softens the sharpness of definition so facial wrinkles can be smoothed over and even eliminated.

star (G). A film actor or actress of great popularity. A *personality star* tends to play only those roles that fit a preconceived public image, which constitutes his or her *persona*. An *actor star* can play roles of greater range and variety. Barbra Streisand is a personality star; Robert De Niro is an actor star.

star system (G). The technique of exploiting the charisma of popular performers to enhance the box-office appeal of films. The star system was developed in America and has been the backbone of the American film industry since the mid-1910s.

star vehicle (G). A movie especially designed to showcase the talents and charms of a specific star.

stock (T). Unexposed film. There are many types of movie stocks, including those highly sensitive to light (*fast stocks*) and those relatively insensitive to light (*slow stocks*).

storyboard, storyboarding (T). A previsualization technique in which shots are sketched in advance and in sequence, like a comic strip, thus allowing the filmmaker to outline the *mise en scène* and construct the *editing* continuity before production begins.

story values (I). The narrative appeal of a movie, which can reside in the popularity of an adapted *property,* the high craftsmanship of a script, or both.

studio (G). A large corporation specializing in the production of movies, such as Paramount, Warner Brothers, and so on; any physical facility equipped for the production of films.

subjective camera. See *point-of-view shot*.

subsidiary contrast (C). A subordinated element of the film image, complementing or contrasting with the *dominant contrast*.

subtext (C). A term used in drama and film to signify the dramatic implications beneath the language of a play or movie. Often, the subtext concerns ideas and emotions that are totally independent of the language of a text.

surrealism (C). An *avant-garde* movement in the arts stressing Freudian and Marxist ideas, unconscious elements, irrationalism, and the symbolic association of ideas. Surrealist movies were produced roughly from 1924 to 1931, primarily in France, though there are surrealistic elements in the works of many directors, and especially in music videos.

swish pan, also **flash** or **zip pan (T).** A horizontal movement of the camera at such a rapid rate that the subject photographed blurs on the screen.

symbol, symbolic (C). A figurative device in which an object, event, or cinematic technique has significance beyond its literal meaning. Symbolism is always determined by the dramatic context.

synchronous sound (T). The agreement or correspondence between image and sound, which are recorded simultaneously, or seem so in the finished print. Synchronous sounds appear to derive from an obvious source in the visuals.

T

take (T). A variation of a specific shot. The final shot is often selected from a number of possible takes.

telephoto lens, long lens (T). A lens that acts as a telescope, magnifying the size of objects at a great distance. A side effect is its tendency to flatten perspective.

thematic montage (C). A type of *editing* propounded by the Soviet filmmaker Eisenstein, in which separate shots are linked together not by their literal continuity in reality but by symbolic association. A shot of a preening braggart might be linked to a shot of a toy peacock, for example. Most commonly used in documentaries, in which shots are connected in accordance to the filmmaker's thesis.

three-point lighting (T). A common technique of lighting a scene from three sources. The *key light* is the main source of illumination, usually creating the *dominant contrast,* where we look first in a shot. *Fill lights* are less intense and are generally placed opposite the key, illuminating areas that would otherwise be obscured by shadow. *Backlights* are used to separate the foreground elements from the setting, emphasizing a sense of depth in the image.

three-shot (T). A *medium shot,* featuring three actors.

tight framing (C). Usually in close shots. The *mise en scène* is so carefully balanced and harmonized that the people photographed have little or no freedom of movement.

tilt, tilt shot (T). See *oblique angle.*

tracking shot, trucking shot. See *dolly shot.*

two-shot (T). A *medium shot* featuring two actors.

V

vertical integration (I). A system in which the production, distribution, and exhibition of movies are all controlled by the same corporation. In America, the practice was declared illegal in the late 1940s.

viewfinder (T). An eyepiece on the camera that defines the playing area and the *framing* of the action to be photographed.

voice-over (T). A *nonsynchronous* spoken commentary in a movie, often used to convey a character's thoughts or memories.

W

wide-angle lens, short lens (T). A lens that permits the camera to photograph a wider area than a normal lens. A side effect is its tendency to exaggerate perspective. Also used for *deep-focus* photography.

widescreen, also **CinemaScope, scope (G).** A movie image that has an *aspect ratio* of approximately 5:3, though some widescreens possess horizontal dimensions that extend as wide as 2.5 times the vertical dimension of the screen.

wipe (T). An *editing* device, usually a line that travels across the screen, "pushing off" one image and revealing another.

women's pictures (G). A film *genre* that focuses on the problems of women, such as career versus family conflicts. Often, such films feature a popular female *star* as protagonist.

Z

zoom lens, zoom shot (T). A lens of variable focal length that permits the cinematographer to change from *wide-angle* to *telephoto shots* (and vice versa) in one continuous movement, often plunging the viewer in or out of a scene rapidly.

Index

H

I

Chapter 6

The Middle Ages: 400–1400

In the Middle Ages, most artistic endeavor was inspired, encouraged, and paid for by the Church. And in each important town, the place where all the medieval arts were concentrated was the cathedral. Medieval cathedrals are marvels of architecture; their doorways and outer walls were graced by superb sculptures; paintings and tapestries adorned their inner walls; and every day the cathedrals were filled with music.

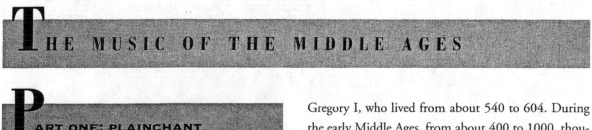

GENERAL CHARACTERISTICS OF MEDIEVAL MUSIC

A huge quantity of music has survived from the Middle Ages. The earliest written examples come from the eighth or ninth century, but much of the music dates from even earlier. This earlier music must have passed from generation to generation by means of an oral tradition. By the year 1000, an enormous amount of medieval music had been composed and was being performed throughout Europe.

Because one of the unifying characteristics of the Middle Ages is the influence of Christianity, it is not surprising that this is also one of the unifying characteristics of medieval music. Most of the surviving music from the medieval period is designed for use in the Christian (Roman Catholic) liturgy. This music is known as **liturgical music**. In addition, there are other pieces used for ceremonies that had a partly religious element, such as processions and coronations. Most of this music is vocal music. The melodies are very smooth and flowing.

Besides religious vocal music, there were probably many other kinds of music as well—folk songs, work songs, dances, and instrumental pieces. We know this from visual evidence in illustrated manuscripts and from poems and books written at the time. Very little of this music, however, has survived in notation. Those pieces we do have are fascinating, with irregular phrase lengths and lively rhythms.

By the later medieval period, two innovations were emerging. One was the rise of written **secular song** ("secular" means "nonreligious"), and the other was the rise of polyphony—music with more than one line or part sounding at a time. Both of these innovations had vital consequences for the entire later history of Western music. The idea that composers could devote their attention to topics outside religion—such as love, political loyalty, or dancing—broadened the scope of music immensely. And polyphony gave rise to harmony, which is one of the main features that distinguishes most Western music from that of other cultures.

Our survey of medieval music is therefore divided into two parts. Part One discusses liturgical chant, and Part Two looks at music of the later Middle Ages—secular song and polyphony.

THE MUSIC OF THE MIDDLE AGES

PART ONE: PLAINCHANT

The vocal music for church services from the early period of the Middle Ages is known as **plainchant**. Many people call it "Gregorian chant" after the famous Pope Gregory I, who lived from about 540 to 604. During the early Middle Ages, from about 400 to 1000, thousands of chants were composed. **(See Listening Guide on page 79.)**

Plainchant is monophonic—that is, it has only one line of music sounding at a time. Several people may be

There are also other ways in which plainchant is varied. It can be varied in the number of singers—with shifts between a solo singer, a small group of singers, and a whole choir. Or it can be varied according to the way the text is set. The text setting may be **syllabic**, with one note for every syllable of the text, or it may be **melismatic**, with a large number of notes sung to a single syllable; or it may be something in between. This middle style, with a small number of notes per syllable of the text, is known as **neumatic**. Most well-known songs today are syllabic ("On Top of Old Smoky," for example). But the Beatles' song "Not a Second Time" starts out quite neumatically. And you may be familiar with the carol "Angels We Have Heard on High," which includes a long melisma on the first syllable of the word "Gloria."

Finally, the most important element of variety in plainchant is given to it by the melodic system in which it is written. This is the system of **modes**. The modes are like colors used in painting. They give richness and variety to the music. There are four main modes in the medieval system, which end, respectively, on D, E, F, and G. All D-mode chants have a similar sound because of the characteristic series of intervals that occur in that mode. The difference in sound

singing that one line in unison, but still only one note is sounded at a time. It may seem very limiting to have music restricted to one line, but in fact plainchant is extremely varied. It ranges from very simple melodies, centered primarily on a single pitch, to highly elaborate ones, with long, flowing lines.

Syllabic.

On top of Old Smo - ky, all cov-er'd with snow,

Partly neumatic.

You know you made me cry— I see no use in won-drin'

why I cried for you.

Melismatic.

Glo - - - - - - - - ri - a

BU-160

Kyrie (plainchant)

Men's choir
Duration: 2:06

Student CD Collection: 1, track 42
Complete CD Collection: 1, track 42

This is a chant from a medieval Roman Catholic Mass. It is one of many settings of this text. Although most of the Mass was in Latin, the words to the Kyrie are in Greek. There are three statements in the text: "Kyrie eleison—Christe eleison—Kyrie eleison" ("Lord, have mercy—Christ, have mercy—Lord, have mercy"). And each of these three statements is sung three times. There is great symbolism in this repetition scheme: the number three represented the Trinity, and three times three was considered absolute perfection.

Corresponding to the three statements of the text, there are three phrases of music. The whole piece begins and ends on G, so it is in the G mode, Mixolydian. As in painting, however, a composition may have a mixture of colors, and there are hints of the Phrygian mode in the first phrase, which ends on E. The shape of the melody is very carefully designed. The first phrase is the shortest and moves in waves. The second phrase starts high, and the motion is mostly descending. The last phrase is in the form of an arch and starts and ends on the same note (G). At the top of the arch, the music reaches up to the highest note in the whole piece. The last time the third statement of the text is sung, the music changes slightly, with the addition of three notes to the beginning of the phrase.

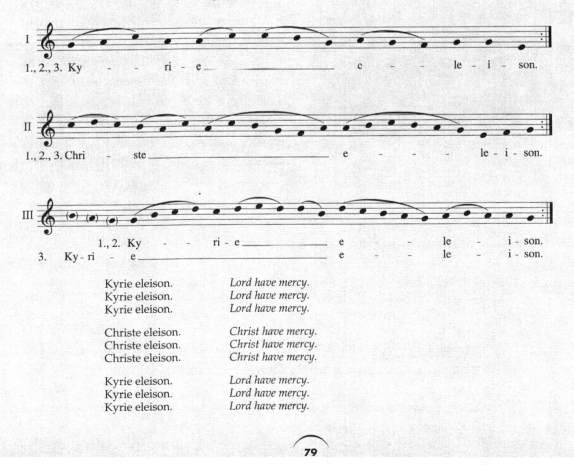

Kyrie eleison.   *Lord have mercy.*
Kyrie eleison.   *Lord have mercy.*
Kyrie eleison.   *Lord have mercy.*

Christe eleison.   *Christ have mercy.*
Christe eleison.   *Christ have mercy.*
Christe eleison.   *Christ have mercy.*

Kyrie eleison.   *Lord have mercy.*
Kyrie eleison.   *Lord have mercy.*
Kyrie eleison.   *Lord have mercy.*

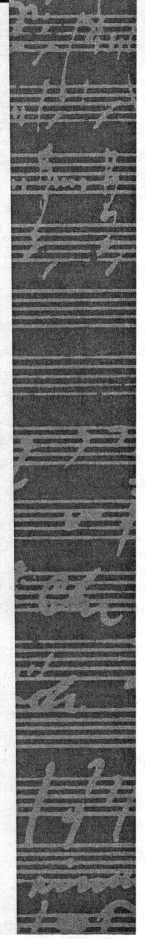

A medieval manuscript from the fifteenth century, showing the music for a Kyrie, with an illumination of monks and a choirboy singing.

folk songs are Dorian. You can hear the special evocative quality of the Dorian mode in a song such as "Scarborough Fair," better known by the words of its refrain, "Parsley, sage, rosemary, and thyme."

The pattern of intervals in E-mode pieces is different. So chants composed in that mode sound different from those composed in the D mode. And the same is true for F-mode and G-mode pieces, because of their characteristic pattern of intervals.

The chart on the next page gives names and the patterns of these four main medieval modes. You will notice that the modes are given with their notes descending, whereas the scales we have looked at were shown in ascending form. This is because most medieval melodies descend to their keynote, giving the music a feeling of relaxation at the end, whereas many later melodies end with a more intense rise to the top of the scale.

This system of modes is very important. It is the basis upon which the music of the Middle Ages is built, and it is this system that makes the world of medieval plainchant so colorful, so rich, and so appealing.

Why does plainchant sound the way it does, with its serene, otherworldly character? The first reason has to do with rhythm. The music flows along without a clearly defined rhythm and with no regular pattern of strong or weak beats. The second reason for the sound of plainchant is the nature of the modes. The modes are very subtle. The colors they impart to the music are not stark or strong: they are gentle pastels. They lack the intense drive of modern scales or keys. Finally, because there is only one musical line, the listener can concentrate entirely on the shape and direction of the melody. Indeed, plainchant is the greatest repository of pure melody in the whole history of Western music and has been called "one of the great treasures of Western civilization."

between the modes is like the difference in sound between major and minor scales. The D mode (usually called the Dorian), from top to bottom, has a whole step, a half step, three whole steps, a half step, and a whole step. None of the other modes has exactly that pattern, so no other mode has the same sound. Many

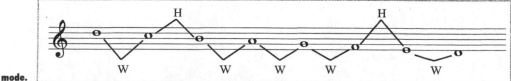

The Dorian mode.

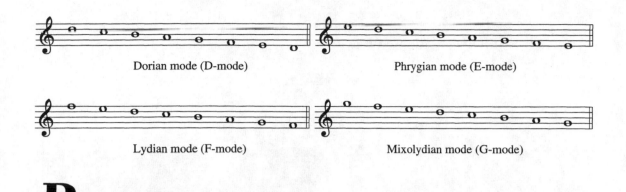

Dorian mode (D-mode)

Phrygian mode (E-mode)

Lydian mode (F-mode)

Mixolydian mode (G-mode)

PART TWO: SECULAR SONG AND POLYPHONY

SECULAR SONG

The rise of secular song can be dated to the twelfth century, when the troubadours were active. Troubadours were poet-musicians who composed songs for performance in the many small aristocratic courts of southern France. (In northern France, such musicians were called *trouvères*.) Troubadours and trouvères wrote their own poetry and music, and the subjects they favored were love, duty, friendship, ceremony, and poetry itself. The primary topic was love. The poems address an idealized vision of a woman, who is remote and usually unattainable. (Most of the troubadours were men.) The lover pines away and pleads for some sign of favor, however slight. There are also a few songs by women troubadours about men, written in the same manner.

This topic is sometimes called "courtly love," because it derived from a conventional code of manners that flourished in the aristocratic courts of the Middle Ages. But it had enormous influence on the whole history of Western love poetry. Eight centuries of love songs, up to and including those of the twentieth century, have been influenced by the conventions and vocabulary of courtly love.

As an example of troubadour music, we shall listen to a song, *A chantar*, by Beatriz de Dia. **(See Listening Guide on page 82.)**

POLYPHONY

It took some time before medieval composers began to be interested in polyphony. The plainchant and secular

Performance of Medieval Music

One of the fascinating things about medieval music is the set of questions it poses for performers today. Plainchant is difficult enough to re-create. But at least we know the context in which it should be sung (a religious service); we know who should be singing (a small choir); and we know that it should usually be sung unaccompanied (that is, without instruments). With secular song, many questions are unresolved. The original manuscripts of the music tell us very little about how to perform it. They provide the words and the notes, but that is all. ✦ There is still a great deal of controversy among modern scholars and performers about the question of accompaniment for medieval secular songs. Some people feel that the songs should be performed as they appear in the manuscripts—that is, with no accompaniment at all. Others point to the elaborate descriptions and pictures of instruments in medieval manuscripts and suggest that performers must have improvised instrumental accompaniments for so sophisticated a repertory.

Beatriz de Dia (late twelfth century)
Song, *A chantar*

Date of composition: c. 1175
Duration: 5:21

Student CD Collection: 1, track 43
Complete CD Collection: 1, track 43

Most of the troubadours of the Middle Ages were men, but a few women troubadours are known. Contrary to popular belief, women in the early Middle Ages enjoyed considerable freedom and political equality. Many of them in all social classes were involved in music, either as patrons, as composers, or as performers. The powerful and charismatic Eleanor of Aquitaine was a great patron of the arts.

Beatriz de Dia, often known as the Comtessa de Dia (Countess of Dia), lived in the late twelfth century. Her medieval biography says that she was the wife of the Count of Poitiers and the lover of a well-known nobleman, who was himself a troubadour. It also states that she was the composer of "many good songs." Only a small number of her poems survive, and only this one has music.

Like almost all the secular songs of the Middle Ages, this one is **strophic**: The same music is repeated for all the stanzas of the poem. The language is that of the south of France; it is known as Occitan, sometimes called Provençal. The poem has five stanzas and a brief two-line ending known as a *tornada*.

Beatriz de Dia addresses her lover, who has scorned her, and expresses her pain at his treating her so badly. It is difficult to gauge the depth of true feeling in this song, because the topic of unrequited love was a highly conventional one in troubadour poetry. Yet beneath the convention, the blending of words and music produces a song of great beauty.

Each line of poetry has its own musical phrase. The first phrase ends with an ornamented half cadence (a cadence that leaves more to be said) on E; the second with a full cadence on D. These two musical phrases are repeated for the third and fourth lines of the poetry. The next two lines are joined and are set higher in the range; they end with the E cadence. The last line, on the other hand, uses the whole musical phrase of lines 2 and 4 with its D ending. The pattern is summarized here:

Line 1	Phrase A
Line 2	Phrase B
Line 3	Phrase A
Line 4	Phrase B
Lines 5 and 6	New higher phrase, with A ending
Line 7	Phrase B

82

Each stanza uses the same arrangement. This pattern gives a rounded feeling to the melody as a whole and a sense of increased intensity before the close. We shall listen to two stanzas.

In this performance, the singer is accompanied by a **vielle** (a bowed instrument—you can see one in the medallion at the top of this listening guide) and a low wooden flute, which provide an introduction and a close to the song as well as some links between stanzas. They are joined for the *tornada* by lute and drum.

43 (43) **0:00**	[vielle prelude]	

STANZA 1

[vielle accompaniment]

0:25	*A chantar m'er de so q'ieu no voldria,*	I must sing, whether I want to or not.
	Tant me rancur de lui cui sui amia,	I feel so much pain from him whose friend I am,
	Car eu l'am mais que nuilla ren que sia;	For I love him more than anything.
	Vas lui nom val merces ni cortesia,	But neither grace nor courtesy has any effect on him,
	Ni ma beltatz, ni mos pretz, ni mos sens.	Nor my beauty, my decency, or my intelligence.
	C'atressim sui engunad'e trahia	I am despised and betrayed,
	Cum degr'esser, s'ieu fos desavinens.	As though I were worthless.

| 1:50 | [flute interlude] | |

STANZA 5

[vielle accompaniment]

3:01	*Valer mi deu mos pretz e mos paratges*	My decency and my ancestry have their value,
	E ma beutatz e plus mos fis coratges,	As do my beauty and the depth of my heart.
	Per q'ieu vos mand lai on es vostr'estatges	So I send to your noble home
	Esta chansson que me sia messatges:	This song: let it be my messenger!
	E voill saber, lo mieus bels amics gens,	And I want to know, my fair friend,
	Per que vos m'etz tant fers ni tant salvatges,	Why you are so savage and cruel to me.
	Non sal si s'es orguoills o mals talens.	I don't know: is it pride or ill will?

TORNADA

[lute and drum join in softly]

| 4:18 | *Mas aitan plus vuoill li digas, messatges,* | But I want even more for you to tell him, messenger, |
| | *Q'en trop d'orguoill ant gran dan maintas gens.* | That pride has been the downfall of many people! |

| 5:01 | [florid ending] | |

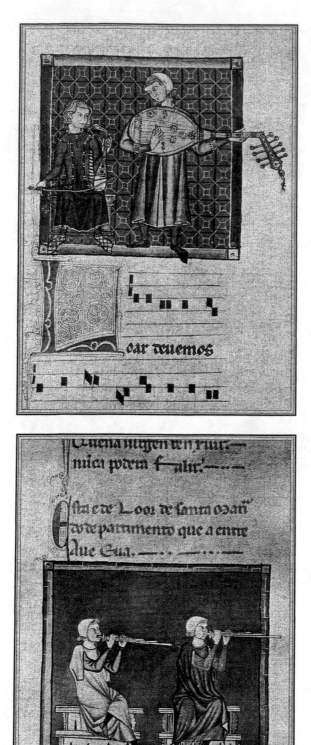

Some medieval song manuscripts have very detailed pictures of musical instruments.

Above: We see a lute and a *rebec* (a high bowed instrument).

Below: Two wind instruments with uneven pipes.

Right: The original medieval manuscript of *Viderunt Omnes*.

song repertories were entirely monophonic, and the subtleties of melodic construction and the text/music relationship in these genres satisfied the musical aims of medieval composers for centuries. Only gradually did the idea of *combining* different notes in music gain popularity in the Middle Ages.

The idea of composing music with two or more independent musical lines first arose in the tenth century and really took hold about 1200, when there was a sudden explosion of polyphonic liturgical composition. The polyphony of this time is striking in its power and grandeur. Compositions of two, three, and even four voices were written to celebrate the major feasts of the church year. At a time when the cycle of life revolved around the church calendar, feasts such as Christmas and Easter must have been spectacular and vivid occasions. People spent days or even weeks preparing for the special celebrations that surrounded the feast days themselves. In the dress that was worn, in the meals that were prepared, in the brief escape from the constant burden of work, these days must have had special significance for the majority of medieval society. It is not surprising, therefore, that such days were marked by very special music.

Below is a sample of this kind of polyphony, showing some of these elements: a bottom voice starting with a sustained tone but turning more rhythmic, a somewhat more complex middle voice, and an extremely elaborate upper voice.

The remarkable thing about this music is the fact that, despite its variety and density, it retains all of the original plainchant embedded in it. All the words are still there, and all the original notes are retained in the lower voice. The composition is a complex and sophisticated edifice, but it is built entirely on the foundation of an ancient structure. This is entirely appropriate, for the music was designed for a cathedral that was one of the glories of the new Gothic age but was erected on the site of a Paris church many centuries old.

LATE MEDIEVAL
POLYPHONIC SONG

By the 1300s, the two main developments of the later Middle Ages had become fused: Secular songs were set to polyphony—often in delicate settings of great sophistication. France and Italy were the two areas at the forefront of the art of polyphonic song at that time. In France, the master composer was Guillaume de Machaut (c. 1300–1377).

Machaut is one of the first composers about whom we know quite a few biographical details. He was educated at Rheims, an important town in north-eastern France. Soon he became quite well known as an administrator, a poet, and a composer. He held positions at the courts of some of the most prominent members of the French ruling aristocracy, including Charles, Duke of Normandy, who later became King Charles V of France. Machaut also was an administrator of the cathedral at Rheims. He died in his late seventies after a busy and productive life.

A great deal of Machaut's work survives. He wrote many long poems and was probably the author of the poems for his own songs. He wrote some sacred music, but most of Machaut's pieces are polyphonic secular songs.

Machaut's musical style is both subtle and intense. The music is full of little rhythmic and melodic motives that tie the composition together and form beautiful melodies. The rhythm is very fluid and depends upon a constant interplay between duple and triple meters. Machaut often uses chromatic notes (unexpected sharps and flats) to make the sound more colorful. **(See Listening Guide on page 88.)**

> **M**usic is a science that would have us laugh and sing and dance.
> —**Guillaume de Machaut**

Di ___   xit   Do-   mi-   nus

Late twelfth-century polyphony in the style of Perotinus.

Guillaume de Machaut (c. 1300–1377)
Secular song (rondeau)
Doulz Viaire Gracieus

Date of composition: Mid-fourteenth century
Voice, lute, and recorder
Duration: 2:00

Student CD Collection: 1, track 46
Complete CD Collection: 1, track 46

This short piece is a good example of Machaut's style. It is a setting of a poem that has a two-line refrain (printed in italics). The refrain comes at the beginning and the end, and its first line comes in the middle of the poem too. This kind of poem is known as a **rondeau**.

The music sounds very simple but is actually quite complex. There are only two sections of music, which alternate in setting each line of the poetry. The first section is five measures long, the second section seven. This contrasts with later music, where the number of measures in each phrase or section tends to be much more regular. A short descending passage on the lute joins the sections together.

There are other aspects of this music that seem unusual to a listener of today. Although the prevailing **meter** of the piece is triple, there are several places where the music moves in duple meter. **Bar lines** were not used in medieval music (although we print them today for the sake of clarity), so the meter could be much more flexible. Also, many of the notes are **chromatic**: even the opening chord contains two sharps. And although the first section ends on G, which leads you to expect that the whole piece will end on G, the final cadence is on B♭.

The voice is accompanied by two instruments: a recorder below the voice and a **lute** above. (A lute is a plucked instrument similar to a guitar.) Although the accompanying parts are quite independent, all three lines together create interesting harmonies, and there is a brief echo among them at the beginning of the B section.

This kind of carefully constructed polyphony, as well as the overall gentle beauty of the piece, are typical of Machaut's music and of fourteenth-century French music in general.

46 (46)	0:00	*Doulz viaire gracieus,*	*Sweet, gracious countenance,*
	0:12	*De fin cuer vous ay servy.*	*I have served you with a faithful heart.*
	0:30	Weillies moy estre piteus,	Take pity on me,
	0:42	*Doulz viaire gracieus;*	*Sweet, gracious countenance;*
	0:55	Se je sui un po honteus,	If I am a little shy,
	1:07	Ne me mettes en oubli.	Do not forget me.
	1:25	*Doulz viaire gracieus,*	*Sweet, gracious countenance,*
	1:38	*De fin cuer vous ay servy.*	*I have served you with a faithful heart.*

Chapter 7

The Renaissance: 1400–1600

A Renaissance painting reveling in the new-found technique of perspective.

GENERAL CHARACTERISTICS OF RENAISSANCE MUSIC

Renaissance music is distinguished from late medieval music in one important way: The overall sound is much smoother and more homogeneous, with less contrast. This change in sound is the result of a change in compositional technique. The highly contrasting and independent lines of late medieval polyphony were replaced by a new polyphonic style based on imitation.

Imitation is a form of polyphony in which all the musical lines present the same musical phrase one after the other. As each line enters, the previous ones continue, so there is a constant sense of overlapping. This technique can be much more varied than it sounds. The strictest kind of imitation is a round, in which all the voices sing exactly the same thing in turn. But often, imitation is much freer than that. In free imitation, only the first few notes of a melodic phrase are sung by each entering voice; the voices then continue freely.

Even though the *style* of music in the Renaissance was very different from that in the Middle Ages, the predominant types of composition were the same. They were these: (1) liturgical music (music for church services, usually Mass settings), (2) motets (settings of Latin texts that are sacred but not liturgical), and (3) secular songs.

Strict imitation (round).

Free imitation.

MUSIC IN THE EARLY RENAISSANCE

The early Renaissance saw a merging of the individual musical characteristics of the different European countries into an international style. Composers throughout Europe began to write similar music—polyphonic, often imitative, and concentrated primarily in the three main types: Mass, motet, and secular song. The foremost composers of the time were John Dunstable of England and Guillaume DuFay of France. Their careers show how the musical style of the Renaissance crossed national boundaries. Dunstable was born in England in 1390 and died there in 1453, but he spent nearly 15 years in France at the height of his career. DuFay (c. 1400–1474) was born in northern France but traveled extensively throughout Europe and spent many years in Italy. He was therefore exposed to the very different musical styles of northern and southern Europe and played an important role in bringing about a fusion of the two in his own music.

Both Dunstable and DuFay and the many other composers who flourished in the early Renaissance wrote music of great beauty and sophistication. Their polyphonic Masses were often unified by musical phrases that reoccur in different movements; their motets are based on Latin texts often taken from the Bible or designed to celebrate an important civic event; and their secular songs are usually three-part gentle love songs in French or Italian.

THE RENAISSANCE MASS

A Roman Catholic Mass as it was celebrated in the 1400s was a long service, with many different readings and prayers, ceremonies and processions, and a large amount of music. Through most of the Middle Ages, all of this music had been sung in plainchant. It was only with the advent of polyphony in the twelfth and thirteenth centuries that some parts of the Mass began to be sung polyphonically. Gradually, composers began to concentrate on those sections of the Mass that remained the same, regardless of the day, feast, or season. There are five of these sections—the Kyrie, Gloria, Credo, Sanctus, and Agnus Dei—and they are known collectively as the Ordinary of the Mass. The tradition of setting these five sections to music began in the fourteenth century and has continued through the Renaissance to the present day. (See Listening Guide on page 99.)

The principal musical characteristic of a Renaissance Mass is polyphony, usually imitation. The flexibility and variety of approach displayed by composers in the fifteenth and sixteenth centuries in using this one compositional technique is remarkable.

THE MID–RENAISSANCE

During the middle part of the Renaissance, the technique of unifying a composition by the use of imitation became fully established. Composers also experimented with ways of linking the five different sections of the Ordinary by drawing the musical material for them from a single source: a piece of plainchant or even a popular song of the day. The source melody usually appears in the tenor voice (the third musical line from the top in a four-voice piece), but the other voices are often derived from it as well.

IOSQVINVS PRATENSIS.

Josquin Desprez in a sixteenth century woodcut.

JOSQUIN DESPREZ (C. 1440–1521)

Josquin Desprez was the most versatile and gifted composer of the mid-Renaissance. He was from northern France and spent much of his career there, as well as at some of the cathedrals and courts of Italy. During his lifetime he became quite famous, and rich noblemen were eager to hire him for their households.

Josquin composed prolifically in the three main genres of Renaissance music: Masses, motets, and secular songs. He brought the Renaissance technique of musical imitation to new heights of clarity and flexibility.

As an example of Josquin's style, we shall study one of his Mass settings: the *Pange Lingua* Mass, composed toward the end of his life. **(See Listening Guide on page 100.)** This composition is known as the *Pange Lingua* Mass because all five movements of the Mass are based on the plainchant hymn *Pange Lingua Gloriosi*. Before examining Josquin's polyphonic Mass setting, let us look at the plainchant that provided the basis for it.

JOSQUIN'S PANGE LINGUA MASS

In his Mass based on the *Pange Lingua* hymn, Josquin took almost all of his musical ideas from the plainchant. Remarkably, each vocal line in every section of the Mass is derived from the chant in some way or another. But it is the way in which he uses the musical material that demonstrates the composer's talent and that enabled Josquin to create a completely new composition from the ancient chant.

In the first place, of course, Josquin's Mass is polyphonic. It is written for four voice lines: sopranos, altos, tenors, and basses. Second, the Mass—unlike the chant—has rhythm (plainchant is usually sung with all the notes equal in length). Every musical phrase has a rhythm especially created by Josquin to fit the words of

> **J**osquin is master of the notes; others are mastered by them.
> —Martin Luther

the Mass. Josquin also molds and varies his phrases by adding notes to or modifying notes from the chant melody. His composition is in five movements, using all five sections of the Ordinary.

The Mass is by no means a lesser piece because of its dependence on earlier melodic material. Indeed, it is precisely in the molding of a well-known original that Josquin shows his ingenuity. The *Pange Lingua* Mass not only stands alone as a composition reflecting the individual genius of its composer. It also is colored throughout with the presence of a sacred tradition, not only in the words of the Mass itself but also in the music and the words of the hymn that stands behind the Mass—a hymn that would have been very familiar to Josquin's audience. The words of the original hymn are not sung in Josquin's Mass, but they would have been called to mind by his audience when they heard the strands of the hymn's melody woven into the polyphony.

Three characteristics of Josquin's special musical style can be heard clearly in this work:

1. Josquin has given each short segment of the music its own **point of imitation**, a musical passage that presents a single tiny musical phrase imitated among the voices. For each new segment of the music, the phrase is different. Each voice states the phrase in turn, and then a cadence follows. The number of statements, the voices that present them, the number of measures between them—all these things may vary.

2. Usually the music is controlled by **overlapping cadences:** The next group of voices begins its statements just as the first group comes to a cadence. This provides articulation for the music while allowing the forward motion to continue.

3. The imitation is usually paired imitation: One pair of voices begins the imitation and another pair answers.

Thomas Aquinas (1225–1274)
Plainchant hymn, *Pange Lingua*

Date of composition: Thirteenth
   century
Choir
Duration: 2:24

Student CD Collection: 1, track 47
Complete CD Collection: 1, track 47

Pan - ge lin - gua __ glo - ri - o - si

Cor - po - ris my - ste - ri - um, _____

San - gui - nis - que pre - ti - o - si,

Quem in mun - di - pre - ti - um _____

Fruc - tus ven - tris ge - ne - ro - si

Rex ef - fu - dit __ gen - ti - um.

The *Pange Lingua* hymn was written by Thomas Aquinas, one of the foremost scholars and theologians of the late middle ages. The hymn is strophic: All four stanzas are sung to the same music. Each stanza has six lines, and they seem to fall into pairs. The chant is in the E (Phrygian) mode, but the only line to end on the E is the last one. This gives the music a sense of continuity until the end. The chant is almost entirely syllabic, and the text urges praise for the miracle of Christ's birth and death.

We shall listen to all four stanzas, but what is important here is the *music*; therefore, the entire text is not given. Remember: All four stanzas have exactly the same music.

47 (47)	0:00	Stanza 1	(*"Pange lingua ..."*)
	0:33	Stanza 2	(*"Nobis datus ..."*)
	1:04	Stanza 3	(*"In supremae ..."*)
	1:39	Stanza 4	(*"Verbum caro ..."*)
	2:12	"Amen"	

Josquin Desprez (c. 1440–1521)
Kyrie from the *Pange Lingua* Mass

Date of composition: c. 1520
Sopranos, altos, tenors, basses
Duration: 2:51

Student CD Collection: 1, track 48
Complete CD Collection: 1, track 48

*A*ll three of the characteristics listed on page 98 may be heard in the opening Kyrie of Josquin's *Pange Lingua* Mass. Let us first look at the phrase that provides the material for the first point of imitation:

This phrase is derived from the first phrase of the plainchant hymn. Notice, however, that Josquin adds a short turning passage between the last two notes to provide intensity and drive to the cadence. Notice, too, the rhythm that Josquin has applied to the notes. It starts out with long notes (which stress the characteristic E–F–E half step of the Phrygian mode) and increases in motion until just before the end. The *meter* of this music is also very flexible. Composers of this era did not use measures or bar lines (as you can see from the facsimile of the original shown below). This creates a very fluid sound without the regularly recurring accents that occur in later music.

The movement as a whole has three main sections:

1. Kyrie eleison.
2. Christe eleison.
3. Kyrie eleison.

Each section begins with a new point of imitation, and all are derived from the original hymn. The "Christe" section is based on the third and fourth lines of the hymn, the final "Kyrie" section on the fifth and sixth lines. Toward the end of the last section, Josquin again adds new rhythmic material to create a strong drive to the final cadence.

48 (48)	0:00	*Kyrie eleison*	(Based on opening of hymn melody.) Tenors and basses; cadence overlaps with entry of altos. Sopranos enter before final cadence.
	0:45	*Christe eleison*	(Based on lines 3 and 4 of hymn melody.) Paired imitation, overlapping entries.
	2:02	*Kyrie eleison*	(Based on lines 5 and 6 of hymn melody.) Sopranos, altos, tenors, basses enter in turn; increase in activity before final cadence.

THE LATE RENAISSANCE

The sixteenth century was a time of remarkable musical achievements. The balance, beauty, and exquisite sound of imitative polyphony were fully explored by composers throughout Europe. In addition, composers began to use more homophonic texture in their compositions. There are few greater contrasts than that between the individual strands of imitative polyphony and the solid chordal texture of homophony, and Renaissance composers from Josquin onward took full advantage of this contrast. They alternated and interwove the two styles in their compositions to achieve ever greater variety of texture and to give expressive emphasis to the words.

In fact, this increasing focus on expressing the meaning of the words marks the progression of music during the Renaissance. During the sixteenth century, the combination of a high degree of technical accomplishment and a new interest in text expression led to the creation of some of the most beautiful works in the history of music. Masses, motets, and secular songs were created by composers throughout Europe: in France and Germany, the Netherlands, Spain, Poland, and England. But probably the main center of musical activity in the sixteenth century was Italy.

Italy was the focal point of the Roman Catholic movement known as the Counter-Reformation, which began partly in reaction to the Protestant Reformation and partly as the result of a genuine desire to reform the Catholic Church from within. The Counter-Reformation had important consequences for music, as we shall see.

One technical change that may be noticed in late Renaissance music is the sound of the last chord at the end of sections. Until this time, final chords contained

Patronage

Music costs money. Composers have to make a living, and so do performers. In the days before public concerts, ticket sales, and commercial recordings, music had to be financed by patrons (supporters). During the Renaissance, most patrons were wealthy aristocrats who could afford to employ musicians at their courts or palaces. Musicians were on the staff at these courts just like doormen, dressmakers, cooks, and other servants.   ¶   Some wealthy aristocrats employed several composers at once. In the later part of the fifteenth century, the duke of Milan appointed the great composer Josquin Desprez to his staff, although he already had four other composers on the payroll.   ¶   Sometimes patrons had to pay handsomely to hire the most famous musicians. When Josquin left Milan, he moved to the court of the duke of Ferrara. He was hired in 1503, against the advice of the duke's private secretary, who urged the duke to hire a composer named Isaac instead. "Isaac gets on better with his colleagues and composes more quickly," he wrote. "It is true that Josquin is a better composer, but he composes only when he feels like it and not when he is asked. Moreover, Josquin is demanding 200 ducats, while Isaac will take 120." The duke decided to go first-class, and Josquin got his 200 ducats.

only the "perfect" intervals (octaves and fifths). But in the late Renaissance, composers began to think that final chords should present the fullest sound possible and therefore should include the third, as well as the root, the fifth, and the octave of the chord. You can clearly hear the difference between a piece that ends with the open sound of an octave and a fifth and a piece that ends with a full chord.

THE COUNTER-REFORMATION AND THE MUSIC OF PALESTRINA

The Counter-Reformation was not primarily concerned with music, but music played a role in the deliberations of the church reformers. In 1534 the reformer Paul III was elected pope, and in 1545 he convened the Council of Trent, a council of cardinals that met from time to time over a period of about 20 years to discuss needed reforms in church administration and liturgy.

Music was discussed only during the last two years of the council. Many complaints were heard:

- ❖ secular songs were being used as the basis for sacred compositions;
- ❖ singers had become too theatrical and were distracting people from the liturgy; and
- ❖ polyphony had become too complicated and florid, obscuring the sacred words.

The council considered banning polyphony altogether, thinking that a return to plainchant was the best solu-

tion. In the end, however, the cardinals agreed that, in addition to the traditional chants, polyphonic music could be used in church, provided that the words could be heard clearly and the style was not too elaborate.

The composer whose music most clearly represents these ideals is Giovanni Pierluigi da Palestrina (c. 1525–1594). Like many people during the Middle Ages and the Renaissance, this man took his name from his home town. He was born in Palestrina, 40 miles from Rome, and was sent to Rome as a choirboy to study and sing. He spent most of his life there at some of the city's greatest musical institutions, including the Sistine Chapel (the private chapel of the pope).

The purity, serenity, and perfection of Palestrina's music have made him the most highly regarded composer of late Renaissance choral music. The principal characteristics of his style are balance, control, evenness, clarity, and perfect text setting. The overall effect conveyed by Palestrina's music is achieved by careful control of two primary elements: the structure of the individual melodic lines and the placement of dissonance.

In the structure of the individual melodic lines for his polyphonic pieces, Palestrina adhered strictly to the following guidelines:

a. The motion of the line is primarily stepwise, with very few leaps.

b. If there is a leap, it is small and is immediately counterbalanced by stepwise motion in the opposite direction.

c. The rhythmic flow is not rigid or regularly accented, but is shifting, gentle, and alive.

Agnus Dei from *Pope Marcellus* Mass

A — gnus — De — i

The second primary element in Palestrina's style is his careful control of dissonance. His music has some dissonances (for without them, the music would be very bland indeed), but they appear only under partic-

ular circumstances. Usually, they are short passing notes or are off the beat. When dissonances do occur on the beat, they are always prepared and immediately resolved.

Four hundred years after Palestrina, the composer Charles Gounod observed: "This severe, ascetic music is as calm and horizontal as the line of the ocean, monotonous by virtue of its serenity; antisensuous; and yet it is so intense in its contemplativeness that it verges sometimes on ecstasy."

1., 2. Passing-tone dissonance of a second.
3., 4. On-the-beat dissonance of a seventh, immediately resolved to a sixth.
5. Passing-tone dissonance of a seventh.

> Contemporary accounts of Palestrina's music: "Chaste and correct style . . . confined with sweet harmony." "His music is extraordinarily acclaimed, and by virtue of its entirely novel character, astonishes even the performers themselves."

It might be thought that such a highly disciplined approach to composition would lead to dull, constricted music. On the contrary, Palestrina's music is so inspiring that it has been taken as a model of perfection for all those wishing to imitate the grace and beauty of Renaissance polyphony. In this case, as so often in artistic endeavors, strict formal rules produced masterpieces of great and lasting value.

Palestrina was a superbly gifted and resourceful composer, and despite the rigor of his approach, he found many ways to introduce variety into his music. In the first place, there is a constant interplay between counterpoint and homophony. And within the sections of counterpoint, Palestrina draws on an almost limitless variety of methods. The imitative entries among the voices can vary in distance, number of entries, voice pairings, and even pitch. Different points of imitation can even be introduced at the same time—something that never happened in Josquin's music. And through it all, the text sounds clearly, with its natural rhythm perfectly conveyed.

Palestrina wrote more than 100 settings of the Mass and several volumes of secular songs, but perhaps his most impressive achievement is the composition of 250 motets. Motets could be written on almost any sacred text: biblical stories, passages from the Psalms, and so on. Almost always, composers chose expressive texts with elements of drama or mystery, and they matched the words with music of remarkable intensity or poignancy. **(See Listening Guide on page 105.)**

THE RENAISSANCE MOTET

The Renaissance motet usually has four voice parts. It is entirely vocal and is usually sung by a small choir rather than by soloists. All the voices sing the same text—a sacred text—in the same language, almost always Latin. Finally, the music may be imitative or homophonic and is usually a mixture of the two.

Motets often have very expressive words. Renaissance composers tended to write richer and more unusual music for motets than they did for the fixed liturgical texts of the Mass. As a result, the music of Renaissance motets is often highly expressive, with a sensitive and compelling approach to the meaning of the text.

THE RENAISSANCE SECULAR SONG

The Renaissance secular song evolved in two phases. In the fifteenth century, secular songs (songs with nonsacred texts) were not very different from those of the late Middle Ages (those of Machaut, for example). And an international musical style had been adopted in most countries. But in the late Renaissance, several European countries developed their own distinct national styles for secular songs.

The most influential of all these countries was Italy, and the distinctive type of secular song that developed there was the **madrigal**. Madrigals are secular vocal pieces

Giovanni Pierluigi da Palestrina
(c. 1525–1594)
Motet, *Exsultate Deo*

Date of composition: 1584
Sopranos, altos I, altos II, tenors, basses
Duration: 2:24

Student CD Collection: 1, track 49
Complete CD Collection: 1, track 49

The motet *Exsultate Deo* was first published in Palestrina's fifth book of motets in 1584. This book contains 21 motets written for five voices. The text is from Psalm 81. Palestrina uses only the first three lines of the psalm, the text of which is given here.

Exsultate Deo adiutori nostro,	Sing out in praise of God our refuge,
iubilate Deo Iacob.	acclaim the God of Jacob.
Sumite psalmum et date tympanum,	Raise a melody; beat the drum,
psalterium iucundum cum cithara.	play the tuneful lyre and harp.
Buccinate in neomenia tuba,	Blow the trumpet at the new moon,
insigni die sollemnitatis vestrae.	and blow it at the full moon on the day
	of your solemn feast.

In his setting Palestrina concentrates only on these exuberant opening verses of the psalm, rather than the fierce later ones. The music is bright and joyful, filled with dotted rhythms and running eighth-note patterns, which help to enliven the work. In addition, the composer uses some word-painting, such as on the opening word "Exsultate," where the musical line rises triumphantly.

With five independent musical lines, the number of possible combinations is large, and Palestrina constantly varies the texture of his music. The clearest examples of this variation are when the sopranos drop out briefly, leaving only the lower voices, or (on the words "psalterium iucundum"—"tuneful lyre") when only three voices are sounding. *Exsultate Deo* is full of imitation, but Palestrina points up the entrance of new lines of text by having them sung homophonically by a pair of voices, which adds an underlying structure to the work as a whole.

Cleverly, he departs from this technique towards the end of the motet on the words "Buccinate" ("blow") and "tuba" ("trumpet"), where there is very close imitation, suggesting the echoing of the turmpet blasts.

This performance is by the choir of Christ Church Cathedral, Oxford, England. The choir, which has been in continuous existence since the early sixteenth century, is made up of the same distribution of voices as it was originally: sixteen boys and twelve men. So all the high voices you hear are those of boys.

Christ Church Cathedral choir.

49 (49)	0:00	*Exsultate Deo adiutori nostro,*	Sing out in praise of God our refuge,	[Imitation in pair of upper voices alone; rising line on "Exsultate."]
	0:11			[Pair of lower voices. Cadence in all five voices; overlaps with:]
	0:28	*iubilate Deo Iacob.*	acclaim the God of Jacob.	[Many entries, suggesting a crowd "acclaiming."]
	0:37			[Lower voices.]
	0:49	*Sumite psalmum et date tympanum,*	Raise a melody; beat the drum,	[Quite homophonic, becoming more imitative. Note dotted rhythm on "tympanum."]
	1:04	*psalterium iucundum cum cithara.*	play the tuneful lyre and harp.	[Elaborate flowering of the voices on "iucundum" ("tuneful").]
50 (50)	0:00	*Buccinate in neomenia tuba,*	Blow the trumpet at the new moon,	[Multiple echoes on "Buccinate;" homophonic climax on "neomenia"]
	0:13			[Running echoes on "tuba."]
	0:23	*insigni die solemnitatis vestrae.*	and blow it at the full moon on the day of your solemn feast.	[Slower, lower, more "solemn."]

for a small group of singers, usually unaccompanied. The favorite topics were love, descriptions of nature, and sometimes war or battles. The music for madrigals mingles chordal and imitative textures and sensitively reflects the meaning of the text. The Italian madrigal became so influential in the course of the sixteenth century that composers of many other nationalities wrote madrigals in Italian, and some composers in England copied the style and wrote madrigals in English.

THE MADRIGAL

As we have seen, matching the words of the text with a musical setting that expresses their meaning was a primary concern of late Renaissance composers. The madrigal is the musical genre that demonstrates this most colorfully.

The madrigal flourished in the courtly atmosphere of Italian aristocratic families. The poetry is serious and elegant, with a sonorous beauty of its own. And the music is carefully designed to reflect the text.

Composers used a variety of techniques to bring out the meaning of the words they set. In general, the same mixture of chordal textures and imitative polyphony is used in madrigals as in motets, but composers went much further in their search for direct expression. If the text had words such as "rising," "flying," or "soaring," then the music would have fast upward scales. "Peace" and "happiness" might be set to sweet major chords, "agony" and "despair" to wrenching dissonances. In fact, contrasts of this kind—between happiness and despair, for example—often appeared in madrigal texts within the same poem. This contrast is known as *antithesis*, and it presented ideal musical opportunities for madrigal composers. A sigh might be represented by sudden, short pauses—to be followed by long flowing lines evoking the elation of love.

In the "Listening" chapter, we heard *Morte, te chiamo*, a sixteenth-century madrigal by Maddalena Casulana that demonstrates these points (pages 72–73). It had a serious text, about love, life, and death, which was clearly expressed by the music. It also had contrast of textures, expressive dissonances, and antithesis.

The madrigal became immensely popular during the sixteenth century and survived well into the seventeenth. Composers strove for ever greater intensity of expression, and the late madrigalists managed to wring every ounce of feeling from each nuance of the text. The technique of depicting the meaning of words through music is known as **word-painting**.

Toward the end of the sixteenth century, a fascination with madrigals had taken hold in England. Italian madrigals sometimes appeared in English translation. One set

Musical Borrowing

The idea that originality is the most important characteristic of a composer is a very modern one. For most of music history, composers borrowed freely from one another. Imitating another composer was considered a mark of respect. ✦ During the Renaissance, composers made widespread use of previously existing material for their works. This included plainchant, popular songs, other people's compositions, and sometimes earlier pieces of their own. Palestrina, one of the greatest composers of the Renaissance era, was a frequent borrower from the works of other composers. Scholars have traced compositions by at least 10 other composers among the building materials of Palestrina's works. ✦ Occasionally you can trace the metamorphosis of the same piece from a chant to a motet to a Mass. For example, Palestrina wrote a motet based on the chant *Assumpta Est Maria*. The motet weaves the original notes of the chant into a beautiful polyphonic whole. Later, Palestrina wrote an entire Mass based on his motet, using the musical fabric of the motet as the basis for an impressive, new, large-scale composition.

was published in 1590 under the title *Italian Madrigalls Englished*. But English composers also wrote their own madrigals with English texts. These were often lighter in tone and more cheerful than their Italian counterparts.

The title page to Thomas Morley's *A Plaine and Easie Introduction to Practicall Musicke*, printed in 1597.

The guiding force for the development of English madrigals was Thomas Morley (1557–1602), a gifted composer, author of an important textbook on music, and owner of the monopoly on music printing for the whole of England. Morley published more madrigals than any other English composer and established a style that was followed by most other English madrigalists.

We shall listen to a pair of extremely short madrigals by Thomas Morley from a collection he published in 1595. Both are for two voices rather than the conventional four. The first (*Sweet Nymph Come to Thy Lover*) is for two women; the second (*Fire and Lightning*) is sung by two men. They make a wonderfully pleasing and varied pair. (**See Listening Guide on page 109.**)

After the work of the late Italian and English madrigalists, the Renaissance polyphonic style had run its course. It had produced works of great beauty and variety, but new composers had new ideas. Their interest in text expression remained paramount, but they felt that new ways had to be found to allow the words to dominate the music. These new ways were the foundation of a new musical style in the seventeenth century, the Baroque style, in which instrumental music became more and more prominent. Let us examine the origins of the style in the rise of instrumental music in the Renaissance.

THE RISE OF INSTRUMENTAL MUSIC

During the Renaissance, instrumental music became more and more popular. A wide range of instruments was in use, from the loud, extrovert trumpets to soft, delicate strings and recorders. Compositions ranged from serious contrapuntal works to lighthearted dances.

One of the former types was the **canzona**, and the master of the canzona was Giovanni Gabrieli (c. 1555–1612), who was an organist and composer at St. Mark's Church in Venice. St. Mark's had two choir lofts facing each other, and Gabrieli took advantage of this to place contrasting groups of instruments in the two lofts, creating an early version of stereo sound. (**See Listening Guide on page 110.**)

The Importance of Dancing
The following extract comes from a dance treatise published in 1859. The treatise is cast as a dialogue between student and teacher.
Student: Without knowledge of dancing, I could not please the damsels, upon whom, it seems to me, the entire reputation of an eligible young man depends.
Teacher: You are quite right, as naturally the male and female seek one another, and nothing does more to stimulate a man to acts of courtesy, honor, and generosity than love. And if you desire to marry, you must realize that a mistress is won by the good temper and grace displayed while dancing. And there is more to it than this, for dancing is practiced to reveal whether lovers are in good health and sound of limb, after which they are permitted to kiss and touch and savor one another, thus to ascertain if they are shapely or emit an unpleasant odor as of bad meat. Therefore, apart from the many other advantages to be derived from dancing, it becomes essential to a well-ordered society.

The largest category of instrumental music during the Renaissance was dance music, since dancing was one of the favorite forms of entertainment. The music was usually binary in form (AABB) and followed the characteristic tempos and rhythms of each dance type. Dances were frequently performed in pairs, contrasting slow with fast, or duple meter with triple meter. (**See Listening Guide on page 111.**)

Thomas Morley (1557–1602)
Two English Madrigals

Date of composition: 1595
Two sopranos (*Sweet Nymph Come to Thy Lover*); two baritones (*Fire and Lightning*)
Duration: 2:31

Student CD Collection: 1, track 51
Complete CD Collection: 1, track 51

The texts for these short pieces were probably written by Morley himself. Each one contains picturesque images, which the music captures beautifully. The first madrigal, *Sweet Nymph*, presents a nightingale, a favorite image for composers. The second, *Fire and Lightning*, is lively and frenetic, with a kicker at the end. Both are primarily imitative, with very close imitation in some sections to liven up the proceedings or intensify the sound. The very last line of *Fire and Lightning* is suddenly homophonic to draw attention to the sting at the end. This last line also exploits antithesis ("fair"/"spiteful") to make its effect.

Both madrigals have such short texts that there are many repetitions of each phrase, and you will hear many instances of word-painting. The fine performances here are by students Sarah Pelletier and Suzanne Ehly, sopranos, and faculty members William Sharp and Mark Aliapoulios, baritones, of the Boston University School for the Arts.

51 (51)	0:00	Sweet nymph come to thy lover,	Imitation.
	0:12	Lo here alone our loves we may discover,	Touches of homophony on "Lo here alone."
	0:20	(*Repeat of first two lines*)	
	0:39	Where the sweet nightingale with wanton gloses,	Imitation; high notes and close harmony on "gloses" [trills].
	0:49	Hark, her love too discloses.	High notes, very close imitation, especially last time through.
	1:03	(*Repeat of last two lines*)	
52 (52)	0:00	Fire and lightning from heaven fall	Lively; very close imitation.
	0:08	And sweetly enflame that heart with love arightful,	Smooth descending scales on "sweetly."
	0:16	(*Repeat of first two lines*)	
	0:31	Of Flora my delightful,	Scales in opposite direction on "delightful."
	0:45	So fair but yet so spiteful.	Last time through: homophonic, close pungent harmony, dissonance on "spite-," incomplete sound on "ful."
	0:47	(*Repeat of last two lines*)	

Chapter 8

The Baroque Era:
1600–1750

Audiences in the Baroque Era

The Baroque era was an important period of transition from the time of small, elite, aristocratic audiences to that of a wider concertgoing public. The trend began in Italy with a new musical invention: opera. Public opera houses were built in Venice and Rome about the middle of the seventeenth century. In the 1670s the first public concert series was organized in London. Toward the end of the Baroque period, similar public concerts began to be held in France (in 1725) and Germany (in the 1740s). ¶ These concerts were funded by subscription. People would sign up for the series, and the organizer could then use the collected money to hire the performers, rent the hall, print programs, and the like. This might be regarded as the first move in the gradually emerging trend from individual patronage to "group patronage." ¶ Some Baroque composers arranged subscription concerts for their own benefit. George Frideric Handel gave many concerts of his own music and made a considerable amount of money during his lifetime. He was also very generous: He inaugurated the idea of giving annual performances of his *Messiah* for charity. A contemporary wrote that *Messiah* "fed the hungry, clothed the naked, fostered the orphan, and enriched succeeding managers of oratorios, more than any single musical production in this or any other country." Handel's *Messiah* performances were very popular. At the 1750 performance, there wasn't enough room for the large audience, despite the request in the announcement that "Gentlemen are desired to come without swords, and the Ladies without hoops."

GENERAL CHARACTERISTICS OF BAROQUE MUSIC

The Baroque era lasted only 150 years, somewhat shorter than the Renaissance and a fraction of the length of the Middle Ages. In spite of this, it is the first period of our musical history that is featured with any frequency in today's concert halls or on radio programs. Even then, only the last half-century of the Baroque era, the period of Bach and Handel and Vivaldi, is generally represented. It is logical, then, to divide our examination of Baroque music into two parts: the early Baroque (1600–1700) and the late Baroque (1700–1750). In fact, this division corresponds to actual musical events, because the early Baroque was the period in which stylistic trends were established, while the late Baroque was the time of the well-known masters and of fixed musical forms.

The early Baroque was a period of excitement and experimentation. The composers of the early 1600s combined expressiveness with great originality. The greatest invention of the age was opera, which displayed the best of all contemporary arts. It featured elaborate stage machinery, gorgeous costumes, and beautiful stage sets. All this was combined with moving stories, expressive acting, and dramatic music.

Early Baroque music was designed to be emotional. Both vocal and instrumental works were written to evoke specific states of mind. Certain melodic turns and harmonic patterns came to be associated with particular feelings. Composers experimented with ways to make music imitate the irregularity, the rise and fall, of impassioned speech.

At the same time, contrary tendencies can be seen in early Baroque music. There was a tendency toward more rigid formal design. Composers began to use bar lines to organize their music into regular metric groupings. And modern tonality began to evolve from the modal system of earlier music.

As the Baroque period progressed, organization and control began to replace experimentation. The forms used in opera and in instrumental music became standardized. The rigid hierarchy of society was reflected in opera plots, which often revolved around the effect on people of a powerful ruler's whims. The growth of tonality, with its carefully organized sequence of keys and harmonic patterns, may also be seen as a mirror of the Baroque social order.

With the Baroque fascination for structure and organization came the development of fixed musical forms. The chief vocal forms of the early Baroque were the opera and the cantata. **Operas** were large-scale productions, expressive and elaborate. They immediately became extremely popular. Great rulers and aristocratic families built their own private theaters for the performance of opera, and opera houses sprang up across Europe.

Cantatas were, in effect, very short unstaged operas: They were written for instruments and one or two voices and portrayed a single scene or situation. Some of the later **church cantatas** (notably those of Bach) were based on liturgical themes and were performed in church on Sundays, but the earlier **chamber cantatas** were secular in nature, telling stories of love lost and found, of nymphs and shepherds. They were perfect for performance in a salon or a small music room.

During the Baroque period, instrumental music gained greatly in importance. Instruments began to take on the shape and sound of their modern counterparts, and instrumental technique began to rival the brilliant speed, expressiveness, and control of the famous opera singers of the day. The most important instrumental forms of the Baroque era were the concerto, the sonata, and the dance suite.

Concertos are based on contrast. Their texture is formed by the interplay between a small group (or soloist) called *solo* and a large group called *ripieno*. The resulting instrumental dialogue allowed Baroque composers to create considerable drama within a purely instrumental form.

Sonatas are chamber works, smaller in scale than concertos and less dependent on contrast. Numbers could range from two or three instruments to a small handful, but a sonata was always designed for a group smaller than an orchestra.

Dance suites were originally designed exclusively to accompany dancing. An evening's entertainment often consisted of a series, or "suite," of contrasting dances, usually in binary form. Later, the dance suite became one of the most popular independent instrumental genres of the late Baroque.

The spread of the Protestant movement had an important influence on music. The most distinctive musical feature of a Protestant service was the **chorale**, a hymn with a steady rhythm and simple tune, usually sung in unison by the whole congregation. Chorale tunes, often dating from the Renaissance or even earlier, found their way into many types of Baroque music, including organ pieces and church cantatas. Another form of sacred music was the **oratorio**. This is a large-scale work like an opera, but it is based on a sacred story, and it is not staged. Instead, a narrator sings the story, and other singers sing the words of people in the story. Similar to the oratorio is the **Passion**, a composition based on the gospel account of the last days of Jesus.

Late Baroque music is characterized by rhythmic vitality. The driving rhythmic pulse of a Vivaldi concerto and the brilliantly organized harmonic motion of a Bach fugue are manifestations of the late style. Again, the vitality is given strength through order and control. But it would be a mistake to think that the emotions that were present in early Baroque music were suppressed in the late period. They were more organized and more formally presented, but they still constituted an essential part of the musical experience.

Stylistically, all Baroque music has one very notable characteristic: a strong bass line. This line not only forms the harmonic underpinning for Baroque music but also provides a strong foundation for the rhythmic momentum often present in music of the time. But whether the upper parts of a Baroque composition have strong rhythmic drive or extended expressive melodies, the bass part is always the driving force, both harmonically and rhythmically. Since the bass line is almost never silent in a Baroque composition, it is known as the **basso continuo** ("continuous bass"), or sometimes just **continuo**. The basso continuo part is usually played by a combination of a keyboard instrument, such as a harpsichord, and a low melody instrument, such as a cello or a bass viol. Whatever the genre, you can recognize a Baroque piece by the strength and powerful sense of direction of its bass line.

THE EARLY BAROQUE (1600–1700)

We saw earlier that the beginning of the Baroque period was a time of experimentation and excitement. Composers were trying out new ideas, and there was a great deal of discussion about music and the way it should be written. Some adhered to the Renaissance ideal of many-voiced polyphony, with its careful shaping of melodic lines and strict control of dissonance. Others felt that music should be subservient to the text, and that the rules of counterpoint and dissonance should be disregarded if they did not serve the primary aim of expressing the text. These composers favored a new song style known as **monody**, a type of music written for solo voice and basso continuo that imitated the natural rhythms of impassioned speech. Monody was composed for both sacred and secular texts; in all cases, the single voice part ranges freely and flexibly above the bass.

One of the early composers of monody was Francesca Caccini (1587–c.1640). She was the principal composer at the court of Tuscany, in northern Italy, and was multi-talented: she could also sing brilliantly, write poetry in both Latin and Italian, and play three different instruments, all equally well. The following brief extract (see below) from one of her sacred songs shows how free and rhapsodic the voice can be in monody. *Maria, dolce Maria*, composed in 1600, expresses the composer's joy in pronouncing the name of Mary.

In the end, both types of music—monody and traditional Renaissance-style polyphony—existed side by side. The most daring experiments in the new compositional style were carried out by a group of composers in Italy and led to the development of a completely new musical genre: opera. Among these composers was a man who was clearly the greatest composer of his age. His name was Claudio Monteverdi. Monteverdi made great contributions in two distinct historical periods. He lived a long life—from 1567 to 1643—and his life cut across the convenient boundaries that historians like to create out of the past. Monteverdi wrote many pieces in Renaissance style, especially madrigals, but he was also the first great opera composer of the Baroque era.

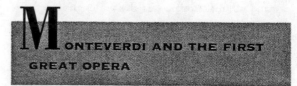

MONTEVERDI AND THE FIRST GREAT OPERA

The first great opera in the history of Western music was Monteverdi's *Orfeo*, written in 1607. The opera is based on the ancient Greek myth of Orpheus and Euridice.

THE STORY OF THE OPERA

Orpheus ("Orfeo" in Italian) and Euridice are in love. Shepherds and nymphs sing and dance together. Suddenly the revelries are interrupted by a messenger who announces that Euridice has been bitten by a snake

Francesca Caccini, *Maria, dolce Maria*

"Mary, sweet Mary, a name so sweet that in saying it my heart is in paradise. A name so sacred and holy that my heart is aflame with heavenly love."

and is dead. Orpheus, a musician, is grief-stricken and decides to travel to the underworld to bring Euridice back to life. The king of the underworld is moved by Orpheus's plea and allows Euridice to return, but on one condition: that Orpheus not turn back and look at her. On their journey, Orpheus becomes anxious and steals a glance at his beloved. She disappears forever.

Monteverdi sets this story with a wide variety of music. There are madrigal-like choruses, dances, and instrumental interludes. But the most striking style of all is called **recitative**, which developed out of the early experiments with monody. Recitative is designed to imitate as closely as possible the freedom and expressiveness of speech.

Recitative is always sung by one singer with accompanying basso continuo. It is very flexible, for it follows the changing meanings of the text, with the bass line supporting the voice and providing punctuation. It can be very simple or quite elaborate and songlike. It is designed to mirror, moment by moment, the emotional state of the singer. In all of his music, but especially in his recitatives, Monteverdi displays the talent that all great opera composers have in common: the ability to capture and reflect the feelings of the human soul. "The modern composer," he said, "builds his works on the basis of truth." **(See Listening Guide on page 122).**

OPERA IN THE SEVENTEENTH CENTURY

In Baroque opera, a distinction gradually arose between those portions of the recitative that were lyrical and songlike and those portions that were more straightforward and conversational. The lyrical part came to be known as **aria**, and the conversational part kept the old name of recitative. Arias were usually written in set forms, with a fixed pattern of repetition, whereas recitatives were freer in form and quite short. The sparse accompaniment and flexible style of recitative made it ideal for setting dialogue and quick interchanges

An Argument over the Future of Music

About 1600, composers and music theorists engaged in a furious debate over the direction that music should take. The most important figures involved were Giovanni Artusi, a prominent Italian music theorist, and the illustrious composer Claudio Monteverdi. They were on opposite sides of the debate. Artusi believed in the conservative Prima Pratica ("First Practice"), whereas Monteverdi was an adherent of the more progressive Seconda Pratica ("Second Practice"). Supporters of the Prima Pratica believed that all composers should adhere to the strict rules of composition adopted by the great composers of the late sixteenth century, most notably Palestrina. Composers should not break those rules regardless of the text they were setting. The slogan "Harmony is the ruler of the text" therefore became Artusi's battle cry. ◆ Monteverdi, however, believed that in passages with very expressive text, the rules could be broken to make the music more intense. He reversed Artusi's slogan to claim that "Text is the ruler of the harmony." In return, Artusi said that Monteverdi and other modern composers had "smoke in their heads" and that their compositions were "the product of ignorance."

Claudio Monteverdi (1567–1643)
Orfeo's recitative, Euridice's recitative,
chorus of nymphs and shepherds,
and instrumental ritornello
from the opera *Orfeo*

Date of composition: 1607
Tenor and soprano solo, chorus,
    instrumental ensemble and basso
    continuo
Duration: 3:55

Student CD Collection: 1, track 58
Complete CD Collection: 2, track 1

The following scene comes from the first act of the opera, in which the love of Orfeo and Euridice is celebrated. In his lyrical recitative "Rosa del Ciel ..." ("Rose of Heaven ..."), Orfeo expresses his passion for Euridice and his happiness that she returns his feelings. Euridice, responding to Orfeo's proclamation of love, affectionately pledges her heart to him in a declamatory passage ("Io non dirò ..."—"I shall not say ..."). A chorus of nymphs and shepherds follows with a celebratory dance ("Lasciate i monti ..."—"Leave the hills ..."), and the scene is closed by an instrumental ritornello.

Monteverdi uses a variety of forms and musical means to depict this pastoral setting. Both Orfeo and Euridice sing in a free, expressive recitative. The melody imitates the rhythms and the inflections of speech and mirrors the meaning of the text. In Orfeo's part, for instance, Monteverdi accentuates significant words such as "fortunato amante" ("happy lover") or "Mio ben" ("My love") by means of rising phrases and matches the musical rhythm with the rhythm of the words:

"fe-li-cís-si-mo" ("happiest")   [♪♪♪♪♪]
"sos-pi-rá-i" ("I sighed"); "sos-pi-rás-ti" ("you sighed")   [♪♪♩♩]

In Euridice's recitative, the composer uses similar lively motives for the words "gioir," "gioia," and "gioisca" ("rejoicing," "rejoice," "enjoys"); employs wide leaps to represent "Quanto" ("How much"); and provides the words "core" ("heart") and "Amore" ("Love") with soothing cadences.

The choral dance consists of two sections: The first, in duple meter, is based on imitative phrases that evoke the movement of dancers; the second provides a distinct contrast, since it is set in triple meter and its texture is completely homophonic. The instrumental ritornello that ensues is a faster dance, which adds variety and brings closure to this short and happy scene.

[soft arpeggiated chords in continuo]

58 (1) 0:00

Rosa del Ciel, vita del mondo, e degna   O Rose of Heaven, life of the world,
Prole di lui che l'Universo affrena,   And worthy offspring of him who rules the
                                                    universe,

[voice becoming more animated]

0:25

Sol, ch'il tutto circondi e'l tutto miri   Sun, you who surround and watch everything
Da gli stellanti giri,   From the starry skies,

[rising melody]

0:34

Dimmi, vedesti mai   Tell me, have you ever seen
Di me più lieto e fortunato amante?   A happier or more fortunate lover than I?

[gentle cadence]

0:45

Fu ben felice il giorno,   Blessed was the day,
Mio ben, [loving phrase] *che pria ti vidi,*   My love, when first I saw you,

0:56

E più felice l'ora   And more blessed yet the hour
Che per te sospirai,   When first I sighed for you,
Poich'al mio sospirar tu sospirasti.   Since you returned my sighs.

[sighing phrases]

1:15

Felicissimo il punto   Most blessed of all the moment
Che la candida mano,   When you offered me your white hand,
Pegno di pura fede, a me porgesti.   As pledge of your pure love.

[many notes]

1:34

Se tanti cori avessi   If I had as many hearts
Quant'occh'il Ciel eterno, e quante chiome   As the eternal sky has eyes, and as
                                                    many as these hills

Han questi colli ameni il verde maggio,   Have leaves in the verdant month of
                                                    May,

1:45 [one "full" note]

Tutti colmi sarieno e traboccanti   They would all be full and overflowing
Di quel piacer ch'oggi mi fa contento.   With the joy that now makes me happy.

[soft cadence]

EURIDICE

[soft lute chords]

59 (2) 2:09   *Io non dirò qual sia*   I shall not say how much

[happy phrases]

2:15   *Nel tuo gioir, Orfeo, la gioia mia,*   I rejoice, Orfeo, in your rejoicing,

2:21   *Che non ho meco il core,*   For my heart is no longer my own

2:27   *Ma teco stassi in compagnia d'Amore;*   But stands with you in the company of Love;

["lui" emphasized]

2:35   *Chiedilo dunque a lui, s'intender brami,*   Ask of *it* then, if you wish to know,

2:42   *Quanto lieto gioisca, e quanto t'ami.*   How much happiness it enjoys, and how
                                                                much it loves you.
[soft cadence]

CHORUS

[happy imitation, duple meter]

60 (3) 2:59   *Lasciate i monti,*   Leave the hills,
                Lasciate i fonti,   Leave the streams,
                Ninfe vezzose e liete,   You charming and happy nymphs,

[same music]

3:09   *E in questi prati*   Practiced in dancing,
        Ai balli usati   And in these meadows
        Vago il bel pie rendete.   Move your pretty legs.

[change of key, homophony, triple meter]

3:18   *Qui miri il Sole*   Here the Sun
        Vostre carole   Sees your dances,
        Più vaghe assai di quelle,   More beautiful yet than those

[same music]

3:26   *Ond'a la Luna*   Which the stars dance
        La notte bruna   To the light of the moon
        Danzano in Ciel le stelle.   In dusky night.

INSTRUMENTAL RITORNELLO

3:33   Faster; recorders, strings, basso continuo

between people in the drama, while arias were reserved for contemplative or passionate moments when the composer wanted to explore the full emotional content of a situation. Recitative usually had simple basso continuo accompaniment; the arias were usually accompanied by full orchestra. The most common forms for arias were ABA form (the B section providing a contrast) and ground bass form, in which a single phrase in the bass is repeated over and over again while the voice sings an extended melody above it.

HENRY PURCELL AND ENGLISH OPERA

While music flourished in Italy, the state of music in England was highly fragmented because of an unstable political situation. The Civil War, which raged from 1642 to 1649, ended with the beheading of the constitutional monarch, Charles I. There followed a period called the Commonwealth, in which the Puritan ethic reigned. As a result, most musical positions were abolished, and theaters and opera houses were closed. In 1660, the son of Charles I returned from exile in France and assumed the throne as Charles II. His return, known as the Restoration, brought with it a rebirth of musical life in England.

Henry Purcell at the age of 36 (the year he died).

The most talented English composer of the late seventeenth century was Henry Purcell, who lived from 1659 to 1695. He held the important position of organist at Westminster Abbey in London and was one of the most prolific composers of his day. In his short life, Purcell wrote a large amount of vocal and instrumental music, including sacred music for the Anglican church, secular songs and cantatas, and chamber music for various combinations of instruments, as well as solo harpsichord music. His best-known work is a short opera called *Dido and Aeneas*, written in 1689.

Dido and Aeneas is a miniature masterpiece. It is based on a part of the great epic poem from antiquity, the *Aeneid* of Virgil. It tells the story of the love affair between Dido, Queen of Carthage, and Aeneas, a mythological Trojan warrior, and it ends with Aeneas's departure and Dido's death. There are three acts—with arias, recitatives, choruses, dances, and instrumental interludes—but only four main singers are required, together with a very small orchestra of strings and harpsichord. The whole opera takes only an hour.

The most famous aria from *Dido and Aeneas* is Dido's lament. Dido has been abandoned by Aeneas and has decided to kill herself. She expresses her determination, her grief, and the pathos of her situation in a deeply moving musical framework. The lament is a ground bass aria—that is, the entire melody is set over a repeated pattern in the bass. **(See Listening Guide on page 126.)**

SONATA AND CONCERTO

Along with the invention of opera, the other major development in the early Baroque was the rise of instrumental music. And the most important instruments were those of the violin family.

Some Italian towns specialized in the making of violins, violas, and cellos, and some makers became very famous. The instruments of Antonio Stradivari and Giuseppe Guarneri are considered the finest ever produced. A genuine "Strad" can be worth several hundred thousand dollars.

The favorite genres of violin music in the last part of the seventeenth century were the sonata and the concerto. A **sonata** was a chamber piece of several contrasting movements, written for a small number of instruments. It could be a **solo sonata**, for a single instrument with basso continuo, or a **trio sonata**, for two instruments and basso continuo. The basso continuo was usually made up of a harpsichord and a low string instrument, such as a cello. The cello would play the bass line and the harpsichord would double the bass line in the left hand and play chords or melodic figures in the right, frequently improvising over the

Gustav Holst, the twentieth-century English composer, called Purcell's *Dido and Aeneas* "the only perfect English opera ever written."

The beauties and graces that are practised on the violin are so great in number that they force listeners to declare the violin to be the king of instruments.
—From a book of instruments published in 1673.

125

Henry Purcell (1659–1695)
Dido's lament from the opera
Dido and Aeneas

Date of composition: 1689
Voice, strings, and harpsichord
Duration: 4:07

Student CD Collection: 1, track 61
Complete CD Collection: 2, track 4

*T*he aria is introduced by a short recitative ("Thy hand, Belinda …") that sets the stage for the emotional intensity of the aria. The recitative has a sparse accompaniment that moves steadily downward, reflecting Dido's grief.

Immediately after this recitative, the ground bass for the aria is heard alone. It is worth looking closely at this phrase, not only because it occurs so many times in the aria (11 times in all), but also because it is very carefully constructed, and the overall effect of the aria depends upon it.

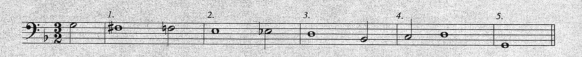

The first important element of this phrase is the fact that it descends chromatically (that is, by half steps). This chromatic descent immediately establishes a sad mood, which continues throughout the piece.

The next thing to notice is the rhythmic shift in the third and fourth measures of the phrase. This is a very subtle shift, but it is very important: it gives the bass line extra interest.

Finally, the ground bass pattern that Purcell establishes for this aria is five measures long, which is quite unusual. Most musical phrases are made up of four or eight measures. But Purcell chose this irregular length deliberately. It sets up a tension in the music, which contributes to the overall sense of strain and grief. It also enables Purcell to allow the vocal line more freedom as it floats over the ground bass. Throughout the aria, the endings of the ground bass pattern and the endings of the vocal phrases sometimes coincide and sometimes are independent. As the intensity increases, the vocal line becomes freer and freer from the constraint of the bass pattern. At the end of the aria, the voice and the ground bass cadence together, and the orchestra provides a short conclusion that is in keeping with the overall mood of the piece.

There are few words in this aria, but, as in most opera arias, they are repeated for dramatic effect. Arias are designed not to convey information or to further the plot but to explore an emotional state. The aria lasts much longer than the opening recitative. It is worth listening to this piece several times to appreciate the skill with which Purcell created it.

61 (4)	0:00	Thy hand, Belinda, darkness shades me,	[slowly descending voice throughout the recitative]
	0:19	On thy bosom let me rest.	
	0:29	More I would, but Death invades me:	
	0:40	Death is now a welcome guest.	[minor chord on "Death;" dissonance on "welcome guest"]
	0:54	[beginning of ground bass: quiet, slow, descending chromatic line heard throughout aria]	

62 (5)	1:08 (1:43)	When I am laid in earth,	[ground bass pattern begins again on "am"]
	1:20 (1:55)	May my wrongs create	[no pause between these two lines]
	1:27	No trouble in thy breast.	[voice falls on the word "trouble"]
	(2:02)	[repeat]	
63 (6)	2:17	Remember me, but ah! forget my fate.	[much repetition; highly expressive rising lines; last "ah" is particularly lyrical]
	2:42	[several repeats]	
	3:30	[cadences of voice and ground bass coincide]	
64 (7)	3:32	[quiet orchestral closing; conclusion of chromatic descent]	
	4:02	[final cadence with trill]	

bass. As in other Baroque music, a strong bass line remained a characteristic feature of Baroque chamber music.

Both the solo sonata and the trio sonata had several contrasting movements. If the movements were based on dance rhythms, the sonata was known as a **sonata da camera** ("chamber sonata"). The movements of a **sonata da chiesa** ("church sonata") were more serious in character.

Apart from the sonata, the favorite form of instrumental music in the Baroque era was the **concerto**.

This was a larger composition, meant for performance in greater spaces such as public halls, and it involved solo players and an orchestra.

The Italian word "concertare" has two meanings. It means to struggle or fight; it also means to cooperate. Both of these contrary meanings are present in a concerto, in which a solo player or a group of solo players is contrasted with an entire orchestra. Sometimes soloists and orchestra all play together, sometimes separately. Sometimes they play contrasting music, sometimes the same music. This dramatic balance and contrast of opposing forces is the essence of the concerto.

The concerto emerged about the end of the seventeenth century. The earliest concertos had a small group of soloists contrasting with the whole orchestra. This type of concerto is known as a **concerto grosso** ("large concerto"). The usual solo group was made up of two violins with basso continuo, but other instrumental groups were possible. The orchestra consisted of violins, violas, cellos, and basso continuo.

The **solo concerto** developed later. In a solo concerto a single soloist is contrasted with the whole orchestra, and the element of drama becomes particularly striking. It was the rise of the solo concerto that led to an increase in technically demanding playing and the **virtuoso** or "show-off" element that has been a characteristic of concertos ever since.

The composer who first brought Italian violin music to international prominence was Arcangelo Corelli (1653–1713). In his compositions, Corelli expanded the technique of violin playing, using repeated notes, fast scales, and double stops (playing more than one string at a time). He once wrote that the aim of his compositions was to "show off the violin." He concentrated entirely on violin music, writing only sonatas and concertos. Corelli was one of the first composers to become famous exclusively from instrumental music, and his compositions were highly influential throughout the remainder of the Baroque era and beyond. **(See Listening Guide on page 129.)**

FRENCH MUSIC

During the seventeenth century, while England was still racked by civil war, France was ruled by one of the most powerful monarchs in European history. Louis XIV reigned for an unusually long time, from 1643 to 1715, and his tastes governed French life for the entire second half of the seventeenth century and well into the eighteenth. Fortunately, Louis XIV was an avid supporter of the arts, and French music flourished under his patronage.

Louis XIV loved to dance, and one of the most important influences on French music was dance. It was featured prominently in French opera and French instrumental music throughout the seventeenth century. By the 1700s, French dances, which were elegant and dignified in their steps, had influenced instrumental music across the whole of Europe. One of the most popular French dances, the minuet, even became established as one of the standard movements of the eighteenth-century Classic symphony.

Dance influenced music in France in two ways. First, French opera included a great deal of ballet. Seventeenth-century French operas were splendid affairs, with elaborate scenery, large choruses, and frequent interludes for dancing. The most important composer of French opera was Jean-Baptiste Lully (1632–1687), the king's music director. Lully's ballet scenes were so popular that the dances from his operas were often played as independent suites. This popularity gave impetus to another trend that had begun late in the Renaissance: the use of dance forms purely as independent instrumental music.

A**ll** Europe knows what a Capacity and Genius the French have for dancing and how universally it is admired and followed.
—Luigi Riccoboni

Louis XIV himself!

Hyacinthe Rigaud (1659–1743). Louis XIV, King of France (1638–1715). Portrait in royal costume (the head was painted on a separate canvas and later added). Oil on canvas, 277 × 194 cm. Louvre, Dpt. des Peintures, Paris, France. © Photograph by Erich Lessing. Erich Lessing/Art Resource, NY.

A grand ball at the French court.

Formalized Baroque depictions of Hope and Fear. Opera singers were trained to depict emotion in highly stylized facial expressions and body gestures.

A Baroque instrumental concert. Notice the central position of the basso continuo players.

tinued to write both concerti grossi (for small group and orchestra) and solo concertos, but the solo concerto became more and more popular. Instruments such as the flute, the oboe, and the trumpet began to be featured in solo concertos. Composers even began to write concertos for keyboard instruments. This was quite revolutionary, because the role of keyboard instruments in concertos had previously been restricted to the basso continuo.

There were many concerto composers active at this time, but the undisputed master of the concerto in the late Baroque period was Antonio Vivaldi.

ANTONIO VIVALDI (1678–1741)

Vivaldi's father was a violinist at St. Mark's in Venice, where Gabrieli and Monteverdi had made their careers, and Antonio learned music at an early age. Like many young men in the Baroque era, Vivaldi trained for the priesthood as well. Because of his red hair, he earned the nickname "The Red Priest." Illness prevented him

THE LATE BAROQUE CONCERTO

By the beginning of the eighteenth century, the concerto had also become fixed in form. Composers con-

A seventeenth-century painting of spring.

A. Diziani. *La Primavera*. Padova, Museo Civico. Sala/Art Resource.

viola, and even mandolin. But most of his concertos are for one or more violins.

By the time of Vivaldi and the late Baroque period, concerto form had become clearly established. There are usually three movements, in the pattern fast–slow-fast. The first movement is usually an Allegro. The second movement usually has an expressive, slow melody that sounds like an opera aria. The third movement is a little faster and livelier than the first.

from continuing his priestly duties, however, and he soon began the job that would carry him through the remainder of his career: He was appointed director of music at the Ospedale della Pietà in Venice. This was a residential school for orphaned girls and young women, which combined basic education with religious training and placed a strong emphasis on music.

Vivaldi wrote a large amount of music for the Ospedale. The girls gave frequent concerts, and people traveled from all over Europe to hear them play. Among the composer's works are solo and trio sonatas, oratorios, sacred music, and nearly 600 concertos! Vivaldi wrote so much music that some of it has still not been published, and many of his pieces have

not been heard since he first wrote them.

Vivaldi must have been inspired by the special talents of the young women in his school, because several of his concertos are for instruments that were then not normally thought of as solo instruments: small recorder, clarinet, bassoon,

Portrait of Vivaldi in his mid-forties.

The first and third movements of a Baroque concerto are in **ritornello** form, which exploits the contrast

Picture of a concert at the Ospedale della Pietà in Venice, where Vivaldi spent most of his career. The girls are playing behind the screen of the organ loft.

Vivaldi was himself an accomplished violinist. A young German law student saw him playing in 1715 and recorded in his diary: "Vivaldi played an improvization that really frightened me. I doubt anything like it was ever done before, or ever will be again."

between the solo instrument(s) and the orchestra in a highly organized way. *Ritornello* is the Italian word for something that returns. The ritornello in a concerto is an orchestral passage that constantly returns. Between appearances of the ritornello, the solo instrument plays passages of contrasting material, which are known as episodes.

At the beginning of a movement in ritornello form, the orchestra plays the entire ritornello in the tonic, or home key. During the body of the movement, the ritornello often will appear only in partial form and will be in different keys, but at the end it will return in its entirety in the tonic key. The solo episodes occur between these appearances. (See accompanying diagram.)

Perhaps the most famous of Vivaldi's concertos today are a group of four concertos known as *The Four Seasons*. They were published in 1725, when Vivaldi was 47 years old. They show Vivaldi's wonderful sense of invention in the concerto medium and his extraordinary flexibility within this seemingly rigid form.

These are solo violin concertos; but in several of the solo episodes, other instruments from the orchestra join in, so that the sound sometimes approaches that of a concerto grosso. There is also constant variety in the handling of the ritornello form, both in the keys employed for the partial returns and in the choice of which part of the ritornello is used. Finally, the *Four Seasons* concertos are an early instance of **program music**—music that is designed to tell a story.

For *The Four Seasons*, Vivaldi wrote four concertos, one for each season of the year. At the head of each concerto, Vivaldi printed a poem describing the season. Beyond that, Vivaldi actually wrote lines from the poem directly into the musical score, so that each musical phrase for the instrumental players is directly tied to the poetic descriptions. For example, there are pas-

sages for thunder and lightning, for a dog barking, for birds singing. But even apart from the poetic texts, the concertos are wonderful examples of the late Baroque violin concerto in their own right. (**See Listening Guide on page 135.**)

The Baroque concerto may seem rather rigid, with its set pattern of movements and its strict ritornello form, but, like pieces such as Vivaldi's *Four Seasons* show, it could be handled with great flexibility to produce music of variety, color, and contrast.

Vivaldi's music was heard and his influence felt not only in his native Italy but throughout Europe. Vivaldi's concertos were studied in great detail and closely imitated by another of the great masters of the late Baroque era: Johann Sebastian Bach.

JOHANN SEBASTIAN BACH (1685–1750)

One of the most influential musicians of all time, and certainly one of the greatest composers in the history of music, was Johann Sebastian Bach. His mastery of musical composition is so universally acknowledged that the date of his death is used to mark the end of the entire Baroque era.

Bach's whole career was spent in one region of Germany. He moved from one small town to another as job opportunities arose. The last part of his life was spent in the somewhat larger town of Leipzig.

Bach did not see himself as an artistic genius, but rather as a hard-working craftsman. He wrote most of his music to order, or to fulfill the requirements of a job. During his life, he was not widely known outside the relatively small circle of his family and acquaintances, and he traveled very little. He never wrote an opera, although that was the most popular

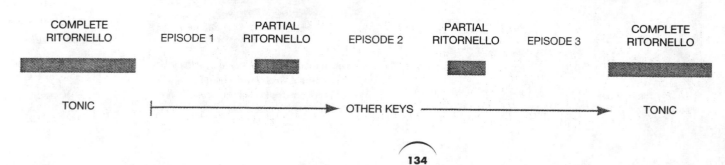

COMPLETE RITORNELLO	EPISODE 1	PARTIAL RITORNELLO	EPISODE 2	PARTIAL RITORNELLO	EPISODE 3	COMPLETE RITORNELLO
TONIC		OTHER KEYS				TONIC

Antonio Vivaldi (1678–1741)
First Movement from Violin Concerto,
    Op. 8, No. 1, *La Primavera* ("*Spring*"),
    from *The Four Seasons*

Date of composition: 1725
Solo violin, strings, and harpsichord
Duration: 3:34

Student CD Collection: 1, track 65
Complete CD Collection: 2, track 12

Like most late Baroque concertos, Vivaldi's *La Primavera* has three movements: fast-slow-fast. Both of the fast movements are in ritornello form and are in a major key (E Major). The slow movement has a long, lyrical melody and is in the minor. In both of the outer movements, instruments from the orchestra join the soloist in some of the solo episodes, giving the impression of a concerto grosso. Both movements are also full of echo effects. The orchestra is made up of first and second violins, violas, cellos, basses, and harpsichord. Like all the *Seasons*, "Spring" is headed by a poem in the form of a sonnet. A sonnet has eight lines of poetry followed by six lines. The six lines are divided into two groups of three. Vivaldi uses the first eight lines for the first movement and the two groups of three for the next two movements.

First movement
(First eight lines of the poem):

> Spring has arrived, and full of joy
> The birds greet it with their happy song.
> The streams, swept by gentle breezes,
> Flow along with a sweet murmur.
> Covering the sky with a black cloak,
> Thunder and lightning come to announce the season.
> When all is quiet again, the little birds
> Return to their lovely song.

The first movement is written in the bright and extroverted key of E Major. The ritornello is made up of two phrases, both of which occur at the beginning of the movement; all the other times, only the second half of the ritornello is played. Between these appearances, the solo violin plays brilliant passages, imitating birdsong and flashes of lightning. Sometimes it plays alone, and sometimes it is joined by two violins from the orchestra.

ALLEGRO		["fast"]	
65 (12)	0:00	"Spring has arrived, and full of joy"	[Ritornello in tonic, first half, loud and then soft]
	0:15		[Ritornello in tonic, second half, loud and then soft]

	0:32	"The birds greet it with their happy song."	[Trills; three solo violins alone, no basso continuo]
	1:08		[Ritornello in tonic, second half, once only, loud]
	1:16	"The streams, swept by gentle breezes, Flow along with a sweet murmur."	[Quiet and murmuring]
66 (13)	1:41		[Ritornello in dominant, second half, once only, loud]
	1:49	"Covering the sky with a black cloak, Thunder and lightning come to announce the season."	[Fast repeated notes; flashing runs and darting passages]
67 (14)	2:17		[Ritornello in C# minor, second half, once only, loud]
	2:25	"When all is quiet again, the little birds Return to their lovely song."	[Long, sustained, single note in bass; rising solo phrases, trills again]
	2:43		[Buildup to:
	3:10		Ritornello in tonic, second half twice, first loud and then soft]

View of Leipzig in Bach's time. The spire of St. Thomas's Church is at the center.

musical genre of the time, because his jobs never required it.

The first jobs Bach held were as church organist in the small towns of Arnstadt and Mühlhausen near his birthplace. At the age of 23, he married and found a better position at the court of the Duke of Weimar, first as organist and later as leader of the orchestra. He stayed there for nine years (until 1717), leaving finally when he was turned down for the position of music director. The Duke of Weimar was so angry at Bach's decision to leave that he had him put in jail for a month!

But Bach got the position he wanted at the court of a nearby prince. The Prince of Cöthen was young, unmarried, and an enthusiastic amateur musician. He kept a small orchestra of his own and made Bach music director. Here, Bach was very happy. He was well paid, he could write a range of varied music, and he was highly regarded by the prince.

In 1720, when Bach was 35, his wife Barbara died. He was married again the following year to a young singer, Anna Magdalena, who, like Bach, was employed at the court of the Prince of Cöthen. Over the years, Bach and his wives had twenty children. Eleven of them died in childhood, as was common in those days, but nine grew to adulthood, and four became famous composers in their own right.

Bach might have stayed at Cöthen for the rest of his life, but the prince also married at this time, and his

BU-204

and direct a new church cantata for every Sunday and feast day of the year. He was also head of the music school attached to St. Thomas's and was responsible for teaching Latin, composition, playing the organ, maintaining all the instruments, and preparing the choirs for the services at the three other main churches in Leipzig.

In 1747, Bach was asked to visit Frederick the Great, the powerful and autocratic King of Prussia. Like Louis XIV of France, Frederick loved music and employed several well-known musicians at his court. He also played the flute and composed a little flute music. One of Johann Sebastian Bach's sons, C. P. E. Bach, was the harpsichordist at Frederick's court. It was the younger Bach who was considered the more up-to-date

The sole surviving portrait of Johann Sebastian Bach.

Stadtgeschichtliches Museum Leipzig

new wife did not like music. The prince's support for Bach and his activities diminished, the orchestra was dismissed, and Bach started looking for a new job.

At this time, the town of Leipzig—a relatively large town with a university, two theaters, and a population of 30,000—was looking for a music director for its St. Thomas's Church. This position involved responsibility for all the town's church music, including that of St. Thomas's and three other churches.

The town council interviewed several musicians and finally settled on Bach as its third choice. (The first choice, composer Georg Philipp Telemann, turned them down, and the second man on the list was not permitted to leave his current post.) But third choice or not, Bach happily accepted the position and moved with his growing family to Leipzig in 1723, when he was 38 years old. He was to remain there for the rest of his life.

Bach was extremely busy in Leipzig. There were several aspects to his job, all of which he fulfilled cheerfully and efficiently. He was required to compose, rehearse,

A contemporary engraving of St. Thomas's Church and its school (left), where Bach worked for the last twenty-seven years of his life.

Frederick the Great playing the flute at a concert in his palace. Bach's son, C.P.E. Bach, is seated at the harpsichord.

composer. Johann Sebastian was known affectionately, but not very respectfully, as "Old Bach." By the middle of the eighteenth century, his music was regarded as old-fashioned and too complicated.

Bach died in 1750, leaving an unparalleled legacy to the musical world. Audiences ever since have been attracted to Bach's music for its careful organization, clear tonal direction, expressive nature, and intellectual brilliance. Bach himself saw his music as a means of supporting his family, instructing his fellow human beings, and glorifying God. For his sons and for his second wife, Anna Magdalena, he wrote books of short keyboard pieces. One book of organ pieces was written "for the instruction of my fellow men." And at the end of many of his compositions, he wrote the letters "S. D. G.," which stand for "Soli Deo Gloria" ("For the Glory of God Alone").

Bach was also exceedingly modest. Toward the end of his life, he said, "I was obliged to work hard. But anyone who is equally industrious will succeed just as well." Family man, teacher, good citizen, humble and pious spirit, Johann Sebastian Bach was also one of the musicians in history on whom we can unhesitatingly bestow the title "genius."

Musical Imitations

Bach's roles as teacher and performer during his years at Leipzig were extremely time-consuming. In addition, he was required to compose regularly. To save time, Bach sometimes reworked existing compositions (both his own and those of other composers) into new pieces. This process has come to be known as "imitation" technique. ✦ "Imitations" can be found both in Bach's instrumental and in his vocal compositions. One of Bach's crowning achievements, written near the end of his life, is the Mass in B minor, much of which consists of movements from his earlier cantatas. Bach welds a diverse range of compositions into a magnificent whole. One scholar has said that the B minor Mass demonstrates that Bach's technique of imitation, adaptation, and compilation must itself be accepted as "a creative act almost on a par with what we normally think of as 'original composition.'" ✦ In 1729, in addition to all his other activities, Bach was appointed director of the Collegium Musicum in Leipzig. During his years directing the Collegium, Bach produced 14 harpsichord concertos. Only one of these, however, was an original work. Most of them are brilliant reworkings of violin concertos by another great eighteenth-century composer: Antonio Vivaldi.

A Musical Offering

In May 1747, Bach traveled to Potsdam, near Berlin, to visit Frederick the Great of Prussia. He displayed his extraordinary skills of improvisation in the presence of the king, and as a result Frederick presented him with a theme to be used as the basis for a composition. When heard alone, the theme seems extremely unpromising. ✦ It is a testimony to Bach's brilliance as a composer that on his return home, he managed to work this theme into an extended and impressive series of pieces, which he entitled *A Musical Offering* and sent with a florid dedication to Frederick the Great. ✦ *A Musical Offering* consists of two fugues, 10 canons (rounds), and a trio sonata. Each of the 13 pieces uses Frederick's theme. The unity that this provides is complemented by the wide variety of canonic procedures employed. These include conventional canons, a canonic fugue, a canon in contrary motion, puzzle canons, and a "crab" canon, in which one player starts at the beginning of the piece and works forward, while the other starts at the end and works backward! Bach's skill and ingenuity in *A Musical Offering* confirm his status as the greatest composer of counterpoint in the history of music.

BACH'S MUSIC

Bach wrote in all the Baroque era's major musical genres, with the exception of opera. His works range from the monumental to the miniature, and they include both sacred and secular music. Every piece is marked by the same careful and faultless construction, the same unerring sense of direction and timing. The Baroque values of rhythmic drive and emotional intensity are vividly present in his compositions. His simple chorale harmonizations are magisterial models for students of harmony. Bach was also an unparalleled master of counterpoint, and composers ever since have studied his works to learn how to combine independent musical lines with conviction and clarity.

The types of music Bach wrote at different periods in his life depended on the kind of job he held at the time. In his early years, he primarily wrote organ music. At the court of the Prince of Cöthen, Bach mostly wrote for keyboard, or for orchestra and other instrumental groups. During the Leipzig years, he produced a large amount of church music, as well as more instrumental compositions.

BACH'S ORGAN MUSIC

Bach's organ music is extremely varied. It includes settings of Lutheran chorales, organ trio sonatas, and preludes and fugues. The chorales are either set in harmony for organ or used as the basis for a series of variations. In the organ trio sonatas, the right hand plays one line, the left hand plays another, and the pedals of the organ are used for the basso continuo.

The prelude and fugue contrast a free type of music

Johann Sebastian Bach (1685–1750)
Prelude and Fugue in E minor

Date of composition: before 1708
Solo organ
Duration: 4:13

Complete CD Collection: 2, track 15

*B*ach, both an accomplished organist and an accomplished composer, makes full use of the organ in his Prelude and Fugue in E minor as well as in his other organ works. In the Prelude and Fugue in E minor, Bach displays the capabilities of both the foot-operated pedal keyboard (which plays the lowest-sounding notes) and the hand-operated keyboard (known as a "manual"). Organs usually have more than one keyboard on which the performer can play different sounds. Changes in timbre can also be produced by pulling and pushing on knobs (known as "stops"). These stops may be used not only to change timbre but also to add an additional line in parallel octaves to the notes (particularly in the pedal keyboard). The common phrase "pulling out all the stops" comes from organ playing.

Changes in timbre are quite evident in this recording. In the Prelude, the first long pedal low note is pure, simple, and flutey. Then the organist pulls out a stop to make the subsequent pedal notes richer and fuller. In the fugue, the organist uses the stops to set up what seem like two different instruments, one with an oboe-like sound and one with a clarinet-like sound. These instruments then compete with each other throughout the piece.

The theme or subject in the fugue is characterized by a special rhythm (dit diddle-DEE, dit diddle-DEE) that makes it easily recognizable.

PRELUDE		
(15)	0:00	Free-flowing music over sustained, soft, low pedal
	0:23	Timbre change; fanfare-like music with flourishes
	0:46	Pedal line alternating with keyboards
	0:55	Switches to top line answered by other voices
	1:10	Music gets "chunky," almost like a slow polka
	1:27	"Chunks" separated by climbing pedal line
	1:44	Pedals and manuals combine for full ending of Prelude

(16)	2:08	First entry of fugue subject (dit diddle-DEE, dit diddle-DEE); instrumental effects created by different stops
	2:14	Second entry of subject (slightly lower)
	2:25	Third entry (high); the other lines are still playing
	2:34	Fourth entry
	2:45	Fifth entry (!) on pedals (in octaves)
	2:54	Change of texture; intervening passage with sixteenth notes
	3:07	Low entry; pedals return to accompany
	3:24	High section with entries spaced out
	3:37	Light section; no pedals
	3:58	Final entry on pedals; the big finale

with a very strict type. The prelude (sometimes called "toccata" or "fantasia") is a rambling, improvisatory piece of the kind that organists play to fill in time before, during, or after a church service. The **fugue** is a carefully worked-out polyphonic composition, that uses a theme (or "subject") that occurs in all the voices, or musical lines, in turn. It begins with a single voice playing the subject unaccompanied. As the second voice brings in the fugue subject, the first one continues playing—and so on, until all the voices are sounding independently. A fugue may have two, three, or four voices. After visiting Frederick the Great, Bach wrote one fugue that has six voices.

Bach was a master of counterpoint, and the fugue is the most demanding type of counterpoint to write. **(See Listening Guide above.)**

BACH'S KEYBOARD, INSTRUMENTAL, AND ORCHESTRAL MUSIC

During his years at the Cöthen court, Bach produced a large amount of music for solo keyboard, other solo in-

struments, and small orchestra. In this music particularly, Bach melded the characteristics of Italian, French, and German styles. Italian music had rhythmic drive and brilliance. French music favored dance forms and ornament. German music was serious and contrapuntal. Bach drew on all these elements to produce an individual style that was the high point of the Baroque era.

Bach wrote much solo music, perhaps inspired by the fine players at the prince's court. There are suites and sonatas for solo violin and solo harpsichord, suites for solo cello, and a suite for solo flute. He also composed several sonatas and trio sonatas.

From the Cöthen years come a large number of orchestral compositions. These include some suites for orchestra, as well as several concertos, including the famous *Brandenburg* Concertos. **(See Listening Guide on page 142.)**

BACH'S VOCAL CHURCH MUSIC

During Bach's stay in Leipzig, he wrote hundreds of cantatas for church services, as well as several other im-

Johann Sebastian Bach (1685–1750)
First Movement from *Brandenburg*
   Concerto No. 2 in F Major

Date of composition: 1721
Instruments: Solo recorder, oboe, horn,
   and violin; with strings and continuo
Tempo: *Allegro*
Key: F Major
Duration: 5:12

Complete CD Collection: 2, track 17

Bach completed the six *Brandenburg* Concertos for the Margrave of Brandenburg in 1721. They show a fusion of national styles, as well as Bach's brilliant mixture of melody and counterpoint.

The *Brandenburg* Concerto No. 2 is in three movements (fast-slow-fast), contrasting solo and ripieno (full ensemble) groups. Bach also explores coloristic possibilities within the solo group (recorder, oboe, horn, and violin) in various combinations of solos, duets, trios, and quartets throughout. Although this piece is often played with flute and trumpet, the word "flute" usually meant recorder in Bach's time, and an early manuscript copy of the score calls for "either trumpet or horn."

The first movement features three rhythmic motives, which combine to form the ritornello:

   a.   mixture of eighth notes and sixteenth notes:

   b.   eighth notes, triadic:

   c.   sixteenth notes, running:

The ways in which these ideas are re-combined, sorted and re-sorted, and moved from one instrument to another, and the ways in which Bach organizes his harmonies and textures are nothing short of astounding.

I		[opening section]
(17)	**0:00**	Ritornello (Tonic: F Major), motives "a," "b," and "c" together
	0:20	Violin solo
	0:25	Ritornello
	0:31	Duet (violin and oboe)
	0:37	Horn solo
	0:41	Duet (recorder and oboe), followed by horn
	0:51	Duet (horn and recorder)
	0:57	Continuation

II		[second section]
(18)	**1:12**	Solo quartet, accompanied by continuo, based on "c"
	1:22	Sequences (fragment of "b"), horn answered by oboe; harmonic modulation
	1:40	Dynamic "echoes" (loud sections followed by soft); based on "a" and "c"

III		[episode]
(19)	**2:07**	Continuing to modulate, steady eighth notes in bass, reaching:
	2:22	Ritornello in B-flat Major
	2:32	Duet (recorder and violin), joined by oboe and horn
(20)	**2:53**	Ritornello, C minor; motive "c" now prominent on top
	3:03	Another harmonically unstable section
	3:16	More sequences between horn and oboe, modulating to:
	3:24	G minor, ritornello
	3:35	Constant changes of texture and harmony (basses get motive "a"!); cadence

		[closing section]
(21)	4:24	Surprise! Everyone in unison on motive "a"; back to home key of F Major
	4:35	Another surprise! One last harmonic excursion
	5:02	Return to original texture
	5:07	Return to original key and ritornello

portant sacred vocal pieces. These include motets, Passions, and the Mass in B minor, which is regarded as one of the greatest traditional Mass settings that has ever been composed.

Bach wrote two Passions for the Lutheran churches of Leipzig. (A third is rumored to exist but has never been found.) A **Passion** is a musical setting of the story from the Gospels of the death and resurrection of Jesus. Bach based one setting on the account in the Gospel of St. John, and the other setting on the account in the Gospel of St. Matthew. Although Bach's musical legacy is full of masterpieces, the *St. Matthew Passion* is universally regarded as one of the most monumental musical masterpieces of all time. It is a huge composition, lasting some three hours, for solo singers, two choruses, one boys' choir, two orchestras, and two organs, and it runs the gamut of human emotion, from grief to awe to despair to spiritual transcendence. With this work alone, Bach shows us how music can reflect and deepen the meaning of human existence. **(See Listening Guide on page 145.)**

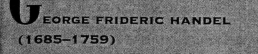

GEORGE FRIDERIC HANDEL (1685–1759)

Although Handel's life overlapped Bach's almost exactly, their careers were remarkably different. As we have seen, Bach lived a quiet, busy life in one small region of Germany. By contrast, Handel traveled extensively and became an international celebrity. Although the central musical genre of the Baroque era was opera, Bach wrote no operas. Handel's career was built on the nearly 40 operas he wrote, mostly for the London stage. Bach was a family man; Handel never married.

Handel was born in Halle, a small town in Germany. His family was not musical, and his father wanted him to study law. He was so obviously gifted in music, however, that he was allowed to study with the music director and organist of the local church. He learned to play the organ, the harpsichord, and the violin, and he studied counterpoint and composition. Handel studied law at the University of Halle for only a year and then left for Hamburg, which was the main center of opera in Germany. He joined the opera orchestra there as a violinist and harpsichordist. At the age of 19, Handel composed his first opera, which was performed at the Hamburg opera house.

Because most operas at this time were Italian operas, Handel decided to travel to Italy, to the center of operatic activity. At 21, he was still only a young man, but he scored a phenomenal success there.

After three years in Italy, Handel was appointed music director to the Elector of Hanover, back in Germany. This was a well-paid position, but Handel was restless. He kept requesting leaves of absence to travel to London, which was fast becoming one of the most important musical centers in the world. In 1712, Handel was granted a short leave to London, which he greatly overstayed, ultimately turning it into a lifelong visit.

Portrait of Handel in his middle years.

Anonymous. Portrait of G. F. Handel. Civico Museo Bibliografico Musicale Rossini, Bologna, Italy. Giraudon/Art Resource, NY.

He made important contacts in London and soon became the favorite of the queen. An embarrassing situation arose two years later, when the queen died, and the Elector of Hanover, Handel's former employer, whose generosity he had exploited, became George I of England. It is said that Handel won his way back into favor by composing his famous *Water Music* suite for a party King George was having on the river Thames. Whether or not this story is true, the king employed Handel again, as he had in Hanover; he was given a sizable salary and was soon composing, conducting at court, and teaching the king's granddaughters. Certainly the king and Handel had much in common. They were both foreigners in England, and they both spoke English with a strong German accent. A contemporary writer made fun of Handel's accent by reporting that one day when there was only a small turnout for one of his concerts, Handel said to the musicians, "Nevre moind; de moosic vil sound de petter."

Handel spent the remainder of his career in London. He was an amazingly prolific composer, a clever politician, and a tough businessman. He made and lost a great deal of money, loved food and drink, and had a quick temper and a broad sense of humor. A contemporary said that "no man ever told a story with more humor than Handel." He was at the center of English musical developments (and rivalries) for 40 years. And in the end, he became an institution. The British people today still regard Handel as an English composer. He is buried in Westminster Abbey—an honor reserved for great English notables such as Chaucer, Queen Elizabeth I, and Charles Dickens.

During his London years (from 1712 until his death in 1759), Handel was involved mainly with opera and oratorio, though he wrote a great deal of other music as well.

Italian opera was very fashionable in London until the 1730s, when public taste began to change. It was at this time that Handel turned his attention to oratorio.

The idea of a musical Bible story sung in English appealed to the English audience. Oratorio was also much less expensive to produce than opera. It was sung on the concert stage and required no costumes, no complicated machinery or lights, and no scenery. Handel's first oratorio was *Saul*, produced in 1739. But his first real success came with *Messiah* in 1741. This soon became his most popular work and remains one of his most frequently performed compositions today. After this, Handel's oratorios became the mainstay of the London concert scene. They were performed during Lent, when opera was not allowed anyway, and they

The writer Dr. Samuel Johnson called Italian opera an "exotic and irrational entertainment." Another critic dubbed it "nonsense well-tun'd."

attracted large audiences, especially from the prosperous middle class, which had always regarded Italian opera with suspicion or disdain. A special feature of Handel's oratorio performances was the appearance of the composer himself playing organ concertos during the intermission.

Toward the end of his life, Handel became blind, but he continued to perform on the organ and to compose by dictation. When he died, 3,000 people turned out for his funeral. He had become a British citizen many years earlier, and the British people had taken him completely into their hearts.

HANDEL'S MUSIC

Handel's music is attractive and easy to listen to. It appeals to a wide range of people because it sounds simple and tuneful. Handel's is the "art that hides art." The skill and brilliant craftsmanship of his music are hidden under the attractive exterior.

Curiously, most people today do not know the compositions on which Handel spent most of his time and for which he was best known in his own day: his Italian operas. These portray events of dramatic and emotional intensity. The main musical forms are the standard ones of opera seria: recitative and aria.

As you read earlier, Baroque arias are usually built in ABA form, with ornaments on the return of the A section. This kind of aria is known as a **da capo** ("from the beginning") aria, because after the B section the composer simply has to write the words "da capo" in the score, and the singer can improvise the embellishments for the repeat of the A section.

Handel's opera *Giulio Cesare* (*Julius Caesar*) was written in 1724 at the height of his involvement with opera. It is based on the story of Caesar and Cleopatra in Egypt. In the opera, Caesar falls in love with Cleopatra and joins forces with her against Ptolemy, King of Egypt. (Baroque operas are full of women controlling men by means of their sexual attractiveness.) In the end, Ptolemy is defeated and Cleopatra is crowned Queen of Egypt.

The excerpt we shall study comes from the third act of the opera, during a temporary setback for Caesar.

After a shipwreck, he is cast up on the shore where his army has been defeated in a battle. He laments his defeat, the loss of his troops, and his separation from Cleopatra.

Handel here deliberately manipulates the conventions of opera seria in order to inject more drama and realism into the situation. What the audience would expect at this point in the opera is a recitative followed by an aria. What Handel does is to begin the scene with "breezy" music—wafting figures on the strings that are appropriate to Caesar's words later in the scene when he calls upon the breezes to soothe him. Then comes recitative *accompagnato*, recitative that is accompanied

The monument to Handel in Westminster Abbey in London.

GEORGE FREDERICK HANDEL Efq.
born February XXIII. MDCLXXXIV.
died April XIV MDCCLIX. *L.F.Roubiliac invt et sct*

by the orchestra to create a more dramatic effect. Finally, the aria starts, with its "breezy" music. All goes conventionally for a while; the A section of the aria continues. Then comes the B section ("Dite, dite dov'è,"—"Tell me, tell me where she is"). But at the point where everyone in the audience would expect the return of the A section (remember, the standard format is ABA), Handel interposes another accompanied recitative ("Mà, d'ogni intorno,"— "But all around me"), which dramatically reflects Caesar's state of mind at his unfortunate situation. It is as though Caesar's reflections are suddenly interrupted by the terrible sight of his surroundings. Handel breaks through the operatic conventions of his time to make his music correspond naturally to the psychological realism of the story. (**See Listening Guide on page 149.**)

Today, Handel's popularity rests mainly on his oratorios. And even in his own time, the oratorios appealed to a very wide public. Why have they always been so popular? First, and most important, the words are in English. Even in the eighteenth century, much of the audience for Italian operas couldn't understand most of the words. Second, the stories are from the Bible (mostly the Old Testament), which was familiar to everyone in those days. Behind the stories, there were political implications as well: references, for example, to the military triumphs and prosperity of Georgian England. Finally, oratorios were less of an aristocratic, snobbish, social event than operas and thus had wider appeal.

The music of Handel's oratorios is vigorous and appealing. It is not so different from the music of his operas. There are recitatives and arias, just as there are in operas. But the main difference is in the choral writing.

Choruses are very rare in late Baroque opera, but they are central to Handel's oratorios. Some of the greatest moments in the oratorios come in the choral pieces, when the chorus comments on the action or summarizes the feelings of the people. Perhaps the best known of Handel's choruses is the "Halleluyah" chorus from *Messiah*.

Messiah was composed in 1741 and soon became the composer's most famous work. It was written in the unbelievably short time of just over three weeks. As he was composing it, Handel said, "I did think I did see all Heaven before me and the great God himself."

Messiah is in three parts, which last some 2½ hours altogether. The music is made up throughout of recitatives, arias, and choruses. The famous "Halleluyah" chorus closes Part II. (**See Listening Guide on page 152.**)

Handel was also an accomplished composer of instrumental music. His two most famous instrumental suites are the *Water Music* and *Music for the Royal Fireworks*.

Handel's music is less complex than that of Bach, with more focus on melody than on counterpoint, and he deliberately appealed to a wider audience than had been traditional. Music was becoming less the preserve of the wealthy and more the delight of everyone who cared to listen.

Hospital for the Maintenance and Education of exposed and deserted young Children.

THIS is to give Notice, that towards the Support of this Charity, the Sacred Oratorio, called,

MESSIAH,

Will be performed in the Chapel of this Hospital, under the Direction of George Frederick Handel, Esq; on Thursday next, the 27th inst. at twelve o'clock at Noon precisely; and, to prevent the Chapel being crowded, no more Tickets will be delivered than it can conveniently hold; which are ready to be had of the Steward of the Hospital; at Arthur's Chocolate-house in St. James's Street ; at Batson's Coffee-house in Cornhill; and at Tom's Coffee-house in Devereux-Court, at Half a Guinea each.   T. COLLINGWOOD, Secretary.

Notice In London newspaper advertising a performance of Handel's Messiah.

Courtesy of the Library of Congress.

An English writer in the eighteenth century complained that the opera house was more of a social than a musical event: "There are some who contend that the singers might be very well heard if the audience was more silent, but it is so much the fashion to consider the Opera as a place of rendezvous and visiting that they do not seem in the last to attend to the music."

George Frideric Handel (1685–1759)
"Halleluyah" Chorus from *Messiah*

Date of composition: 1741
Chorus and orchestra
Duration: 3:49

Student CD Collection: 2, track 8
Complete CD Collection: 2, track 33

*T*he "Halleluyah" chorus comes as the climax of Part II of *Messiah*. In it Handel displays extraordinary ingenuity in combining and contrasting all the possible textures available to him: unison, homophonic, polyphonic, and imitative. In setting the word "Halleluyah" itself, he also uses a tremendous variety of different *rhythms*. Finally, much of the strength of the movement comes from its block alternation of simple tonic and dominant harmonies, as well as its triumphant use of trumpets and drums. The jubilant feeling is immediately evident and is a direct reflection of the text: "Halleluyah" is a Hebrew word that means "Praise God."

The text itself is treated in two ways:

1. Declamatory statements (e.g., "For the Lord God omnipotent reigneth") characterized by longer note values and occasional unison singing.
2. Contrapuntal responses (e.g., "forever and ever, halleluyah, halleluyah"), characterized by faster notes, and offering musical and textual commentary on the declamatory statements.

The "Halleluyah" chorus falls into nine relatively symmetrical sections, each featuring a single texture or combination of textures.

8 (33)	**0:00**	Instrumental opening ("pre-echo").

HOMOPHONIC

[Two phrases, each with five statements of "Halleluyah." Notice the changing rhythms.]

	0:07	First phrase, tonic.
	0:16	Second phrase, dominant.

UNISON

[With homophonic "halleluyah" responses: "For the Lord God omnipotent reigneth."]

	0:25	First phrase, dominant.
	0:37	Second phrase, tonic.

POLYPHONIC

9 (34)	**0:49**	Statement by sopranos, tonic.
	0:56	Statement by tenors and basses, dominant.
	1:05	Statement by tenors and altos, tonic.
	1:14	Short instrumental interlude.

HOMOPHONIC

[With noticeable change in dynamics: two phrases, one soft (*piano*), one loud (*forte*).]

1:16   *piano:* "The kingdom of this world is become ..."

1:27   *forte:* "... the kingdom of our God and of His Christ."

IMITATION

[Four entries, "And He shall reign forever and ever."]

10 (35)   1:38   Basses, tonic.

1:43   Tenors in counterpoint with basses, dominant.

1:49   Altos in counterpoint with basses and tenors, tonic.

1:55   Sopranos in counterpoint with all other voices, dominant.

UNISON

[Three declamatory statements ("King of Kings and Lord of Lords") against homophonic responses ("forever and ever, halleluyah, halleluyah"), each at a different pitch, moving higher and higher.]

11 (36)   2:01   Sopranos and altos, answered by other voices.

POLYPHONIC

[Two statements of "And he shall reign forever and ever," against contrapuntal responses ("and he shall reign . . .").]

2:42   Basses, dominant.

2:48   Sopranos, tonic.

UNISON/ HOMOPHONIC

[Combination of unison and homophonic textures—"King of Kings" . . . ("forever and ever") "and Lord of Lords" . . . ("halleluyah, halleluyah").]

2:54   Tenors, answered by other voices.

HOMOPHONIC

[Statements by all voices.]

3:03   "And He shall reign forever and ever."

3:10   "King of Kings and Lord of Lords" (twice).

3:19   "And he shall reign forever and ever."

[Final statement of "King of Kings and Lord of Lords."]

3:26   Tenors and sopranos, answered by other voices.

3:34   Pause; one final drawn-out homophonic statement: plagal cadence (IV–I).

It was during the Baroque era that many elements of what we recognize today as "classical" music were formed. These include regular patterns of meter and a formalized hierarchy of keys and chord progressions. Instrumental music came to be regarded on a par with vocal forms, and two influential instrumental genres – the sonata and the concerto – were established.

The great new musical invention of the Baroque era was opera. Opera brought together all the arts, combining carpentry and painting (for the scenery), costume design, dramatic acting, instrumental music, and, of course, beautiful singing, into one superb spectacle. The main topics of Baroque opera were stories from Classical antiquity – from Greek and Roman myths or history. And the principal vocal forms used in opera were recitative and aria.

Recitatives are relatively simple, with sparse accompaniment and with flexible and irregular rhythms designed to imitate speech. They are designed for dialogue and for moving the story along. Arias occur when the action stops and a character expresses his or her emotional reaction to the situation. Arias are lyrical and expressive; they can be about love or rage or grief, and they are the emotional high points of the music.

The most common form for arias is ABA form. The central (B) section offers a contrast, and the return of the A section can provide an opportunity for the singer to ornament the melody. In the Baroque period, audiences liked to hear high voices on the great arias, so the male roles were usually sung by castratos, whose voices were as high as those of the women.

The development of instrumental music was helped along by the great skill of the Italian makers and players of stringed instruments, especially the violin. Sonatas and concertos for violins are the most important instrumental works of the Baroque era. Sonatas were composed for one violin and basso continuo (solo sonata) or for two violins and basso continuo (trio sonata). Since the basso continuo is usually played by both a keyboard and a low stringed instrument, the solo sonata is performed by three players and the trio sonata by four.

Concertos exploit the Baroque love of contrast. They employ many different types of contrast, between loud and soft, fast and slow, and fiery and lyrical; however, the most important contrast is between the sound of the solos and that of the whole orchestra. There may be a small group of solo players (usually from two to four) or a single soloist. In the outer (first and third) movements of a Baroque concerto, the contrast is made explicit by using ritornello form.

An early print of an aria from Purcell's *Dido and Aeneas*.

Chapter 9

The Classic Era: 1750–1800

THE EARLY CLASSIC PERIOD

Although the end of the Baroque era is generally given as 1750 (the date of Bach's death), the origins of the Classic style date from earlier than that. Starting about 1730, a new musical style began to appear that was lighter, more accessible, more varied, and less demanding. The name given to this musical style at the time was *galant*, which we might translate as "fashionable" or "up-to-date." Two of the composers involved in this stylistic change were Bach's sons: C. P. E. Bach, who was at the court of Frederick the Great in Berlin, and J. C. Bach, who made his career in London. Other important composers of this early Classic style were Johann Stamitz in Mannheim and Giovanni Battista Sammartini (1701–1775) in Italy.

These composers rejected the dense contrapuntal style of the late Baroque era in favor of music that was lighter in texture, easier to listen to, and more varied. Early Classic music has far more variety than Baroque music. There are frequent changes of texture, of dynamics, of instrumentation. The phrases are shorter, and each phrase may be quite different from the one that precedes it.

Many early Classic compositions have three movements instead of four because the minuet did not become a standard feature of sonatas and symphonies until the second half of the eighteenth century.

THE CLASSIC MASTERS

The masters of the Classic style were Haydn and Mozart. Since their own time, these two composers have been regarded as the most accomplished among a large number of highly skilled musicians active in the second half of the eighteenth century. Both men were extraordinarily prolific, completing many hundreds of superb compositions during their lifetimes. Although the musical language and techniques they used were common throughout Europe at the time, their individual abilities were so remarkable, their grasp of harmony, form, and expression so assured, and their melodic invention so rich that they stand out from their contemporaries. Both men were so fluent in music and created so many masterpieces that they may rightly be regarded as among the greatest geniuses of the age.

FRANZ JOSEPH HAYDN (1732–1809)

Anyone can see that I'm a good-natured fellow.
—Haydn

Haydn was born in a small village in Austria. His father was a wheelmaker—an important trade in the eighteenth century—and Haydn was one of 12 children. There was much music-making at home and in the village, and Haydn displayed an early talent for music. At the age of eight, he was accepted as a choirboy at St. Stephen's Cathedral in Vienna, the biggest city in the Austrian empire. Here he stayed until he was 18, when his voice changed. (In those days, the onset of puberty

Above: Haydn at 60.

Below: Mozart at 33.

Haydn in full dress.

[I was never so devout as when I was at work on *The Creation*. —Haydn]

Haydn's Contract

When Haydn was appointed to the Esterházy court, his contract was very specific about his duties. He was required to dress "as befits an honest house officer in a princely court," that is, with brocaded coat, powdered wig, white stockings, and silver buckles on his shoes. He was to be in charge of all the musicians, serve as an example to them, and "avoid undue familiarity with them in eating and drinking or in other relations, lest he should lose the respect due to him." He was responsible for looking after all the music and the instruments. And he was required to compose music as the prince demanded, and forbidden to give away or sell copies of his music or compose for anyone else "without the knowledge and gracious permission of his Serene Princely Highness." ◆

Haydn was quite content with this arrangement. He said later: "My Prince was happy with all my works; I received approval; I could, as head of an orchestra, make experiments in my music. I was cut off from the world: there was no one to confuse or annoy me, and I was forced to become original."

for both boys and girls was many years later than it is today.)

While he was at the cathedral, he had learned to play the harpsichord and the violin, so for the next 10 years (about 1750 to 1760) Haydn made a living giving harpsichord lessons and playing in local orchestras. During this time, he lived in a small room in an apartment building in Vienna. Luckily for him, some of the grander apartments were occupied by people who became very useful in furthering his career. One was Pietro Metastasio, the most famous poet and opera librettist (opera text writer) of his time; Metastasio introduced Haydn to many prominent figures in the musical world. Another was a woman who was the head of one of the most prominent aristocratic families of the time. Her name was Maria Esterházy, and the Esterházy family was to play a significant role in Haydn's life and career.

In 1761, Haydn was hired as assistant music director to the household of Prince Paul Anton Esterházy. The prince had a sizable retinue of servants, including a small orchestra of about 12 players. Haydn was responsible for composing music on demand, supervising and rehearsing the other musicians, and caring for the instruments.

Prince Paul Anton died in 1762 and was succeeded by his brother Nikolaus. Prince Nikolaus Esterházy was an avid music lover who spent a great deal of money on his court and entertainment. In the countryside, Prince Nikolaus built a magnificent palace that had two large music rooms and two small theaters for opera. He called this palace Esterháza after the family name.

In 1766 Haydn was promoted to music director at Esterháza. He was responsible for directing all the music at the palace. There were usually two full operas as well as two big concerts given each week. Extra concerts were put on whenever an important visitor came to the palace. Music was performed at meals, and the prince had chamber music played in his own rooms almost every day. Haydn wrote much of this music himself.

Over the course of his lifetime, Haydn wrote about a dozen operas, more than 100 symphonies, nearly 70

Left: The palace of Esterháza, where Haydn spent most of his life.

Below: The music room in the palace of Esterháza.

string quartets, more than 50 keyboard sonatas, and a large amount of choral music, songs, and other chamber music. Haydn stayed in the service of the Esterházy family until 1790, when Prince Nikolaus died. The new prince, Nikolaus II, did not like music and disbanded the orchestra. Haydn, now nearly 60, moved back to Vienna.

By this time, his work was internationally known, and he traveled twice to London—first from 1791 to 1792, then from 1794 to 1795. For his visits to London, Haydn wrote his last 12 symphonies, brilliant and fascinating works, which were performed there to wild public acclaim. They are known as the *London Symphonies.*

In his late years, back in Vienna, Haydn wrote mostly string quartets and vocal music. His quartets are varied and masterful, covering the entire range of expression from playfulness to profundity. The vocal works include six Mass settings for chorus and orchestra and the two great oratorios of his last years, *The Creation* (1798) and *The Seasons* (1801).

Haydn died in 1809 at the age of 77. His reputation transcended even national disputes. Vienna was under siege by the French army at the time, but Napoleon posted a guard of honor outside Haydn's house to pay homage to the greatest composer of the age.

HAYDN'S MUSIC

For a long time, Haydn's music was regarded as genial and lively, and much of its depth, wit, and brilliance went unnoticed. This was because only a few of his compositions were performed regularly at concerts. Nowadays, however, much more of Haydn's music is being performed, and the extraordinary range of his achievement is being recognized.

His operas are full of beautiful music—lyrical, inventive, and moving. His symphonies range from ceremonious public works with trumpets and drums to compositions of great delicacy, charm, and even tragedy. The string quartets explore an enormous range of expression, with a masterful handling of the intimate medium and brilliant writing for the four instruments. The early quartets usually give most of the melodic material to the first violin, but in the later quartets the other instruments are more fully integrated, with each of the four players contributing much to the discourse. When the great German poet Goethe compared a string quartet to a conversation among four equally interesting individuals, he must have been thinking of the Haydn quartets.

The Haydn Masses are noble, grand structures, combining a conservative choral style appropriate to the traditional texts with his own individual orchestral

LISTENING GUIDE

Franz Joseph Haydn (1732–1809)
Minuet and Trio from Symphony No. 45
** in F-sharp minor**

Date of composition: 1772
Orchestration: 2 oboes, 2 horns, violins
  I and II, viola, cello, double bass
Tempo: *Allegretto* ("Moderately fast")
Meter: $\frac{3}{4}$
Key of movement: F♯ Major
Duration: 4:53

Student CD Collection: 2, track 12
Complete CD Collection: 2, track 40

We studied a fairly simple minuet and trio in the Listening chapter at the beginning of this book. This movement is more fascinating and complex. Understanding its many levels can take dozens of repeated hearings, and yet it is also graceful and lively, and a pleasure to listen to.

Among the standard features of minuet form and style—a fixed pattern of repetition, triple meter, moderate tempo—Haydn has incorporated several others that make this particular minuet unique. The most striking is the amount of contrast he has written into this piece. There is contrast of dynamics, texture, instrumentation, and key.

The first—contrast of dynamics—is evident from the outset. In the first section of the movement, which takes only about 13 seconds to play, Haydn changes dynamics four times. These dynamic contrasts are reinforced by textural contrasts: Haydn tends to use monophony or very thin counterpoint for the quiet passages and thick polyphony for the loud. For this first section the instrumentation also follows suit. We hear violins alone in the quiet passages and the whole orchestra playing when the music is loud. All these contrasts continue throughout the piece. As for contrast of key, there is a move to the dominant key for sections B and C and a sudden and unexpected shift to F-sharp *minor* in the middle of the D section.

In some ways it seems as though Haydn is deliberately trying to confuse his listeners. Usually in minuet movements the form is easy to hear. But in this movement, the form is quite difficult to hear. Haydn tries every trick in the book to confuse us. He does this by (1) putting the strong cadences in the wrong place, (2) using linking phrases across the section divisions, (3) syncopating the rhythm, and (4) using internal repetitions. For example, he repeats some of the A section inside the B section and so on (this is known as *rounded binary*).

There is more. In his internal repetitions of the rounded binary form (repeating A inside B, and C inside D), instead of repeating exactly, Haydn rewrites the music each time.

Let's look at the D section first, since that is the easiest one. The D section contains a shortened restatement of C. Haydn actually repeats only the first half of C (compare 1:41–1:56 with 2:33–2:40). But if you listen closely, you will hear that Haydn has actually rewritten the passage to make it sound fresh. In its first appearance, the instrumentation involves only the two horns, with a tiny touch of strings at the end. In its restatement, oboes, horns, and all the strings play the music.

The rewriting of the A section within the B section is even more subtle. Compare 0:00–0:14 with 0:49–1:05. Listening carefully, you'll find many differences involving dynamics, phrase lengths (including the length of the whole passage), and instrumentation. Haydn is really trying to keep his audience on their toes!

The best way to untangle all of this is by means of the timed listening guide. If you glance frequently at your watch or CD timer while you are listening, follow the listening guide carefully, and listen to the piece several times, you'll be able to get some sense of what a brilliant and sophisticated composer Haydn really was.

MINUET			
A	12 (40) **0:00**	The first section of the minuet, in F♯ Major. Graceful dancelike character; full of contrasts; syncopation. Ends with quiet linking passage on violins alone.
A	**0:14**	Repeat of first section of the minuet.
B (+A')	13 (41) **0:30**	The second section of the minuet, longer than the first. Dominant key (C♯ Major). Short loud passage, longer quiet syncopated passage on strings alone. Then a crescendo into a restatement (A') of the first section of the minuet (0:49).
B (+A')	**1:05**	Repeat of entire second section, including its restatement of A.

TRIO			
C	14 (42) **1:41**	First section of trio. Rising phrase for horns, graceful answering phrase for violins.
C	**1:56**	Repeat.
D (+C')	15 (43) **2:11**	Second section of trio, longer than the first. Back to tonic key (F♯ Major). Divided into three parts: beginning, with descending phrases in horns; (2:21) oboes replace the horns, sudden shift to F♯ *minor*; (2:33) shortened restatement (C') of the first section of the trio.
D (+C')	**2:40**	Repeat of entire second section of trio, including its restatement of C.

MINUET			
		[The entire minuet is repeated exactly.]
A	16 (44) **3:10**	A section.
A	**3:24**	Repeat of A section.
B (+A')	**3:39**	B section, including restatement of A.
B (+A')	**4:14**	Repeat of B section with restatement of A.

and symphonic brilliance. And Haydn's two oratorios, *The Creation* and *The Seasons*, display a wit and a liveliness together with the kind of exquisite pictorial writing that never fails to captivate audiences. In *The Creation*, for example, which describes the creation of the world, Haydn begins with a depiction of Chaos, in which darkness and void are represented by murky harmonies and unsettled rhythm. On the last word of the choral proclamation "And there was *light!*," there is a loud, radiant climax on a C-Major chord. Both *The Creation* and *The Seasons* contain cleverly realistic musical descriptions of nature: a cooing dove, a flashing storm, a slithery worm.

In the middle of Haydn's career at Esterháza, in the early 1770s, there was an interesting change of style that affected his string quartets, piano sonatas, and symphonies. Quite suddenly, some of Haydn's works began to display a mood of melancholy and longing that had not been there before. Haydn experimented with this style by writing several compositions in un-usual minor keys, with sudden changes of dynamics, remote harmonic excursions, and burdened, intense, slow movements. We shall listen to a movement from one of Haydn's symphonies from this period. Possibly because the prince did not react favorably to the new style, Haydn abandoned it after a few years. **(See Listening Guide on page 176.)**

All of Haydn's pieces adopt Classic formal procedures. Nevertheless, Haydn showed great ingenuity in exploiting the fixed forms of Classic music for his own expressive purposes. One device that he invented was the "false recapitulation." You remember that in sonata form, the opening music of the movement comes back again—after the development section—with the same melody and harmony that it had at the beginning. Haydn sometimes liked to play games with the expectations of his audience by *pretending* to start the recapitulation in the middle of the development section. The music of the opening of the movement is played, leading us to think that the recapitulation has started.

LISTENING GUIDE

**Franz Joseph Haydn (1732–1809)
Fourth Movement from String Quartet,
Op. 33, No. 2, in E-flat Major**

Tempo: *Presto* ("Very fast")
Meter: $\frac{6}{8}$
Key: E♭ Major
Duration: 3:08

Student CD Collection: 2, track 17
Complete CD Collection: 2, track 45

This movement is in the form of a rondo. There is a catchy main theme, which constantly returns in the course of the movement. Between appearances of the main theme are passages of contrasting material known as episodes. In this rondo Haydn adopts the following form, with A as the main theme and B, C, and D as the three episodes:

A B A B A C A B A D A Coda

Haydn has written this movement in the attractive and bouncy meter of 6/8 and in a fast tempo, which makes the music particularly lively and fun. But the joke comes in the final measures, as the listener has no idea where the ending really is.

178

A 17 (45) **0:00**	Main theme.
0:06	Repeat.
B **0:12**	First episode.
A **0:28**	Main theme.
B **0:34**	Repeat of first episode.
A **0:50**	Main theme.
C 18 (46) **0:57**	Second episode, many key changes.
A **1:25**	Main theme.
B **1:31**	First episode again.
A **1:48**	Main theme.
D **1:54**	Third episode.
2:13	Pace slows down, anticipation, then:
A **2:23**	Main theme again.
CODA **2:30**	Final cadence?
19 (47) **2:32**	Sudden change of texture and tempo.
2:45	Final cadence?
2:46	Main theme, broken up into four separate phrases.
2:58	Ending?
3:01	First phrase of main theme!

Mozart at the age of 7.

Lorenzoni, Pietro Anton (attributed to). Young Mozart wearing court-dress. 1763. Mozart House, Salzburg, Austra. Erich Lessing/Art Resource, NY.

But then the harmonies change, the development continues, and we realize we've been tricked. A little while later, the true recapitulation occurs.

Haydn liked to play other kinds of tricks on his listeners. In 1781 he published a set of six string quartets, which have come to be called the "Joke Quartets." The quartets contain serious music and emotionally expressive passages, but there are many witty moments, too: cadences in the "wrong" places, oddly shaped melodies, and unexpected rhythms. At the end of the second quartet of the set (Opus 33, Number 2), there is a "false ending." The music seems to stop, suddenly moves on, stops again, and then seems to begin again. Then the movement ends. **(See Listening Guide on page 178.)**

This kind of manipulation of audience expectations could occur only in a period in which formal procedures were strict. When there are no rules, breaking the rules is no fun!

Even today, much of Haydn's music is only rarely performed. But as time goes on, and more of his compositions become familiar, we realize that Haydn was one of the most versatile and gifted composers of his time.

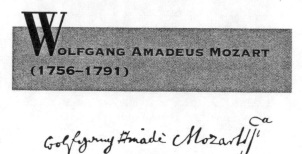

WOLFGANG AMADEUS MOZART (1756–1791)

For most listeners, Mozart's music is easier to appreciate than Haydn's. Compared with Haydn, Mozart wears his heart on his sleeve. His music is more colorful, more intense.

Mozart was born into a musical family. His father,

> I pay no attention whatever to anybody's praise or blame. . . . I simply follow my own feelings.
> —Mozart, in a letter to his father

Leopold Mozart

Leopold Mozart is often mentioned only in relation to his illustrious son, Wolfgang Amadeus Mozart. This is a little unfair, because he was a distinguished performer, composer, author, and music theorist in his own right. ✦ In 1756, Leopold published a treatise entitled *Versuch einer grundlichen Violinschule* (*Essay on a Fundamental Violin Method*), designed partly as an aid for teaching the violin and partly as a discussion of musical performance and analysis. It represents one of the most important contributions to music theory in the mid-eighteenth century. ✦ Unfortunately, a large number of Leopold's compositions remain unresearched, uncatalogued, and unpublished. Those that are documented include Masses, symphonies, divertimenti, partitas, serenades, and a wide variety of chamber music. Much of Leopold's music exhibits a strong naturalistic tendency and employs instruments such as bugles, bagpipes, the hunting horn, the hurdy-gurdy, and the dulcimer. Leopold sometimes asks for dog noises, human cries, pistol shots, and whistles! ✦ Leopold composed little after 1762. This sudden decrease in productivity can be attributed to the huge amount of time he devoted to teaching his son and to the numerous tours of Europe they undertook together in an attempt to promote Wolfgang's extraordinary talents. In short, Leopold sacrificed his own considerable career to further that of his son. No one was better qualified to recognize Wolfgang's gifts than his own father.

Leopold, was a distinguished violinist and composer who held the post of deputy music director at the court of the Prince-Archbishop of Salzburg in Austria. He was also the author of an important book on violin-playing.

He decided to devote his career to promoting the abilities of young Wolfgang. Wolfgang was uniquely, breathtakingly gifted. His father piously referred to him as "this miracle God has caused to be born in Salzburg."

Mozart was born in 1756. By the age of four, he was already displaying amazing musical ability. At six, he had started to compose and was performing brilliantly on the harpsichord. For the next ten years, his father took him on journeys to various courts, towns, and principalities around Europe, where he played for noblemen, princes, and even the Empress of Austria, Maria Theresa.

These constant travels in his formative years had a valuable effect on the young boy. Mozart's principal teacher at this time was his father, but he absorbed other

"This boy will cause us all to be forgotten."
—composer Johann Adolf Hasse

Portrait of the Mozart family from about 1780. Mozart plays a duet with his sister, while his father listens, and his mother Is remembered in a painting behind them.

Painting, Baroque, 18th Century. Johann Nepomuk Della Croce, *The Mozart Family* (1780–1781). Oil on canvas. 140 × 186 cm. Mozart House, Salzburg, Austria. Erich Lessing, Art Resource.

The Boy Genius

Mozart's genius as a child caused such a sensation in London that he was examined and tested by a scientist. The scientist wrote a report attesting to Mozart's musical ability and age. The proof that he was indeed a boy and not a midget came at the end of a rigorous series of musical examinations:

While he was playing to me, a cat came in, upon which he immediately left his harpsichord, nor could we bring him back for a considerable time. He would also sometimes run about the room with a stick between his legs for a horse.

Engraving from Leopold Mozart's *Violin Method*, published in 1756, the year of Wolfgang's birth.

The city of Salzburg, Mozart's birthplace, in the mid-eighteenth century.

musical influences like a sponge. Wherever he went, he picked up the musical style of the region and of the prominent local composers.

From all these sources and from his own teeming imagination, Mozart fashioned an individual style. By the time he was eight, Mozart had already had some music published. By 10, he was writing symphonies. At 14, he had produced his first full-length opera. By the time he was 17 years old, when he and his father returned home to Salzburg to try to find Wolfgang a job, he was a mature and fully formed creative artist.

Finding Mozart a job was not easy. The Prince-Archbishop of Salzburg was an autocratic ruler, and his patience had already been tried by the constant leaves of absence of his deputy music director (Mozart's father). The archbishop agreed to employ Mozart, but only in a junior position. Mozart wrote a fair amount of music in these years, but both he and his father felt that Salzburg was too stifling for him. After a few years, Mozart traveled again to try to find a position elsewhere. This time he traveled with his mother, since his father could not afford to leave his post for any more trips. He went to Munich, Mannheim (where Stamitz's great orchestra was centered), and Paris. But in none of these places was a job forthcoming. Most of Mozart's prospective employers thought he was too young and too talented ("overqualified" is the word we would use today) for a normal position. Indeed, any music director would have been threatened by this brash and brilliant youngster. In Paris he encountered not only disap-

pointment but also tragedy: his mother died. He wrote to his father and sister:

> I hope that you are prepared to hear with fortitude one of the saddest and most painful stories.... I can only judge from my own grief and sorrow what yours must be.

Although Mozart was given a promotion upon returning to Salzburg, he was still unsatisfied. In 1780 he accompanied the archbishop on a visit to Vienna.

SEI
QUARTETTI
PER DUE VIOLINI, VIOLA, E VIOLONCELLO
Composti e Dedicati
al Signor
GIUSEPPE HAYDN
Maestro di Cappella di S.A.
il Principe d'Esterhazy &c &c
Dal Suo Amico
W. A. MOZART
Opera X.

In Vienna presso Artaria Comp.
Mercanti ed Editori di Stampa Musica,
e Carte Geografiche.

The ending of Mozart's dedication to Haydn: "I remain with all my heart, dearest friend, your most sincere friend."

Title page of Mozart's six string quartets dedicated to Haydn.

Composers and Patrons in the Classic Era

Music patronage was at a turning point when Mozart went to Vienna in the last part of the eighteenth century. Many patrons of music continued to be wealthy aristocrats. Haydn's entire career was funded by a rich prince. Mozart's father and, for a time, Mozart himself were in the employ of another prince. But when Mozart went to Vienna in 1781, he contrived to make a living from a variety of sources. In addition to performances at aristocratic houses and commissions for particular works, Mozart gave piano and composition lessons, put on operas, and gave many public concerts of his own music. ¶ The eighteenth century saw a considerable rise in the number and availability of public concerts. Three types were common: charity concerts to raise money for local poorhouses and orphanages; subscription concerts, for which tickets were sold in advance; and benefit concerts, at which composers played for their own profit. Music was becoming more and more the province of the general public, and composers less and less the servants of the rich.

Mozart was outraged when he was forced to eat in the servants' quarters and infuriated when the archbishop refused to let him go to the houses of other aristocrats who had invited him to perform for them. Mozart angrily demanded his release from the archbishop's employ and received it, as he wrote to his father, "with a kick on my ass from our worthy Prince-Archbishop."

Thus began the freelance career of one of the most brilliant musicians in history. At first Mozart supported himself by giving piano lessons. He also wrote several sonatas for the piano and some piano concertos. Piano music was very popular in Vienna. Mozart had some success with a German comic opera he wrote in 1782 called *The Abduction from the Seraglio* (so called because the action takes place in a Turkish *seraglio*, or harem). Also in 1782 he married his landlady's daughter, a young soprano named Constanze Weber. His father, to whom he continued to write regularly, disapproved strongly of the marriage.

For the next few years, Mozart was highly successful. He undertook a set of string quartets that were designed to emulate those of Haydn, and he dedicated them in a warm and heartfelt style to the older master. We know the two composers met a few times at string quartet parties. Haydn played the violin, Mozart the viola.

In these years Mozart won great fame—and made quite a lot of money—by means of piano concertos. Between 1784 and 1786, he wrote 12 piano concertos. This was a fine opportunity for him to appear before the Viennese public as both composer and pianist, because he played the solo parts in the concertos himself. The concertos were very successful, and Mozart was at the height of his career.

Gradually, however, Mozart's popularity began to wane. The Viennese were always eager for some new sensation, and Mozart had been around for a while. In addition, the city was undergoing a recession, and concert dates and composing contracts were hard to come by. Mozart's correspondence from the late 1780s is full of letters requesting loans from friends, and, despite his dislike of authority, he made attempts to find a secure position at the Viennese court.

Mozart did not write many new symphonies during this period, but in the summer of 1788, in the space of about eight weeks, he wrote three symphonies in a row. These last three symphonies, Nos. 39, 40, and 41, are the culmination of his work in the genre. They are very different from each other, but all three are richly orchestrated, enormously inventive, and full of subtle details that repay frequent rehearings.

Perhaps the greatest achievement of Mozart's last years is represented by his operas. Mozart had been interested in opera since his boyhood travels to Italy. He had already written several youthful pieces and, since coming to Vienna, both an opera seria (serious Italian opera) and a German comic opera. Now, in what would be the last five years of his life, he completed five great operas. The best known of these are *The Marriage of Figaro* (1786), *Don Giovanni* (1787), and *The Magic Flute* (completed in the year of his death, 1791). These operas are all very different, but in each of them Mozart displays his remarkable understanding of human nature in all its richness. In Figaro, he depicts with the finest subtlety the urgent adolescent sexuality of a servant boy and the deeply moving despair of a neglected wife. In *Don Giovanni*, Mozart explores the richly human traits of determination, pride, grief, comedy, and seduction. In *The Magic Flute*, the themes are noble ambition, marital harmony, and pure love. In Mozart's hands, these ideals and emotions are transformed from the conventions of the opera stage into the deepest expression of human feelings.

In November of 1791, while he was working on a Requiem Mass (Mass for the Dead), Mozart became ill. And on December 5, at the age of 35, with half a lifetime of masterpieces still uncomposed, Wolfgang Amadeus Mozart died.

Mozart's Music

Mozart's music is a remarkable combination of the accessible and the profound. As Mozart wrote to his father, his music appeals to experts and amateurs alike. Another reason so many people are so attached to Mozart's music is its extraordinary breadth. There is an

> **I** swear before Almighty God that your son is the greatest composer I know either in person or by reputation.
> —Haydn to Mozart's father

Musical Forgeries

The fame of Haydn and Mozart and other great composers has led to great excitement whenever one of their music manuscripts turns up in an attic or an old desk drawer. Sometimes these documents are authentic. But often they are forgeries, and some of them are good enough to fool even the experts (for a while). In 1994, some "newly discovered" Haydn piano sonatas, authenticated by a world-renowned Haydn scholar and due for performance at Harvard University's Music Department, were declared to be fakes. ✦ The name of one of the great composers on the title page virtually guarantees a favorable reception for a work. For nearly a hundred years, a well-known symphony was thought to be by Mozart (his "37th Symphony"). It was hailed by critics as "typical of the master." But when the symphony turned out to be not by Mozart at all but by a less famous contemporary of his, critics immediately described it as "obviously not on a par with the work of the master." The work hadn't changed—it was the same music!—only people's preconceptions had changed.

Autograph manuscript of a work for voice and piano by Mozart. Notice the speed and clarity of Mozart's handwriting.

incredibly wide range of music to choose from—more than 800 compositions, from the lightest little comic pieces to works that explore the great themes of human existence: life and death, love, tragedy, romance, despair and hope.

Mozart wrote in all the main genres of Classic music: opera, symphony, string quartet, and sonata. He wrote solo concertos for a wide variety of instruments: violin, flute, oboe, clarinet, bassoon, and horn. But for his own instrument, the piano, he composed more than 20 concertos, which are among his greatest masterpieces. We shall listen to a slow movement from one of these piano concertos. (See Listening Guide on page 186.)

Mozart wrote dozens of sonatas, both for solo piano and for combinations of instruments, including piano, strings, and winds. He also composed many great string quartets. In addition to these works, Mozart wrote several string quintets, in which an extra viola is added to the two violins, viola, and cello of the string quartet. This makes the music richer and the counterpoint fuller.

Mozart also greatly enriched the expressive power of opera. In *The Magic Flute, Don Giovanni,* and *The Marriage of Figaro,* Mozart transcends convention by portraying people in all their psychological complexity.

Of *The Magic Flute:* "This opera . . . is the only one in existence that might conceivably have been composed by God."
—Neville Cardus, music critic, 1961

O Mozart, immortal Mozart, how many, how infinitely many inspiring suggestions of a finer, better life have you left in our souls!
—Franz Schubert

Even in his purely instrumental works, Mozart wrote music that flouted convention. He created works of great depth and seriousness for "background music" at garden parties. He wrote slow movements of heartbreaking simplicity for his piano concertos. Often he used counterpoint to intensify his music in places where counterpoint was not usual. And his melodies often have passages that are chromatic (moving by half steps) at a time when most composers wrote melodies that are entirely diatonic (using only notes from the scale). Finally, Mozart's music often passes briefly into the minor mode, even in major-mode passages, which creates added depth and emotional resonance. It is like the shadow of a small cloud passing over a sunny meadow.

Only a very small number of his works use a minor key as the tonic. Among these is the Symphony No. 40 in G minor, written in 1788. **(See Listening Guide on page 189.)**

Although Mozart's music is richer, more versatile, and more varied than most eighteenth-century music, it does use the same basic conventions as other music of the time. The instruments are the same, the forms are the same, and the primary genres that Mozart cultivated are the same. But Mozart's music speaks deeply to more people, covers a wider range of feeling, and resonates with more human significance than that of almost any other composer before or since. In that sense, Mozart's music is truly "classic."

A scene from a production of Mozart's opera *The Magic Flute.*

Wolfgang Amadeus Mozart
(1756–1791)
First Movement from Symphony No. 40
in G minor, K. 550

Date of composition: 1788
Orchestration: Flute, 2 oboes, 2 clar-
    inets, 2 bassoons, 2 horns, and
    strings
Tempo: *Allegro molto* ("Very fast")
Meter: $\frac{2}{2}$
Key: G minor
Duration: 8:16

Student CD Collection: 2, track 20
Complete CD Collection: 3, track 1

In the space of eight weeks during the summer of 1788, Mozart completed three large-scale symphonies. Though there was no reason for him to have known this, they were to be his last. Perhaps he intended them to be published and performed together.

The G-minor Symphony, the middle one of the three, is one of Mozart's best-known works, representing one of his greatest achievements in the symphonic realm. It is marked by perfect balance and control, a wealth of harmonic and instrumental color, and a brilliant use of formal structure.

The first movement is a superb example of these characteristics. In it, Mozart takes advantage of the dramatic possibilities of sonata form, while also playing with its conventions for expressive purposes. The basic structure of sonata form is easy to hear, but we can also see how Mozart *manipulated* the form to surprise and delight his listeners. There are many examples, but the most obvious one is the way he leads us to expect the recapitulation at a certain point, only to pull the rug out from under us.

You should first listen to the piece a few times simply to enjoy the fine expressive writing—the brilliant balance between loud and soft, woodwinds and strings, descending and ascending phrases, and minor and major keys. Notice, too, how Mozart spices up the sound with chromatic passages and surprise notes. Next, listen for the structure, the basic template of sonata form, which is so clearly articulated in this movement. The next couple of times, listen for how Mozart plays with this structure (and with his audience's expectations) for expressive purposes. Finally, try putting all these things together and listen for them all at once.

Don't stop listening after that, however. For you may find, as many of the most experienced listeners do, that you will hear something new in this movement every single time you listen to it. And there are three other movements in this symphony . . . three other symphonies in the group . . . dozens of other symphonies by Mozart.

EXPOSITION		
		[timings for the repeat are in parentheses]
20 (1)	0:00	Opening theme: violins, quiet, G minor; closed by full orchestra, loud.
22 (3)	(2:02)	

Allegro molto

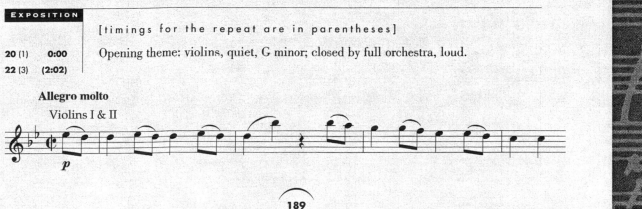

0:24 (2:27)	Restatement of opening theme, woodwinds added, beginning modulation to second key.
0:34 (2:37)	Energetic bridge passage, loud, full orchestra, preparing for second key. (Central to this passage is a strong rising figure, which appears later in the movement.)

Violins I & II

0:50 (2:53)	Cadence in new key (B♭–relative major).
21 (2) **0:52** (2:56)	Second theme, also quiet, smooth alternation of strings and woodwinds, quite chromatic.

Violins   Clarinets   Violins

1:10 (3:14)	Odd surprise notes.
1:20 (3:23)	Cadence.
1:27 (3:31)	Spinning-out section (clarinet, bassoon, strings).
1:47 (3:50)	Ending passage, loud, whole orchestra.
2:00 (4:04)	Final cadences of exposition.
22 (3) **2:02**	(Exact repetition of entire exposition.)

DEVELOPMENT

23 (4) **4:09**	Many key changes, by means of first theme dropping down.
4:23	A "blender" passage, in which the themes are cut up and tossed around; whole orchestra, loud.

190

24 (5) 4:52		Music gets quiet ... quieter (we are expecting the recapitulation ... but:)
5:09		Suddenly loud (we've been fooled: no recapitulation here).
5:19		Another preparation, quiet woodwind descent (watch out: is this real ... ?)

RECAPITULATION

25 (6) 5:24		YES! (But notice how Mozart sneaks it in ever so quietly.) All goes normally here, though there are some changes from the exposition.
5:57		New material, loud, whole orchestra (sounds like it's left over from the development). It uses the rising figure from the opening bridge passage (shown above at 0:34).
6:29		Back on track ...
26 (7) 6:40		Second theme: quiet, winds and strings, this time in tonic key (G minor).
6:58		Surprise notes.
7:05		New material.
7:14		Back on track ...
7:21		Spinning out.
7:44		Music opens out to:

CODA

27 (8) 7:53		Confirming tonic key, floating, quiet.
8:03		Repeated definitive cadences, loud.
8:09		Three final chords.

Classic music presents a notable contrast from that of the Baroque era. Classic music is lighter, more delicate, with simpler harmonies and clearer textures. The most obvious difference is in the bass. We pointed out in the style summary of the previous chapter that a Baroque piece's most characteristic feature is the strength and powerful sense of direction of its bass line. (This is usually played in chamber music by at least two instruments, a keyboard and a low stringed instrument, and in orchestral music by a keyboard and all the low strings.) In Classic music, the accompaniment is usually much lighter, with the chords broken up into patterns or with the bass notes more separated, with some "air" between them.

Second, Classic music tends to stick to simpler harmonies, usually staying within the home key or using closely related keys, without some of the dissonant chords sometimes used for expressive effect in Baroque music. A standard pattern of key relationships within a movement or among the movements of a work became clearly established in this period.

Third, Classic music uses a symmetrical arrangement of musical phrases. Phrases tend to be two or four measures long and to be arranged into pairs. This symmetry is used as the basis for simple, attractive melodies.

Finally, the ruling force in Classic music is convention. Convention governs the number of movements in a piece, the forms in which they are cast, and the tempos at which they are played. The key relationship among movements is set by convention, as is the order and approximate length of the key areas within movements. Individual keys are associated with particular moods and even with particular instruments.

The most important musical genres of the Classic era are opera, symphony, and chamber music — especially the string quartet and sonata. Symphonies and chamber works follow a four-movement format: a moderately fast first movement, a graceful or lyrical slow movement, a minuet and trio, and a fast final movement. The first, third, and last movements are usually in the tonic key. The slow movement might be in the dominant key (V), the subdominant key (IV), or the relative minor key (vi). Sonata form is used in the first movement. Aria form, theme and variations form, or sonata form in the second; minuet-and-trio form in the third; and either rondo or sonata form in the fourth.

In concertos, the convention is that the piece should contain only three movements: moderately fast, slow, and fast. Historically, concertos did not take on the minuet-and-trio movement of the symphonic format. The piano became one of the principal solo instruments featured in Classic concertos.

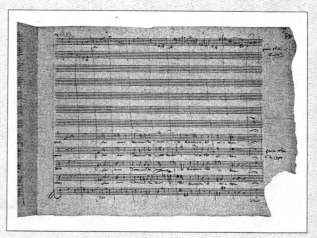

The last page of music Mozart wrote before his death.

Chapter 10

Beethoven

Sometimes there are composers who simply do not fit conveniently into pigeonholes or our conveniently constructed time periods. We say that the Classic era in musical style ended about 1800 and that the Romantic era began about the same time. But there is one composer whose life spanned that boundary by about a quarter century in either direction and whose individuality was so strong that he simply cannot be labeled. That composer was Beethoven.

Beethoven grew up at a time when both Haydn and Mozart were still alive and actively composing. The music he heard and studied was strictly Classic in style. But he died in 1827, well into the nineteenth century, when Romanticism was in full flower.

Like all great artists who live at a time of change, Beethoven was both a beneficiary of that change and partly responsible for it. He took the forms, procedures, and ideals that he had inherited from the Classic era and developed them beyond their previously accepted limits. He brought Classic genres—symphony, concerto, sonata, string quartet—into the nineteenth century and transformed them into the vehicles of musical expression for a new age. He burst through the boundaries of Classic restraint to create works of unprecedented scope and depth. He enlarged the orchestra, changed musical structure, added a chorus to the symphony, and told

narratives with some of his purely instrumental works—all things that had wide-ranging repercussions for a century and more. Finally, he invested instrumental music with a personal subjectivity and with the stamp of his own extraordinary personality in such a way that music was never the same again. He was both the child of one era and the founding father of another. That is why Beethoven has a chapter of his own.

The history of Beethoven is tantamount to an intellectual history of the nineteenth century.
—Karl Dahlhaus

Portrait of Beethoven at the age of 49.

Ludwig van Beethoven, portrait by Joseph Karl Stieler, 1820. Beethoven–Haus Bonn.

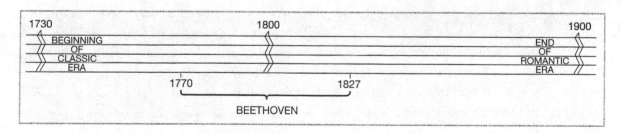

1730   1800   1900
BEGINNING OF CLASSIC ERA   END OF ROMANTIC ERA
1770   1827
BEETHOVEN

BEETHOVEN'S LIFE

Beethoven is perhaps the most famous musician of all time. Ever since his death in 1827, he has been revered as the principal figure in the history of Western music. His influence

on later composers was enormous, to the extent that many of them actually found his accomplishments intimidating.

Who was this man?

The only composer's name over the stage of Symphony Hall (built 1900) in Boston.

BEETHOVEN'S EARLY LIFE

Ludwig van Beethoven was born in 1770 into a family of musicians. Both his grandfather and his father were professional musicians at the court of the Elector (the local ruler) in the German town of Bonn. His grandfather was highly respected, but his father became something of a problem at the court because he was an alcoholic. As a teenager, Beethoven was put in charge of the family finances and started a job at the court. He studied organ and composition and helped look after the instruments. About the same time, he began to write music, mostly songs and chamber works.

In 1790, an important visitor passed through Bonn. This was Haydn, on his way to London for the first of his successful visits. He met the young Beethoven and agreed to take him on as a student when he came back from London to Vienna. In 1792, Beethoven moved to Vienna to study with the great master. He was 22; Haydn was 60.

Apparently the lessons did not go well. Haydn was old-fashioned and a little pompous, Beethoven rebellious and headstrong. But Beethoven was a formidable pianist, and he soon found support among the rich patrons of the arts who lived in Vienna. Prince Lichnowsky gave him board and lodging at his palace, in return for which Beethoven was to compose music and play the piano at evening parties ... at least that was the arrangement. In fact, Beethoven hated being dependent and often refused to play. But the prince was very tolerant; he finally set Beethoven up with his own apartment so that he could work as he pleased.

In the early years, Beethoven wrote mostly keyboard and chamber-music pieces. As time went on, however, he decided to start composing in the larger musical forms of the day—string quartet, piano concerto, and symphony. By the time Beethoven was 32, he had written—among other works—piano sonatas, a great deal of chamber music, a set of six string quartets, three piano concertos, and two symphonies. The string quartets, concertos, and symphonies owe a great debt to Haydn and Mozart.

But Beethoven's music was already starting to show signs of considerable individuality. The First Symphony deliberately begins in the wrong key, before turning to the right one. The Third Piano Concerto features a powerful unifying rhythm. And the last movement of one of the early string quartets has a deeply expressive slow introduction entitled *La Malinconia* (*Melancholy*).

Beethoven had every reason to feel melancholic at this time of his life. For it was in 1802 that he discovered the tragic truth that was to haunt him for the rest of his life: He was going deaf. He contemplated suicide but, overcoming his despair, decided that his first responsibility lay with his music. He had to produce the works that were in him.

His disease progressed gradually. It took some years for him to become totally deaf, and there were periods when normal hearing returned. But by 1817, Beethoven could not hear a single note, and his conversations were carried on by means of an ear trumpet and a notebook slung around his neck. His deafness eventually prevented him from performing and conducting, but he continued to compose until the end of his life. He could hear everything inside his head.

> Though I had some instruction from Haydn, I never learned anything from him.
> —Beethoven

THE HEROIC PHASE

The middle period of Beethoven's life was marked by a vigorous concentration on work and the sense of triumph over adversity. For these reasons, it is often called the "heroic" phase. "I will seize Fate by the throat," he said. This was also a period of extraordinary productivity. In the ten years between 1802 and 1812, Beethoven wrote six more symphonies, four concertos, five more string quartets, an entire opera, some orchestral overtures, and several important piano sonatas as well as other pieces of chamber music.

The music Beethoven wrote during this time is strong and muscular, with contrasting passages of great lyricism. This contrast exists *between* works (Symphonies Nos. 4, 6, and 8, for example, are gentle, whereas Symphonies Nos. 3, 5, and 7 are more powerful) and also *within* works. Some compositions build to aggressive climaxes and then move into moments of purest beauty and radiance. (The first movement of the Fifth Piano Concerto does this.) Like Mozart, Beethoven wrote his piano concertos to display his own virtuosity, but soon his deafness prevented him from playing in public, and he became increasingly introverted and antisocial. He was sometimes seen striding around the countryside without a coat or a hat, ignoring the weather and muttering to himself.

The most striking thing about the compositions from the heroic phase is their length. From the Third Symphony on, Beethoven was writing works much larger in scope than those of his predecessors. The Third Symphony has a first movement that is by itself as long as many complete symphonies of Haydn and Mozart.

During this phase, Beethoven became very famous. His works were regarded as strong and patriotic at a time when his homeland was at war with France. He even wrote some overtly political pieces, such as

Beethoven's Personality

Beethoven is often portrayed as a wild, aggressive individual, intolerant in the extreme, and prone to violent fits of rage. There is an element of truth to this image of the composer, though it hardly does justice to the complex nature of his personality. ◆ He lived at a time when the established hierarchy of European society was in question, and he held ambivalent views toward authority. When he was asked to play in aristocratic homes, he insisted that no one be in the same room with him. He hated the idea of conforming to fixed social etiquette. His deafness, naturally enough, also made him more withdrawn and unsociable. ◆ There were many contradictory strands to Beethoven's personality. At times he was warm and welcoming; on other occasions he could be cold and hostile. He was a loner, yet he enjoyed the company of a number of intimate friends. He appeared content to work in his cramped quarters in Vienna, yet he relished long walks in the countryside and often spent summers in country villages. He often expressed the desire for a tranquil home life, yet he never married. Perhaps we should expect such contradictions from a genius as extraordinary as Beethoven.

I must confess that I live a miserable life.... I live entirely in my music. —Beethoven, in a letter to a friend, 1801

a *Battle* Symphony—complete with brass fanfares and cannon fire—to celebrate an early victory of the Duke of Wellington over Napoleon. He also became quite wealthy. His music was published and performed more than ever, and his income from these sources as well as from aristocratic and royal patrons was substantial.

PERSONAL CRISIS AND HALT TO PRODUCTIVITY

After the extraordinarily productive years of the heroic phase, Beethoven found himself embroiled in a family crisis, which robbed him of his creativity for several years. In 1815 came the death of Beethoven's brother, who left his widow and Beethoven with joint custody of his son—Beethoven's nephew, Karl. This caused Beethoven great turmoil and distress. Having never married himself, he yearned often for a normal family life, with a wife to comfort him and a child of his own. He once said to a friend that such intimacy was "not to be thought of—impossible—a dream. Yet… I cannot get it out of my mind."

To be thrust suddenly into a position of paternal responsibility for a child and into close contact with a young woman completely undermined Beethoven's equilibrium. He threw himself into a series of devastating legal battles with his brother's widow to obtain sole custody of Karl. The conflict dragged on for years, sapping Beethoven's energy and destroying his peace of mind (not to mention that of the boy and his poor mother). Ultimately, Beethoven won the legal battles (he had powerful friends), and Karl came to live with him. The relationship was a stormy one, however, because Beethoven was appallingly strict and possessive. At the age of 19, Karl pawned his watch, bought two pistols, and tried to kill himself. This action, from which Karl soon recovered, brought some sense back to the situation. Karl was allowed to return to his mother's house, and he escaped from Beethoven's domination by joining the army.

Beethoven's funeral procession in Vienna. There were 20,000 people in attendance at this event.

LATE YEARS

After the most intense period of the battle over Karl, Beethoven only gradually regained his productivity. The most important works of his late years are the last three piano sonatas, the Ninth Symphony, and a series of string quartets. The piano sonatas are remarkable pieces, unusual in form and design, and most moving in their juxtaposition of complexity and simplicity. The Ninth Symphony, finished in 1824, continued Beethoven's tradition of breaking barriers. It is an immense work with a revolutionary last movement that includes a choir and four vocal soloists. This was unheard of in a symphony at this time, although many later composers imitated the idea in one way or another. The text for the last movement of the Ninth Symphony is a poem by the great German poet Schiller: the *Ode to Joy*. It is a summation of Beethoven's philosophy of life: "Let Joy bring everyone together: all men will be brothers; let all kneel before God."

Beethoven's last three years were devoted entirely to string quartets. In this most intimate of genres, he found a medium for his most personal thoughts and ideas. Many people have found Beethoven's late string quartets to be both his greatest and his most difficult music. Yet there are moments of tenderness and great

beauty, as well as passages of dissonant harmonies and rhythmic complexity, and some of the most profound music in the Western tradition. Beethoven died on March 26, 1827, at the age of 56, leaving an indelible mark on music and the way it has been experienced by listeners ever since.

BEETHOVEN'S MUSIC

Beethoven's music has always represented the essence of serious music. In the twentieth century, people who know of only one classical composer know of Beethoven. And his music is played more, written about more, and recorded more than the music of any other composer in the world.

His music is appealing, moving, and forceful. It reaches something inside us that is elemental. It has a unique combination of the simple and the complex, the emotional and the intellectual. We recognize, on hearing it, that it comes from the spiritual side of a man, but also from a man who was entirely, and sometimes painfully, human.

There are some stylistic traits in Beethoven's music that might be regarded as his "fingerprints"—traits that can be instantly recognized and that mark the music

> I shall hear in Heaven.
> —Beethoven's last words

Beethoven's Work Habits

As Beethoven grew older and withdrew more and more from society, he became wholly absorbed in his art. He would habitually miss meals, forget or ignore invitations, and work long into the night. He himself described his "ceaseless occupations." Beethoven felt the strongest urge to produce the music within him, and yet he suffered the same creative anxiety as lesser mortals: "For some time past I have been carrying about with me the idea of three great works .... These I must get rid of: two symphonies, each different from the other, and also different from all my other symphonies, and an oratorio .... I dread beginning works of such magnitude. Once I have begun, then all goes well." ✦ We are fortunate in possessing many of the sketchbooks in which Beethoven worked out his musical ideas. They present a vivid picture of the composer at work.

> In his final illness, Beethoven is reported to have said: "Strange—I feel as though up to now I have written only a few notes."

A page from one of Beethoven's manuscripts.

as unmistakably his. These include the following: (1) long powerful *crescendos* that seem to carry the music inexorably forward, (2) themes that sound exactly right both quiet and very loud, (3) *dramatic* use of Classic structures such as sonata form, and (4) sudden key changes that nonetheless fit into a powerful harmonic logic.

The most famous of Beethoven's compositions come from the middle part of his life: the heroic phase. These include Symphonies Nos. 3–8, the middle string quartets, Piano Concertos Nos. 4 and 5, the Violin Concerto, and the opera *Fidelio*. Some of the pieces are actually *about* heroism: The Third Symphony is entitled the *Eroica* (*Heroic*), and *Fidelio* (*The Faithful One*) displays the heroism of a woman who rescues her husband from unjust imprisonment. As

a result, much of this music is strong, dramatic, and powerful.

But there is another side to Beethoven: the lyrical side. Some of the middle symphonies are very tuneful and smoothly contoured, like the Sixth Symphony, known as the *Pastoral*. And even in the more dramatic pieces, there are often contrasting passages of great tenderness. One of the secrets of Beethoven's style is the way he juxtaposes strong and tender passages within the same work.

Less well known are the compositions from Beethoven's early period. These include pieces that he wrote before moving to Vienna and some compositions from his first years in that city. Some are deliberately modeled on the works of his great forebears, Haydn and Mozart; others already show signs of re-

Music Critics

During the latter part of Beethoven's life, music journalism began to appear. Daily newspapers started to carry articles and reviews of music, and journals devoted to music were established. Then, as now, critics were not always well disposed toward new music. Here are a few early reviews of Beethoven's compositions: ◆ On the overture to Beethoven's opera *Fidelio*: "All impartial musicians and music lovers were in perfect agreement that never was anything as incoherent, shrill, chaotic, and ear-splitting produced in music." ◆ On the Third Symphony: "It is infinitely too lengthy. . . . If this symphony is not by some means abridged, it will soon fall into disuse." ◆ On the Fifth Symphony: ". . . a sort of odious meowing." ◆ On the Ninth Symphony: ". . . crude, wild, and extraneous harmonies." ". . . ugly, in bad taste, cheap." ◆ On the late music: "He does not write much now, but most of what he produces is so impenetrably obscure in design and so full of unaccountable and often repulsive harmonies that he puzzles the critic as much as he perplexes the performer." ◆ On all his music: "Beethoven always sounds to me like the upsetting of bags of nails, with here and there also a dropped hammer."

markable originality. There are songs, piano pieces, and much chamber music.

Finally, there are the works from the last part of Beethoven's career. These are all very different, and there are fewer of them. They include the Ninth Symphony, the *Missa Solemnis*, the late piano sonatas, and the last five string quartets. Beethoven's late music is very rich. There is a sense of great depth juxtaposed with an extraordinary, almost heartbreaking, innocence and simplicity. In his last years, Beethoven was no longer concerned with drama and heroism but with pursuing the path of his own creativity, wherever it might lead. Some of the music from this period is demanding and difficult to listen to, but with repeated hearings it can provide listeners with a lifetime of enjoyment and reward.

LISTENING EXAMPLES

To get an idea of the range of Beethoven's achievement, we shall listen to compositions from each of the three main periods of his life. The first is a set of variations on a theme, written by Beethoven in 1790 for solo piano. Next we shall study the whole of the Fifth Symphony, perhaps the most famous of Beethoven's compositions. It was written in 1807–8, right in the middle of the heroic phase. Finally, we shall listen to one movement from a late piano sonata, to see how profound and compelling Beethoven's late music can be.

A giant goblin crossing time and space.—E. M. Forster in *Howard's End*, describing the Fifth Symphony

Beethoven at about the time he wrote the Fifth Symphony.

Ludwig van Beethoven, miniature by Christian Horneman, 1802. Beethoven-Haus Bonn, Collection H. C. Bodmer.

LISTENING GUIDE

Ludwig van Beethoven (1770–1827)
Six Easy Variations on a Swiss Tune in F Major for Piano, WoO 64

Date of composition: 1790
Tempo: *Andante con moto* ("Fairly slow but with motion")
Meter: ¼
Key: F Major
Duration: 2:47

Student CD Collection: 2, track 28
Complete CD Collection: 3, track 9

This is one of many sets of variations that Beethoven wrote in his early years. Variations on melodies are an easy way for a composer to learn his or her craft, since the tune and the harmony already exist and all the composer has to do is think of ways to decorate or vary them.

The little Swiss tune that Beethoven uses as the basis for this composition is very simple and attractive. Underlying its simplicity, however, is an interesting quirk: It is made up of unusual phrase lengths. This is probably the feature that attracted Beethoven to the theme in the first place. Instead of the usual four-measure phrases, this tune is made up of two three-measure phrases answered by a phrase of five measures.

This phrase structure, as well as the skeleton of the tune and its harmony, are carried through all the six variations. Beethoven uses triplets, march rhythms, dynamic changes, eighth notes, sixteenth notes, and even the minor key to decorate and vary the music; however, if you play the recording of just the theme a few times first, before listening to the variations, you will be able to follow its outline throughout the piece.

THEME		
		[Andante con moto—"Fairly slow but with motion"]
28 (9)	**0:00**	The theme is simple and pleasant. Notice how it ends very much as it begins.

VARIATION 1		
	0:23	Beethoven introduces triplets (three notes to a beat) in both the right and the left hand.

VARIATION 2		
	0:40	The melody is mostly unchanged in the right hand, but the left hand has jerky, marchlike accompanying rhythms.

VARIATION 3		
29 (10)	**1:02**	This variation uses the minor key, and Beethoven indicates that it should be played "smoothly and quietly throughout."
	1:28	The last part of this variation is repeated.

VARIATION 4		
	1:48	Back to the major and loud again. Octaves in the right hand, triplets in the left.

VARIATION 5		
	2:04	The fifth variation is mostly in eighth notes with a little syncopation and some small chromatic decorations.

VARIATION 6		
	2:26	Dynamic contrasts, sixteenth-note runs, and trills mark the last variation, which ends with a two-measure coda to round off the piece.

BEETHOVEN'S FIFTH SYMPHONY

Beethoven's Fifth Symphony was written in the middle of his heroic period, when the composer was in his late thirties. It is his most famous piece and probably the most famous symphony ever written. The music is taut and expressive, and unified to an unusual degree. The opening four-note motive, with its short-short-short-LONG rhythm, pervades the whole symphony in one form or another. There is a cumulative sense of growth right from the beginning of the first movement to the end of the last movement, and many commentators have noted the feeling of personal triumph that this gives. Underlying this feeling is the motion from C minor to C Major. Symphonies almost always end in the key in which they begin, but Beethoven's Fifth starts out tense and strained in C minor and ends up triumphant and exuberant in C Major. Beethoven also adds several instruments to the orchestra for the last movement, to increase the power and range of the music and add to the sense of triumph.

The feeling of unity in the symphony is reinforced by two further techniques. Instead of being separate, the last two movements are linked, with no pause between them. And Beethoven actually quotes the theme of the third movement in the last movement, thus further connecting them.

All these things—the progression from minor to major, the larger orchestra, the linking of movements, the reference back to earlier movements toward the end—were new to symphonic music at the time and had an enormous influence on later composers throughout the remainder of the nineteenth century.

In the Fifth Symphony, Beethoven set the stage for an entirely new view of music. Music was now seen as the expression of a personal and subjective point of view, no longer as the objective presentation of an artistic creation. This new view was the basis of Romanticism.

> Two opinions of Beethoven's Fifth Symphony:
> "How big it is—quite wild! Enough to bring the house about one's ears!"
> —Goethe
> "Ouf! Let me get out; I must have air. It's incredible!"
> —Jean François Le Sueur

LISTENING GUIDE

Ludwig van Beethoven (1770–1827)
Symphony No. 5 in C minor

Date of composition: 1807–8
Orchestration: 2 flutes, 2 oboes, 2 clarinets, 2 horns, 2 trumpets, timpani, strings
Duration: 33:06

Student CD Collection: 2, track 30
Complete CD Collection: 3, track 11

FIRST MOVEMENT

Tempo: *Allegro con brio* ("Fast and vigorous")
Meter: $\frac{2}{4}$
Key: C minor
Form: Sonata-Allegro
Duration: 7:26

The first movement of Beethoven's Fifth Symphony is dense and concentrated. There is not a note or a gesture too many in the whole movement. The exposition begins with a short-short-short-LONG motive that colors almost every measure of the movement.

The second theme is announced by a horn call. The theme itself starts quietly and smoothly, but underneath it, on cellos and basses, the initial rhythmic motive quietly makes itself heard. Quickly another climax builds, and the exposition ends with the whole orchestra playing the original motive together.

During the development section, the horn call that introduced the second theme is gradually broken down into smaller and smaller elements until only a single chord is echoed quietly between the strings and the woodwinds. Then the recapitulation brings back the music of the movement's first part with crashing force. A short coda brings the movement to a powerful conclusion.

Throughout the movement, long crescendos (from *pianissimo*, **pp**, to *fortissimo*, **ff**) and short passages of quiet music (*piano*, **p**) serve to increase the intensity and drive. The overall effect is one of great power and compression.

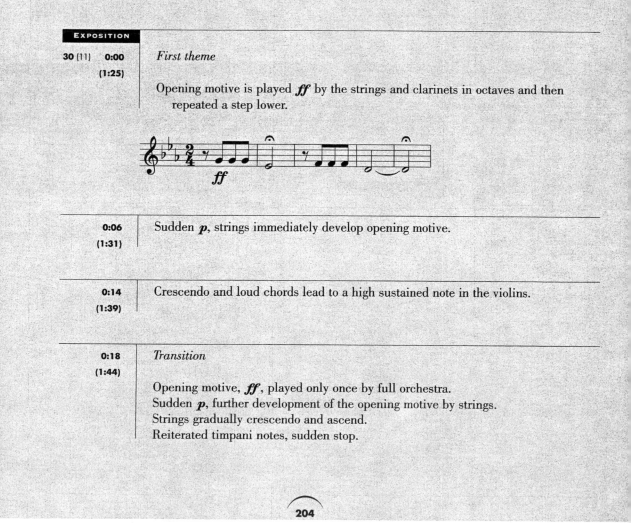

EXPOSITION

30 (11) **0:00**
(1:25)

First theme

Opening motive is played **ff** by the strings and clarinets in octaves and then repeated a step lower.

0:06
(1:31)

Sudden **p**, strings immediately develop opening motive.

0:14
(1:39)

Crescendo and loud chords lead to a high sustained note in the violins.

0:18
(1:44)

Transition

Opening motive, **ff**, played only once by full orchestra.
Sudden **p**, further development of the opening motive by strings.
Strings gradually crescendo and ascend.
Reiterated timpani notes, sudden stop.

0:43 (2:08)		Horn-call motive, *ff*.

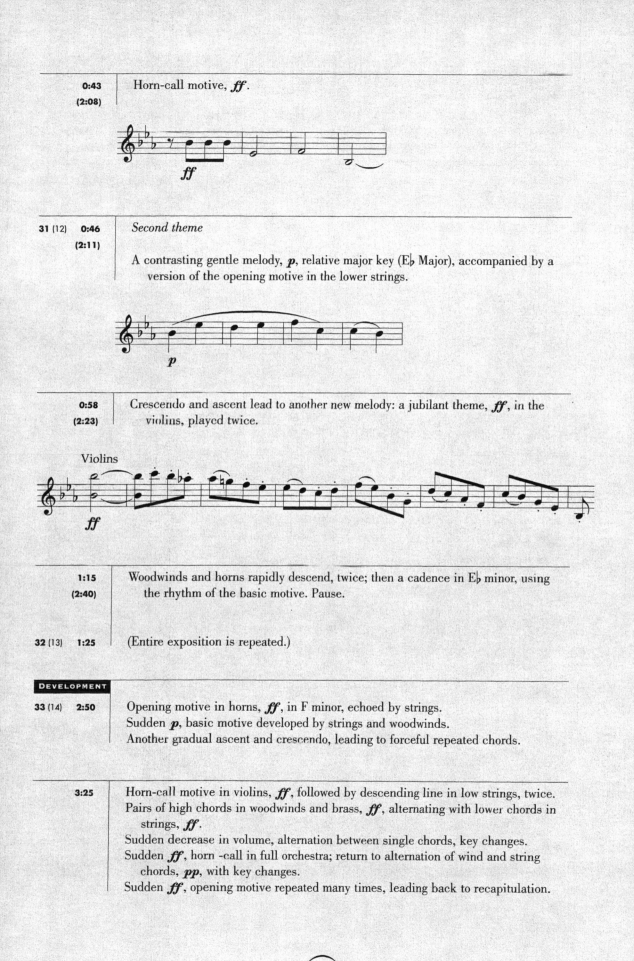

31 (12) **0:46** (2:11)		*Second theme*

A contrasting gentle melody, *p*, relative major key (E♭ Major), accompanied by a version of the opening motive in the lower strings.

0:58 (2:23)	Crescendo and ascent lead to another new melody: a jubilant theme, *ff*, in the violins, played twice.

Violins

1:15 (2:40)	Woodwinds and horns rapidly descend, twice; then a cadence in E♭ minor, using the rhythm of the basic motive. Pause.

32 (13) **1:25**	(Entire exposition is repeated.)

DEVELOPMENT

33 (14) **2:50**	Opening motive in horns, *ff*, in F minor, echoed by strings. Sudden *p*, basic motive developed by strings and woodwinds. Another gradual ascent and crescendo, leading to forceful repeated chords.

3:25	Horn-call motive in violins, *ff*, followed by descending line in low strings, twice. Pairs of high chords in woodwinds and brass, *ff*, alternating with lower chords in strings, *ff*. Sudden decrease in volume, alternation between single chords, key changes. Sudden *ff*, horn-call in full orchestra; return to alternation of wind and string chords, *pp*, with key changes. Sudden *ff*, opening motive repeated many times, leading back to recapitulation.

34 (15)   **4:08**   *First theme*

Opening motive, **ff**, in tonic (C minor), full orchestra.
Opening motive developed, strings, **p**, joined by slow-moving melody on one oboe.
Oboe unexpectedly interrupts the music with a short, plaintive solo.

4:39   *Transition*

Development of opening motive resumes in strings, **p**.
Gradual crescendo, full orchestra, **ff**, repeated timpani notes, sudden stop.
Horn-call motive, **ff**, in horns.

35 (16)   **5:02**   *Second theme*

Contrasting gentle melody, **p**, in C Major (the *major* of the tonic!), played
    alternately by violins and flutes. (Basic motive accompanies in timpani when
    flutes play.) Gradual buildup to the return of:
Jubilant string theme, **ff**, in violins, played twice.
Woodwinds and horns rapidly descend, twice, followed by a cadence using the
    rhythm of the opening motive. Then, without pause, into:

36 (17)   **5:52**   Forceful repeated chords, **ff**, with pauses.
Horn-call motive in lower strings and bassoons, along with flowing violin melody,
    f, in tonic (C minor).
Descending pattern, violins, leads to:
6:17   A completely new theme in the strings, rising up the minor scale in four-note
    sequences.

Violins

f

Four-note fragments of the new theme are forcefully alternated between woodwinds
    and strings.
A short passage of fast, loud, repeated notes leads into a return of the opening
    motive, **ff**, full orchestra.
Suddenly **pp**; strings and woodwinds develop the motive for a few seconds.
A swift and dramatic return to full orchestra, ending with **ff** chords.

Chapter 11

The Nineteenth Century

PART ONE: EARLY ROMANTICISM

In addition to Beethoven, five great composers were active in the first half of the nineteenth century: Franz Schubert, Hector Berlioz, Felix Mendelssohn, Fryderyk Chopin, and Robert Schumann. Also important were the women Clara Schumann (1819–1896) and Fanny Mendelssohn Hensel (1805–1847), though their achievements are harder to assess, as we shall see.

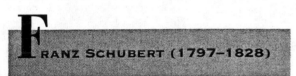

FRANZ SCHUBERT (1797–1828)

Schubert was the son of a Viennese schoolmaster and lived most of his life in Vienna. It is extraordinary to think that Schubert and Beethoven lived at the same time and in the same city and that they met only once.

The two men could not have been more different. Whereas Beethoven was proud, assertive, and difficult to get along with, Schubert was shy, retiring, and exceedingly modest, with a large number of good friends. Their music, too, is very different: Beethoven's dramatic and intellectually powerful, Schubert's gentle, relaxed, and lyrical, with a magical harmonic gift. Finally, whereas most of Beethoven's music was published during his own lifetime, only a small percentage of Schubert's enormous output was published while he was alive, much of it having to wait decades for publication. Schubert wrote more than 900 works in his very short life (he died at the age of 31), a level of productivity that surpasses even that of Mozart.

Schubert sang as a choirboy when he was young and

Franz Schubert.

also played the violin, performing string quartets with his father and brothers at home and playing in the orchestra at the choir school, where he came to know the symphonies of Haydn, Mozart, and Beethoven firsthand. Schubert's gift for composition was already evident, and when his voice changed, he left the choir and was accepted as a composition student by the composer at the Imperial Court in Vienna, Antonio Salieri. His father wanted Schubert to become a schoolmaster like himself; he tried briefly, but he was a poor teacher and soon gave it up. Schubert then embarked on his quiet career as a composer, living in Vienna and working every morning. He seemed to be a limitless fountain of music. "When I finish one piece," he said, "I begin the next." In the afternoons, he went to one or another of the Viennese cafés and spent time with his friends.

Schubert occasionally tried to win recognition by writing opera, the most popular (and lucrative) genre of his day; but although he composed many operas, they met with little success. He also applied for some important musical positions, with the same disappointing result. It seemed as though Vienna had room for only one brilliant composer, and the powerful figure of Beethoven cast a long shadow. In spite of these setbacks, Schubert's talent and modest personality won the affection of many people, who gave him moral and, occasionally, financial support. At one time, several of his friends banded together to pay for the publication of a group of his songs. Toward the end of his life, however, Schubert's essential loneliness often overcame him, and he despaired of achieving happiness. Some of Schubert's most profound works come from this period of his life.

In his last year, Schubert's productivity increased even further. Perhaps he knew that he did not have much time left. A month before he died, Schubert arranged to take lessons in counterpoint! "Now I see how much I still have to learn," he said. He died of syphilis on November 19, 1828. According to his last wishes, he was buried near Beethoven in Vienna. His epitaph, written by a friend, reads: "Here the art of music has buried a rich possession but even more promising hopes."

SCHUBERT'S MUSIC

"Everything he touched turned to song," said one of his friends about Schubert. Schubert's greatest gift was his genius for capturing the essence of a poem when he set it to music. In fact, his song settings seem to transcend the poetry that he put to music. The melodies he devised for the voice, the harmonies and figuration of the piano part—these turn mediocre poetry into superb songs and turn great poetry into some of the most expressive music ever written. During his pathetically short life, Schubert composed *more than 600 songs*. These range from tiny poems on nature, to dramatic dialogues, to folklike tunes, to songs of the deepest emotional intensity. In addition to this enormous number and variety of individual songs, Schubert also wrote two great song cycles, *Die schöne Müllerin* (*The Pretty Miller-Maid*, 1824) and *Winterreise* (*Winter's Journey*, 1827). The first tells the story of a love affair that turns from buoyant happiness to tragedy; the second is a sequence of reflections on nostalgia, old age, and resignation. Both contain music of the greatest simplicity as well as the greatest sophistication. Whether expressing the joys of youthful love or the resignation of old age, Schubert's music goes straight to the heart.

Schubert's gift for lyricism influenced everything he wrote, even his instrumental music. He composed a great variety of music for solo piano and some wonderful chamber music. Apart from the innate lyricism of "everything he touched," two of his chamber works are actually based on songs he wrote. One is called the *Death and the Maiden* String Quartet, the other the *Trout* Quintet. Each has a movement that is a set of variations on a melody from one of those songs. (**See Listening Guides on pages 243 and 245.**)

Among the larger works are several operas, a number of choral works, and eight symphonies. The best known of Schubert's symphonies are his last two, the so-called *Great* C-Major Symphony (1828) and the *Unfinished* Symphony (Schubert completed only two movements).

From his tiny, moving, earliest songs to the expansiveness and grandeur of his late symphonies, Schubert's music is finally emerging from the enormous shadow cast by Beethoven. It is fascinating to contemplate how highly we would regard Schubert's music today if Beethoven hadn't been there at all.

"**M**y peace is gone, my heart is heavy, and I will never again find peace." I may well sing this every day now, for each night, on retiring to bed, I hope I may not wake again; and each morning but recalls yesterday's grief. —Letter of Franz Schubert, 1824, quoting from one of his own songs

Franz Schubert (1797–1828)
Song, *Die Forelle* (The Trout)

Date of composition: 1817
Voice and piano
Tempo: *Etwas lebhaft* ("Rather lively")
Meter: $\frac{2}{4}$
Key: D♭ Major
Duration: 2:10

Student CD Collection: 2, track 59
Complete CD Collection: 4, track 1

"The Trout," written to the poem of a German poet, Christian Friedrich Schubart, appeals to today's listeners just as it did to Schubert's contemporaries. Part of the song's charm lies in the composer's remarkable ability to depict the atmosphere of the poem by blending the melody with its accompaniment, both of which have an equal share in the musical interpretation of the poem.

The song begins with a piano introduction based on a "rippling" figure that evokes the smooth flow of a stream. This figure becomes the dominant feature of the accompaniment, over which the voice sings an animated and lighthearted melody.

The song represents a modified strophic form with an unexpected change of mood in the last stanza. The first two stanzas are sung to the same music simply because the scene remains the same: As long as the water in the stream is clear, the fish is safe. In the third stanza, however, when the fisherman grows impatient and maliciously stirs up the water to outwit the trout, the music becomes more agitated and unsettled. After the fish is finally hooked, the smoothing of the water's surface is represented by the return of the gentle "rippling" figure, which gives a sense of artistic unity and makes the song a highly organic work.

The subtlety of expression, the perfect matching of feeling to music, and the gentle pictorial touches all combine to make of this song a complete miniature masterpiece.

59 (1)	0:00	Piano introduction based on the rippling figure.	

STANZA 1

	[rippling accompaniment continues]	
0:08	*In einem Bächlein helle,*	In a limpid brook
	Da schoss in froher Eil'	In joyous haste
	Die launische Forelle	The whimsical trout
	Vorüber wie ein Pfeil.	Darted about like an arrow.
0:20	*Ich stand an dem Gestade*	I stood on the bank
	Und sah in süsser Ruh'	In blissful peace, watching
	Des muntern Fischleins Bade	The lively fish swim around
	Im klaren Bächlein zu.	In the clear brook.
	[last two lines repeated]	
0:39	Piano interlude	

[same music]

60 (2)   **0:45**

Ein Fischer mit der Rute   An angler with his rod
Wohl an dem Ufer stand,   Stood on the bank,
Und sah's mit kaltem Blute,   Cold-bloodedly watching
Wie sich das Fischlein wand.   The fish's flicker.

0:57

So lang' dem Wasser Helle,   As long as the water is clear,
So dacht' ich, nicht gebricht, I thought, and not disturbed,
So fängt er die Forelle   He'll never catch that trout
Mit seiner Angel nicht.   With his rod.

[last two lines repeated]

1:17   Piano interlude

STANZA 3

[sudden change of rhythm, harmony, and accompanying
figures]

61 (3)   **1:23**

Doch endlich ward dem Diebe   But in the end the thief
Die Zeit zu lang. Er macht   Grew impatient. Cunningly
Das Bächlein tückisch trübe,   He made the brook
                                    cloudy,   [diminished sevenths]

Und eh ich es gedacht,   And in an instant [suspense gaps
                                                       in piano]

1:37

So zuckte seine Rute,   His rod quivered,
Das Fischlein zappelt dran,   And the fish struggled on it. [crescendo]
Und ich mit regem Blute   And I, my blood boiling,   [earlier music
                                                                  returns]

Sah die Betrog'ne an.   Looked at the poor tricked creature.

[last two lines repeated]

1:58   Piano postlude

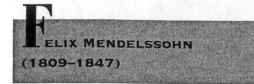

FELIX MENDELSSOHN (1809–1847)

Mendelssohn is one of the two composers in this chapter (the other being Gustav Mahler) who illustrate the uncomfortable position occupied by Jews in nineteenth-century Europe. His grandfather had been the famous Jewish philosopher Moses Mendelssohn. His father was a banker, a prominent member of German middle-class society. And his mother was also from a distinguished family; she was cultivated and very musical. In 1811 the Mendelssohn family was forced to flee from Hamburg to Berlin for political reasons, and when Felix was seven years old, his father had the children baptized; a few years later, his father converted to Christianity himself. Despite the increasing toler-

> **A**rt and Life are not two different things.
> —Felix Mendelssohn

ance of nineteenth-century society, it was still easier to make your way in an "enlightened" age if you were not Jewish.

After that, the family enjoyed increasing prosperity and social status. The Mendelssohn home was a focal point for writers, artists, musicians, and intellectuals in Berlin society. Among the regular guests were the famous philosopher Hegel and the brilliant biologist Humboldt. Chamber concerts were held every weekend, and under the tutelage of their mother, Felix and his older sister Fanny soon proved to be especially gifted in music.

About Fanny we shall say more later. Felix was precocious in everything he undertook. At the age of 10, he was reading Latin and studying arithmetic, geometry, history, and geography. He played the piano and the violin, and he started music theory and composition lessons with a distinguished professor of music in Berlin. He began to compose, write poetry, and paint. Several of his early compositions were performed at the Sunday concerts in his parents' home.

As a youth, Mendelssohn was introduced to the most famous literary figure in Germany, Goethe, and a great friendship developed between the old man and the gifted teenager. Mendelssohn also traveled widely in Europe, either on holidays with his family or in the company of his father.

All of this time, Mendelssohn was composing prolifically. He had an extraordinary fluency and control. By the time he was 20 he had written more than 100 pieces.

Mendelssohn was very interested in music of the past. It was at the age of 20 that, together with a family friend who was a professional actor, he arranged for a performance of one of the great masterpieces of Bach that had not been heard for nearly a century—the *St. Matthew Passion*. The performance, with Mendelssohn conducting, was a landmark in the revival and appreciation of Bach's music in the modern era. "To think," said Mendelssohn, "that it should be an actor and a Jew who give back to the people the greatest of all Christian works."

Felix Mendelssohn about 1829.

In his twenties, Mendelssohn continued to perform as a conductor and a pianist, to compose prolifically, and to travel a great deal, in Italy, Scotland, and England. In 1835, he was appointed conductor of the Leipzig Gewandhaus Orchestra, where he worked hard to improve the quality of performances and the working conditions of the musicians. He revived many important works of the past and also championed the music of his contemporaries. When the score of Schubert's *Great* C-Major Symphony was discovered, the world premiere was given by Mendelssohn and his orchestra.

Mendelssohn was married in 1837, and the couple had five children. In 1843 he was appointed director of the Berlin Cathedral Choir and director of the Berlin Opera. He continued to divide his time between Berlin and Leipzig, and in the same year he was appointed director of the newly opened music conservatory in Leipzig. Despite all these activities, Mendelssohn continued to compose. Among the many works he wrote at this time were an opera, two large oratorios, symphonies, concertos, chamber music, and numerous pieces for solo piano.

In May of 1847, his closest friend and confidante, his sister Fanny, suddenly died. Felix was shattered. His last great work, the String Quartet in F Minor, Op. 80, was composed as a "Requiem for Fanny." He became ill and tired and could no longer conduct. A series of strokes in October led to his death on November 3, 1847, at the age of 38. Mendelssohn was buried in Berlin, near Fanny's grave.

MENDELSSOHN'S MUSIC

Mendelssohn was a composer who continued the Classic tradition in his works, while adopting some of the less extreme ideas of Romanticism. He wrote in most of the traditional genres of the Classic era, and the formal outlines of his works are clear and easy to follow. Mendelssohn maintained the greatest respect for the past—especially the music of Bach, Handel, Mozart, and Beethoven—and his music shows the influence of these composers. His style is more transparent and lighter than that of many early Romantic composers, certainly less extroverted and smaller in scale than that of Berlioz; it ranges from lively and brilliantly animated to lyrical and expressive.

Mendelssohn's main orchestral works include five symphonies and several overtures. Many of these are programmatic, though only in a general sense: They do not tell a detailed story but evoke scenes and landscapes. The best known of these are the *Scottish* Symphony (Symphony No. 3), the *Italian* Symphony (Symphony No. 4), and the *Hebrides* Overture, all written after Mendelssohn's travels. The *Hebrides* Overture was inspired by his trip to Scotland and evokes a rocky landscape and the swell of the sea. Like many early Romantics, Mendelssohn read and admired Shakespeare, and another overture often performed today is the Overture to Shakespeare's *A Midsummer Night's Dream*. Listening to this piece, it is hard to believe it was written when the composer was only 17.

Mendelssohn also wrote several concertos, mostly for piano but also for violin. His Violin Concerto in E minor is certainly the most popular of all his works, because of its beauty and lyricism. (**See Listening Guide on page 256.**)

Mendelssohn's admiration for Bach and Handel led to his interest in choral writing. After the famous revival of Bach's *St. Matthew Passion*, Mendelssohn studied Handel's oratorios and composed two major oratorios of his own, *Elijah* and *St. Paul*. He also wrote a great deal of other choral music, and his sacred music includes works for Jewish, Catholic, Lutheran, and Anglican services.

His chamber music includes songs, string quartets, sonatas, and piano trios. Perhaps the most popular of these works is the Piano Trio in D minor. In addition, Mendelssohn wrote a large number of miniatures for solo piano; in the typical mold of early Romanticism, he called them *Songs Without Words*. They are gentle, delightful, and lyrical—expressive without being deeply profound. In these ways, they capture the essence of Felix Mendelssohn's music.

ver since I began to compose, I have remained true to my starting principle: not to write a page because the public or a pretty girl wanted it a certain way, but to write solely as I thought best.
—Felix Mendelssohn

Felix Mendelssohn (1809–1847)
First Movement from Concerto in
  E minor for Violin and Orchestra,
  Op. 64

Date of composition: 1844
Orchestration: Solo violin and orchestra
Tempo: *Allegro molto appassionato*
  ("Fast and very passionate")
Meter: $\frac{2}{2}$
Key: E minor
Duration: 13:17

Complete CD Collection: 4, track 19

This concerto, one of Mendelssohn's most popular works, was composed three years before his death. It has remained one of the favorites of all the Romantic violin concertos for its combination of lyricism and dazzling virtuosity. There are many innovative features. First, all the movements follow one another without a break. Second, in contrast to the Classical concerto, melodies are initially stated by the soloist instead of by the orchestra. Finally, the cadenza in the first movement is placed immediately after the development section, instead of coming at the end like an afterthought.

There are many demanding sections throughout this concerto. Particularly challenging are those places where the violin soloist is required to finger and bow *two* strings simultaneously. This technique is termed "double-stopping" and is featured in all movements. Octave double-stops present even more difficulties, since precise fingering is extremely difficult.

FIRST MOVEMENT	[sonata form]
	Allegro molto appassionato

EXPOSITION

(19)	0:00	FIRST THEME (solo violin), high, over quiet accompaniment.

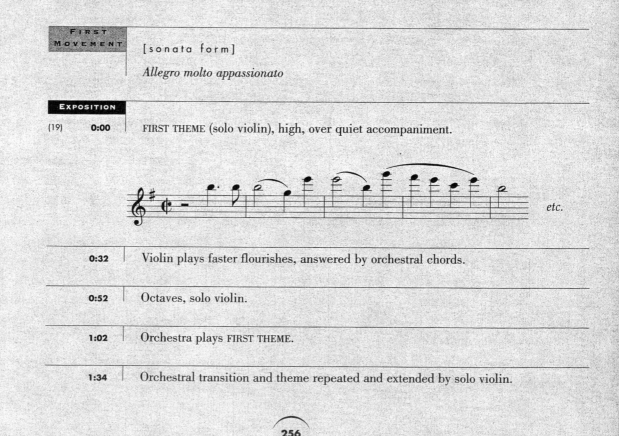

	0:32	Violin plays faster flourishes, answered by orchestral chords.
	0:52	Octaves, solo violin.
	1:02	Orchestra plays FIRST THEME.
	1:34	Orchestral transition and theme repeated and extended by solo violin.

	2:06	More flourishes, featuring double-stops (solo violin), and an orchestral climax. Gradually the music calms and leads to a cadence.

(20)	**3:03**	SECOND THEME, initiated by woodwinds, answered and extended by solo violin.

	4:24	Return to FIRST THEME, virtuosic passages, crescendo, big orchestral chords.

DEVELOPMENT

(21)	**5:38**	Fragmentation of themes, including transitional material and first and second themes. Contrasts of loud and soft, violin descends, everything calms down before a big crescendo into the:
(22)	**7:20**	*Cadenza* (violin alone), featuring difficult trills, double-stops, and extremely high notes.

RECAPITULATION

(23)	**8:54**	Orchestra plays FIRST THEME while solo violin continues virtuosic flourishes.
	9:13	Traditional material, loud, orchestra, repeated and extended by violin, quietly. Cadence.
(24)	**9:48**	SECOND THEME, woodwinds, then solo violin with extension. Cadence.
	11:08	Motion increases, brilliant running passages on solo violin, fragments of themes and pizzicatos on the orchestra.
	11:59	Stratospheric climbs by solo violin, punctuated by big orchestral chords. Speed and intensity gradually increase to:
	12:09	Subsidiary Theme, solo violin.
	12:44	*Presto* (very fast) section, hurried-sounding, signaling ending of the movement.
	13:10	End of movement, but bassoon holds a single note (to lead into the beginning of the next movement).

FANNY MENDELSSOHN HENSEL (1805–1847)

Fanny was four years older than Felix, and they were very close throughout their lives. Fanny was a talented pianist and also a gifted composer, but her career as a composer illustrates the distance women still had to travel for equality of opportunity in the nineteenth century.

Her father strongly disapproved of the idea of her pursuing a career in music. Like many people of his time, he felt that a professional career was unsuitable for a woman. Amateur music-making was entirely acceptable—indeed, it was the province of a cultivated young woman—but making a living as a performer or a composer was out of the question. Even her brother Felix agreed with this view.

Fanny Mendelssohn about 1830.

So Fanny led the more conventional life of a well-educated middle-class woman. At 24, she married Wilhelm Hensel, a painter and artist at the court in Berlin. Fanny had a son and ran the family household. She continued to play the piano, and after her mother's death she took over the organization of the famous Sunday concerts at her parents' home. She often played the piano at the concerts and directed a choral group that performed there. One day, at the age of 41, while rehearsing the chorus for a performance of a cantata composed by Felix, she had a stroke. She died that same evening.

Despite discouragement from her father and her brother, Fanny had composed a great deal. She wrote many songs, some cantatas and oratorios, chamber music, and small piano works, which, like Felix, she called *Songs Without Words*. **(See Listening Guide on page 259.)**

Some of her early songs were published in collections with pieces by her brother, though they carried Felix's name. After the death of her father, she did arrange for publication of one or two works under her own name.

All in all, Fanny composed about 400 works, though most of them have never been published. They remain in manuscript in American and European libraries. In the last few years, with increasing focus on the contributions of women to the history of music, more and more of her works are being published and recorded. It is impossible to assess her true contributions or to compare her achievement with Felix's until her compositions have received the same attention as those of her brother.

Fanny Mendelssohn Hensel
  (1805–1847)
Lied from *Songs without Words*, Op. 8,
  No. 3

Date of composition: 1840?
Tempo: *Larghetto* ("Fairly slow")
Meter: $\frac{4}{4}$
Key: D Major
Duration: 3:05

Student CD Collection: 2, track 69
Complete CD Collection: 4, track 25

 he *Lieder ohne Wörte* (*Songs Without Words*) were not published until after Fanny's death. The third of this four-piece set, entitled *Lied* (*Song*), is also marked *Lenau*, the name of a German poet, suggesting that an actual poem may have inspired her to write this song. The tuneful, flowing phrases are indeed highly singable and memorable. The form is a typical one for a song: ABA. Throughout the piece, there is an accompaniment of gentle, repeated chords in the middle range, and slow, isolated bass notes. The atmosphere suggests a reflective inner dialogue.

A		
69 (25)	0:00	Melody repeats a gently curving motive, followed by an ascending leap, as a kind of questioning idea. This is followed by a balanced descending motive. The mood is one of contemplation.
	0:30	Questioning idea in low range, response in higher range.
B		
70 (26)	1:03	Modulating, unstable B section—shorter, faster exchanges of questioning idea, answered by descending arpeggios.
	1:20	Minor version of questioning idea in low range. Crescendo, then decrescendo, leads to:
A'		
71 (27)	1:39	Clear return of the beginning, moving quickly to faster sequential phrases.
	2:15	Closing section using questioning idea, including crescendo and leap to highest note of the piece. Ends with gentle decrescendo.

The nineteenth century witnessed the rise, across Europe, of a large, primarily urban, middle class. Members of this class not only formed the largest audience for music, but also became music "consumers," buying sheet music of songs or chamber music for performances at home. An evening was not complete without a song recital or an amateur piano performance after dinner. Nineteenth-century novels, such as those of Eliot or Thackeray, are full of references to such performances, mostly by women. ¶ Composers, too, belonged mostly to the middle class. They were small entrepreneurs in their own right, negotiating fees with publishers and concert promoters. Many composers made a comfortable living from their music. They were also freer from the constraints of employers, such as the church or aristocratic courts, which often had dictated terms of style or content to composers in previous eras. The artistic freedom of composers in the nineteenth century was therefore the result of economic as well as aesthetic conditions.

FRYDERYK CHOPIN (1810–1849)

Chopin was the first of the great piano virtuosos in the Romantic era. Most composers before Chopin played the piano, and many of them actually composed at the keyboard, even if they weren't writing piano music. But after Beethoven, Chopin was the first important nineteenth-century composer to achieve fame as a performing pianist, and almost all his compositions are written for solo piano.

Chopin was born in 1810 to a French father and a Polish mother. His father taught French, and his mother taught piano at a school in Warsaw. Chopin began formal piano lessons at the age of seven, and his first composition was published the same year. At the age of eight, he gave his first public concert, and at the age of 15 he was sufficiently accomplished to play before Tsar Alexander I of Russia, who presented him with a diamond ring.

When Chopin was 19, he heard the great violinist Paganini play and was inspired to become a touring virtuoso himself. Most of his compositions at this time were designed for his own use. Chopin would improvise for hours at the keyboard and only occasionally write down what he had played. His music was often based on Polish dances such as the polonaise or the mazurka.

In 1830, Chopin completed two piano concertos, which he performed in public concerts, and toward the end of the year he left Poland, unaware that he would never see it again. From a distance he heard of the Warsaw uprising and the storming of Warsaw by the Russian army. From this time on, the Polish quality of his music deepened, and his compositions became more intense and passionate. A review stated: "Chopin has listened to the song of the Polish villager, he has made it his own and united the tunes of his native land in skillful composition and elegant execution."

In 1831, at the age of 21, Chopin settled in Paris, the center of European artistic activity. Soon he was caught up in the whirl of Parisian society, and his brilliant and poetic playing made him very much in demand in the city's fashionable salons. He had a wide circle of friends, including some of the great cultural figures of the time, such as Berlioz, Liszt, and the artist Delacroix.

In his late twenties, Chopin was introduced by Franz Liszt to Aurore Dudevant, a well-known novelist who published under the male pseudonym George Sand. They soon started living together, and the years they spent together were among the most productive of Chopin's life. He was often ill, however, displaying the first signs of the tuberculosis that would later kill him. George Sand looked after him devotedly, though Chopin was a difficult patient, and there is a rather unflattering portrait of him in one of her novels.

The relationship ended in 1847, after which Chopin's health rapidly deteriorated. He composed little but gave public recitals in London and Paris. It was reported that he was too weak to play louder than *mezzo-forte*. Chopin died in 1849 at the age of 39. At his request, Mozart's Requiem was played at his funeral.

Portrait of Chopin at the age of 28 by the famous French painter Eugène Delacroix.

Eugène Delacroix (1798–1863). *Portrait of Frederic Chopin* (1810–1860), 1838. Oil on canvas, 45.5 × 38 cm. Louvre, Dpt. des Peintures, France. © Photograph by Erich Lessing. Erich Lessing/Art Resource, NY.

CHOPIN'S MUSIC

The best way to think of Chopin's music is as poetry for the piano. In an English newspaper, he was once called a "musical Wordsworth." He wrote no program music, and almost all his works are for solo piano. The two piano concertos are really piano solos with rather sketchy orchestral accompaniment.

Chopin's style is entirely a personal one, as might be expected from one who improvised so freely. Most of his pieces are fairly short, and they fall into several categories. First there are the dances—polonaises, mazurkas, and waltzes. The **waltz** was fast becoming the favorite ballroom dance of the nineteenth century. Chopin managed to create enormous variety of mood with the basic format of this one dance. (**See Listening Guide on page 264.**) **Mazurkas** and **polonaises** are both Polish dances, and Chopin invested them with the spirit of Polish nationalism. Mazurkas are in triple meter with a stress on the second or third beat of the bar. Polonaises are stately and proud.

261

Chopin also wrote in free forms without dance rhythms: preludes, études, nocturnes, and impromptus. The **preludes** follow the pattern established by Bach in his *Well-Tempered Clavier*: There is one in each major and minor key. (**See Listening Guide below**.) **Étude** literally means "study piece," and each of Chopin's études concentrates on one facet of musicianship or piano technique. The **nocturnes** are moody, introspective pieces, and the **impromptus** capture the essence of improvisation ("impromptu" means "off the cuff").

The formal structure of these pieces is fundamentally simple, relying upon the ABA pattern common to aria or song form. However, Chopin usually varied the return of the opening section quite considerably, creating instead an ABA' structure.

In all these genres, Chopin wrote highly individual pieces, each one with an elegiac or rhapsodic quality, and each one expressive and pianistic—that is, perfectly suited to the special sound and capabilities of the piano. Chopin's works are carefully designed for the instrument of his day. They depend upon the new tech-

nology of the early nineteenth-century piano, which allowed the rapid repetition of single notes. The sound of the instrument was softer, less brilliant than it is today, and Chopin's melodies and chords exploited this quality. Often, the melodies are highly lyrical and dreamy, and the sustaining pedal allows widely spaced notes to blend together as chords in the left hand. Chopin's left-hand harmony is varied and expressive, and sometimes the main melody can appear in the left hand with the accompaniment above it in the right. There is often much delicate, rapid ornamentation in the right hand, with short free passages or runs or trills that add to the impression of improvisation. Finally, Chopin's written directions often call for a special expressive device called **rubato**. Literally, this Italian word means "robbed." Using this technique, the player keeps the tempo going in the accompaniment while the melody slows down slightly before catching up a moment later. Carefully applied, rubato can suggest the kind of expressive freedom that must have characterized the playing of Chopin himself.

> Compared with Berlioz, Chopin was a morbidly sentimental flea by the side of a roaring lion.
> —J. W. Davison

LISTENING GUIDE

Fryderyk Chopin (1810–1849)
Prelude in E minor, Op. 28, for Piano

Date of composition: 1836–39
Tempo: *Largo* ("Broad")
Meter: $\frac{2}{2}$
Duration: 2:27

Student CD Collection: 3, track 1
Complete CD Collection: 4, track 28

Chopin composed 24 preludes between 1836 and 1839. They follow the same idea as Bach's two sets of preludes and fugues, presenting all 24 major and minor keys of the scale system.

This particular piece features an ABA' structure. In the A section, an almost static melodic line is accompanied by steady chords that constantly descend. Notice the use of "neighbor" tones in the right-hand melody: the melody goes to an adjacent pitch and then returns. The B section is marked by melodic arpeggios and has more rhythmic movement. The return of the A section is varied, and there is a wonderfully expressive silence before the end.

A SECTION		
1 (28)	**0:00**	Opening melody. Focus is on descending left-hand accompanying chords. Upper neighbor tone is heard several times in right hand.
	0:20	New note, melodic motion continues to descend.
B SECTION		
2 (29)	**0:46**	More motion in melody and change in accompanying figures.
	1:01	End of section, little flourish in melody, returning to:
A¹ SECTION		
3 (30)	**1:07**	Variation of A.
	1:22	More rhythmic activity in both hands.
	1:25	Loudest section.
	1:35	Feeling of stasis.
	1:48	"Goal" reached.
	2:01	Final chord?
	2:04	Expressive silence.
	2:09	Real final cadence (three chords).

Fryderyk Chopin (1810–1849)
Waltz in D-flat Major, Op. 64, No. 1,
  for Piano Solo (*Minute* Waltz)

Date of composition: 1847
Tempo: *Tempo giusto* ("Exact tempo")
Meter: $\frac{3}{4}$
Duration: 1:47

Complete CD Collection: 4, track 31

This is the sixth of 14 waltzes Chopin wrote for the piano. Each one is based on the characteristic "ONE-two-three ONE-two-three" waltz rhythm, but each one is different.

The D♭-Major Waltz is known as the *Minute* Waltz because it is so short, though it actually takes about two minutes to play. Chopin marks it *Molto vivace—leggiero* ("Very fast and lively—light"). The opening theme, in which the melody seems to circle around itself, has been compared to a dog chasing its own tail. The overall scheme is ABCAB, with repetitions of melodic phrases within each section. This gives form to the delicate and swirling music.

A			
(31)	0:00	Around and around, right hand only.	
	0:04	Waltz rhythm enters in left hand, right-hand melody in eighth notes.	
B			
(32)	0:12	New melody, rapid key changes, continuing fast eighth notes.	
	0:22	Repeat of B section.	
C			
(33)	0:33	Lower melody in A♭, slower in effect (melody in half and quarter notes).	
	0:48	Ornamented repeat; slow down.	
	1:01	Trill, return to:	
A			
	1:06	Around and around, opening music and melody.	
B			
(34)	1:19	B section again; repeated.	
	1:38	Very high descent to closing chords.	

A typically Romantic painting of Liszt at the piano. Those listening (from left to right) are the great figures of nineteenth-century music and literature: the poet Alfred de Musset, authors Victor Hugo and George Sand, fabled violinist Paganini and composer Rossini, and (seated) author Marie d'Agoult, Liszt's common-law wife. The entire scene is dominated by the almost surreal figure of Ludwig van Beethoven.

RICHARD WAGNER (1813–1883)

Richard Wagner is a perfect example of the contradictions inherent in genius. His importance as a composer was enormous, and his writings on music, literature, and politics exerted a tremendous influence on artistic and intellectual thought throughout the second half of the nineteenth century. Yet he was an appalling egoist, a home-wrecker, and an outspoken and virulent anti-Semite.

Wagner was born in Leipzig. His father died when Wagner was an infant, and when his mother married again, Wagner was educated under the influence of his stepfather, who was a writer and an artist. Wagner studied Shakespeare and Homer and was overwhelmed by hearing Beethoven. At Leipzig University he studied music, but, before completing his degree, left to take a job in a small opera house. For the next six years, Wagner learned about opera from the inside, as a chorus director and as a conductor. He married an actress, Minna Planer, and composed his own first operas. From the beginning, Wagner wrote his own librettos and was thus able to achieve remarkable cohesion between the drama and the music.

From the beginning, too, Wagner spent more than he earned. In 1839, he was forced to flee Germany rather than end up in debtor's prison. His passport and Minna's had been revoked, so they crossed the border at night and made a harrowing journey to Paris.

The two were extremely poor, and the Paris Opera would not accept Wagner's latest work, *Rienzi*, for production. He made a living by selling some music—and most of Minna's clothes! He also composed another opera, based on the folk tale of *The Flying Dutchman*.

Discouraged by his reception in Paris, Wagner suddenly received news that both *Rienzi* and *The Flying Dutchman* had been accepted for production in Germany. He was overwhelmed with gratitude and swore never to leave his native land again. The operas were a great success. At the première of *Rienzi* at the Dresden

opera house, Wagner "cried and laughed at the same time, and hugged everyone he met." At the age of 30, Wagner was appointed court conductor in Dresden.

The couple was financially comfortable for the first time, and Wagner was able to compose two more operas: *Tannhäuser* (1845) and *Lohengrin* (1848). In both operas, Wagner continued to base his librettos not on historical drama but on folk legend. *Tannhäuser* is the story of a medieval German troubadour; *Lohengrin* is based on Grimm's fairy tale of the Swan Knight of the Holy Grail.

After joining a failed coup against the monarchy in 1848, Wagner again had to leave the country. And despite his earlier vow, the next 12 years were years of exile. He and Minna settled in Zurich, and from this period date his most important writings: an essay called *The Art Work of the Future* (1849) and a book entitled *Opera and Drama* (1851). In these works, he called for a renewal of the artistic ideals of Greek antiquity, in which poetry, drama, philosophy, and music would be combined into a single work of art: the "complete art work," as Wagner called it. Music and words should be completely interwoven in a retelling of old myths, which could carry the resonance of profound human truth. This new type of opera was known as **music drama**.

Wagner spent the next 35 years fulfilling this vision. But before he did so, he revealed a far less attractive side of his personality by publishing a vicious anti-Semitic essay entitled *Jewishness in Music*. He attacked the music of Mendelssohn and other Jewish composers and went on to call for the removal of the entire Jewish community ("this destructive foreign element") from Germany.

Wagner next started composing the poetry and the music for the largest musical project of the entire Romantic period: his cycle of music dramas entitled *The Ring of the Nibelungs*. This was to be a series of four long operas based on medieval German legend, involving gods and goddesses, dwarfs and giants, and human heroes. The central symbol of the cycle is a

The French poet Baudelaire on Wagner's music: "I love Wagner, but the music I prefer is that of a cat hung up by its tail outside a window and trying to stick to the panes of glass with its claws."

The Ring Cycle

Wagner's *The Ring of the Nibelungs* is a cycle of four music dramas: *The Rhinegold, The Valkyries, Siegfried*, and *The Twilight of the Gods*. It represents one of the greatest achievements in the history of Western music. Its creation took Wagner more than 25 years. The four dramas together take more than 15 hours to perform. ✦ Wagner wrote the music *and* the poetry for *The Ring*. Although the poetry is itself an impressive achievement, it is the manner in which the music describes and illuminates the poetry that is most extraordinary. Wagner's dense network of **leitmotivs**—musical phrases associated with objects, characters, events, thoughts, and feelings—adds meaning to the text and offers psychological insights into the characters and the reasons behind their actions. ✦ *The Ring* explores universal and contradictory themes: love and hate, heroism and cowardice, good and evil, greed and selflessness, naïveté and unscrupulousness. Power, symbolized by the ring itself, is exposed as a corrupting force. The English playwright and critic George Bernard Shaw interpreted parts of *The Ring* as a political allegory of the oppressed masses in the nineteenth century. The German author Thomas Mann, a profound admirer of Wagner, considered the huge *Ring* cycle the equivalent of Émile Zola's cycle of novels or the epic Russian novels of Tolstoi and Dostoevski. Like those great literary masterpieces, *The Ring* is still powerfully relevant today.

magic ring made of stolen gold that dooms all who possess it.

Wagner set about this enormous task with no hope of performance. Halfway through, he broke off work to write two other operas unconnected to the Ring cycle: *Tristan and Isolde* (1859) and *The Mastersingers of Nuremberg* (1867). He was in the grip of an unstoppable creative urge. Speaking of these years later in life, he said: "The towering fires of life burned in me with such unutterable heat and brilliance that they almost consumed me."

He had affairs with other women: the wife of a French patron (her husband threatened to put a bullet through Wagner's head), the wife of a wealthy merchant who lent him money (she was the inspiration for *Tristan and Isolde*), and the new wife of a good friend, the conductor and enthusiastic Wagner supporter Hans von Bülow. Cosima von Bülow was the daughter of Franz Liszt, another loyal friend of Wagner's. The affair gradually deepened, and Wagner and Minna separated. But it was not until eight years later that Wagner and Cosima could be married, after overcoming the objections of both Liszt and Hans von Bülow. By then the couple had already had two daughters and a son. Cosima was 32, Wagner 57.

During these last eight years, Wagner had despaired of having his new operas produced, but his hopes were suddenly realized beyond his wildest dreams. In 1864 an 18-year-old youth ascended the throne of Bavaria as King Ludwig II of Bavaria. Having read Wagner's writings and admired his operas, King Ludwig was an ardent fan of Wagner's. He was also in love with Wagner. "An earthly being cannot match up to a divine spirit," the king wrote to Wagner. "But it can love; it can venerate. You are my first, my only love, and always will be."

For the rest of Wagner's life, his extravagant financial demands were met with unparalleled generosity by the young king. Wagner's work prospered. He was able to finish the gigantic *Ring* cycle, and he made plans for a new theater in which the four-evening event could be staged. These plans finally came to fruition in a new opera house in Bayreuth (pronounced "BYE-royt"), a small town in Bavaria.

On February 13, 1883, Wagner died of a heart attack. Since Wagner's death, his memory has inspired a cult. Worshippers make the pilgrimage to Bayreuth for the annual Wagner festival. Wagner societies exist in countries around the world. The Bayreuth Festival has been run by members of Wagner's family since his death.

The Bayreuth Festival

Wagner laid the foundation stone for his own *Festspielhaus* ("Festival Theater") in Bayreuth on May 22, 1872. Initially, money for the project was hard to come by. However, King Ludwig's generous financial assistance enabled the theater to be completed. The first production—the entire *Ring* cycle—took place in August of 1876. The next Bayreuth Festival did not take place until 1882. At a performance of *Parsifal* that year, Wagner conducted the final scene—his only conducting appearance at the theater. ¶ Since Wagner's death in 1883, the Bayreuth Festival has been run by members of Wagner's family. His widow and son, Cosima and Siegfried, were in charge until they both died in 1930, whereupon Winnifred, Siegfried's widow, took over. The ensuing years, 1930–44, were clouded by Adolf Hitler's association with Winnifred and with Bayreuth. ¶ The Bayreuth Festival closed in 1944 as a result of the Second World War. It reopened in 1951 with extraordinarily successful productions of *Parsifal* and *The Ring*, directed by Wieland Wagner, the composer's grandson. Under Wieland, Bayreuth attained a new acceptability, distancing itself from its Nazi association. Wolfgang Wagner, another of Wagner's grandsons, assumed responsibility for the Festival in 1966, following Wieland's death.

Wagner's art is diseased.
—Friedrich Nietzsche

BU-274

WAGNER'S MUSIC

Wagner's only important works are for the opera stage. His first two operas, *Rienzi* and *The Flying Dutchman*, are in the tradition of German Romantic opera, with grand scenes and with separate arias, duets, ensembles, and choruses. Already, however, we see Wagner writing his own librettos and concentrating on human beings as symbols of grand ideas. (Verdi, by contrast, concentrated on human beings for their expression of humanity.) By the time of *Tannhäuser* and *Lohengrin*, Wagner had developed his poetic skill and found fertile ground in ancient legend. His poetry is terse and powerful. In both operas, the individual items (aria, recitative, chorus) are less distinct in musical style, and there is much more musical continuity.

For the works up to *Lohengrin*, we can still use the term "opera"; the later works are music dramas. In the *Ring* cycle (made up of four music dramas: *The Rhinegold*, *The Valkyries*, *Siegfried*, and *The Twilight of the Gods*), Wagner developed his technique of continuity

to the fullest. The music is absolutely continuous, and the orchestra carries the main musical content. The voices sing in an **arioso** style (that is, halfway between speechlike recitative and lyrical aria), blending into the instrumental fabric. *Tristan and Isolde* and *The Mastersingers*, which Wagner composed in the middle of *The Ring*, and *Parsifal*, which he composed after it, also display this technique.

The orchestra is central to Wagner's music, and he wrote for a large one. He particularly enjoyed using brass instruments. He even invented a new musical instrument to cover the gap between the horns and the trombones. This instrument is known as a **Wagner tuba**. The orchestra of the *Ring* uses four of them. Their sound is rounder, a little deeper, and more solemn than that of the horns.

Musical continuity in Wagner's music dramas is also achieved through harmonic means. In this, too, Wagner was a revolutionary. Instead of ending each phrase with a cadence, he tends to melt the end of one phrase into the beginning of the next. And whereas most music of the time is clearly in a specific key, Wagner's music is tonally very ambiguous. Often it is so chromatic that it is hard to say which key is being used at any one point. In Wagner's *Tristan and Isolde*, for example, there seems to be no fixed key or clear-cut cadence until the very end of the work! This perfectly suits the sense of unfulfillment and longing that is the subject of the drama. **(See Listening Guide on page 292.)**

Finally, Wagner's music depends upon a technique that he himself invented (though it might be seen as the logical outcome of earlier musical developments). This technique is the use of **leitmotiv** (pronounced "LIGHT-moteef"). This is a German word that means **leading motive**. A leitmotiv is a musical phrase or fragment that carries associations with a person, object, or idea in the drama.

You may remember that Berlioz used a recurrent theme (*idée fixe*) to refer to the beloved in his *Symphonie fantastique*. And other composers used themes associated with particular characters in their operas. Wagner's leitmotiv technique is different. First, leitmotivs can refer to many things other than a person.

Photographic portrait of Richard Wagner in velvet coat and hat.

Leitmotivs in Wagner's music dramas are associated with a spear, longing, fate, and the magic ring itself. Second, Wagner's leitmotivs are flexible, undergoing musical transformation as the ideas, objects, or people change in the course of the drama. Finally, Wagner uses his leitmotivs like threads in a tapestry. They can be combined, interwoven, contrasted, or blended to create an infinity of allusions and meanings.

Wagner, the political revolutionary, revolutionized music by his brilliant writing for orchestra, by making the orchestra the central "character" of his dramas, and by his development of the leitmotiv technique. In addition, Wagner's continuity of writing and tonally ambiguous harmonic style laid the foundation for the completely new language of twentieth-century music.

A spectacular production of Verdi's *Aida* in the Roman amphitheatre at Verona.

I want subjects that are novel, big, beautiful, varied, and bold—as bold as can be.
—Giuseppe Verdi

Grieg specialized in piano miniatures inspired by Norwegian tunes. His well-known orchestral *Peer Gynt* Suite was written for the play of the same name by the Norwegian writer Henrik Ibsen. The Danish composer Carl Nielsen (1865–1931) was a highly individual composer, whose main works (operas, symphonies, and string quartets) belong to the first two decades of the twentieth century. The leading composer of Finland was Jan Sibelius (1865–1957). He wrote seven superb symphonies and a deeply emotional string quartet, but his most famous work is the symphonic poem *Finlandia* (1899), whose intense national flavor caused it to be banned by the foreign rulers in Finland, though it was an immense success throughout the rest of Europe.

SPAIN

The principal nationalist composers of Spain were Enrique Granados (1867–1916), Isaac Albéniz (1860–1909), and Manuel de Falla (1876–1946). Granados and Albéniz wrote piano suites in lively Spanish rhythms and with colorful melodies. De Falla is best known for his wonderful *Nights in the Gardens of Spain*, a series of three evocative and atmospheric pieces for piano and orchestra.

FRANCE

After the end of the Franco-Prussian War in 1871, a National Society for French Music was founded to encourage French composers. The most gifted of these were Camille Saint-Saëns (1835–1921) and Gabriel Fauré (1845–1924). Saint-Saëns' *Carnival of the Animals* for chamber orchestra is great fun; his Symphony No. 3 is a more serious work but also very attractive. Fauré wrote exquisite French songs to poems by some of the leading French poets of his day.

PYOTR ILYICH TCHAIKOVSKY (1840–1893)

The Russian composer Pyotr Ilyich Tchaikovsky wrote operas in Russian based on works of Russian literature and also made use of Russian folk songs—but he was not as committed a nationalist as some of his contemporaries. It may be partly for this reason that he achieved an international success.

Tchaikovsky was the son of a mining engineer and a mother of French extraction, to whom he was very close. He had piano lessons as a child and did some composing, but he turned to music as his main emotional outlet only after his mother died when he was 14. Tchaikovsky began to earn a living as a government clerk at the age of 19, but when the new St. Petersburg Music Conservatory was founded, he quit his job and entered the Conservatory as a full-time student. A family friend described him as "poor but profoundly happy" at having chosen music as a career. His talents were such that a year after graduating, he was appointed professor at the music conservatory in Moscow. From that time on, he devoted his life to music.

In Moscow he met many other composers and publishers and flourished in the lively atmosphere of the cosmopolitan city. He also traveled abroad. He wrote articles and a book on music and composed prolifically.

All this time, however, Tchaikovsky lived with a secret: He was gay. He was tormented by self-hatred and the fear of being exposed. In 1877, at the age of 37, he suddenly decided to get married. Partly he may have felt that this step might "cure" him of his nature; partly he may have thought he needed the cover. The marriage was an instant disaster. Tchaikovsky fled, attempted suicide, and had a nervous breakdown.

After some months of convalescence, Tchaikovsky gradually recovered and turned once more to music. Both his Fourth Symphony and his opera *Eugene Onyegin* date from this time, and both contain powerful reflections of his emotional state.

A strange turn of events helped to provide emotional and financial support for Tchaikovsky. A wealthy widow named Madame von Meck decided to become his patron. She said she would commission some pieces and provide the composer with an annual income. There was only one condition: The two must never meet. This suited Tchaikovsky perfectly, and for the next 13 years Madame von Meck and Tchaikovsky

From Tchaikovsky's review of a performance of *Das Rheingold*, from Wagner's *Ring* cycle: "From the scenic point of view it interested me greatly, and I was also much impressed by the marvelous staging of the work. Musically it is inconceivable nonsense."

carried on an intense personal relationship without ever seeing each other. They shared their innermost thoughts, but only by letter, and they wrote to each other every day.

Tchaikovsky was able to resign his teaching post, and he composed a great deal of music during those years. In 1890, Madame von Meck suddenly broke off the relationship and the patronage. No explanation was offered, though her family may have put pressure on her to direct her funds elsewhere. Tchaikovsky was deeply hurt, but by now he had a substantial income from his music, and the Russian czar had provided him with a life pension.

In his last years, Tchaikovsky wrote some of his best-known music, including a ballet entitled *The Nutcracker* and his Sixth Symphony, subtitled *Pathétique*. Tchaikovsky died in 1893, apparently of cholera, though it has been suggested that, threatened with public exposure of his homosexuality, he committed suicide.

TCHAIKOVSKY'S MUSIC

Tchaikovsky's music is highly emotional. It surges with passion and appeals directly to the senses. The range of expression is very great, from the depths of despair to the height of joy. There is sensuousness, delicacy, nobility, tenderness, and fire. *The Nutcracker* is one of the most popular ballet scores in the world, though it is followed closely by *Sleeping Beauty* and *Swan Lake*, both also by Tchaikovsky. The Fourth and Sixth Symphonies are deeply emotional utterances, and his operas, such as *Eugene Onyegin* and *The Queen of Spades*, though less well known, are powerfully dramatic works. Tchaikovsky also wrote three piano concertos as well as a violin concerto that enraptures audiences every time it is played.

Tchaikovsky used an orchestra of moderate size; he never went to the extremes of some other Romantic composers. But he was very interested in orchestral color. There is little in music to match the stirring brass fanfare at the beginning of the Fourth Symphony or the

Copyright

Before the first international convention on the issue of copyright, held in Berne, Switzerland, in 1886, composers' works were unprotected. There was little that famous composers could do to prevent "pirate" editions of their works from circulating. Unscrupulous publishers would simply get hold of a copy of the work and then print and sell copies of it. A fundamental principle was established at Berne, namely that a published work (including a musical one) is protected under copyright during the author's or composer's lifetime and for 50 years following his or her death; the principle has remained more or less intact to the present day. In addition, regarding musical works, a fee must be paid for each *performance* of a work, whether it be live or recorded.

Tchaikovsky in 1888.

> Repulsive and barbaric.
> —a Viennese newspaper on Tchaikovsky's Violin Concerto

paired clarinets at the beginning of the Sixth. For "The Dance of the Sugar-Plum Fairy" in *The Nutcracker*, Tchaikovsky contrasts the delicate shimmery sound of the celesta with the deep richness of a bass clarinet.

Tchaikovsky was a master of melody. Some of his tunes have become a part of the Western consciousness, featured in famous popular songs or as soundtracks to movies. He sometimes used folk tunes, but most of his melodies came from his own inexhaustible lyrical gift. Tchaikovsky was a Russian composer, as he always insisted, but his music speaks to millions of people as the expression of a human heart.

> Where words fail, music speaks.
> —Tchaikovsky, quoting the German writer Heinrich Heine

301

Pyotr Ilyich Tchaikovsky (1840–1893)
First Movement from Symphony No. 4
   in F minor

Date of composition: 1877–78

Orchestration: 2 flutes, 2 oboes,
   2 clarinets, 2 bassoons, 4 horns,
   2 trumpets, 2 trombones, bass
   trombone, tuba, timpani, strings

Tempo: *Andante sostenuto* ("Fairly slow
   and sustained")

Meter: ¾

Key: F minor

Duration: 18:43

Complete CD Collection: 5, track 24

*T*chaikovsky's Symphony No. 4 is a powerful, impassioned work, written at the time of Tchaikovsky's disastrous marriage. The composer described it as a "musical confession of the soul." The first movement particularly has an enormous expressive range. Its two most striking elements are a powerful brass fanfare that opens the work (and returns to interrupt the music at crucial points) and a radical reinterpretation of Classic sonata form. Tchaikovsky described the brass fanfare as "inescapable Fate," and the whole movement as "a perpetual alternation between grim reality and dreams of happiness."

To mold the passion and intensity of his music, Tchaikovsky casts his first movement in a sonata form that has been forcefully reshaped. The development of the first theme occurs mostly *within* the exposition; the development section itself is correspondingly brief; and the recapitulation is foreshortened and condensed, leading to a frantically accelerated coda. At major structural points in this form (at the beginnings of the development, recapitulation, and coda), the Fate motive intrudes forcibly and inexorably. Finally, for this movement, Tchaikovsky adopts a highly unconventional key-scheme that traces a circle of minor thirds beginning and ending on F: F, A♭, C♭ (=B), D, and F. As a true Romantic, Tchaikovsky created his own individual blend of tradition and innovation as a vehicle for his most personal utterances.

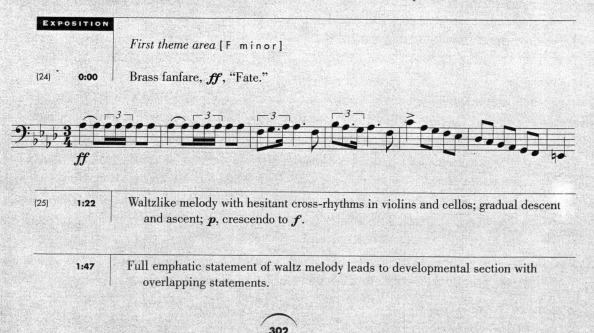

EXPOSITION		
		First theme area [F minor]
(24)	**0:00**	Brass fanfare, **ƒƒ**, "Fate."
(25)	**1:22**	Waltzlike melody with hesitant cross-rhythms in violins and cellos; gradual descent and ascent; **p**, crescendo to **ƒ**.
	1:47	Full emphatic statement of waltz melody leads to developmental section with overlapping statements.

	3:06	Full emphatic statement of waltz melody.
	3:36	More fragmentary versions of waltz melody.
	4:09	Full statement, strings with repeated sixteenth notes.
	4:37	Suddenly quiet, transition to:
(26)	5:20	*Second theme area* [A♭ minor] Clarinet, rhythmically jumpy theme and fast, falling chromatic scales echoed by other winds.
	5:43	Jumpy theme again with new lyrical countermelody in cellos.
	6:34	[C♭ = (B)] ***pp***; timpani articulate gradual accelerando and crescendo; new lyrical idea in violins alternates with waltz melody in winds.
	7:13	Lyrical idea in flutes; waltz melody in strings; accelerando and crescendo continue.
(27)	7:54	Closing theme: bold descending arpeggios in strings linked by rising scales, accompanied by *rhythms* of waltz melody in brass.
	8:12	Descending arpeggios in brass.
	8:29	Closing material: waltz theme.

DEVELOPMENT

(28)	9:02	Fanfare idea, "Fate." Sounds like repeat of the exposition but moves directly into:
	9:21	Developmental treatment of waltz melody.
	9:55	Ascending version of waltz melody in cellos.
	10:02	Lyrical idea in cellos now as countermelody to waltz melody.
	10:27	Lyrical idea again.
	10:50	Long crescendo; building and gradually ascending.

(29)	**11:26**	Fanfare idea used developmentally.
	11:46	Fanfare, again, at higher pitch; illusion of ever-ascending pitch and growing intensity.
	12:14	Descending scales.

RECAPITULATION

[D minor]

(30)	**12:18**	Fanfare returns, "Fate."
	12:30	Powerful return of waltz idea, decrescendo to:
(31)	**13:04**	Quiet return of second theme; jumpy rhythms in bassoon, followed by fast falling chromatic line.
	13:28	Lyrical idea in French horn as countermelody.

[F minor]

	14:21	Lyrical idea and waltz melody alternate quietly; timpani articulates a long gradual crescendo and accelerando.
	15:31	Building intensely to:
	15:43	Closing material built on waltz theme.

CODA

(32)	**16:13**	Return of fanfare, "Fate," with timpani roll. [Slower tempo]
	16:36	New sustained ascending flute line.
	16:55	Sustained line moves to oboe; waltz rhythms build.
	17:13	Suddenly *pp* and quicker; waltz rhythms accelerate even more.
	17:36	Previous passage repeated.
	18:04	Tremolo version of waltz melody; conclusion with timpani rolls and heavy octave chords.

PART THREE: LATE ROMANTICISM

Toward the end of the nineteenth century, a new atmosphere reigned in Europe and the United States. Independence and unification brought more stability to many countries, and there were moves toward greater democracy, with monarchies being replaced by parliamentary governments. Free compulsory education led to a more educated public, and the early horrors of the sweat shops were gradually replaced by better working conditions. Commerce and industry were central preoccupations, and a more down-to-earth attitude replaced the dreamy fantasyland of high Romanticism. The movement known as Realism affected all culture, from the novels of Dickens, Flaubert, and Zola to the plays of Henrik Ibsen, the paintings of Gustave Courbet, and the philosophy of William James. Music was also affected, as we shall see. As the end of the century approached, a spirit of general dissatisfaction and uneasiness took hold.

The major composers of late Romanticism were Johannes Brahms, Giacomo Puccini, and Gustav Mahler. All these composers reflected the new atmosphere in different ways. Brahms found new force in the rigor of Classic and Baroque musical genres and forms. Puccini wrote dramatic realist operas of acute psychological insight. Mahler created a new synthesis of song and symphony in a mood tinged with resignation.

JOHANNES BRAHMS (1833–1897)

Johannes Brahms was born in Hamburg in 1833. His father was an orchestral and band musician; his mother came from a wealthy family and was 44 when Brahms was born, a fact that may have colored Brahms's later relationship with Clara Schumann, who was 14 years older than he.

Brahms was a child prodigy. He gave his first piano recital at the age of 10, and an American entrepreneur tried to book him for a concert tour of the United States, but his piano teacher refused. Brahms spent much of his youth playing the piano at bars and coffee houses; he also wrote pieces for his father's band. While still a youth, he was exposed to Hungarian gypsy music as a result of the flight of many nationalist rebels from Hungary after the Hungarian uprising of 1848. This led to a fascination with gypsy tunes and rhythms. Brahms also met the great violinist Joseph Joachim, with whom he developed a lifelong friendship. But the real turning point for Brahms came when he was 20 and he met Robert Schumann. Brahms played some of his own compositions for the great Romantic master in

Johannes Brahms as a young man.

Schumann's study. After a few minutes, Schumann stopped him and went to fetch Clara. "Now you will hear music such as you have never heard before," he said to her. During the time of Schumann's illness, Brahms and Clara Schumann became very close. Their friendship lasted until Clara's death 43 years later, one year before Brahms's own.

Throughout his life, Brahms compared himself, mostly unfavorably, with other great composers of the past, especially Beethoven. He said that he felt the presence of Beethoven as "the step of a giant over my shoulder." It took him 20 years to summon the courage to publish his First Symphony.

Brahms settled in Vienna, the imperial capital, where he made a name for himself as a pianist. "He plays so brightly and clearly," wrote Joseph Joachim. "I have never met such talent." He also worked as a conductor. Brahms lived a quiet, reserved life, and although he enjoyed the company of many friends, he also needed a great deal of solitude. He usually hid his feelings. Clara Schumann, who knew him better than anyone else, called him "a riddle." In his musical life, he was not pleased to be seen as a symbol of conservatism and the leader of an "anti-modern" movement in music. Wagner attacked him mercilessly in print, calling him a "street-musician," a "hypocrite," and a "eunuch."

Brahms deliberately avoided the innovative genres of modern music, such as the symphonic poem and music drama, preferring instead solo piano pieces, songs, choral works, chamber music, concertos, and symphonies. He continued to be conscious of the great achievements of the past. The last movement of his First Symphony makes a deliberate reference to Beethoven's Ninth, and the last movement of his Fourth Symphony uses a Baroque form and is based on a theme by Bach.

Throughout the years, Brahms continued to rely on Clara Schumann for advice and comments on his compositions. Her enormous enthusiasm undoubtedly bolstered his self-confidence. But in the spring of 1896 came terrible news: Clara had died of a stroke. Brahms traveled to Bonn to attend her funeral. On his return, he wrote one of his most beautiful works, the *Four Serious Songs* for piano and voice on texts that Brahms selected from the Bible. The fourth song, with a text from Corinthians, describes the immortality of love: "These three things endure: faith, hope, and love; but the greatest of these is love." A month after Clara's funeral, Brahms was diagnosed with cancer. He died on April 3, 1897, at the age of 64. Large crowds attended his funeral, and messages of sadness poured in from all over Europe. In the great port city of Hamburg, where Brahms had been born, all the ships lowered their flags to half mast.

BRAHMS'S MUSIC

Brahms was a Romantic who expressed himself in Classic and sometimes even Baroque forms; within these forms, his music is highly original. Brahms avoided the fashionable genres of Romantic music, such as opera and symphonic poems. And he wrote no program music, though he liked to hide references to women he admired in his compositions. He adored the human voice, and his Romantic songs follow directly in the line of Schubert and Schumann. The main themes of his songs are love, nature, and (toward the end of his life) death. He also set many folk songs to music. The most famous of these is the exquisite *Lullaby*, Op. 49, No. 4 (sometimes called "Brahms's Lullaby"). We shall listen to this work. **(See Listening Guide on page 308.)**

His four symphonies are masterpieces—the first and the fourth powerful and intense, the second and the third more lyrical and serene. We shall study a movement from the Fourth Symphony. **(See Listening Guide on page 309.)** The Violin Concerto stands with those of Beethoven, Mendelssohn, and Tchaikovsky as one of the great violin concertos of the nineteenth century. It is technically impressive, powerful, and lively, but it also has passages of great calm and beauty. Written for himself to play, Brahms's two piano concertos are also masterpieces. In all his orchestral works, Brahms used an orchestra not much bigger than Beethoven's, avoiding the huge, showy sounds of Wagner and Liszt. One characteristic of Brahms's style is his thick orchestral textures. He liked to "fill in" the sound between treble and bass with many musical lines, and to double melodies in thirds or sixths. He especially favored instruments that play in the middle range, such as clarinet, viola, and French horn.

This warmth of sound may be found in his chamber music as well. Because he was a fine pianist, Brahms wrote several chamber works for piano and strings, but he also composed some excellent string quartets. His love of rich textures is shown in the two string *quintets* and two string *sextets*. Toward the end of his life, after he had decided to give up composition, Brahms met a fine clarinetist who inspired several chamber works featuring the clarinet. In all these works there is passion, but the passion is mingled with resignation and an autumnal sense of peace. Brahms's solo piano music was written mostly for his own performance. The early pieces are strong and showy, but the later ones are much more delicate and extremely profound.

Brahms composed several choral works. The most important of these is the *German Requiem*, for soprano and baritone soloists, chorus, and orchestra, for which Brahms chose his own texts from the German Bible. It was not written for a religious service but for concert performance. Nevertheless, the music is sincere and deeply felt. Brahms was a man who did not believe in organized religion, yet he was privately devout and read every day from the Bible he had owned since childhood.

Brahms has been called a conservative composer because of his adherence to models from the past. Yet he was an innovator in many ways. His rhythms are always complex and interesting, with syncopation and offbeat accents and with a very frequent use of mixed duple and triple meters. His phrases are often irregular—expanded or contracted from the usual four- or eight-bar format. And he was a master of variation, in which something familiar is constantly undergoing change. Indeed, in Brahms's music there is very little exact repetition or recapitulation: the music seems to grow organically from beginning to end. Brahms himself was both complex and fascinating, and the same can be said of his music.

Because of the beauty and sweetness of his tone, Brahms called clarinetist Richard Mühlfeld *Fräulein Klarinette* ("Miss Clarinet"). He also described him as "the greatest artist there is on the instrument."

Johannes Brahms (1833–1897)
Wiegenlied (Lullaby), Op. 49, No. 4

Date of composition: 1868
Tempo: *Zart bewegt* ("Moving tenderly")
Meter: ¾
Key: E♭ Major
Duration: 2:07

Complete CD Collection: 5, track 33

*B*rahms wrote this, perhaps his most famous song, for the baby son of a woman who sang in his choir in Hamburg. It is strophic: The two stanzas are sung to the same music. The poem (an old German folk song) has three pairs of lines, but Brahms repeats the last pair to make a balanced four pairs, with four phrases of music, given four measures each. There are an additional two measures of piano introduction. Brahms uses every means at his disposal to create a peaceful musical setting for this lullaby. The vocal line is smooth and wafting; the piano part has transparent texture, a rocking, hazy rhythm, and extremely stable harmonies. There is the slightest intensification of the piano part in the second half of each stanza ("Morgen früh...")/("Schlaf nun...").

---

9 (33)   **0:00** | [Two measures piano introduction, setting the mood]

STANZA 1

0:06 | *Guten abend, gut' Nacht,*   Good night, good night,
           | *Mit Rosen bedacht,*   (Those covers) decorated with roses,
           | *Mit Näglein besteckt,*   Embroidered with carnations,
           | *Schlupf unter die Deck.*   Slip under them.

           [ends high]

0:31 | *Morgen früh, wenn Gott will,*   Tomorrow morning, God willing,
           | *Wirst du wieder geweckt.*   You will wake again.
           | *Morgen früh, wenn Gott will,*   Tomorrow morning, God willing,
           | *Wirst du wieder geweckt.*   You will wake again.

           [ends low]

STANZA 2

[music repeated for second stanza]

1:05 | *Guten Abend, gut' Nacht,*   Good night, good night,
           | *Von Englein bewacht,*   You are watched over by angels,
           | *Die zeigen im Traum*   Who will show you in your dreams
           | *Dir Christkindleins Baum.*   The Christ child's tree.
           | *Schlaf nun selig und süss,*   Sleep now, blessed and sweet,
           | *Schau im Traum's Paradies.*   And look at Paradise in your dreams.
           | *Schlaf nun selig und süss,*   Sleep now, blessed and sweet,
           | *Schau im Traum's Paradies.*   And look at Paradise in your dreams.

Chapter 12

The Twentieth Century I: The Classical Scene

The French writer Romain Rolland, describing Debussy: "The great painter of dreams."

The composer whose music most closely parallels these developments was Debussy, who was also French and lived in Paris. He attended many of the first exhibitions of Impressionist painting and was a personal friend of several of the Symbolist writers.

Claude Debussy was a talented pianist as a child and was accepted as a student at the Paris Conservatory of Music at the age of 10. When he was 18, he began to study composition, and in 1884 he won the prestigious Prix de Rome, the highest award for French composers. One of the influences on his music was the distinctive sound of the Indonesian gamelan. (We heard an example of gamelan music in the opening chapter of the book.)

Debussy's most famous orchestral composition is the *Prelude to the Afternoon of a Faun* (1894), which is based on the poem by the Symbolist poet Mallarmé. The music is dreamy and suggestive, using a large orchestra primarily for tone color. Other orchestral pieces by Debussy include *Trois Nocturnes* (*Three Nocturnes*) and *La Mer* (*The Sea*). *Trois Nocturnes* has three sections, entitled "Clouds," "Festivals," and "Sirens." *La Mer* also consists of three sections, evoking sun and sea, the play of waves, and the sound of the wind on the water. Later, Debussy wrote his only opera, *Pelléas et Mélisande*, to a Symbolist play by Maeterlinck. **(See Listening Guide on page 333.)**

Debussy's piano music is highly varied and includes some of his greatest compositions. There are pieces of pure Impressionism, such as *Jardins sous la pluie* (*Gardens in the Rain*) or

La Cathédrale engloutie (*The Sunken Cathedral*), but also humorous pieces, technical studies, and music for children. The best-known piece for children is *Golliwog's Cake-Walk*. Debussy also wrote some non-Impressionist chamber music, including a fine string quartet and sonatas for violin and piano, cello and piano, and flute, viola, and harp.

Debussy's music was little known until he was about 40. After the premiere of *Pelléas et Mélisande*, he became quite famous and traveled around Europe conducting performances of his work. He loved fine food and fancy clothes and as a result was often short of money. He had two wives and a mistress, though not all at the same time! Debussy died of cancer in his native Paris at the age of 56.

Claude Debussy in a portrait by Marcel Baschet, 1884.

Claude Debussy (1862–1918)
Prélude à l'après-midi d'un faune

Date of composition: 1894
Orchestration: 3 flutes, 2 oboes,
    English horn, 2 clarinets,
    2 bassoons, 4 horns, 2 harps,
    antique cymbals, strings
Duration: 11:10

Complete CD Collection: 6, track 5

Debussy's *Prelude to the Afternoon of a Faun* is an evocation of natural scenes, sense-impressions, and moods. It suggests the thoughts and feelings of a mythical creature of the forest, who is half man and half goat (not to be confused with "fawn"). He is half asleep in the hot sun and his mind dwells on sexual fantasies. He expresses his feelings by playing his panpipes.

Debussy matches the mood of the poem with sensuous, dreamy music that often swells up with emotion. He uses a large orchestra, with two harps but no trumpets, trombones, or timpani. The only percussion instruments are antique cymbals—very small cymbals that resonate quietly near the end of the piece. Other special orchestral colors are created by harp glissandos and horn calls played with mutes to make them sound far away. Most of the time, the strings play very quietly, and sometimes they use special effects, such as playing with a mute or bowing over the fingerboard, which creates a hushed tone. In this context of a piece that is mostly quiet, the few passages of crescendo sound emotional and surging.

The opening flute melody is sensuous, chromatic, and vague. This melody serves as the basis for much of the piece. It is shaped as a series of curves, gently rising and falling. Debussy deliberately modeled the shape of this melody on medieval plainchant, which he thought could serve as an inspiration for composers in the Modernist era.

The composition falls into three sections in an ABA pattern, though each section merges imperceptibly with the next, and the return of the opening A section is modified. One of Debussy's aims was to break down the clear formal outlines of traditional music.

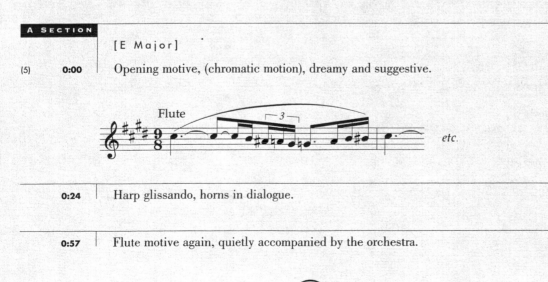

A Section		
		[E Major]
(5)	0:00	Opening motive, (chromatic motion), dreamy and suggestive.

| | 0:24 | Harp glissando, horns in dialogue. |
| | 0:57 | Flute motive again, quietly accompanied by the orchestra. |

	1:15	Horns play quick little figures. Oboe elaborates flute motive.

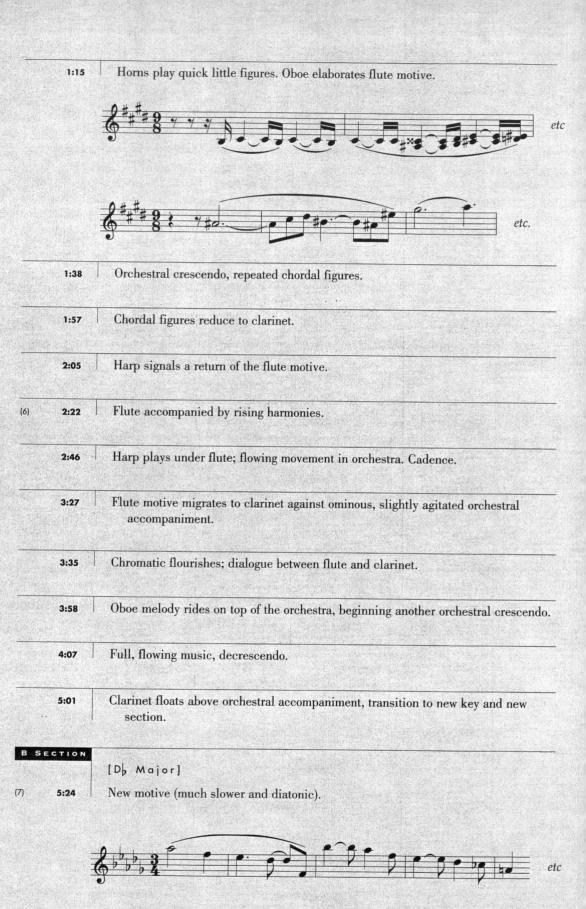

	1:38	Orchestral crescendo, repeated chordal figures.
	1:57	Chordal figures reduce to clarinet.
	2:05	Harp signals a return of the flute motive.
(6)	2:22	Flute accompanied by rising harmonies.
	2:46	Harp plays under flute; flowing movement in orchestra. Cadence.
	3:27	Flute motive migrates to clarinet against ominous, slightly agitated orchestral accompaniment.
	3:35	Chromatic flourishes; dialogue between flute and clarinet.
	3:58	Oboe melody rides on top of the orchestra, beginning another orchestral crescendo.
	4:07	Full, flowing music, decrescendo.
	5:01	Clarinet floats above orchestral accompaniment, transition to new key and new section.

B SECTION

[Db Major]

(7)	5:24	New motive (much slower and diatonic).

	5:50	Crescendo.
	6:04	New motive becomes slow-moving melody for strings.
	6:14	Crescendo, decrescendo; music is constantly moving and pulsating.
	6:54	Horn melody in duet with solo violin, harp accompaniment.
(8)	**7:23**	Flute introduces abbreviated, slower form of the opening motive, at a slightly higher pitch; harp accompaniment continues.

	7:44	Oboe, faster motion with trill; lively conversation with other woodwinds.
	8:00	Oboe plays slow version of motive.
	8:22	English horn reiterates the oboe motive, with similar comments from the other woodwinds.

A¹ SECTION

[return to E Major]

(9)	**8:40**	Flute melody returns, along with E-Major tonality. Diatonic accompaniment against chromatic solos of the woodwinds.
	9:02	Antique cymbals.
	9:54	Ending chords; oboe melody; mixed orchestral colors.
	10:20	Single descending notes from harp. Brief nostalgic reminiscences of motive.
	10:59	Pizzicato (low strings).

PRIMITIVISM

Primitivism is the name given to a movement in painting at the beginning of the twentieth century. Artists were attracted by what they saw as the directness, instinctiveness, and exoticism of non-urban cultures. This was a time during which writers such as Sigmund Freud were exploring the power of instinct and the unconscious.

Among the painters of Primitivism were Paul Gauguin, Henri Rousseau, and Pablo Picasso. Again, the center of this artistic movement was Paris. Paul Gauguin was fascinated by "primitive" cultures and eventually went to the South Sea Islands to live and work among the islanders. His paintings are bold and bright, and they use symbols of cultural primitivism. Henri Rousseau's paintings are deliberately naive but highly imaginative. Their vivid scenes are not designed as representative of nature but as evocations of a state of mind. Pablo Picasso was one of the greatest painters of the twentieth century, and he changed his style many times during his lifetime. But in the early 1900s, he, too, was interested in Primitivism, and his painting *Les Demoiselles d'Avignon* (*The Young Women of Avignon*) is an example of this style. It is also a landmark in twentieth-century art. The painting is raw, primitive, and deliberately shocking. Its flat planes, deconstruction of the bodies, angularity of form, and especially the use of African masks for some of the faces had a revolutionary impact on the development of modern painting.

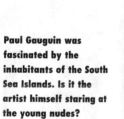

Paul Gauguin was fascinated by the inhabitants of the South Sea Islands. Is it the artist himself staring at the young nudes?

Paul Gauguin (1848–1903), *Contes barbares*. 1902. Oil on canvas, 130 × 89 cm. Essen, Museum Folkwang. Archiv für Kunst und Geschichte, Berlin.

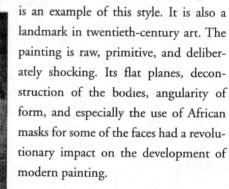

IGOR STRAVINSKY (1882–1971)

The musical equivalent of Picasso was Stravinsky. He, too, lived a long life, evolved several distinct styles during his career, and had a lasting impact on twentieth-century culture.

Igor Stravinsky was born in St. Petersburg, Russia. His father was an opera singer, but he insisted that Igor study law at the university instead of music. Stravinsky used to compose on the sly. At the age of 21, he gave up law altogether and began formal music lessons with the great Russian nationalist com-

Igor Stravinsky in 1925.

poser Rimsky-Korsakov. From his mentor, Stravinsky learned how to obtain vivid colors and strong effects from an orchestra.

In 1910, Stravinsky moved to Paris, at that time the undisputed center of European culture. Stravinsky was asked to produce some works for the Ballets Russes, a famous and influential ballet troupe based in Paris and headed by the great Russian impresario Serge Diaghilev. Stravinsky wrote three of his most important ballet scores as commissions for the Ballets Russes: *The Firebird* (1910), *Petrushka* (1911), and *The Rite of Spring* (1913). All three are inspired by the prevailing style of Primitivism. The primitive atmosphere in Stravinsky's music is enhanced by his use of **polyrhythms** (different meters sounding at the same time), **bitonality** (two different keys sounding at the same time), and **ostinato** (constantly repeated phrases).

The Rite of Spring, a composition of tremendous power and boldness, is one of the most revolutionary works of the twentieth century. It depicts the rituals of ancient pagan tribes, and it caused a riot at its first performance in Paris in 1913. The audience was profoundly shocked by the violent and overtly sexual nature of the choreography on stage as well as by the pounding rhythms and clashing dissonances from the orchestra. Soon thereafter, the work was recognized as a masterpiece. **(See Listening Guide on page 338.)**

Stravinsky lived in Switzerland during the First World War, and then returned to Paris in 1920. His most important compositions from this period took a different direction entirely. Smaller and more transparent, they relied on small groups of varied instruments and sometimes were influenced by the new music emanating from America—jazz. The jazz-influenced pieces from this period include *Ragtime* for 11 instruments (1918) and

> S travinsky's music used to be original. Now it is aboriginal.
> —Ernest Newman, 1921

> S travinsky looks like a man who was potty-trained too early, and his music proves it as far as I'm concerned.
> —Russell Hoban

Picasso's revolutionary painting *Les Demoiselles d'Avignon* (1907).

Pablo Picasso, *Les Demoiselles d'Avignon*. Paris (June–July 1907). Oil on canvas, 8' × 7'8" (243.9 × 233.7 cm). The Museum of Modern Art, New York. Acquired through the Lillie P. Bliss Bequest. Photograph © 1998 The Museum of Modern Art. © 2002 Estate of Pablo Picasso/Artists Rights Society (ARS), New York.

Igor Stravinsky (1882–1971)
Le Sacre du Printemps (The Rite of Spring), **Opening Section**

Date of composition: 1913

Orchestration: Piccolo, 3 flutes, alto flute, 4 oboes, English horn, E♭ clarinet, 3 clarinets, 2 bass clarinets, 4 bassoons, contrabassoon, 8 horns, D trumpet, 4 trumpets, 3 trombones, 2 tubas, 2 timpani, bass drum, side drum, triangle, antique cymbals, strings

Duration: 8:50

Complete CD Collection: 6, track 10

Some of Stravinsky's most memorable works were written for the Ballets Russes in Paris within 10 years before World War I. *Le Sacre du Printemps*, the third of a group of ballets (with *The Firebird*, 1910, and *Petrushka*, 1911), was finished in 1913. It features the largest orchestra ever used by Stravinsky and presents bold, daring, and often alarming moments that shocked the first audiences. *Le Sacre du Printemps* was one of the musical masterpieces that was visually realized in Walt Disney's animated feature *Fantasia*, as musical background to the creation of the world. See how your own imagination compares with that of the Disney classic, or even that of Stravinsky's own conception, which was a succession of tribal rites. Even without pictures, the music is brilliantly imaginative, colorful, and striking. Maybe even more so!

We will listen only to the first several minutes, beginning with a solo bassoon, playing in its eerie highest register:

(10)	0:00	
	0:10	Horn enters.
	0:20	Descending woodwinds; clarinet.
	0:44	English horn enters. More bassoon.
	0:58	Woodwinds gather momentum.
	1:12	Trills, fuller texture; small high clarinet.

1:32	Bubbling bass clarinet.
1:45	Section comes to a close, trills in violins.
1:55	Small clarinet, interplay with English horn.
2:16	Flute response.
2:24	Oboe.
2:29	Small clarinet in high register.
2:47	Muted trumpet.
2:51	Begin orchestral crescendo.
3:01	Stop!
3:02	Bassoon reappears, high-register solo.
3:10	Clarinet trill, pizzicato strings, chords. Monotonous two-note figure starts and continues through the following:
(11) 3:34	Pounding, steady orchestral chords, irregular accents.

3:44	Movement in woodwinds, arpeggios.
3:53	Trumpet, triplet figures, quick runs on winds.
4:13	Orchestral pounding returns.

	4:22	Bass melody: bassoons interspersed with orchestra rhythms.
	4:32	Trombone, orchestral flashes of color.
(12)	4:53	Big brass chord; timpani; return of two-note figure; orchestral flashes.
	5:17	Horn melody.
	5:21	Flute response.
	5:28	Dialogue between flute and muted trumpet.
	5:36	Flutes enter, accompanied by other woodwinds; two-note figure continues.
(13)	5:53	Brass chords, parallel motion up and down; much louder now.
	6:09	Agitated strings; piccolo.
	6:17	Woodwind melody.
	6:27	Orchestral crescendo, with short blasts.
	6:53	Loud drum crashes, rhythmic activity increases over static accompaniment.
(14)	7:03	Brass chords.
	7:29	Triplet rhythms, horn calls, high flutes, dissonant wild trumpet calls, very fast strings punctuated by drum strokes.
	8:17	Clarinets in octaves, melody over flute trills.
	8:42	Pulse slows down to a low-pitched trudge.

Piano-Rag-Music (1919). Stravinsky was attracted to jazz because of its clear, clean textures and lively rhythms.

In 1920, Diaghilev invited Stravinsky to arrange some eighteenth-century music for a ballet called *Pulcinella*. Stravinsky took some chamber sonatas by Classic composers and not only orchestrated them but also subtly reworked them, transforming the Classic style into a modern idiom. He organized the accompanying figures into ostinatos, rewrote some of the harmonies to make them slightly more biting, and changed the phrase-lengths to make them slightly irregular. The result is a remarkable work that was also extraordinarily influential on the development of twentieth-century music. Indeed, *Pulcinella* ushered in a completely new compositional style known as Neo-Classicism.

STRAVINSKY AND NEO-CLASSICISM

Stravinsky's work on *Pulcinella* led him to a new consideration of Western musical traditions, and he used the past as a means of renewing the present. He said: "*Pulcinella* was my discovery of the past, the epiphany through which the whole of my late work became possible."

Neo-Classical composers in the twentieth century adopted ideas not only from the Classic period, but also from the Baroque era. In place of the big, wild, expressive orchestral sounds of the 1910s (like those in *The Rite of Spring*), the focus now was on formal balance, clarity, and objectivity. Many Neo-Classical compositions use small ensembles, and some of them have titles that deliberately recall Classic and Baroque genres, such as Concerto or Symphony.

As well as adopting the genres (concerto, concerto grosso, symphony) of eighteenth-century music, Stravinsky adopted their formal structures. In the music from his Neo-Classical period, you can find patterns that are like sonata form, theme-and-variations form, aria form, and rondo form. In no way, however, could one of Stravinsky's Neo-Classical compositions ever be mistaken for an original piece from the eighteenth century. Although the aesthetic

of the past is clearly there, the style of the music has been updated and modernized. Harmonies are modern, accompanying figures are new, phrase-lengths are irregular, and the rhythm is lively, bouncy, even a little quirky. **(See Listening Guide on page 342.)**

In 1939, as Europe headed once again toward the catastrophe of a world war, Stravinsky moved to America. He settled in Los Angeles and was engaged by Hollywood to write some film scores. Unfortunately, none of these was ever completed. He did finish a Mass, as well as an opera called *The Rake's Progress* (1951). *The Rake's Progress* is the last composition of Stravinsky's Neo-Classical style and one of the finest.

After 1951 Stravinsky began to experiment with twelve-tone techniques and again radically changed his musical style. Many of his late compositions use twelve-tone methods of composition. They include an elegy for President John F. Kennedy (completed in 1964) and a Requiem written in anticipation of Stravinsky's own death. Stravinsky died in 1971, near the age of 90, having undertaken several stylistic shifts in his compositional career and having profoundly influenced the course of music during the greater part of a century.

STRAVINSKY'S MUSIC

Igor Stravinsky
USA 2c

As we have seen, Stravinsky's personal style underwent several changes during the course of his career. He wrote in the splashy, colorful orchestral style of the Russian nationalists, composed music with the force and power of Primitivism, adopted jazz techniques, invented a new musical style known as Neo-Classicism, and turned finally to twelve-tone techniques.

Stravinsky took ideas from the medieval, Baroque, and Classic periods, as well as from contemporary music. He wrote for almost every known musical combination, both instrumental and vocal, choral and orchestral, chamber and stage. His genres included opera, ballet, oratorio, symphony, concerto, chamber music, sonata, piano solo, song, chorus, and Mass.

And yet some things remained common to all of

Igor Stravinsky (1882–1971)
First Movement from Concerto in E-flat
    (*Dumbarton Oaks*) **for Chamber**
    Orchestra

Date of composition: 1938
Orchestration: Flute, clarinet, bassoon,
    2 horns, 3 violins, 3 violas, 2 cellos,
    2 basses
Meter: $\frac{2}{4}$
Key: E♭
Tempo: *Tempo giusto*
Duration: 4:11

Student CD Collection: 3, track 28
Complete CD Collection: 6, track 15

This concerto is from Stravinsky's Neo-Classical period, during which he imitated the clarity and transparency of earlier masters. It is scored for a chamber group of winds and strings, in three movements, and is known as *Dumbarton Oaks* because it was commissioned by some wealthy patrons of the arts whose home near Washington, D.C., had that name.

Stravinsky modeled the work after Bach's *Brandenburg* Concertos, which provided him with the inspiration for both the texture and the liveliness of the music. Compare the Bach extracts with those of Stravinsky:

etc.

FIGURE 1A: Bach, *Brandenburg* Concerto No. 6, first movement, mm. 1–2.

FIGURE 1B: Stravinsky, Concerto in E♭, first movement, mm. 15–16.

etc.

FIGURE 2A: Bach, *Brandenburg* Concerto No. 3, third movement, m. 1.

342

FIGURE 2B: Stravinsky, Concerto in E♭, first movement, m. 155.

A slow, chordal section recurs several times, functioning much like the ritòrnello of a Baroque concerto grosso. The piece is saturated with the lively rhythms and quirky sense of humor that are typical of Stravinsky, and it combines great clarity with pungent modern harmonies. Its jazzy swing and transparency of texture create a wonderful listening experience. The following comments just provide a few "signposts" along this delightful journey.

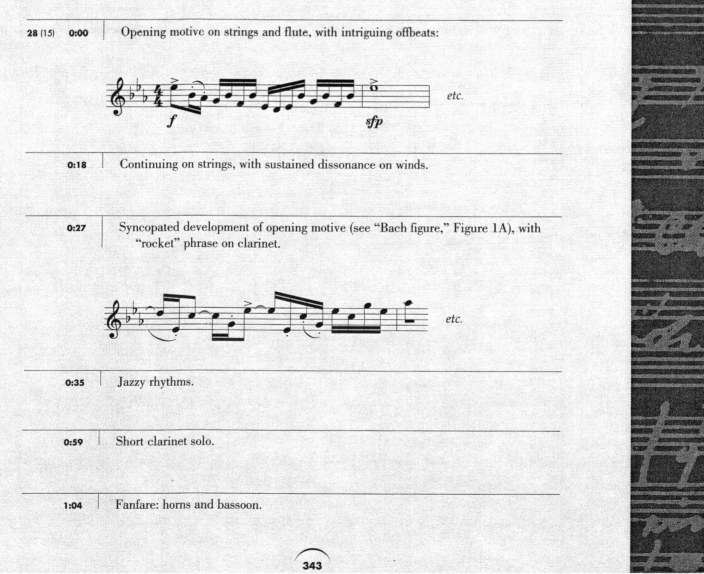

28 (15)	0:00	Opening motive on strings and flute, with intriguing offbeats:
	0:18	Continuing on strings, with sustained dissonance on winds.
	0:27	Syncopated development of opening motive (see "Bach figure," Figure 1A), with "rocket" phrase on clarinet.
	0:35	Jazzy rhythms.
	0:59	Short clarinet solo.
	1:04	Fanfare: horns and bassoon.

343

1:21	Clarinet again, followed by strings and bassoon.
1:38	Crescendo: syncopated rhythmic figure in all parts except basses.
1:52	Climax. Unison playing, winding down to:
29 (16) 2:02	An extended fugue on strings alone; violas, followed by violins, basses, and cellos.
2:47	Louder, horns and strings, with fanfare.
3:05	New melody in horns, with busy, bubbling accompaniment on bassoon and clarinet.
3:26	Crescendo. Sixteenth-note figure in strings against cross-rhythms in winds. (See Figure 2B.)

| 3:55 | Ritornello: slow chords. |

etc.

| 4:11 | Soft ending. |

Stravinsky's periods and compositional styles. First of all was his interest in rhythm. His rhythms are highly individual—catchy, unexpected, and fascinating. Stravinsky used syncopation with great effect, and often a short rest or silence appears, to throw the rhythm off balance. He often used several different meters, one right after the other or even simultaneously.

Second, Stravinsky had an acute ear for tone color. He used unusual combinations of instruments to get exactly the effect he wanted, and he also used instruments in novel ways. *The Rite of Spring*, for example, begins with a bassoon, which is a low instrument, playing at the very top of its range, producing a strange, eerie sound. (This passage is used at the start of Walt Disney's *Fantasia* to suggest the beginning of Creation.)

Finally, Stravinsky's use of harmony was highly original. Much of his music is tonally based, and yet he often used *two* key centers instead of one. Another very characteristic harmonic effect is the use of an ostinato (repeated pattern) as an accompaniment. Above the ostinato, the harmonies may change, but the ostinato remains as a kind of tonal anchor.

Stravinsky used to compose carefully and consistently every day in his study, which was filled with the tools of his trade: paper, pencils, erasers, rulers, ink, scissors, and a large desk. He worked regular hours—"like a banker," he said. But his lasting legacy is his music.

Stravinsky in later life.

Britten was gay, and he lived with Peter Pears, a fine tenor singer, who remained his lifelong companion. During World War II, the couple was invited to America by the poet W. H. Auden, who was also gay and who had formed an artists' community in New York. But after only two years, Britten and Pears returned to England.

Peter Pears (left) and Benjamin Britten in 1949.

Then began the remarkable series of operas on which Britten concentrated for the next ten years. The first was *Peter Grimes* (1945), then came *Billy Budd* (1951), *Gloriana* (1953), written for the coronation of Queen Elizabeth II, and *The Turn of the Screw* (1954). In most of his vocal works, a central role is designed for tenor Peter Pears.

During the 1960s, Britten concentrated on two major projects. The first was the production of several cello works for the great Soviet cellist Mstislav Rostropovich, who had recently been allowed to travel from the Soviet Union and whose great artistry Britten admired.

The other project of Britten's from this time was the *War Requiem* (1961). This is certainly the most important achievement of Britten's career, and it stands as one of the great works of the century. Britten's *War Requiem* was written for the dedication of the new cathedral in Coventry, England, which had been constructed to replace the great medieval church destroyed

I always try to make myself as widely understood as possible; and if I don't succeed, I consider it my fault.—Dmitri Shostakovich

BENJAMIN BRITTEN (1913–1976)

Benjamin Britten was born in a small English country town in Suffolk. He was a child prodigy and began turning out compositions at the age of five. Later, he arranged some of these childhood pieces into the *Simple Symphony* (1934), which is one of his most attractive works. Britten's *The Young Person's Guide to the Orchestra* (1946) is designed to display all the different instruments of a symphony orchestra.

The new cathedral at Coventry, England, merged into the ruins of the old.

Benjamin Britten (1913–1976)
Sanctus from *War Requiem*

Date of composition: 1962
Duration: 9:52

Complete CD set: 6, track 37

Britten's *War Requiem* is a modern setting of the Catholic Mass for the Dead. Interspersed throughout the Mass are poems written by Wilfred Owen, who was killed in the First World War. These poems act as a kind of commentary on the different Mass movements. The work calls upon a large number of disparate musical forces: soprano soloist, chorus, boys' choir, organ, and orchestra for the Latin text; tenor and baritone soloists and instrumental chamber group for the English poems.

We will listen to the fourth movement, *Sanctus*. The Mass text appears unaltered in the original Latin and is set in musical styles appropriate to Gregorian chant (syllabic, neumatic, recitational, and melismatic), as well as in the Renaissance styles of imitative and free counterpoint. Owen's poetry (in English), in contrast to the ecclesiastical style of the Latin sections, uses operatic forms (recitative, aria, etc.) and is performed by a baritone soloist. There is a striking contrast between the exaltation of the *Sanctus* text and the profound despair of the poetry. The texts are as follows:

(Soprano soloist and chorus, with full orchestra):

Sanctus, sanctus, sanctus,
Dominus Deus Sabaoth.
Pleni sunt coeli et terra gloria tua.
Hosanna in excelsis.
Benedictus qui venit
in nomine Domini.
Hosanna in excelsis.

Holy, holy, holy,
Lord God of hosts.
Heaven and earth are full of your glory.
Hosanna in the highest.
Blessed is He who comes
in the name of the Lord.
Hosanna in the highest.

(Baritone soloist, with chamber orchestra):

After the blast of lightning from the East.
The flourish of loud clouds, the Chariot Throne;
After the drums of Time have rolled and ceased,
And by the bronze west long retreat is blown,

Shall life renew these bodies? Of a truth
All death will He annul, all tears assuage?—
Fill the void veins of Life again with youth,
And wash, with an immortal water, Age?

When I do ask white Age he saith not so:
"My head hangs weighed with snow."
And when I hearken to the Earth, she saith:
"My fiery heart shrinks, aching. It is death.
Mine ancient scars shall not be glorified,
Nor my titanic tears, the sea, be dried."

(37)	0:00	Beginning; vibraphone, glockenspiel, antique cymbals, bells, and piano; short crescendo. This group continues throughout the opening section.

0:04	*Sanctus*, (syllabic).
0:17	*Sanctus*,
0:24	*Sanctus*, (melismatic).
0:40	*Dominus Deus Sabaoth, Dominus Deus Sabaoth* (neumatic).
1:00	*Sanctus*, (long melisma).

CHORUS

1:15	*Pleni sunt coeli et terra gloria tua* (recitative, beginning with orchestral sounds piling up, then parts of the chorus layered on top of one another in a large crescendo, then . . .)
1:53	Stop!

CHORUS

	[new section, jubilant feeling with brass fanfares]
1:55	*Hosanna in excelsis* (sopranos, altos, tenors) against *Sanctus* (basses, doubled by orchestral basses, fairly long section). Horns leap and trumpets blast. Becomes quieter.

SOPRANO & CHORUS

		[lyrical with responses by chorus]
(38)	3:11	*Benedictus, benedictus qui venit in nomine, in nomine Domini, in nomine Domini, Benedictus qui venit, qui venit in nomine Domini* (long melisma), *qui venit in nomine* (neumatic) *Domini, Domini, Domini* (extremely long melismas).
	5:35	Stop!
	5:36	*Hosanna in excelsis* (sopranos, altos, tenors) against *Sanctus* (basses, doubled by orchestral basses). Brass fanfares; horn and trumpet calls, similar to previous *Hosanna*. Long crescendo, ending with big splash.
	6:15	Stop!

(39)	6:17	[new section, baritone solo]
		Single pitch heard on horn and low strings.

BARITONE

6:21	*After the blast of lightning from the East*, (recitative), harp glissando, flutes, lively woodwind figures.
6:36	*The flourish of loud clouds, the Chariot Throne;*
6:41	Harp glissando, lively woodwind figures.

6:46	*After the drums* (timpani roll) *of Time have rolled and ceased*, (harp glissando, woodwind figures), *And by the bronze west* (harp glissando) *long retreat is blown*, (woodwind figures, leading into . . .)

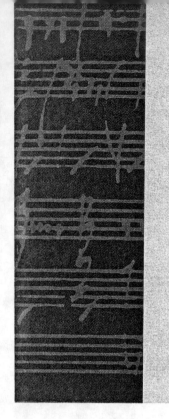

BARITONE

[New section, beginning with staccato strings, repeating woodwind motive]

	7:21	*Shall life renew these bodies?* (snare drum taps, horn note) *Of a truth* (accompaniment continues) *All death will He annul, all tears assuage?* (more motion) *Fill the void veins of Life again with youth, And wash, with an immortal water, Age?* (climax)
	7:53	Instrumental interlude (strings, oboe, insistent timpani strokes, continuing through:)
	7:59	*When I do ask white Age he saith not so:*
	8:11	(over soft high-pitched flute) *"My head hangs weighed with snow."*
	8:24	Motion continues.
(40)	8:28	*And when I hearken to the Earth, she saith:*
	8:40	(accompanied by woodwinds in long notes, and pizzicato strings, slow) *"My fiery heart shrinks, aching. It is death. Mine ancient scars shall not be glorified, Nor my titanic tears,* (slower) *the sea, be dried."*
	9:29	Slow, descending, sparsely orchestrated tones, deeper and deeper, quieter and quieter ... dying away ...
	9:52	End of movement.

during World War II. For this event, Britten mingled lamentation for Britain's war dead with a powerful call for peace. He alternates settings of the age-old, timeless Latin Mass for the Dead with settings of poems by Wilfred Owen, who had been killed a week before the end of the First World War at the age of 24. The *War Requiem* is richly varied and, with its expressive tension between the old and the new, both powerful and moving. We shall listen to a section of this work. **(See Listening Guide on page 370.)**

Britten's very individual sound is based on many factors: the directness and lack of pretension in the melodic lines, the common use of high tenor voice (this range seems to affect even his instrumental compositions), and an almost constant tension between conflicting tonalities. This can extend sometimes to clear instances of bitonality.

THE AMERICAN SCENE

The history of classical music in America reaches back to Colonial times, during which period the most significant composer was William Billings (1746–1800), a composer of rough-hewn (he called himself a "carver") and highly original settings of psalms and songs for unaccompanied chorus. His publication in 1770 of *The New-England Psalm-Singer* marked the appearance of the very first published collection of American music.

In the nineteenth century, the American tradition was kept alive in the South and the Midwest by means of "shape-note" books, in which pitches are indicated (for people who cannot read music) by simple signs such as small triangles, circles, and squares. One of the best-known of these shape-note hymn collections is *The Sacred Harp*, published in 1844. African-American spirituals were sung widely throughout the nineteenth century, although the first published collection of spirituals did not appear until 1867. And in the Midwest, one of the most original American composers, Anthony Heinrich (1781–1861, known as "the Beethoven of Kentucky") wrote elaborate and complex orchestral works descriptive of nature on the frontier.

But the rough-and-ready style of American music was soon overwhelmed by more "proper," European-trained composers. One of these was Lowell Mason (1792–1872), who wrote over a thousand hymn settings, some of which may still be found in Protestant hymnals.

About the beginning of the twentieth century, American music and music-making were still strongly influenced by the mid-nineteenth-century European tradition. The United States had not participated in the nationalist wave that swept through many other countries from the 1860s to the 1890s. During this period, America was absorbed by its own inner turmoil: the Civil War, the assassination of President Lincoln, and Reconstruction. American composers, mostly trained in Europe, paid little attention to the enormously varied indigenous music around them: African-American spirituals, New England hymn tunes, Native American songs and dances, the music of jazz bands, revival-meeting songs, and Irish-Scottish-English-American folk melodies. And the American public was interested only in imported music: Italian operas, Handel's English oratorios, and above all, German symphonies and chamber music.

Music was, however, becoming better established on the American scene. Conservatories of music were founded, concert halls were built, and music began to be taught as a serious discipline on university campuses. Most composers in the years around the turn of the century began or concentrated their careers in Boston. They included John Paine (1839–1906), who was the first professor of music ever to be appointed in the United States (at Harvard University); Edward MacDowell (1860–1908), a fine pianist as well as a composer; Horatio Parker (1863–1919), a choral composer on mostly religious texts; George Chadwick (1854–1931), a symphonist and American opera composer, who was for more than 30 years director of the newly founded New England Conservatory of Music in Boston; and Arthur Foote (1853–1937), whose best works are his beautiful solo songs and chamber music.

Boston was also the home of several women composers. They included Helen Hood, Mabel Daniels, Helen Hopekirk, and Margaret Lang, who was born in 1867 and died in 1972 at the age of 104.

Perhaps the best-known woman composer in Boston at the turn of the century was Amy Beach (1867–1944). She began her musical career as a concert pianist but also composed a wealth of important music,

including a Mass, a piano concerto, an opera, a symphony, chamber music, piano works, and songs. She was the piano soloist in the first performance of her Piano Concerto (1899), which was premiered by the Boston Symphony Orchestra. Her symphony, entitled the *Gaelic Symphony* (1896) because it is based on Irish folk tunes, was also first performed by that orchestra and carries the distinction of being the first American symphony by a woman.

Today, although there are some attempts at an American music revival, little of this late nineteenth- and early twentieth-century music receives regular concert performance. Perhaps the inferiority complex vis-à-vis music from Europe has still not quite disappeared.

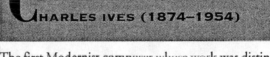

CHARLES IVES (1874–1954)

The first Modernist composer whose work was distinctively American was Charles Ives, who grew up in a small Connecticut town. He was the son of a bandmaster and music teacher whose approach to music was fun-loving and unconventional. Ives's father used to play tunes in two different keys at once, and he sometimes asked Charles to sing a song while he played the accompaniment in the "wrong" key on the piano. This open-minded and experimental approach stayed with Ives all his life.

Ives went to Yale as an undergraduate and then went into the insurance business, devoting his spare time to music. Over the next 10 years, he wrote an enormous quantity of music, while his business prospered, too. Although he lived until 1954, most of his music dates from before the First World War.

Ives's music is a remarkable, unique mixture. He was a radical experimentalist, who nonetheless believed in the values of small-town America. Most of his compositions are based on American cultural themes: baseball, Thanksgiving, marching bands, popular songs, the Fourth of July, fireworks, and American literature. Working alone, Ives developed some of the avant-garde innovations that would not take hold in the broader musical scene until the 1960s. He wrote music with

Charles Ives, composer and insurance agent.

> An Old Testament prophet crying a New Mythology in the American wilderness.—David Woodridge on Ives

Charles Ives (1874–1954)
Second Movement from *Three Places*
in New England ("Putnam's Camp,
Redding, Conn.")

Date of composition: 1903–11
Orchestration: Flute/piccolo,
    oboe/English horn, clarinet,
    bassoon, 2 or more horns, 2 or more
    trumpets, 2 trombones, tuba, piano;
    timpani; drums; cymbals; strings
Duration: 5:38

Student CD Collection: 3, track 37
Complete CD Collection: 6, track 41

"*P*utnam's Camp" captures a child's impression of a Fourth of July picnic
with singing and marching bands. In the middle of the picnic, the boy falls asleep and dreams
of songs and marches from the time of the American Revolution. When he awakes, he again
hears the noise of the picnic celebration.

Ives's piece is a type of aural collage. Contrasting sounds and textures are overlaid and
connected. Moments of simplicity provide the listener with a point of repose and orientation
before one is thrown back into the vivacious tumult. The moments of thinner texture—when
one or a few instruments stand out with a clear and simple melodic idea—separate passages of
fervent, strident, jumbled polyphony. Although Ives combines every melody and every rhythm
very precisely, the effect is (and it is an effect he strove for) one of varying successions of vigorous, raucous noise. Audiences today delight in the energy of the work, and different ideas
surface with every rehearing.

37 (41)	**0:00**	*Introduction:* full orchestra with dissonant but rhythmically unified descending scales, leading to repeated notes; a vigorous marchlike pulse.
	0:10	*Allegro* ("quick-step time"): a bouncy, accessible melody accompanied by a regular thudding bass. The conventional harmonies contrast with the harsh introduction.
		Flutes and trumpets can be heard with competing melodies as Ives evokes the atmosphere of a chaotic festive event.
	0:47	After a fanfare by a single trumpet, the confused fervor of the different simultaneous events continues even more energetically, with strong melodies in trombones and trumpets, and heavy use of cymbals and snare drum.
38 (42)	**1:00**	Thinner texture and softer dynamics lead to parodied quotation of "Rally Round the Flag" and "Yankee Doodle," with:
	1:08	Disjunct melody in violins with conflicting piano and percussion, leading to:
	1:50	Softly throbbing cellos and basses, gradually slowing down, illustrating the child gradually falling asleep.
	1:55	Decrescendo, then quiet.

39 (43)	**2:06**	*Dream section:* Begins with an ethereal sustained high chord (the Goddess of Liberty), then continues with a legato but energetic melody (first flute, then oboe). But the regular pulse (percussion and piano) accompanying this melody accelerates and takes off on its own (the soldiers march off to pipe and drum). Different melodies in the violins, oboes, clarinets, and trumpets, in a number of different meters and keys, combine with a building tension. The conflicting pulse of the piano and snare drum against the slower pulse of the repetitive low strings can be clearly heard. This gradually dies down, and then:
40 (44)	**3:10**	A bold, new, brass melody emerges and leads to another section of conflicting melodies; simultaneously, "The British Grenadiers," a favorite revolutionary tune, is heard in the flutes.
	3:36	A strongly accented and repetitive tune ascends in the brass and starts another dense passage.
	3:57	*Awakening:* This comes to an abrupt halt (the boy suddenly awakes), and a lively tune is revealed in the violins (the boy hears children's songs in the background). This builds to another complex passage (different bands, songs, and games combine). Heavy, low rhythms and several meters combine. Fragments of lively string melody, "The British Grenadiers," and other tunes.
	4:47	Repeated notes in trumpets and brass cut in suddenly.
	4:54	Another swirl of melodies and rhythms, oscillating notes crescendo, frantic scales, as all the instruments push their dynamic limit, leading to the final jarring chord.

wild dissonances; Ives wrote a note to his music copyist, who had "corrected" some of the notes in his manuscript: "Please don't correct the wrong notes. The wrong notes are right." He wrote for pianos specially tuned in quarter tones; in his *Concord* Sonata he called for the pianist to use an elbow to press down notes and, in one place, a wooden board to hold down 16 notes at once. "Is it the composer's fault that a man has only ten fingers?" he asked. Ives's most famous composition is *The Unanswered Question* (1908), in which two different instrumental groups, sitting separately, play different music at the same time. And in his program piece called *Putnam's Camp*, the music depicts two marching bands passing each other, playing different tunes. (**See Listening Guide on page 374.**)

The music of Charles Ives was virtually unknown in its own time. It was only in the 1940s that Ives's work began to be performed, and only many years later that he began to be recognized as the first truly original American musical genius.

AARON COPLAND (1900–1990)

If Ives represents the avant-garde in American music, Aaron Copland represents a more mainstream approach. Copland was born into a Jewish immigrant family in Brooklyn and decided to become a composer at the age of 15. When he was 20, he went to Europe—specifically to Paris, where he studied with Nadia Boulanger.

Boulanger was perhaps the most famous composition teacher of the twentieth century. She was also a composer, pianist, organist, and conductor. She was extremely strict in her teaching, insisting that her stu-

Composer, conductor, and author Aaron Copland conducting his own work at Tanglewood, Massachusetts.

dents learn all aspects of music, including careful and detailed analysis of musical scores. A large number of American composers of the twentieth century studied with Boulanger, forming in this way a thorough and rigorous background for their own work.

When Copland returned from Paris in 1924, he decided to write works that would be specifically American in style. To do this, he drew on the most recognizably American musical style: jazz. And many of his compositions are marked by the syncopated rhythms and chord combinations of American jazz. One of these is the Clarinet Concerto (1948), which he wrote for the famous jazz clarinetist Benny Goodman.

Another way Copland strove to put America into his music was by the use of purely American cultural topics. His ballet suites *Billy the Kid* (1938) and *Rodeo* (1942) are cowboy stories, and *Appalachian Spring* (1944) depicts a pioneer wedding in rural Pennsylvania.

Appalachian Spring also demonstrates a third technique used by Copland to make his music sound American: quoting from folk songs, hymns, and coun-

try tunes. The fourth scene of *Appalachian Spring* sounds like country fiddling, and the seventh scene is a series of variations on the exquisite Shaker melody "Simple Gifts."

Finally, Copland made his music sound American by a rather more sophisticated technique. He used very widely spaced sonorities—deep basses and high, soaring violins—to evoke the wide-open spaces of the American landscape. In addition, he often used the interval of a fifth in his music, a very open-sounding interval, and his chord changes are slow and static, suggesting the more gradual pace of nature's clock. Copland said that he wanted to write music "that would speak of universal things ... music with a largeness of utterance wholly representative of our country."

Two of Copland's more accessible and popular works are *Lincoln Portrait* and *Fanfare for the Common Man*, both composed in 1942. For the *Lincoln Portrait*, Copland arranged extracts from Lincoln's speeches and letters to be recited with orchestral accompaniment. The *Fanfare for the Common Man* is a wonderful piece; written for brass instruments and percussion, it is rousing and strong. Both works were composed to provide patriotic encouragement at a time of national anxiety. **(See Listening Guide on page 377.)**

Copland wrote books on music, gave lectures, conducted around the world, composed film scores, and was the mentor of such luminaries as Leonard Bernstein. Copland's leading position in the world of twentieth-century American musical life led to his being called "the dean of American music."

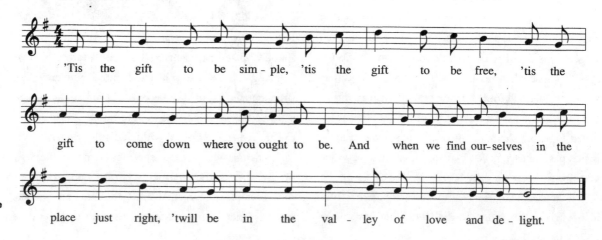

'Tis the gift to be sim - ple, 'tis the gift to be free, 'tis the gift to come down where you ought to be. And when we find our-selves in the place just right, 'twill be in the val - ley of love and de - light.

The Shaker song "Simple Gifts."

BU-310

Aaron Copland (1900–1990)
Fanfare for the Common Man

Date of composition: 1942
Orchestration: 3 trumpets, 4 horns,
  3 trombones, tuba, timpani, bass
  drum, tam-tam
Duration: 3:36

Student CD Collection: 3, track 41
Complete CD Collection: 7, track 1

Perhaps today we might find Copland's piece more aptly titled *Fanfare for the Average American*. Certainly Copland did not consciously intend his "common man" to be conceived in terms of gender exclusivity. And although Copland's title does not mention any nationality, this piece has become almost a sound icon for America—specifically, for the spirit of the American pioneer, facing vast challenges and wide vistas, from the open prairie to outer space.

Much of the piece's bold, assertive mood comes from its instrumentation, as it is scored entirely for brass and percussion. The simplicity of its motives—using triads, fifths and octaves—gives an open, spacious quality to the piece.

41 (1)	**0:00**	Somber strokes on the bass drum, timpani, and gong (tam-tam); gradual decrease in volume.
	0:25	Fanfare idea in a steady, deliberate tempo—ascending triad; then the fifth outlining that same triad leads to a high note and a slower, descending arpeggio. Stark, unison trumpets.
	0:54	Timpani and bass drum.
42 (2)	**0:59**	Fanfare idea, louder, now harmonized with one additional contrapuntal line in the French horns.
	1:39	Tam-tam, timpani, and bass drum.
43 (3)	**1:50**	Accented low brass take up the fanfare, imitated by timpani, then by trumpets and French horns. Harmony expands richly to three and more chord tones. Rising fifth and octave intervals in timpani.
44 (4)	**2:38**	Another series of statements of the fanfare motive begins. This moves to a series of stepwise descents from the highest pitch of the piece.
	3:04	A contrasting harmonic area is introduced, but with the same rising fifth–octave motive.
	3:27	The work ends with a bold crescendo but an unsettled harmonic feeling, evoking a restless spirit, the spirit of exploration.

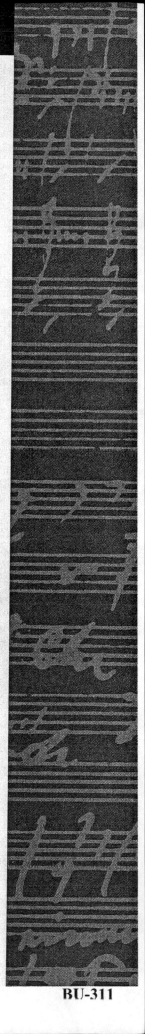

BUILDING BRIDGES

Much of Copland's music is the result of an attempt to bridge the gap between "serious" music and its audience. Two other American composers did this in different ways; these composers were George Gershwin and Leonard Bernstein.

GEORGE GERSHWIN (1898–1937)

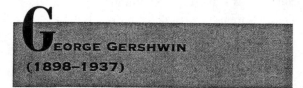

George Gershwin was primarily a composer of popular songs and a jazz pianist. But he was also attracted to the world of the concert hall, and he wrote four works that reach across the cultural divide between popular and classical music. The first was *Rhapsody in Blue* (1924), a highly attractive and successful mixture of the jazz idiom and concert music, scored for solo piano and orchestra. Next came the jazzy Piano Concerto in F (1925). Both compositions were designed for Gershwin's own brilliant piano playing.

In 1928, Gershwin composed *An American in Paris*, a programmatic symphonic poem. The music is colorful, lively, and drawn from Gershwin's own experience in visiting Paris several times.

The last of Gershwin's works to bridge the gap between popular and classical music was by far the most ambitious: It was a full-length opera, in which Gershwin combined elements of jazz, church meetings, street cries, lullabies, and spirituals. The opera was *Porgy and*

LISTENING GUIDE

George Gershwin (1898–1937)
"Bess, You Is My Woman Now" from
Porgy and Bess

Date of composition: 1935
Duration: 5:59

Complete CD Collection: 7, track 5

The boundaries between opera and musical are frequently blurred in the twentieth century, but Gershwin conceived of his work as an opera and envisioned its performance at the Metropolitan Opera in New York. To write it, he steeped himself in black culture, living on a small island in South Carolina and working with the Charleston writer DuBose Heyward (author of the original story *Porgy*) as the work was being planned.

"Bess, You Is My Woman Now" celebrates a moment of happiness in Porgy's struggle for the love of Bess. Porgy is portrayed as a straightforward, hardworking man with a physical handicap, who must compete with the rough gambler Crown and the smooth, sophisticated drug dealer Sportin' Life for Bess's affection.

The song's larger structure is of three varied stanzas, with a short refrain employed after the second and third. In the Listening Guide, lowercase letters attached to the phrases serve to identify related melodic ideas. The broad, sustained sweep of the "a" phrase, with its large leaps, is contrasted with phrases of faster rhythms and more scalar motion. Repeated notes and a declamatory style distinguish the simple, striking refrain; in its second appearance, it is expanded and serves as a conclusion.

The "togetherness" of Bess and Porgy is emphasized musically by their singing alternating stanzas with very similar music and wording, and by their singing a duet at the end of the extract. The Southern black dialect is imitated by the spelling and dropped consonants of the text. Gershwin's musical vocabulary includes many elements of jazz, including the slide and the "blue note" on "woman" and the syncopated rhythmic patterns on "you is, you is."

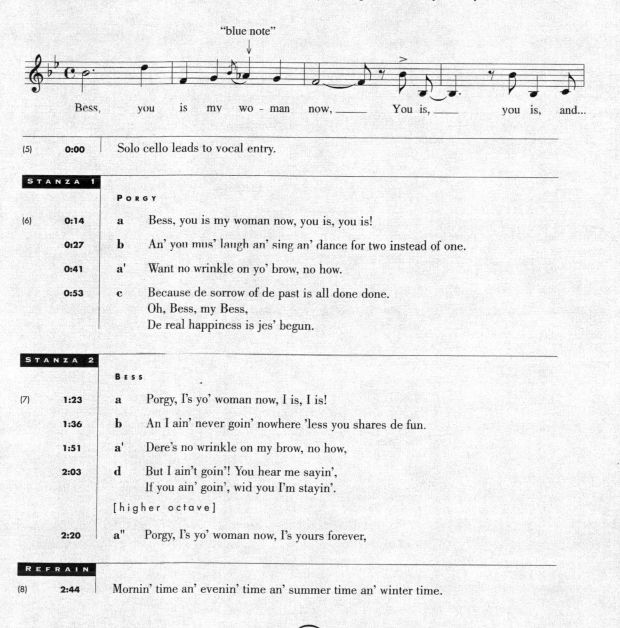

| (5) | 0:00 | Solo cello leads to vocal entry. |

STANZA 1

PORGY

(6)	0:14	**a**	Bess, you is my woman now, you is, you is!
	0:27	**b**	An' you mus' laugh an' sing an' dance for two instead of one.
	0:41	**a'**	Want no wrinkle on yo' brow, no how.
	0:53	**c**	Because de sorrow of de past is all done done. Oh, Bess, my Bess, De real happiness is jes' begun.

STANZA 2

BESS

(7)	1:23	**a**	Porgy, I's yo' woman now, I is, I is!
	1:36	**b**	An I ain' never goin' nowhere 'less you shares de fun.
	1:51	**a'**	Dere's no wrinkle on my brow, no how,
	2:03	**d**	But I ain't goin'! You hear me sayin', If you ain' goin', wid you I'm stayin'.
			[higher octave]
	2:20	**a"**	Porgy, I's yo' woman now, I's yours forever,

REFRAIN

| (8) | 2:44 | | Mornin' time an' evenin' time an' summer time an' winter time. |

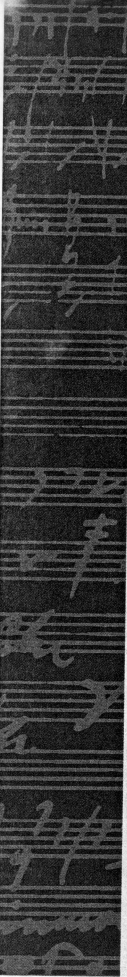

PORGY

2:52	Mornin' time an' evenin' time an' summer time an' winter time,
3:01	Bess, you got yo' man.

STANZA 3

BESS

[Porgy sings a countermelody]

(9) **3:15** **a'** Porgy, I's yo' woman now, I is, I is!

> **PORGY**
>
> Bess, you is my woman now an' forever.
> Dis life is jes' begun.

3:27 **b** An I ain' never goin' nowhere 'less you shares de fun.

> Bess, we two is one now an' forever.

3:42 **a'** Dere's no wrinkle on my brow, no how,

> Oh, Bess, don' min' dose women.
> You got yo' Porgy, you loves yo' Porgy,
> I knows you means it, I seen it in yo' eyes, Bess.

3:54 **d** But I ain't goin'! You hear me sayin',
If you ain' goin', wid you I'm stayin'.

[slower]

4:10 **a"** Porgy, I's yo' woman now, I's yours forever,

> We'll go swingin' through de years asingin'.
> Hmmm...

REFRAIN

(10) **4:37** Mornin' time an' evenin' time an' summer time an' winter time. Hmmm...

4:46 > Mornin' time an' evenin' time an' summer time an'
> winter time.

CODA

(11) **5:03** Oh, my Porgy, my man Porgy,

> My Bess, my Bess,

[voices declaim in harmony over "a" idea then over refrain in orchestra; long decrescendo]

5:24 From dis minute I'm tellin' you, I keep dis vow;

Porgy, I's your woman now.

> Oh, my Bessie, we's happy now,
> We is one now.

[peaceful cadence with lowered leading tone]

Bess, which contains some of Gershwin's best-known tunes, including "It Ain't Necessarily So" and "Summertime." Many people know these songs, but not so many have heard the entire opera, which is one of Gershwin's greatest achievements. *Porgy and Bess* was completed in 1935. A year and a half later, the brilliant young composer was dead, cut off in the midst of his career by a brain tumor at the age of 38. **(See Listening Guide on page 378.)**

Leonard Bernstein (1918–1990)

The person who best represented American music and music-making in the second half of the twentieth century was also one of the most famous musicians in the world. His name was Leonard Bernstein, and he continued the tradition, started by Copland and Gershwin, of blending popular and "serious" styles. Like Copland and Gershwin, Bernstein was Jewish. Like them, he was a brilliant pianist and a prodigiously gifted all-round musician. Like Copland, Bernstein lectured and wrote books about music and loved to

Passion, commitment, intensity—Leonard Bernstein conducting.

teach. Like Gershwin, Bernstein enjoyed fast cars, fancy clothes, and all-night parties.

Bernstein got his start in music at Tanglewood, where he became a protégé of the conductor and music patron Serge Koussevitsky. In 1943, Bernstein caused a sensation when he took over a New York Philharmonic concert as conductor on only a few hours notice. From then on, his career was assured.

Bernstein was enormously versatile, and he had the energy of three men. He used to sleep only two or three hours a night. He could have been a great pianist, a great conductor, or a great composer. Instead, he was all three.

As a pianist, Bernstein enjoyed playing everything from Mozart to Gershwin. As a conductor, Bernstein's career was unparalleled. He was for 10 years the permanent conductor of the New York Philharmonic, but he was in demand by orchestras all over the world. His conducting was manically energetic: He would throw his arms around, shake his fists, twist and cavort. Sometimes he would leap into the air to express his excitement. But underneath the showmanship, there was a profound musical intelligence.

As a composer, Bernstein was highly versatile. Like Stravinsky and Copland, he wrote ballet music. Bernstein also wrote musicals, including *On the Town* (1944), *Wonderful Town* (1953), and *Candide* (1956). His most successful musical, and his most famous composition, was *West Side Story*, written in 1957. An updating of Shakespeare's *Romeo and Juliet*, it tells the story of lovers separated by the gulf between rival gangs on Manhattan's West Side. The score is brilliant,

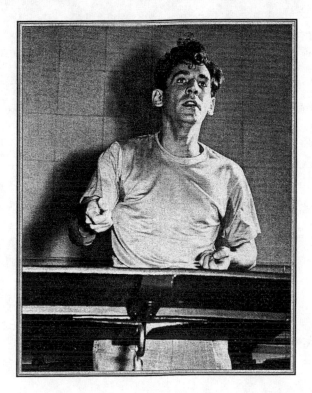

Leonard Bernstein in 1947.

combining jazz, snappy dances, and moving lyricism. Bernstein had an uncanny ability to write immensely moving music that seems simple and direct and completely hides the craft that went into it. **(See Listening Guide below.)**

In addition to ballets and musicals, Bernstein wrote gentle songs and delicate piano pieces, as well as big choral works, three symphonies, two operas, and a Mass. Multiple reconciliations are attempted in his *Mass*, written in 1971. It is a rock setting of the Catholic Mass with singers and orchestra; it is a concert piece that is designed to be staged; and some of the text is in Hebrew.

LISTENING GUIDE

Leonard Bernstein (1918–1990)
"Make Our Garden Grow"
from *Candide*

Date of composition: 1956
Orchestration: 2 flutes, oboe, 2 clarinets,
  bass clarinet, bassoon, 2 horns,
  2 trumpets, 2 trombones, tuba, timpani
  and percussion, harp, strings
Duration: 3:58

Complete CD Collection: 7, track 12

The comic operetta *Candide* is based on the satire by the eighteenth-century author Voltaire. It was set in two acts by Lillian Hellman, with lyrics by Richard Wilbur, John Latouche, and Dorothy Parker, and first produced in 1956.

The comical story of Candide follows him through several countries as he searches for Cunegonde, the beautiful daughter of a European baron. The lovers were separated when they were "discovered" by her brother, who reported the incident to their father. The story recounts the wild and steamy escapades of Candide and Cunegonde as they go their separate ways but ultimately meet again somewhere in Turkey, where they adopt the "work ethic" philosophy, buy a small farm, and vow a life of simplicity.

This selection comes at the end of the production and features all the principal characters. The entire ensemble is joined by the chorus (in a moving unaccompanied section) toward the end of the dramatic finale.

The musical structure Bernstein adopts for this number is a fairly simple, strophic, song form. The overall tonal scheme outlines a dissonant augmented chord (C–E–A♭–C), which lends a strong sense of resolution to the final verse. This feeling of conflict resolved is also played out in the orchestral section.

		[C Major]
(12)	**0:00**	Orchestral prelude, (strong resolving dissonances).

CANDIDE

		[E Major]
	0:15	You've been a fool and so have I, But come and be my wife, And let us try before we die To make some sense of life.

Refrain:

We're neither pure nor wise nor good;
We'll do the best we know; [gentle]

0:57   We'll build our house, and chop our wood,
And make our garden grow, [climax]
And make our garden grow.

1:21   Orchestral interlude.

CUNEGONDE

[A♭ Major; same melody, more motion in accompaniment]

(13)   **1:30**   I thought the world was sugarcake,
For so our master said;
But now I'll teach my hands to bake
Our loaf of daily bread.

**CUNEGONDE
& CANDIDE**

[duet]

1:55   *Refrain:*

We're neither pure nor wise nor good,
We'll do the best we know;
We'll build our house, and chop our wood,
And make our garden grow,
And make our garden grow.

2:30   Orchestral interlude.

**PRINCIPAL
CHARACTERS**

[return to C Major—louder]

2:35   Let dreamers dream what worlds they please,
Those Edens can't be found.
The sweetest flow'rs, the fairest trees
Are grown in solid ground.

**WITH
CHORUS**

[unaccompanied voices; orchestra suddenly drops out]

Refrain:

(14)   **3:02**   We're neither pure nor wise nor good;
We'll do the best we know; [gentle]

3:14   We'll build our house, and chop our wood,
And make our garden grow, [high C in sopranos!]
And make our garden grow. [orchestra rejoins]

3:36   Huge orchestral climax.

3:46   Final cadence.

Audiences for Music in the Twentieth Century

Audiences for music expanded enormously in the twentieth century, largely as a result of new technology. The radio and the phonograph brought music to millions of people who would otherwise not have been able to hear it. The commercialization of popular music also brought with it an exponential increase in the number of people hearing music of all kinds, in dance halls and nightclubs as well as on radio and on recordings. From the earliest cylinders invented before the turn of the century to the compact discs and CD-ROMs of today, recording technology has turned music into a business worth billions of dollars. ¶ In this atmosphere of popularization, classical music, with its greater subtlety and deeper intellectual challenges, had to struggle for survival. The audiences for live classical music are still dwindling. Many orchestras have had to disband. Others have had to rely more and more on a small repertoire of orchestral "standards" to ensure a viable level of attendance. This, in turn, has turned most orchestras (as well as opera houses and chamber-music groups) into highly conservative organizations, rather than the places of excitement and experimentation they used to be. In Mozart's time, most performances were of new music; now they are mostly of old music. The 2,000-year-old tradition of Western music, with its treasury of musical masterpieces and proven ability to express the human soul in ways that words cannot reach, is at a turning point. Will it survive our new century?

Chapter 13

The Twentieth Century II: Jazz, An American Original

What is jazz? Most of us recognize it when we hear it, but it's not so easy to list the essential ingredients of jazz. First of all is the rhythm. Jazz usually has a steady rhythm that continues from the very beginning of a piece to the end. That rhythm is often underscored by percussion instruments, which play a central role in the performance of jazz. The most characteristic part of jazz rhythm is syncopation: the accentuation of "offbeats," or beats that are unstressed in other types of music. The combination of these rhythmic elements contributes to what is known as "swing." Swing is the *feeling* generated by the steady rhythm and accented offbeats of the music and by the lively, spirited playing of jazz performers. Swing is what makes you want to move to the music.

Another primary ingredient of jazz is the use of "blue notes." Blue notes are notes that are played or sung lower or flatter than the pitches in a conventional Western scale. Common blue notes in jazz are the third, fifth, and seventh notes of a scale. Often, these notes are not exactly a half step low but rather indeterminate in pitch, and they can be "bent" or "scooped" by many instruments and by singers. These blue notes contribute to the expressive nature of much jazz performance.

Third, jazz often contains special sounds or conventional instruments playing in unusual ways. Trumpets playing "wah-wah" with a mute, trombones making slides, clarinets squealing in the high register — these are sounds directly associated with jazz but avoided in "straight" concert music. Jazz singers also deliberately make use of unusual sounds. A special kind of singing in which the vocalist improvises with nonsense syllables ("doo-be-doo dah," etc.) is known as "scat" singing. There are also instruments rarely used in concert music that are central to jazz. Foremost among these is the saxophone, which comes in many sizes, from the small soprano sax to the enormous contrabass. Most common in jazz are the alto and tenor instruments.

Finally, most people would say that improvisation is a necessary element in jazz. Certainly in many forms of jazz, improvisation plays a central role in the creation of the music, and some of the best jazz performers have been spontaneous and inventive improvisers. There is a difference, however, between genuine improvisation and the performance of a free-sounding melodic line that has been worked out in advance. Some of the most famous jazz performers would repeat their best solos night after night. This does not mean that they were not playing jazz. Perhaps the best approach is to say that improvisation is a typical but not an absolutely necessary ingredient of jazz.

Great jazz artists, however, are often great improvisers. This means that they are not just performers but *composers* as well.

> A jazz musician is a juggler who uses harmonies instead of oranges.
> —Jazz author Benny Green

The saxophone family (from left to right): bass, baritone, two tenors, two altos, and soprano.

Jazz combo at the Village Vanguard club in New York City.

Marching band in New Orleans, 1900.

Courtesy of Hogan Jazz Archive, Howard-Tilton Memorial Library, Tulane University.

THE HISTORY OF JAZZ

ORIGINS

Both the place and the time of the emergence of jazz can be fixed with some certainty. The place was New Orleans, the time was the 1890s.

In the late nineteenth century, New Orleans was one of the most culturally diverse and thriving cities in the United States. Its people were of African, French, Spanish, English, and Portuguese origin. There were first-, second-, and third-generation Europeans; African-Americans who were former slaves or descendants of former slaves; Haitians; Creoles; and a constant influx of new immigrants from Europe, the Caribbean, and other parts of the United States. Being a flourishing port, New Orleans also attracted sailors and visitors from all over the world.

The city had one of the liveliest musical cultures of any city in America. There was opera and chamber music. European ballroom dances were heard side by side with sailors' songs and hornpipes. Street sellers advertised their produce with musical cries. Work songs and "field hollers" mingled with the piano music of elegant salons. The bars, gambling joints, dance halls, and brothels were filled with smoke, liquor, and music.

BAND MUSIC

Everywhere in New Orleans were the bands: marching bands, dance bands, concert bands, and society orchestra bands. Bands played at weddings, funerals, parades, and political rallies, or just for the joy of it. Some of the musicians were classically trained; most could not read a note. But almost everybody played. Bands often held competitions among themselves to see which could play the best. And the sound of a band in the street was an excuse for children (and adults) from all the neighborhoods to come and join the fun.

The standard instruments in late nineteenth-century American bands were the trumpet (or cornet), clarinet, trombone, banjo, drums, and tuba. This instrumentation provided the proper balance between melody instruments, harmony instruments, bass, and percussion. All these instruments were, of course, portable. Only later, when band music moved indoors, did the instrumentation include piano and string bass.

Band music was the first of the three major musical influences on early jazz. The other two were ragtime and the blues.

RAGTIME

Ragtime was a type of piano music (sometimes also played on other instruments) that also became popular in the 1890s. It was originally played mostly by African-American pianists in saloons and dance halls in the South and the Midwest. "Ragging" meant taking a popular or classical melody and playing it in characteristic syncopated style. Later the style caught on, developing a form of its own, and ragtime was played by both black and white musicians to audiences all over the country.

Ragtime music is usually in duple meter and has the feel and tempo of a march. The left hand plays a steady, regular beat while the right hand plays a lively melody in syncopated rhythm. A ragtime composition usually consists of a series of related sections with a repetition pattern, most often AA BB A CC DD or something similar.

The most famous composer and performer of ragtime was Scott Joplin, whose father was a slave but who himself received a formal music education and composed classical music as well as a large number of piano rags.

Scott Joplin was born in 1868 and eventually got a job as a pianist in the Maple Leaf saloon in Sedalia, Missouri. His most famous piece, the *Maple Leaf Rag*, was published in 1899 and sold so well that Joplin moved to St. Louis to concentrate on composition. **(See Listening Guide below.)** In 1909 he settled in New York and composed a full-length opera, *Treemonisha*, which he attempted (without success) to have professionally produced. Joplin died in 1917, completely unrecognized by the musical establishment.

The notorious Basin Street of New Orleans in the 1890s, lined with saloons and brothels.

Courtesy of Hogan Jazz Archive, Howard-Tilton Memorial Library, Tulane University.

> Ragtime: white music, played black.—Author Joachim Berendt

LISTENING GUIDE

Scott Joplin (1868–1917)
***Maple Leaf Rag*, for piano solo**

Date of composition: 1899
Tempo: *Tempo di marcia* ("March tempo")
Meter: $\frac{2}{4}$
Key: A♭ Major
Duration: 3:12

Complete CD Collection: 7, track 38

Scott Joplin's *Maple Leaf Rag* sold hundreds of thousands of copies after it was published in 1899. It is typical of much ragtime music written around the turn of the century. A steady left-hand accompaniment keeps the march beat going throughout the piece while the right hand plays a lively, syncopated melody against this steady beat. The sections are repeated in the usual pattern: AA BB A CC DD. Each section is 16 measures long. The slight changes between sections, the standard but slightly irregular repetition pattern, the contrast between the rock-steady left hand and the dancing right hand—all these make for a composition of great attractiveness and help to explain the enormous popularity of ragtime in the early years of the history of jazz. In this recording, we hear a piano roll made by Joplin himself in 1916.

A		
(38)	**0:00**	Strong, steady chords in left hand; syncopated rhythm in right hand; short arpeggiated phrases.
A		
	0:21	Repeat.
B		
(39)	**0:42**	Melody begins higher and moves down; *staccato* articulation.
B		
	1:03	Repeat.
A		
	1:24	Opening section is played only once here.
C		
(40)	**1:45**	Change of key to D♭ Major (IV); rhythmic change in right hand; left-hand leaps.
C		
	2:06	Repeat.
D		
(41)	**2:28**	Return to original key; strong final cadence.
D		
	2:48	Repeat.

THE BLUES

The blues is a form, a sound, and a spirit, all at the same time. It began as a type of vocal music that crystallized in the 1890s from many elements. Among these were African-American spirituals, work songs, and street cries. The blues began as unaccompanied song but soon came to use banjo or guitar accompaniment. The common themes of early blues are sadness in love, betrayal, abandonment, and sometimes humor.

There is great variety in sung blues, but if there is a "standard" form, it is this: a series of three-line stanzas, in each of which the first two lines are the same:

I followed her to the station, with a suitcase in my hand.

I followed her to the station, with a suitcase in my hand.

Well, it's hard to tell, it's hard to tell, when all your love's in vain.

When the train rolled up to the station, I looked her in the eye.
When the train rolled up to the station, I looked her in the eye.
Well, I was lonesome, I felt so lonesome, and I could not help but cry.

(From Robert Johnson, "Love in Vain")

Each line is set to four measures, or bars, of music, so this pattern is known as **12-bar blues** (4 bars × 3 lines = 12 bars). The chord progressions in 12-bar blues are very simple, using only tonic (I), subdominant (IV), and dominant (V) chords. The overall pattern of 12-bar blues looks like this:

	MEASURE 1	MEASURE 2	MEASURE 3	MEASURE 4
LINE 1	I	I	I	I
LINE 2	IV	IV	I	I
LINE 3	V	V (or IV)	I	I

Every stanza of the song follows the same pattern. The singer may occasionally vary the accompaniment a little by introducing other chords or extra beats, but the basic pattern stays the same. Also, the singer has ample opportunity for varying the melodic line according to the expression of the text and his or her own personal feeling. The best blues singers use the rigid structure of blues for the most subtle variations in pitch (blue notes) and rhythm. Slight shadings of the pitch, little ornaments, and especially deliberate "misplacement" and constant manipulation of the rhythm are part and parcel of blues singing. The effect is of a very flexible and very personal vocal style against a square and simple background.

The form of the blues, with its special combination of flexibility and rigidity, began to be widely used by instrumentalists in the 1920s and has strongly influenced other types of popular music and jazz ever since.

Our example of blues singing is by Bessie Smith (1894–1937), known as the "Empress of the Blues." **(See Listening Guide on page 416.)** Bessie Smith grew up in Tennessee and from an early age helped support the family by singing on street corners. After false starts as a dancer and a vaudevillian, she devoted herself full-time to singing blues.

Smith had a hit in 1923 with her very first recording. Audiences were stunned by the mature, tragic quality of her voice and by her sensitive, personal style, which seemed to speak directly to the listener. On her way to a singing session in 1937 her car crashed into the side of the road, and by the next day Bessie Smith was dead.

DIXIELAND

Dixieland jazz (sometimes known as New Orleans jazz) flourished in the city of New Orleans, especially in the red-light district called Storyville. Small bands played in the brothels and saloons, and a standard form of "combo" arose: a "front line" of trumpet, clarinet, and trombone, and a "rhythm section" of drums, banjo, piano, and bass. Every instrument in a Dixieland band has a specific function. The main melody is played by the trumpet, while the clarinet weaves a high countermelody around it. The trombone plays a simpler, lower tune. In the rhythm section, the drums keep the beat, the piano

She had this trouble in her, this thing that wouldn't let her rest sometimes, a meanness that came and took her over.—Sidney Bechet about Bessie Smith

Bessie Smith (1894–1937)
Florida-Bound Blues

Date of performance: 1925
Duration: 3:13

Student CD Collection: 3, track 54
Complete CD Collection: 7, track 42

Bessie Smith often recorded with a small ensemble, but many of her performances feature piano and voice alone. Some of the great jazz pianists of the day recorded with Smith, and this recording features pianist Clarence Williams, who was also active as a songwriter, music publisher, and record producer.

Florida-Bound Blues is a standard 12-bar blues with words and music in an AAB pattern. Listen, though, for subtle changes in the words and melody between the first two lines of each stanza. In the first stanza, for example, "North" and "South" are sung as short notes in the first line but extended in the second line.

Among Smith's many vocal trademarks found in this recording is the addition of a chromatic note before the last note of a line.

The bare-bones melody:

Bessie Smith's version:

Sometimes she makes a quick slide, but sometimes she stretches out the added note.

Another common effect is a sudden pitch drop at the end of a line, producing a more intimate spoken sound. This sort of trick was a dependable way of creating a bond with an audience that was often doing plenty of talking on its own.

Florida-bound Blues also shows the broad, world-weary tone that permeates her work and provides glimpses of her offhand sense of humor. Above all, this recording provides a clear picture of her masterful control of pitch, rhythm, and volume.

54 (42)	0:00	Piano introduction	Piano immediately puts listener off balance before settling into a solid key and rhythm.
55 (43)	0:11	*Goodbye North, Hello South,*	Strict rhythm in piano is offset by Bessie's extra beat in the first line.
		Goodbye North, Hello South.	Vocal control: Listen to the change of volume on "North" and "South."
		It's so cold up here that the words freeze in your mouth.	Compare the heavily blued note on "words" to the centered pitch on "freeze."

56 (44)	0:46	*I'm goin' to Florida where I can have my fun,* *I'm goin' to Florida, where I can have my fun.* *Where I can lay out in the green grass and look up at the sun.*	Piano introduces a smooth, more melodic response to vocal. Listen for the added chromatic note on "fun." Note the piano "roll" filling in the space after "grass."
57 (45)	1:22	*Hey, hey redcap, help me with this load.* *Redcap porter, help me with this load (step aside).* *Oh, that steamboat, Mr. Captain, let me get on board.*	Listen for the deliberate variety and humor in these two lines. Each of the repeated notes is approached from below, creating a pulse in the line.
58 (46)	1:58	*I got a letter from my daddy, he bought me a sweet piece of land.* *I got a letter from my daddy, he bought me a small piece of ground.* *You can't blame me for leavin', Lord, I mean I'm Florida bound.*	Heavily blued notes on "from my daddy" ("daddy" means "lover"). Bessie varies this line by not taking a breath in the middle, making the ending breathless.
59 (47)	2:35	*My papa told me, my mama told me too.* *My papa told me, my mama told me too:* *Don't let them bell-bottom britches make a fool outa you.*	A new ending for the melody of the first two lines. Vocal line moves up on "fool," highlighting the punchline at the end.

and banjo play chords, and the bass plays the bass line (usually on plucked strings).

The sound of Dixieland jazz is of many lines interweaving in a complex but organized way. The effect is of collective improvisation but with every instrument having a carefully defined role. The most common musical forms are 12-bar blues and **32-bar AABA form** (the standard form of thousands of pop songs throughout the twentieth century).

The 32-bar AABA form has four eight-measure sections:

◆ A eight measures
◆ A eight measures
◆ B eight measures
◆ A eight measures

The first statement of the tune takes up the first 32 measures. Then the band plays variants of the tune or improvises on its basic chord progressions, while keeping to the 32-measure format. Each statement of the tune or the variation on it is known as a "chorus." In Dixieland jazz, a piece usually begins with the whole band playing the first chorus, and then features alternations of (accompanied) solo and collective improvisation. Some-

The King Oliver Creole Jazz Band, 1921.

Frank Driggs Collection/Archive Photos.

The recordings of the Hot Five and the Hot Seven contributed more than any other single group of recordings to making jazz famous and a music to be taken seriously.—Jazz historian Gunther Schuller

Louis Armstrong's Hot Five,
Exclusive Okeh Record Artists.

Louis Armstrong's Hot Five, Chicago, 1925 (from left to right): Armstrong, Johnny St. Cyr, Johnny Dodds, Kid Ory, Lil Hardin.

Frank Driggs Collection/Archive Photos.

except for a single soloist. This is known as a "break."

Some of the most famous musicians and bandleaders of early jazz were Jelly Roll Morton (piano), Louis Armstrong (trumpet), Joe "King" Oliver (trumpet), Bix Beiderbecke (trumpet), Sidney Bechet (clarinet and soprano saxophone), and Jack Teagarden (trombone).

The most important figure in jazz from the 1920s was Louis Armstrong (1901–1971). After he left New Orleans, Armstrong settled in Chicago, where, with his composer and pianist wife, Lil Hardin, he made a series of groundbreaking recordings. His brilliant trumpet-playing and enormously inventive improvisations paved the way for a new focus in jazz on solo playing. Armstrong's career spanned more than 50 years in American music, and in later years, when asked to speak about his life, he would simply point to his trumpet and say: "That's my living; that's my life."

Armstrong's Chicago music brought jazz from the dense polyphony of New Orleans, with many simultaneous lines, to an era of the astonishing solo. The performance we will hear is a Hot Five recording—trumpet, clarinet, and trombone for the musical lines, and piano (Lil Hardin), guitar, and banjo for rhythm and fill-in harmony.

Hotter Than That is a remarkable performance on

many levels. It might be seen as a ____ner on early jazz: It contains bits of the earlier polyphonic New Orleans style as well as the flashy solos that became popular in the 1920s, and it displays breaks, stop-time, and call-and-response, all standard parts of the vocabulary of early ensemble jazz. Beyond that, it is one of the first truly great jazz recordings, showing Armstrong at his exuberant best on both trumpet and vocals. **(See Listening Guide on page 419.)**

SWING

In the 1930s and early 1940s, the most popular jazz style was **swing**. The Swing Era takes its name from the fact that much of the music of the time was dance music. Because swing was usually played by large bands with as many as 15 or 20 musicians, the Swing Era is also called the Big Band Era. This period also saw the growth of much solo playing, such as that of tenor saxophonists Coleman Hawkins and Lester Young, trumpeter Roy Eldridge, and pianists Fats Waller and Art Tatum.

The most important changes from Dixieland jazz to the big bands were the larger number of performers, the use of saxophones in the band, and the use of written (composed or "arranged") music. For the first time, jazz was mostly written out, rather than mostly improvised. Swing music became extraordinarily popular during these years, and huge ballrooms would be filled with enthusiastic crowds dancing to the music. Some of the great swing bands of the time were those of Fletcher Henderson, Count Basie, Duke Ellington, and Benny Goodman.

The instruments of the big bands were divided into three groups: the saxophones, the brass section, and the rhythm section. The saxophone group included alto and tenor saxophones, and saxophone players ("reedmen") could usually also play clarinet. The brass section included both trumpets and trombones. The rhythm section included guitar, piano, bass, and drums. In addition, the bandleader (usually a pianist, a clarinetist, or a trumpeter) would often be featured as a soloist.

Visual presentation was an important element of

H*earing* Louis Armstrong play, I stood silent, almost bashful, asking myself if I would ever be able to attain a small part of Louis Armstrong's greatness.—Tenor saxophonist Coleman Hawkins

Louis Armstrong (1900–1971)
Hotter Than That

Date of performance: 1927
Instruments: Trumpet, clarinet,
    trombone, piano, banjo, guitar
Duration: 3:00

Complete CD Collection: 7, track 48

Hotter Than That is built around a 32-measure tune written by Lil Hardin. The 32-measure chord pattern is repeated several times, and the performers improvise all their melodic lines over this stable chord structure. The end of each 16-measure section is played as a break: everyone drops out except the soloist, who leads the song into the next half of the chorus or into the next chorus itself. The basic structure of the performance is shown here:

Intro:	full ensemble (8 bars)
Chorus 1:	trumpet solo with rhythm section (32 bars)
Chorus 2:	clarinet solo with rhythm section (32 bars)
Chorus 3:	vocal with guitar (32 bars)
New material:	vocal and guitar duet (16 bars)
Chorus 4:	trombone solo with rhythm section (16 bars)
	full ensemble (16 bars)
Coda:	trumpet and guitar

In the third chorus, Armstrong sings instead of playing, scatting through the entire 32 bars. Pay special attention to the similarity between his trumpet-playing and his singing: he uses the same clean attack, the same "shake" at the end of a long note, the same "rips" up to a high note, and the same arpeggiated style of melody. He also builds a string of 24 equal syncopated notes, intensifying the swing in the rhythm.

After the scat chorus, Armstrong and guitarist Lonnie Johnson play a call-and-response chorus, imitating each other's notes, inflections, and rhythms. In this section, as in the whole song, every note drives the song forward, producing a work of great energy and unity.

INTRO		
(48)	**0:00**	Full ensemble, New Orleans–style polyphony. Listen for the individual instruments.

CHORUS 1		
(49)	**0:08**	Trumpet solo. Listen for Armstrong's confident rhythm and occasional "burbles."
	0:24	Break: background drops out, Armstrong "rips" to a high note.
	0:26	Armstrong improvises on arpeggios. "Shake" on long notes.

| | 0:42 | Break: clarinet jumps in on trumpet line, prepares for solo. |

CHORUS 2

(50)	0:44	Clarinet solo. Same tempo, but not as much rhythmic variety.
	1:00	Break: Clarinet dives into a long blued note.
	1:02	Clarinet solo continues.
	1:17	Break: Armstrong jumps in, preparing the scat chorus.

CHORUS 3

(51)	1:20	Scat chorus. Listen for variety of sound: jagged lines vs. smooth lines, notes hit perfectly vs. notes slid.
	1:35	Break: "rip" to high note.
	1:39	Scat in syncopation with guitar.
	1:53	Break: whining scat, preparing for:

NEW MATERIAL

(52)	1:55	Scat/guitar dialogue. Call-and-response.
	2:08	"Rip" to high note in voice, imitated in guitar.
	2:13	Piano transition to:

CHORUS 4

(53)	2:17	Trombone solo, ending with chromatic climb to:
	2:32	Break: Armstrong on an energetic climbing sequence into:
	2:35	New Orleans–style polyphony by full ensemble, Armstrong on top.
	2:43	Multiple breaks ("stop-time").

CODA

| (54) | 2:47 | Full group, followed by: |
| | 2:49 | Guitar/trumpet interchange. |

The Duke Ellington Orchestra, 1949.

the big bands. Similarly, the sound of the big bands of the Swing Era was smooth and polished. This was partly because of the prominence of the smooth-sounding saxophones, and partly because the music was almost all written down. The polyphonic complexity of collective improvisation had given way to an interest in a big homophonic sound, lively presentation, and polish.

One of the most important and influential composers in the history of jazz was Duke Ellington (1899–1974). He is said to have been responsible for as many as 1,000 jazz compositions. Ellington was a man of many talents, being at one and the same

LISTENING GUIDE

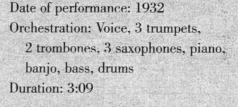

Duke Ellington (1899–1974)
It Don't Mean A Thing
(If It Ain't Got That Swing)

Date of performance: 1932
Orchestration: Voice, 3 trumpets,
2 trombones, 3 saxophones, piano,
banjo, bass, drums
Duration: 3:09

Student CD Collection: 3, track 60
Complete CD Collection: 7, track 55

The title of *It Don't Mean A Thing (If It Ain't Got That Swing)* became a motto for an era—and has survived as a catch-phrase in the jazz world up through today. The song is an exceptionally lively and infectious number that displays numerous hallmarks of the Ellington sound at the beginning of the swing era: the unique interplay between vocals and orchestra, the growling wah-wah brass contrasted with the sultry saxophones, the driving slap of the bass, the sensational solos by Joe "Tricky Sam" Nanton on muted trombone and Johnny Hodges on saxophone, and the superb instrumental arrangement and wide palette of instrumental timbres used throughout each variation of the principal theme.

60 (55)	0:00	Introductory vamp between Ivie Anderson's scat improvisation and the driving bass and drum.
	0:11	Joe "Tricky Sam" Nanton plays a muted trombone solo atop a subdued chorus of saxophones and muted trumpets that blare out in brief response to each phrase of Nanton's solo. This solo elaborates on the entire tune *before* the band's initial statement.

61 (56)	0:46	Entry of the first chorus (see below). Blue note on "ain't." Note the call-and-response interplay between vocals and orchestra.
	0:54	Second chorus.
	1:03	Transitional section of contrasting character.
62 (57)	1:13	Restatement of first chorus.
63 (58)	1:22	Entry of Johnny Hodges's saxophone solo. Notice how Ellington's arrangement accelerates the shifts in the orchestral timbres behind Hodges. Ellington veers further and further away (in texture, harmony, and counterpoint) from the original statement of the vocal model in each variation. Notice also the prearranged backing and elaborate responses to the solo.
64 (59)	2:43	Scat improvisation by Anderson.
	2:52	Return to first chorus and fadeout by muted trumpets on the motive from their response.

It Don't Mean A Thing
(If It Ain't Got That Swing)

Duke Ellington

time a master songwriter, an innovative composer and arranger, an imaginative and capable pianist, and an extraordinary bandleader.

Ellington was the first to make full use of the rich palette of colors available to the jazz orchestra. Similarly, Ellington's harmony was years ahead of that of his contemporaries, using extended chords, deft chromatic motion, and novel combinations of disparate sonorities. **(See Listening Guide on page 421.)**

The bandleader who did the most to popularize swing was Benny Goodman (1909–1986). Known as the "King of Swing," clarinetist Goodman led a band that was heard by millions across America on a weekly radio show, and he achieved the unprecedented in 1938 by bringing his band to Carnegie Hall, the traditional home of classical music. Goodman was also the first to break through what was then known as the "color barrier" by hiring black musicians such as pianist Teddy Wilson and vibraphonist Lionel Hampton to play among white musicians. This was an important step in what was still an officially segregated country.

Another influential aspect of Goodman's work was his formation of small groups—sometimes a trio or a quartet, most often a sextet. Goodman's sextet and his other small groups paved the way for the virtuoso solo playing and small combos of bebop.

Bebop

In the early 1940s, a reaction to the glossy, organized sound of some of the big bands set in. Some jazz musicians began to experiment again with smaller combos and with a type of music that was more intellectually demanding, more for listening than for dancing. This style is known as **bop** or **bebop**. The name probably derives from some of the nonsense syllables used in scat singing ("Doo-wah doo-wah, be-bop a loo-wah"). And the most frequent phrase-ending in bebop solos is, ♪ which fits the word "bebop" perfectly. There is also a composition by Dizzy Gillespie that is called *Bebop*.

The pioneers of bebop were Charlie "Bird" Parker (alto saxophone), Dizzy Gillespie (trumpet), and The-

lonious Monk (piano). In turn, these three players influenced other musicians, including Stan Getz, Miles Davis, Sarah Vaughan, and John Coltrane. In fact, it would be difficult to find a jazz musician who has not been influenced by Parker, Gillespie, and Monk.

Benny Goodman in 1938, with manic drummer Gene Krupa.

Bebop is a very different kind of music from swing. It is harder, irregular, and less predictable. It is played by a small group (for example, saxophone and trumpet with piano, bass, and drums). The tempo is generally faster, and there is far more solo improvisation. The chord progressions and rhythmic patterns are complex and varied. Bop is generally considered the beginning of modern jazz.

With its fast pace and its emphasis on solo improvisation, bebop depended on the inventiveness, quick thinking, virtuosity, and creativity of individual musicians. Charlie Parker, Dizzy Gillespie, and Thelonious Monk began playing independently, but had a similar approach to the new music. They also performed together and developed considerable complexity in their playing. Their solo improvisations were quick and unpredictable, full of fiery fast notes, lengthy pauses, and sudden changes of direction. Although bop was still based on popular songs (AABA form) or on the 12-bar blues pattern, the simple harmonies were enriched with new and more dissonant chords, and the

Jazz is freedom. Think about that. You think about that.— Thelonious Monk

Beboppers in 1948. From Left to Right: Thelonious Monk, Howard McGhee, Roy Eldridge, Teddy Hill.

Charlie Parker and Dizzy Gillespie in 1950, with John Coltrane (tenor saxophone) and Tommy Potter (bass).

accompanying rhythms were more complex. Soloists often deliberately overran the underlying sectional patterns and began and ended phrases at unexpected and unconventional places.

Bebop musicians sometimes wrote new tunes themselves, but more often they improvised around well-known songs of the day. Beboppers avoided improvising on the melody; their solos were built strictly on the chord patterns and often made no reference to the tune. As a result, their music could sound quite different from the original song.

A distinct culture surrounded bebop. It was a music of rebellion. Swing had been accepted, and even taken over, by the white establishment, and bebop was, in a sense, a reaction to this. It was designed to be different.

For such controversial music, bebop is based on a remarkably conservative structure. Normally it begins with a 32-bar tune. Often the melody instruments play the tune in unison. Then each instrument improvises over the chords of the tune.

The great genius of bebop was Charlie Parker (1920–1955), a brilliant, self-destructive saxophonist who died at the age of 34 from alcoholism and drug addiction. His improvisations changed the way a generation

LISTENING GUIDE

The Charlie Parker Quartet
Confirmation

Date of performance: July 30, 1953
Personnel: Charlie Parker, alto
    saxophone; Al Haig, piano; Percy
    Heath, bass; Max Roach, drums.
Duration: 2:58

Student CD Collection: 3, track 65
Complete CD Collection: 7, track 60

*C*onfirmation is one of the most stunning of Parker's many extraordinary performances. The studio tapes show that the piece was recorded straight through, with no splicing, no alternative takes, and no errors. It is important to remember that although the first few measures (the initial A of the AABA form) and the third group of eight measures (the B section) have been worked out beforehand, all the rest of what Parker plays is made up on the spot. All the running notes, the rhythmic figures, the cascades of musical gestures—all these are created in the very moment of performance. Not only that, but each time Parker plays the A section—every single time—he varies it considerably. It is hard to imagine that anyone could display such rich and instantaneous creativity.

Charlie Parker's alto saxophone is accompanied by piano, bass, and drums. These serve to create a harmonic foundation and keep a consistent beat, against which Parker's ingenuity,

424

flexibility, and expressive flights can shine. Toward the end of the piece, each of the other players gets a few measures to improvise on his own: first the pianist, then the bass player, and then the drummer. Parker wraps everything up with everyone playing together again.

The form of the piece is the favorite one of the bebop era: AABA form. Just to remind you, each section of this form lasts for 8 measures. So each statement or *chorus* of the whole form lasts for 32 measures. There are three whole choruses with Parker, then the piano plays the A section twice (= 16 measures), the bass player has 8 measures, the drummer has 8, and then Parker returns to play B and A once more (the final 16 measures). To keep your place, keep counting measures (*1*, 2, 3, 4; *2*, 2, 3, 4; etc.) all the way through (it's easier if you focus on the bass, which plays on the beat all the way through).

INTRODUCTION		
65 (60) 0:00		There is a brief 4-measure introduction by the piano.
CHORUS 1		
66 (61) 0:05		The tune is a typical bebop composition: angular, irregular, and offbeat. Yet Parker makes it sound melodic as well as deeply rhythmic. The rhythm section is rock-solid, though the drummer manages to be splashy and interesting at the same time. Although the chorus altogether contains three statements of the A section, Parker makes them sound different each time. The B section (0:25–0:34) is not as highly differentiated in this piece as it is in some bebop compositions, though its harmonies are different.
CHORUS 2		
67 (62) 0:44		Parker really starts to fly on this chorus (hence his nickname, "Bird"). He also plays in the lower register of the saxophone to give variety to his solo.
CHORUS 3		
68 (63) 1:22		The third chorus is unified by rapid, descending chromatic phrases, which in turn are balanced by arch-shaped arpeggios. A triplet turn is a common motive, and Parker plays right across the "seams" of the AABA form to make long, compelling musical statements of his own.
PIANO SOLO (AA)		
69 (64) 2:00		Al Haig takes 16 measures for his improvisation, which is quite musical for a normal human being, but which sounds pretty flat after listening to Charlie Parker!
BASS SOLO (B)		
2:16		Percy Heath gets to play some different rhythms for 8 measures with hints of the tune.
DRUM SOLO (A)		
2:28		Amazingly, Max Roach manages to suggest the melody on his 8 measures. (Try humming it along with him.)
FINAL HALF-CHORUS (BA)		
70 (65) 2:35		Parker repeats the B and A sections as a final half-chorus, playing with intensity but closer to the original melody. Percy Heath (who was said to be overwhelmed by Parker's playing on this recording date) gets in the last word!

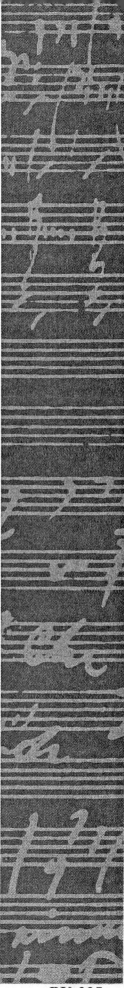

thought about jazz. His playing was profound, dizzying, subtle, and complex; his phrasing unconventional and inspired; his tone edgy and intense, liquid in one line and sandpaper in the next. Parker absorbed music of all kinds, including Stravinsky and Bartók; he loved painting and dance. And he was both loyal and inspiring: Dizzy Gillespie called him "the other half of my heartbeat."

We shall listen to a remarkable performance by Parker, entitled *Confirmation*, which he recorded in 1953. Like the jazz piece *Crazeology* that we studied in the Listening chapter at the beginning of this book, Charlie Parker's *Confirmation* is based on the chord changes of Gershwin's *I Got Rhythm*, known familiarly as "rhythm changes." Also like *Crazeology*, *Confirmation* is a 32-bar AABA form. But these aspects of the piece, though they are important, pale in comparison with the extraordinary creativity and brilliance of the saxophonist. **(See Listening Guide on page 424.)**

COOL JAZZ

Cool jazz was really a subcategory of bop. It continued to use small combos, and the rhythmic and harmonic styles were similar. Cool-jazz pieces also were based on popular tunes or blues patterns. The departures from bop can be noted immediately in the overall sound of the groups and in the improvised solos. The playing is more subdued and less frenetic. Pieces tend to be longer, and they feature a larger variety of instruments, sometimes including the baritone saxophone, with its deep, full sound, and even some classical instruments, such as the French horn and the cello, which are characteristically mellow in sound.

Some groups specializing in cool jazz became quite popular in the 1950s. Miles Davis formed a group with nine instruments; the George Shearing Quintet used piano, guitar, vibraphone, bass, and drums; and perhaps the most popular group of all (certainly one of the longest lasting) was the Modern Jazz Quartet, which featured Milt Jackson on vibraphone. The vibraphone (an instrument like a xylophone, with metal bars and an electrically enhanced, sustained, fluctuating tone) is the perfect instrument for projecting the "coolth" of cool jazz.

FREE JAZZ

At the end of the 1950s, the move away from preset chord progressions led to the development in the 1960s and 1970s of what is known as free jazz. This style depended both on original compositions and on creative improvisation. The most influential musician of this period was Ornette Coleman, alto saxophonist, trumpeter, violinist, and composer. Several pieces have been named for him, and an album of his, made in 1960 and entitled *Free Jazz*, gave its name to the whole period.

Free jazz is abstract and can be dense and difficult to follow. Besides abandoning preset chord progressions, it often dispenses with regular rhythmic patterns and melody lines as well. Drumming is energetic, full of color and activity, without a steady and constant pattern of beats. Melodic improvisations are full of extremes: very high notes, squawks and squeals, long-held tones, fragmented phrases, and sudden silences. Many free-jazz groups have experimented with the music of other countries. Idioms borrowed from Turkish, African, and Indian music appear in many free-jazz compositions, and some groups have made use of non-Western instruments, such as sitars, gongs, and bamboo flutes.

The Modern Jazz Quartet.

Free jazz in its purest form was not popular. It could be difficult to listen to and was often raucous and dissonant. Totally free collective improvisation must necessarily have many moments of complete chaos. (Coleman's *Free Jazz* has two bands improvising simultaneously with no predetermined key, rhythm, or melody.) Free-jazz composers responded to this problem by writing compositions that would begin and end with a set theme or melody, allowing room for free improvisation in between. Obviously, in these cases the melody provides a common basis for the intervening improvisations and eliminates the randomness of complete freedom. Also, the influence of Eastern and African music brought to free jazz a common language of drones and new scale patterns.

FUSION

Fusion is the name given to the musical style of the 1970s and 1980s that combined elements of jazz and rock music. Perhaps it was the lack of an audience for free jazz or the overwhelming popularity of rock that encouraged jazz musicians to incorporate elements of rock into their performances and compositions during this period.

Rock and jazz have some origins in common: early blues, gospel music, and popular ballads. But they developed along separate lines. Rock is largely vocal music and is based on simple and accessible forms and harmonies. Jazz is mostly instrumental music, and some forms of jazz are quite complex, ignoring popular appeal.

Fusion was the first jazz style to achieve wide popularity since the mass appeal of swing in the 1930s and 1940s. Its most influential proponent was Miles Davis, who made two records in 1969 that established the fusion style for the 1970s and 1980s: *In a Silent Way* and *Bitches Brew*.

The primary characteristics of fusion are the adoption of electric instruments (electric piano, synthesizer, and electric bass guitar) in place of their traditional ancestors, a large percussion section (including several non-European instruments such as hand drums, bells, gongs, shakers, and scrapers), and simplicity of form

> A jazz musician who plays fusion is selling out.
> —Wynton Marsalis

Jazz singer Betty Carter performing in Carnegie Hall.

Jazz and Classical

Some of the elements of jazz—syncopation, for example—appear in classical music. Some Bach melodies are fascinating in their syncopations and cross-rhythms; Beethoven wrote some variations that sound like ragtime; and Debussy invented many of the chords used later in jazz. But jazz brought to the musical scene an art that was highly original and full of vitality. And many classical composers of the twentieth century turned to the inspiration of jazz in their own work. ✦ Jazz exerted a strong influence on Stravinsky. His first work to incorporate elements of jazz was *L'Histoire du Soldat* (1918); subsequent compositions that employ jazz techniques include *Ragtime*, of the same year, *Piano-Rag-Music* (1919), and the *Ebony* Concerto for clarinet and jazz band (1945). ✦ Ravel, Milhaud, Copland, and Bernstein were four other famous twentieth-century composers influenced by jazz. The Ravel piano concertos each contain jazzlike episodes, and his Violin Sonata has a second movement entitled "Blues." Milhaud's *Création du Monde* incorporates influences from the jazz he heard in Harlem nightclubs in the early twenties. Copland's music is full of jazzy rhythms and harmonies, as is that of Bernstein, who moved especially freely between the two worlds. ✦ The composer who most successfully brought together elements of jazz and classical music was George Gershwin. His *Rhapsody in Blue* (1924) is a perfect example of a symphonic work permeated by elements of the jazz style.

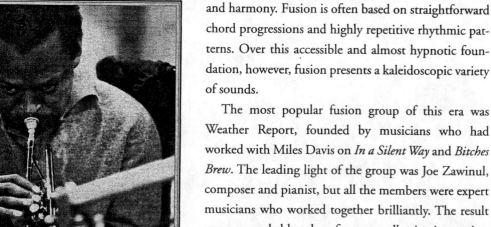

Miles Davis.

and harmony. Fusion is often based on straightforward chord progressions and highly repetitive rhythmic patterns. Over this accessible and almost hypnotic foundation, however, fusion presents a kaleidoscopic variety of sounds.

The most popular fusion group of this era was Weather Report, founded by musicians who had worked with Miles Davis on *In a Silent Way* and *Bitches Brew*. The leading light of the group was Joe Zawinul, composer and pianist, but all the members were expert musicians who worked together brilliantly. The result was a remarkable talent for true collective improvisation, with a combination of solo lines merging into a rich group sound. Other important groups were founded by Herbie Hancock and Chick Corea.

GLOSSARY AND MUSICAL EXAMPLE LOCATOR

(Fuller discussions of these terms may be found on the pages indicated.)

ABA or aria or da capo form   Tripartite form, found in opera arias and some slow movements of instrumental works, featuring an opening A section, a contrasting B section, and a return to the A section, which is often sung with embellishments. (See p. 148.) (Musical example: George Frideric Handel, *Giulio Cesare*, p. 149.)

Alberti bass   Accompaniment in which the chords are broken up into individual short notes played in a repeated rhythm. (See p. 162.)

arch form   Five-part form in which part one corresponds to five, part two corresponds to four, and part three is the apex. (See p. 366.)

aria   Lyrical section of opera for solo singer and orchestra, usually in ABA form. (See p. 121.) (Musical example: George Frideric Handel, *Giulio Cesare*, p. 149.)

atonality   The lack of a key system or tonal center in music. (See p. 328.) (Musical example: Arnold Schoenberg, *Madonna* from *Pierrot Lunaire*, p. 350.)

Baroque   The period in European music from about 1600 to 1750. (See p. 115.)

basso continuo   Single instrument or small group of instruments, usually including a harpsichord, playing the bass line in Baroque music. (See p. 119.) (Musical examples: Arcangelo Corelli, Trio Sonata, Op. 3, No. 7, p. 129, and Johann Sebastian Bach, *Brandenburg* Concerto No. 2 in F Major, p. 140.)

bebop or bop   Form of jazz that developed in the 1940s for small combos, with harder, more improvisatory music. (See p. 423.) (Musical examples: Charlie Parker, *Confirmation*, p. 424, and Benny Harris, *Crazeology*, p. 70.)

binary form   A form with two sections, each of which is repeated, as in the pattern AABB. (See p. 67.) (Musical examples: Wolfgang Amadeus Mozart, Minuet and Trio from Symphony No. 18 in F Major, K. 130, p. 66, and Franz Joseph Haydn, Minuet and Trio from Symphony No. 45 in F-sharp Minor, p. 176.)

bitonality   Two different keys sounding simultaneously. (See p. 337.) (Musical example: Charles Ives, "Putnam's Camp" from *Three Places in New England*, p. 374.)

blue note   Flattened or "bent" note played or sung in jazz. (See p. 411.) (Musical examples: Bessie Smith, *Florida-Bound Blues*, p. 416, and Duke Ellington, *It Don't Mean a Thing (If It Ain't Got That Swing)*, p. 421.)

bunraku   Traditional Japanese puppet theater. (See p. 15.)

caccia   Medieval Italian secular song in which two voices sing in a round. (See p. 87.)

cantata   *Chamber* cantatas were unstaged dramatic works for a single singer or a small group of singers and accompanying instruments. *Church* cantatas involved solo singers, choir, and instruments and focused on the liturgical theme of a particular day. (See p. 118.)

canzona   Renaissance instrumental work, often involving counterpoint. (See p. 108.) (Musical example: Giovanni Gabrieli, *Canzona Duodecimi Toni*, p. 110.)

castrato   Male singer castrated before puberty to retain high voice. Castratos were common in the eighteenth century. (See p. 150.)

character piece   Short programmatic piece usually for solo piano. (See p. 267.) (Musical example: Robert Schumann, *Träumerei* (*Dreaming*) from *Kinderszenen*, Op. 15, p. 267.)

chorale   A Protestant hymn sung in unison by the entire congregation in even rhythm. Often harmonized for use by church choir. (See p. 119.) (Musical example: Johann Sebastian Bach, *St. Matthew Passion*, p. 145.)

Classic   The period in European music from about 1730 to 1800. (See p. 157.)

comic opera   (Italian: *opera buffa*; French: *opéra comique*; German: *Singspiel*.) Light opera, with amusing plots, down-to-earth characters, simpler music, and spoken dialogue. (See p. 162.) (Musical example: Giovanni Pergolesi, *La Serva Padrona*, p. 163.)

concerto   Instrumental work, usually in three movements, highlighting contrast. Baroque concertos were usually written in the pattern fast-slow-fast, featuring ritornello form. A *concerto grosso* featured a small group of instruments contrasted with the whole group. A *solo concerto* featured a single instrument contrasted with the whole group. (See p. 118.) (Musical examples: Antonio Vivaldi, *La Primavera* ("*Spring*") from *The Four Seasons*, p. 135, and Johann Sebastian Bach, *Brandenburg* Concerto No. 2 in F Major, p. 142.) Classic and Romantic concertos tended to be solo concertos, retaining the fast-slow-fast pattern, and combining ritornello form with Classic forms, such as sonata form or aria form. (See pp. 172, 256.) (Musical example: Felix Mendelssohn,

Concerto in E minor for Violin and Orchestra, Op. 64, p. 256.)

concerto form Three movements, in the pattern fast-slow-fast. (See p. 127.)

continuo See **basso continuo**.

courtly love Stylized convention of poetry and code of behavior developed in the medieval courts of southern France. (See p. 81.) (Musical example: Beatriz de Dia, *A chantar*, p. 82.)

didjeridoo Wooden wind instrument in use among the Australian aborigines. (See p. 13.)

divertimento A chamber work meant as a "diversion"; generally lighter in style and with five, six, or more movements. (See p. 160.)

double-stopping Playing more than one string at a time on a string instrument. (See p. 256.) (Musical example: Felix Mendelssohn, Concerto in E minor for Violin and Orchestra, Op. 64, p. 256).

Enlightenment Eighteenth-century philosophy that favored a rational and scientific view of the world. (See p. 157.)

ensemble Usually used to refer to opera scenes in which several individuals sing together.

étude Solo instrumental piece focusing on a particular aspect of technique. (See p. 262.)

Expressionism Artistic and musical movement focusing on extreme emotions, such as fear or anguish. (See p. 345.) (Musical example: Alban Berg, *Wozzeck*, Act III, Scenes 3, 4, and 5, p. 355.)

fanfare A stirring phrase or a complete short work that is written primarily or entirely for brass instruments. (See p. 61.) (Musical examples: Paul Dukas, Fanfare from *La Péri*, p. 62, and Aaron Copland, *Fanfare for the Common Man*, p. 377.)

fugue Highly organized contrapuntal work featuring a theme or "subject" that occurs in all the musical lines in turn until all the lines are sounding at once. (See p. 141.) (Musical example: Johann Sebastian Bach, Prelude and Fugue in E minor, p. 140.)

fusion Music combining elements of both jazz and rock. (See p. 427.)

fuzz box Device that adds distortion to the sound of an electric guitar. (See p. 459.)

gagaku Ancient Japanese orchestral music. (See p. 15.)

gamelan Indonesian musical ensemble involving mostly metal percussion. (See pp. 17–19.) (Musical example: *Gangsaran - Bima Kurda - Gangsaran*, p. 18.)

German song A work for voice and piano set to a German text. (See p. 63.) (Musical example: Franz Schubert, *Gretchen am Spinnrade*, p. 63.)

grand opera Spectacular type of nineteenth-century

French opera, with elaborate stage sets, ballet, and crowd scenes. (See p. 272.)

Gregorian chant See **plainchant**.

ground bass A phrase in the bass that is repeated over and over again. (See p. 125.) (Musical example: Henry Purcell, Dido's Lament from *Dido and Aeneas*, p. 126.)

hardingfele Norwegian folk violin. (See p. 12.)

Impressionism Movement in painting of the late nineteenth and early twentieth centuries in which the outlines are vague and the pictures dreamy and suggestive. Also refers to a parallel movement in music. (See p. 330.) (Musical example: Claude Debussy, *Prélude à l'après-midi d'un faune*, p. 333.)

impromptu Instrumental piece, usually for piano, that gives the impression of being improvised. (See p. 262.)

jali Official singer and historian of the Mandinka tribe of West Africa. (See p. 5.)

kabuki Japanese style of traditional musical theater, involving an all-male cast. (See p. 15.)

koto Japanese instrument plucked like a zither. (See p. 15.)

leitmotiv Musical phrase or fragment with associations to a character, object, or idea. (See p. 291.) (Musical example: Richard Wagner, Prelude and *Liebestod* from *Tristan und Isolde*, p. 292.)

libretto The text for an opera. (See p. 174.)

liturgical music Music for a religious ceremony. (See p. 77.)

lute A plucked instrument with a rounded back, short neck, and frets. (See p. 72.) (Musical example: Guillaume de Machaut, *Doulz Viaire Gracieus*, p. 88.)

lyric opera Type of French opera midway between grand opéra and opéra comique, usually featuring plots of tragic love. (See p. 272.)

madrigal Secular vocal work, often in Italian, for a small group of singers. (See pp. 72, 106.) (Musical example: Maddalena Casulana, *Morte, te chiamo*, p. 72.)

Magnus Liber Organi "Great Book of Polyphony." Late twelfth-century collection of polyphonic compositions designed for the Cathedral of Notre Dame in Paris. (See p. 85.) (Musical example: Perotinus, *Viderunt Omnes*, p. 86.)

mbira African instrument made of a small wooden box or gourd with thin metal strips attached. (See pp. 12, 20–21.) (Musical example: *Chemetengure/Mudendero*, p. 21.)

melismatic Musical setting of text with a large number of notes to a single syllable. (See p. 78.)

Middle Ages   The period in European music from about 400 to 1400. (See p. 76.)

minimalism   Musical style of the 1960s to the 1990s involving very limited materials, constant repetition, and very gradual change. (See p. 397.)

minuet (and trio)   An instrumental work in the tempo (moderate) and meter (triple) of a favorite seventeenth- and eighteenth-century dance, in binary form. The trio is in form and structure like another minuet, but it usually has a contrast of texture, instrumentation, and sometimes key. (See p. 66.) (Musical example: Wolfgang Amadeus Mozart, Minuet and Trio from Symphony No.18 in F Major, K.130, p. 66, and Franz Joseph Haydn, Minuet and Trio from Symphony No. 45 in F-sharp Minor, p. 176.)

minuet-and-trio form   Often used for third movements of Classic instrumental works. Both minuet and trio are in two parts, each of which is repeated. The minuet is played twice, once before and once after the trio. (See p. 171.) (Musical examples: Wolfgang Amadeus Mozart, Minuet and Trio from Symphony No.18 in F Major, K.130, p. 66, and Franz Joseph Haydn, Minuet and Trio from Symphony No. 45 in F-sharp Minor, p. 176.)

Modernism   The cultural movement, stressing innovation, that dominated the first sixty to seventy years of the twentieth century. (See p. 323.)

modes   System of melodic organization used in music of the Middle Ages and early Renaissance. There are four main medieval modes, designating pieces ending on D, E, F, and G, respectively. (See p. 78.) (Musical example: Kyrie, p. 79.)

monody   Type of early Baroque music for solo voice and **basso continuo** with vocal line imitating the rhythms of speech. (See p. 119.) (Musical example: Claudio Monteverdi, extracts from *Orfeo*, p. 122.)

motet   (Renaissance) A vocal setting of a Latin text, usually sacred. (See p. 104.) (Musical example: Giovanni Pierluigi da Palestrina, *Exsultate Deo*, p. 105.)

movement   Large, separate section of a musical work.

music drama   Term coined by Wagner to refer to his operas, which involve ancient myth, resonant poetry, and rich, dramatic music. (See p. 288.) (Musical example: Richard Wagner, Prelude and *Liebestod* from *Tristan und Isolde*, p. 292.)

nationalism   A nineteenth-century movement that stressed national identity. In music, this led to the creation of works in native languages, using national myths and legends, and incorporating local rhythms, themes, and melodies. (See p. 227.) (Musical example: Bedřich Smetana, *The Moldau*, p. 298.)

neumatic   Musical setting of text with varying numbers of notes per syllable. (See p. 78.)

nocturne   Moody, introspective piece, usually for solo piano. (See p. 262.)

noh   Ancient Japanese theatrical genre, with highly stylized acting. (See p. 15.)

octatonic scale   Scale with eight notes within the octave, separated by a series of alternating whole and half steps. (See p. 329.)

opéra comique   Small-scale French nineteenth-century opera, with humorous or romantic plots. (See p. 272.)

opera seria   ("Serious opera") Italian Baroque form of opera in three acts, with conventional plots, and alternating recitatives and arias. (See p. 131.) (Musical example: George Frideric Handel, *Giulio Cesare*, Act III, Scene 4, p. 149.)

oral tradition   The practice of passing music (or other aspects of culture) orally from one generation to another. (See pp. 2 and 8.)

oratorio   An unstaged dramatic sacred work, featuring solo singers (including a narrator), choir, and orchestra, and usually based on a biblical story. (See p. 119.)

orchestral song cycle   Song cycle in which the voice is accompanied by an orchestra instead of a piano. (See p. 318.)

Ordinary of the Mass   The collective name for those five sections of the Catholic Mass (Kyrie, Gloria, Credo, Sanctus, Agnus Dei) that occur in every Mass. (See p. 97.)

ostinato   Constantly repeated musical phrase. (See p. 337.) (Musical example: Igor Stravinsky, *Le Sacre du Printemps* (*The Rite of Spring*), p. 338.)

pantonality   Term referring to the simultaneous existence of all keys in music. (See p. 328.)

Passion   Similar to the oratorio. An unstaged dramatic sacred work, featuring solo singers (including a narrator), choir, and orchestra, and based on one of the Gospel accounts of the last days of Jesus. (See p. 119.) (Musical example: Johann Sebastian Bach, *St. Matthew Passion*, p. 145.)

pentatonic scale   A scale with five notes; the most common form has the following intervals: whole step, whole step, minor third, whole step. (See p. 328.)

plainchant   Monophonic liturgical vocal music of the Middle Ages. (See p. 77.) (Musical example: Kyrie, p. 79.)

point of imitation   Section of music presenting a short phrase imitated among the voices. (See p. 98.) (Musical example: Josquin Desprez, Kyrie from the *Pange Lingua* Mass, p. 100.)

polyphony   Music with more than one line sounding at the same time. (See p. 81.) (Musical example: Perotinus, *Viderunt Omnes*, p. 86.)

polyrhythms   Different meters sounding simultaneously. (See p. 337.)

polytonality   The existence in music of two or more keys at the same time. (See p. 328.)

Postmodernism   A cultural movement of the last part of the twentieth century, involving a juxtaposition of past and present, popular and refined, Western and non-Western styles. (See p. 326.)

prelude (toccata)   Free, improvisatory work or movement, usually for organ. (See p. 141.) (Musical example: Johann Sebastian Bach, Prelude and Fugue in E minor, p. 140.)

Primitivism   Artistic movement of the early twentieth century concentrating on nonurban cultures and untamed nature. (See p. 336.)

program music   Instrumental music that tells a story or describes a picture or a scene. (See pp. 134, 238.) (Musical example: Antonio Vivaldi, *La Primavera* (*"Spring"*) from *The Four Seasons*, p. 135.)

protest song   A song devoted to a social cause, such as the fight against injustice, antiwar sentiment, etc. (See p. 455.)

quartal chords   Chords based on fourths rather than thirds. (See p. 329.)

quarter tones   Pitches separated by a quarter of a step rather than a half or a whole step. (See p. 330.)

ragtime   Early jazz in which the melody is highly syncopated, usually in duple meter and march tempo. (See p. 413.) (Musical example: Scott Joplin, *Maple Leaf Rag*, p. 413.)

rap   Popular music style of the 1980s and 1990s with fast, spoken lyrics and a strong, and often complex beat. (See p. 469.)

recitative   Music for solo voice and simple accompaniment, designed to reflect the irregularity and naturalness of speech. (See p. 121.) (Musical example: Claudio Monteverdi, extracts from *Orfeo*, p. 122.)

recitative accompagnato   Dramatic recitative accompanied by the orchestra. (See p. 148.) (Musical example: George Frideric Handel, *Giulio Cesare*, Act III, Scene 4, p. 149.)

reggae   Popular music style from Jamaica, with a light, catchy sound, characterized by offbeats played on the rhythm guitar. (See p. 464.)

Renaissance   The period in European music from about 1400 to 1600. (See p. 94.)

Requiem Mass   Mass for the dead. (See p. 184.)

riff   A short, repeated, melodic phrase often found in popular music. (See p. 453.) (Musical example: The Beatles, *It Won't Be Long*, p. 453.)

ritornello   An orchestral passage in a concerto that returns several times, in the same or in different keys. (See p. 133.) (Musical example: Antonio Vivaldi, *La Primavera* (*"Spring"*) from *The Four Seasons*, p. 135.)

rondo form   Often used for last movements of Classic instrumental works. A theme constantly returns, alternating with constrasting passages (episodes). (See p. 172.) (Musical example: Franz Joseph Haydn, String Quartet, Op. 33, No. 2, in E-flat Major, p. 178.)

scat   To sing with made-up syllables. (See p. 411.) (Musical example: Louis Armstrong, *Hotter Than That*, p. 419.)

secular music   Music that is nonreligious. (See p. 77.)

shakuhachi   Japanese end-blown bamboo flute. (See pp. 10, 15–16.) (Musical example: *Koku-Reibo*, p. 16.)

shamisen   Japanese plucked instrument with three strings and a long neck. (See p. 15.)

sinfonia   Three-movement instrumental introduction to eighteenth-century Italian opera. (See p. 168.)

sitar   A long-necked, resonant, plucked string instrument from India. (See p. 10.)

sonata   Baroque: A work for a small group of instruments. Sonatas include solo sonatas (one instrument and basso continuo) and trio sonatas (two instruments and basso continuo). Also divided by style into *sonata da camera* ("chamber sonata"), whose movements were based on dance rhythms, and *sonata da chiesa* ("church sonata"), whose movements were more serious in character. (See p. 119.) Classic and Romantic: Work for solo piano or piano and another instrument in three or four movements. (See p. 170.) (Musical examples: Arcangelo Corelli, Trio Sonata, Op. 3, No. 7, p. 129, and Ludwig van Beethoven, Piano Sonata in E Major, Op. 109, p. 218.)

sonata form   Organizing structure for a musical work or movement. It has three main parts: an *exposition*, in which the main themes are presented and the primary key moves from tonic to dominant; a *development* in which many keys are explored and the themes are often presented in fragments; and a *recapitulation*, in which the music of the exposition returns, usually staying in the tonic key throughout. (See p. 170.) (Musical examples: Wolfgang Amadeus Mozart, Symphony No. 40 in G minor, K. 550, p. 189, and Ludwig van Beethoven, Symphony No. 5 in C minor, p. 203.)

song cycle   Series of songs linked together. (See p. 241.)

Sprechstimme ("speechsong")   Technique of singing, halfway between speech and song. (See p. 355.) (Musical example: Arnold Schoenberg, *Madonna* from *Pierrot Lunaire*, p. 350.)

string quartet   Work, usually in four movements, for two violins, viola, and cello. (See p. 168.) (Musical examples: Franz Joseph Haydn, String Quartet, Op. 33, No. 2, in E-flat Major, p. 178, and Béla Bartók, String Quartet No. 4, p. 366.)

strophic song   Song in which all stanzas are sung to the same music. (See p. 240.) (Musical examples: Beatriz de

Dia, *A chantar*, p. 82, and Franz Schubert, *Gretchen am Spinnrade*, p. 63.)

suite A series of short pieces, usually based on various Baroque dance forms. (See p. 119.)

swing (1) The feeling generated by the regular rhythm and the syncopated accents of jazz. (See p. 411.) (2) Dance music played by jazz bands in the 1930s and early 1940s. (See p. 418.) (Musical example: Duke Ellington, *It Don't Mean a Thing (If It Ain't Got That Swing)*, p. 421.)

syllabic Musical setting of text with one note per syllable. (See p. 78.)

Symbolism Literary movement of the late nineteenth and early twentieth centuries concentrating on suggestion rather than description. (See p. 331.)

symphonic poem Programmatic orchestral work in one movement. (See p. 239.) (Musical example: Franz Liszt, *Hamlet*, p. 279.)

symphony Orchestral work, usually in four movements, the first being moderate in tempo, the second slow, the third a minuet or a scherzo, and the fourth fast. (See p. 168.) (Musical example: Ludwig van Beethoven, Symphony No. 5 in C minor, p. 203.)

thematic transformation Technique of changing or varying a theme in its different appearances throughout a work. (See p. 275.) (Musical example: Franz Liszt, *Hamlet*, p. 279.)

theme and variations Form of a work or a movement in which successive statements of a melody are altered or embellished each time. (See p. 43.) (Musical examples: Ludwig van Beethoven, *Six Easy Variations on a Swiss Tune*, p. 201, and Franz Schubert, Quintet in A Major (*The Trout*), p. 245.)

32-bar AABA form Format involving four eight-measure phrases, the first two and the last being the same. This form is very common in popular songs and jazz. (See p. 69.) (Musical example: Benny Harris, *Crazeology*, p. 70.)

through-composed song Song in which the music is continually evolving. (See p. 240.) (Musical example: Arnold Schoenberg, *Madonna* from *Pierrot Lunaire*, p. 350.)

tone color The distinctive sound of an instrument or voice. (See p. 10.)

total serialism Strict organization of all musical elements (dynamics, rhythm, pitch, etc.) of a musical composition by arranging them into series. (See p. 385.) (Musical example: Pierre Boulez, *Structures I* for two pianos, p. 387.)

troubadour Poet-musician of medieval southern France. (See p. 81.) (Musical example: Beatriz de Dia, *A chantar*, p. 82.)

trouvère Poet-musician of medieval northern France. (See p. 81.)

twelve-tone system Twentieth-century compositional technique in which the composer treats all twelve pitches as equal and uses them in a highly organized way. (See p. 328.) (Musical example: Arnold Schoenberg, Theme and Sixth Variation, *Variations for Orchestra*, Op. 31, p. 352.)

verismo Literary and operatic style featuring down-to-earth plots and characters. (See p. 272.)

virtuoso A performing musician (usually instrumentalist) who is outstandingly gifted. (See p. 218.)

Wagner tuba Brass instrument with a range between French horn and trombone. (See p. 291.)

wah-wah pedal Device for electric guitar that changes frequencies on the same note. (See p. 459.)

whole-tone scale A scale with six notes, each separated from the next by a whole step. (See p. 329.)

word-painting The technique of depicting the *meaning* of words through music. (See p. 107.) (Musical example: Thomas Morley, *Sweet Nymph Come to Thy Lover* and *Fire and Lightning*, p. 109.)

C R E D I T S

18 "Gangsaran-Bima Kurda-Gangsaran." Reprinted by permission of the Department of Ethnomusicology, University of California at Los Angeles.

30, 34, 39 "Happy Birthday to You," by Mildred J. Hill and Patty S. Hill. © 1935 (renewed) Summy–Birchrard Music, a division of Summy–Birchard, Inc. All rights reserved. Used by permission. Warner Bros. Publications U.S. Inc., Miami, FL 33014.

74 "A Lesson in Music." Copyright Alastair Reid. Reprinted by permission.

78 "Not a Second Time." Words and music by John Lennon and Paul McCartney. Copyright 1963, 1964 Northern Songs Ltd. Copyright renewed. All rights controlled & administered by EMI Blackwood Music Inc. under license from ATV Music Corp. (Maclen Music). All rights reserved.

92 Handwritten score, "Introit & Kyrie, Missa for Sancti Ylarionus Abbatis." Torino, Biblioteca Nationale Universiteria. Lucca: Libreria Musicale Italiana © 1990. Used by permission.

112 Ockeghem "Missa mi mi," by Johannes Ockeghem. Vatican City, Biblioteca Apostolica Vaticana, MS Chigi CVIII 234. Used by permission.

113 "Missa mi mi" from "Masses and Mass Sections" by Johannes Ockeghem, edited by Jaap van Benthem. Copyright 1994 Koninklijke VNM. Used by permission.

154 Handwritten score, "Ah, Ah Belinda" by Purcell, from the opera "Dido and Aeneas" from Orpheus Brittanicus. From "Monuments of Music and Music Literature in Facsimile" 1st series, music 1, pg. 193, Orpheus Brittanicus by Henry Purcell, Broude Brothers, NY © 1965. Used by permission.

155 "Ah, Ah Belinda" by Purcell. © 1961 (renewed) by Novello & Co. Ltd. 8/9 Frith Street, London W1D 3JB. International copyright secured. All rights reserved. Reprinted by permission of G. Schirmer, Inc. (ASCAP)

192 Handwritten score, "Requiem" by Mozart, Classical Era score KV 626, Bildarchiv der Oesterreichische Nationalbibliothek.

193 "Requiem" by Mozart. Copyright 1992 Breitkopf & Haertel. Weisbaden. Excerpts from EB 5210. Used by permission.

222 Handwritten score, "Symphony No. 6" ("Pastoral") by Beethoven, © 2000 Verlag Beethoven-Haus Bonn. Used by permission.

223 "Symphony No. 6" ("Pastoral") by Beethoven, edited by Jonathan Del Mar. Publisher: Baerenreiter-Verlag, Kassel. Used by permission.

322 "Symphony No. 2" by Gustav Mahler, 1st page—Fourth Movement: Urlicht. Original autograph score. Gilbert Kaplan Collection, New York.

323 "Symphony No. 2" by Gustav Mahler. Copyright 1971 (renewed) by Universal Edition Vienna. All rights reserved. Used by permission of European American Music Distributors LLC, sole U.S. and Canadian agent for Universal Edition Vienna.

338 Le sacre du printemps ("The Rite of Spring") by Igor Stravinsky. Copyright 1912, 1921 by Hawkes & Son (London) Ltd. Copyright renewed. Reprinted by permission of Boosey & Hawkes, Inc.

342 Concerto in E-flat for Chamber Orchestra ("Dumbarton Oaks") by Igor Stravinsky. Copyright 1938 (renewed) by G. Schirmer (ASCAP). International copyright secured. All rights reserved. Reprinted in the U.S. by permission of G. Schirmer, Inc. Copyright 1938 (renewed) B. Schott's Soehne, Mainz. All rights reserved. Used by permission of European American Music Distributors, LLC, sole Canadian agent for B. Schott's Soehne, Mainz.

347 "Five Pieces for Orchestra" by Arnold Schoenberg. Used by permission of Belmont Music Publishers, Pacific Palisades, CA 90272.

350 "Pierrot Lunaire" by Arnold Schoenberg. Used by permission of Belmont Music Publishers, Pacific Palisades, CA 90272.

352 "Variations for Orchestra" by Arnold Schoenberg. Used by permission of Belmont Music Publishers, Pacific Palisades, CA 90272.

366 "String Quartet No. 4" by Bela Bartok. Copyright 1929 by Boosey & Hawkes, Inc. Reprinted by permission of Boosey & Hawkes, Inc. and for the USA and by Universal Edition for Canada. Copyright renewed in the territory of Canada by Derissin of European American Distributors Corp.

370 "War Requiem" by Benjamin Britten, text by Wilfred Owen from *The Collected Poems of Wilfred Owen.* Copyright 1963 by Chatto & Windus Ltd. Reprinted by permission of New Directions Publishing Corp.

378 "Bess, You Is My Woman Now," from "Porgy and Bess" by George Gershwin, DuBose and Dorothy Heyward and Ira Gershwin. © 1935 (renewed 1962). George Gershwin Music, Ira Gershwin Music, and DuBose and Dorothy Heyward Memorial Fund. All rights administered by WB Music Corp. All Rights Reserved. Used by Permission. Warner Bros. Publications, U.S. Inc., Miami, FL 33014.

382 "Make our Garden Grow" from "Candide," music by Leonard Bernstein (1918–1990) lyrics by Richard Wilbur (1921–) Copyright 1955, 1957, 1958, 1976, 1982, 1990, 1994 by Amberson Holdings LLC. Publisher: Boosey & Hawkes, Inc. Sole agent. Reprinted by permission.

386 "Structures I" by Pierre Boulez. Copyright 1955 by Universal Edition (London) Ltd. London. Copyright renewed. All rights reserved. Used by permission of European American Music Distributors LLC, sole U.S. and Canadian agent for Universal Edition (London) Ltd.

388 "Polonius Platitudes" by Edwin London. Copyright 1971 Edwin London (ASCAP). Used by permission of the composer.

395 "Renaissance Concerto" by Lukas Foss. Copyright Carl Fischer Inc. Used by permission of the composer.

400 "Sound Patterns" by Pauline Oliveros. Copyright Tonos Musikverlag, GmbH, Darmstadt, Germany.

405 "Symphony No. 1" by Ellen Taaffe Zwilich. Copyright 1983 by Associated Music Publishers, Inc. International Copyright Secured. All Rights Reserved. Reprinted by permission.

408 "Me he perdido muchas veces por el mar" by George Crumb, © 1971 C. F. Peters Corporation. Used by permission.

415 "Love in Vain Blues," words and music by Robert Johnson. Copyright 1978, 1990, 1991 King of Spades Music. All rights reserved. Used by permission.

416 "Florida-Bound Blues" by Clarence Williams. © Universal–MCA Music Publishing, a division of Universal Studios, Inc. All Rights Reserved. Used by Permission. Warner Brothers Publications U.S. Inc., Miami, FL 33014

422 "It Don't Mean a Thing (If It Ain't Got That Swing)" by Duke Ellington and Irving Mills. © 1932 (renewed 1960). EMI Mills Music, Inc. and Famous Music Corporation. All rights outside USA controlled by EMI Mills Music, Inc. and Warner Brothers Music. All Rights Reserved. Used by Permission. Warner Bros. Publications, U.S. Inc., Miami, FL 33014.

432 "Satin Doll" handwritten score from "Music is My Mistress" by Duke Ellington. © 1973 by Duke Ellington, Inc. Used by permission of Doubleday, a division of Random House, Inc.

433 "Satin Doll" by Johnny Mercer, Duke Ellington and Billy Strayhorn, © 1953, 1958 (copyrights renewed) WB Music Corp., Famous Music Corporation and Tempo Music Inc. All

The author and publisher wish to acknowledge, with thanks, the following photographic sources.

ON ALL LISTENING GUIDES:
Beethoven's handwritten sketches for the Fifth Symphony. Gesellschaft der Musikfreunde, Vienna.

CHAPTER 1
1 Steve Cole, PhotoDisc, Inc.
2 Pierpont Morgan Library/Art Resource, NY
3 (bottom left) Ramey/Stock Boston
3 (top right) Lisa Quinones/Black Star
3 (bottom right) Ramey/Stock Boston
4 (left) eStock Photography LLC
4 (right) Jack Vartoogian
5 (left) Jack Vartoogian
5 (right) Jack Vartoogian
6 (left) Wolfgang Kaehler Photography
6 (right) Jay Blakesberg/Retna, Ltd.
7 (left) John Lei/ Stock Boston
7 (bottom right) Steve Vidler/eStock Photography LLC
9 Jagdish Argarwal/Dinodia Picture Agency
10 Jack Vartoogian
11 (top right) Musée de l'Homme, Phototheque
11 (second from top) Culver Pictures, Inc.
11 (middle right) Paolo Koch/Photo Researchers, Inc.
11 (bottom right) Courtesy of the author.
12 (left) Musser, a Division of The Selmer Company
12 (top right) Sarah Errington/The Hutchinson Library
12 (middle right) Jitendra Arya
13 (top left) José Azel/Woodfin Camp & Associates
13 (bottom left) Wolfgang Kaehler Photography
13 (right) Lester Sloan/Woodfin Camp & Associates
14 Wolfgang Kaehler Photography
15 (left) Jack Varoogian
15 (top right) Jack Vartoogian
15 (bottom right) Jack Vartoogian
16 Jack Vartoogian
19 Steve Vidler/eStock Photography LLC
20 Marc & Evelyne Bernheim/Woodfin Camp & Associates
21 Shanachie Entertainment

CHAPTER 2
23 Ben Christopher/Performing Arts Library
44 (top right) Stephen Morley/Retna, Ltd.
44 (left) Eric Simmons/Stock Boston
44 (bottom right) UPI/Corbis
45 (top left) Volkman Kurt Wentzel/National Geographic Society
45 (middle right) CTK/Sovfoto/Eastfoto
47 (top) Walter H. Scott
47 (bottom) Institut Royal du Patrimoine Artistique (IRPA-KIK)
48 (top) Fritz Henle/Photo Researchers, Inc.
48 (bottom) Walter H. Scott
49 (top) Jon Blumb
49 (bottom left) Index Stock Imagery, Inc.
49 (bottom right) Tony Freeman/PhotoEdit
50 (top left) Walter H. Scott
50 (top right) Walter H. Scott
50 (bottom) Walter H. Scott
51 (top right) Walter H. Scott
51 (middle right) Walter H. Scott
51 (bottom extreme right) Walter H. Scott
51 (bottom left) John Bacchus/Pearson Education Corporate Digital Archive
51 (bottom middle) Todd Powell/Index Stock Imagery, Inc.
51 (bottom right) Robert Ginn/PhotoEdit
52 (top left) Walter H. Scott
52 (top right) Royal Ontario Museum
52 (bottom) Walter H. Scott
53 (left) Steinway & Sons
53 (middle) Royal Ontario Museum
53 (right) Steinway & Sons
54 (left) Art Rewsource, NY
54 (right) Corbis
54 (bottom right) Janet Gillies/Experimental Musical Instruments
55 (top right) Walter H. Scott
55 (bottom right) Walter H. Scott
56 (top) Walter H. Scott
56 (top left) Walter H. Scott
56 (top left) Walter H. Scott
56 (bottom) John Abbott Photography
57 (top left) Walter H. Scott
57 (top right) Walter H. Scott
57 (bottom) John Abbott Photography
58 (top left) The Granger Collection
58 (right) French Government Tourist Office
58 (bottom left) Snark International/Art Resource, NY

CHAPTER 3
60 Mary Kate Denny/PhotoEdit
63 Archiv/Photo Researchers, Inc.

BU-346